Contemporary Tableware

First published in Great Britain in 2013
Bloomsbury Publishing Plc
50 Bedford Square
London WC1B 3DP
www.bloomsbury.com

ISBN: 978-1-4081-5395-6

Published simultaneously in the USA by
The American Ceramic Society
600 N. Cleveland Ave., Suite 210
Westerville, Ohio, 43082, USA
http://ceramicartsdaily.org

ISBN: 978-1-57498-330-2

CIP Catalogue records for this book are available from the British Library and the US Library of Congress.

Typeset in Adobe Caslon Pro
Book design by Saffron Stocker
Cover design by Sutchinda Thompson
Edited by Kate Sherington

Printed and bound in China.

This book is produced using paper that is made from wood grown in managed, sustainable forests. It is natural, renewable and recyclable. The logging and manufacturing processes conform to the environmental regulations of the country of origin.

Cover image: Bodo Sperlein for Nikko, Blossom plates, bowls and cup, 2011. Bone china, diameter: 26 cm (10¼ in). *Photo: Graeme Duddridge.*
Back cover image: Linda Bloomfield, thrown porcelain tableware, 2011. Max. plate diameter: 26 cm (10 in). Stylist: Twig Hutchinson. *Photo: Emma Lee.*
Contents page image: Pigeon Toe Ceramics, Portland, Oregon, Scribble Nesting Bowls designed by Lisa Jones, 2010. Thrown porcelain, glazed on the inside, width: 20 cm (8 in.). *Photo: Lisa Warninger.*
Image p. 6/7: See p. 31.
Image p. 68/69: See p. 153.

Contemporary Tableware

Linda Bloomfield

BLOOMSBURY
LONDON • NEW DELHI • NEW YORK • SYDNEY

THE AMERICAN CERAMIC SOCIETY • OHIO

Contents

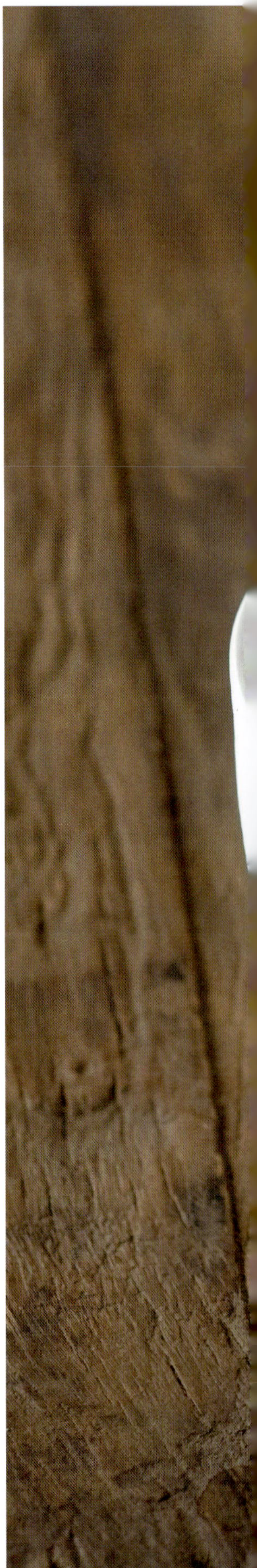

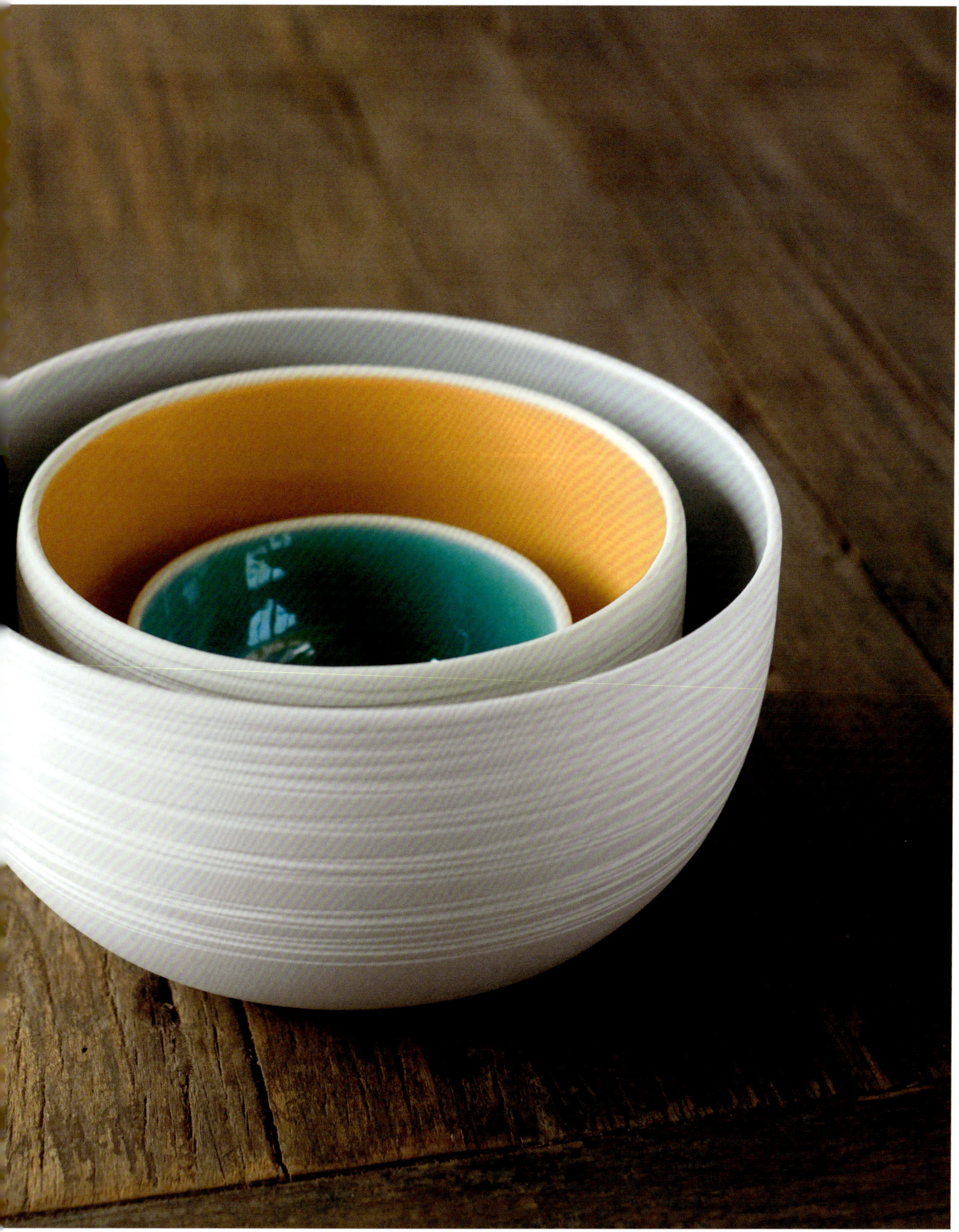

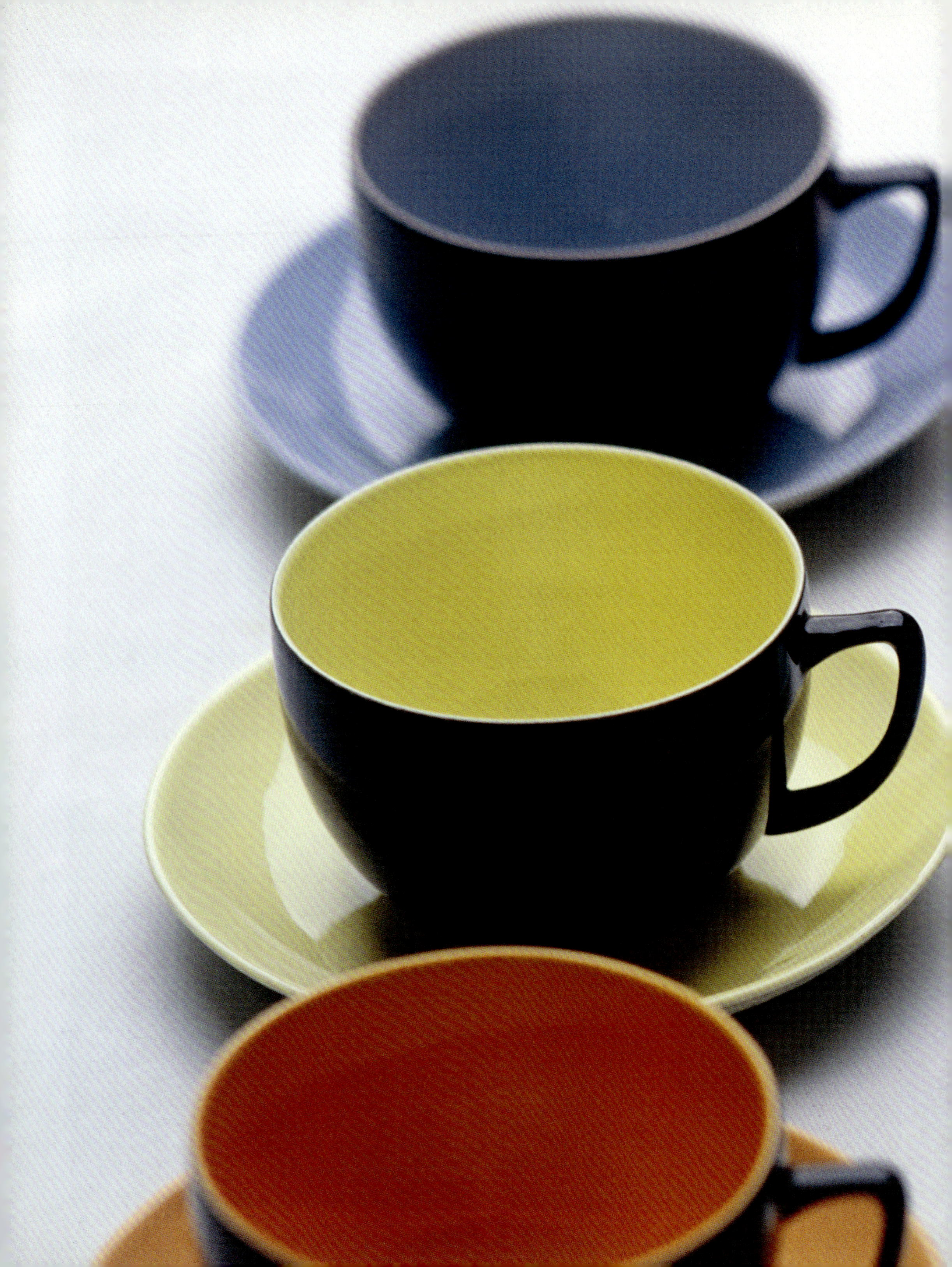

Part 1

A MODERN APPROACH TO TRADITION

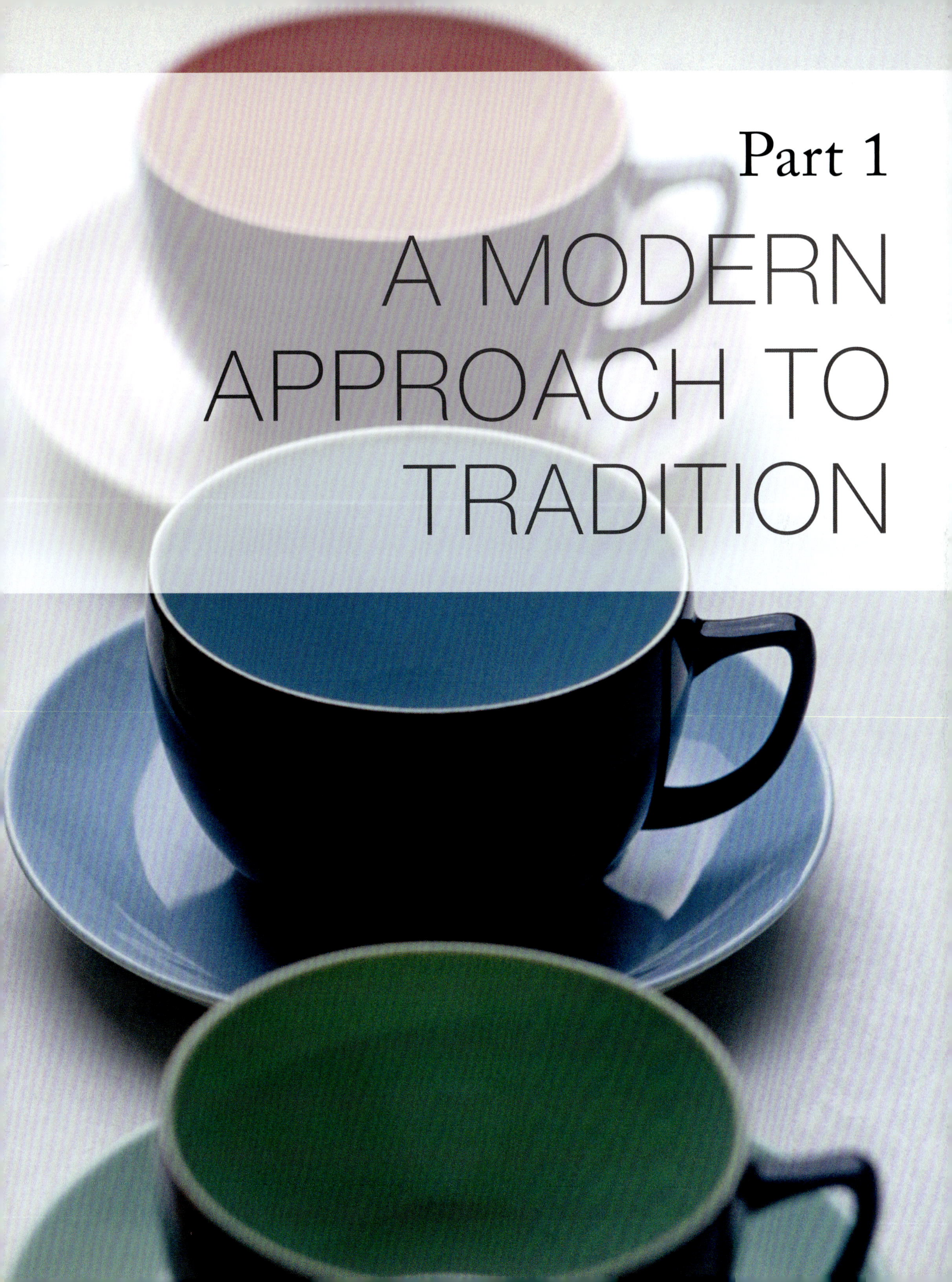

1 Introduction

Handmade tableware

In the 19th century, at the end of the Industrial Revolution, John Ruskin and William Morris criticised industrially produced wares and inspired the Arts and Crafts movement. They proposed a return to hand-crafted decorative arts, which should be both beautiful and useful. The concept of the handmade object being made available to all was raised again in the 20th century by potter Bernard Leach, who established the studio pottery movement. His vision of the individual artist making pots in a studio or workshop inspired many to become potters in the 1960s and '70s. Craft has again become popular in the 21st century as people tire of manufactured wares and crave the qualities of handmade work, realising that beautifully designed and made tableware can enhance everyday life.

Nowadays there are designer-makers who not only make things themselves, but whose understanding of the materials and making processes enables them to design pieces for industrial manufacture. These potters produce thrown or hand-built prototypes for industrial production, bringing a handmade feel to mass-produced wares. Making by hand can become a fulfilling way of life, although it is hard work to earn a living from a craft. For this reason, many studio potters tire of tableware production and make higher-priced individual pieces instead, encouraged by craft organisations trying to raise the profile of craft to that of art. The resulting pots are often too expensive to use and end up sitting on a shelf, while the humble handmade mug or bowl continues to be used every day. This book aims to showcase the work of those potters who are committed to making tableware.

Changing habits

Naturally, changing attitudes and habits in food preparation and service and the rituals of mealtimes have also led to changes in the way tableware is used and produced. The way we eat now is less formal than during the previous century and a traditional matching dinner service might only be used on special occasions. This gives rise to new categories of tableware and new roles for familiar pieces. Besides formal dinnerware, there is a new category of 'casual tableware' for everyday use. We use mismatched pieces, combining mass-produced plates and bowls alongside handmade pottery, bringing art into a domestic setting. Using handmade pots can bring a similar feeling of warmth and human contact to eating a home-cooked meal, and this current appreciation of the handmade is very encouraging for makers of tableware.

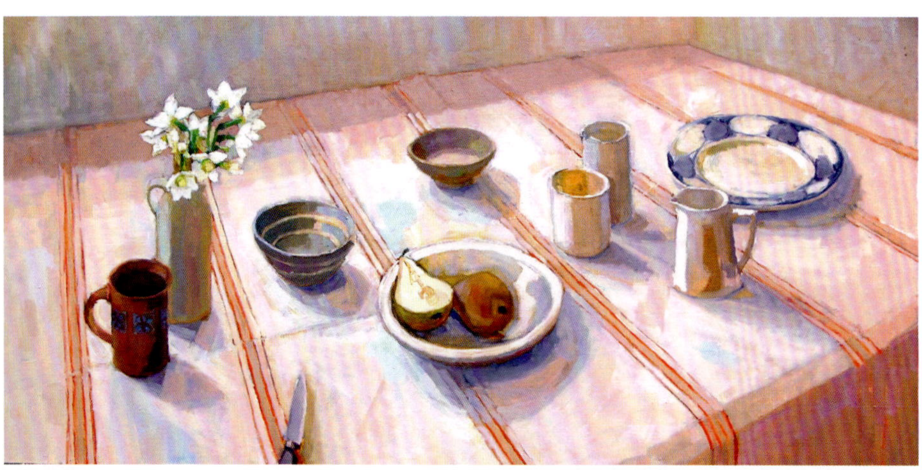

Sarah Spackman, *After they'd gone*, 2010. Oil painting, 60 x 101 cm (23½ x 40 in.). *Photo: by the artist.*

Design sources

Today's makers and designers draw on a rich history of pottery and industrial design for ideas, and there is greater awareness today of the different design traditions. One of the aims of this book is to bring together a number of different strands which have influenced contemporary tableware design.

During the Sung dynasty (AD 960–1279), the Chinese were the first to make durable, mass-produced porcelain tableware and by the 16th century were exporting it around the world. The Japanese adapted pottery-making techniques from China and Korea and added their own unique character from the 16th century onwards. Meanwhile in post-medieval Europe, a rustic style of country pottery was evolving, which ended with the Industrial Revolution. At the beginning of the 20th century, the many strands that were to influence contemporary tableware came together. The studio pottery movement was established by Bernard Leach in England, while modernism took hold across Europe. Then the Second World War forced many talented artists and designers to flee to England and America, where they were able to exert a subsequent influence on design. In Scandinavia, folk art and textile design influenced the decoration of mass-produced tableware, with artists and studio potters collaborating with industry.

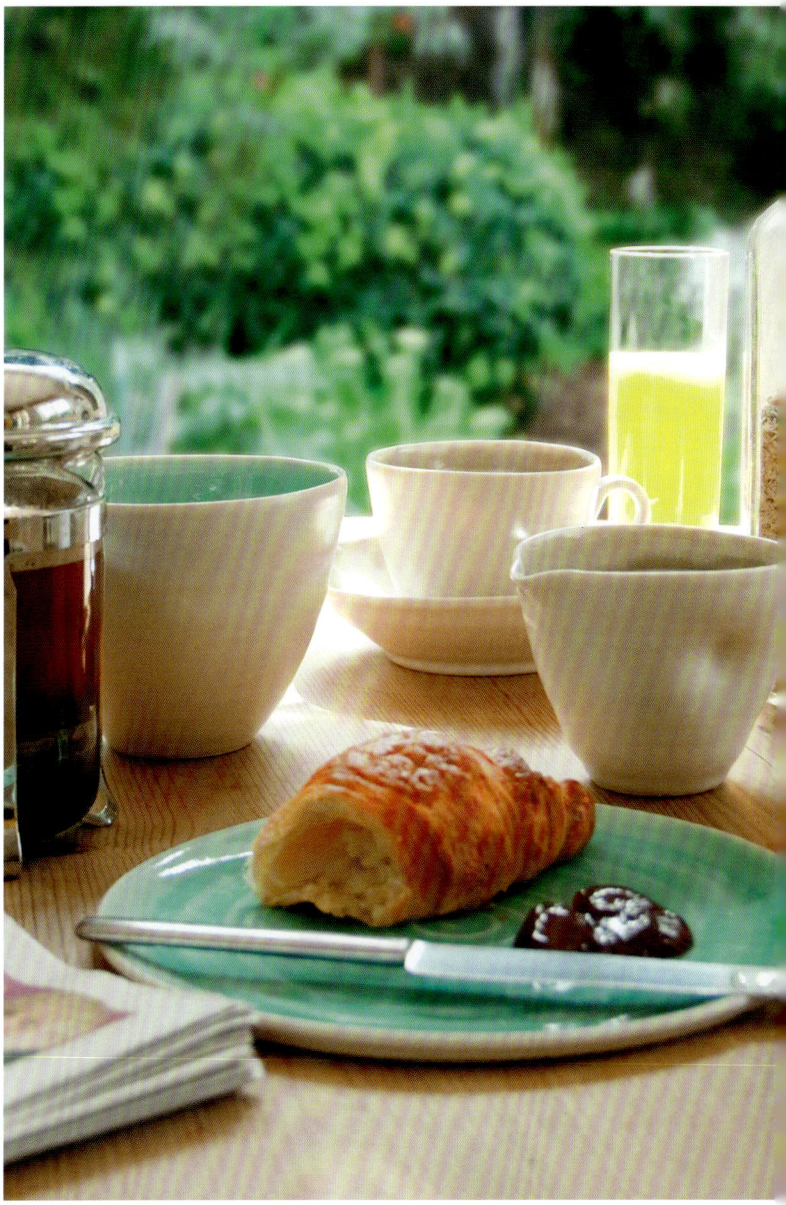

Linda Bloomfield, plate, bowl, cup and saucer, and dimpled jug, 2011. Thrown porcelain, plate width: 21 cm (8¼ in.). *Photo: David Fawcett, Seek and Adore.*

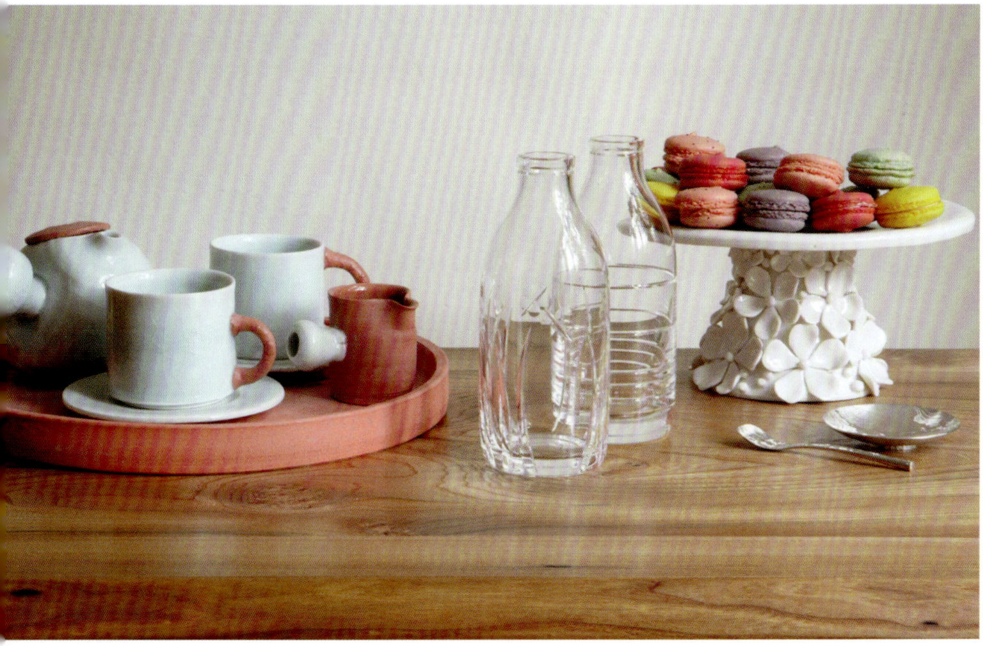

Adam Frew, tea set, celadon and stained porcelain, 2011; Sam Sweet, cut-crystal milk bottles, hand-blown lead crystal, 2011; Emma Clegg, cake stand, thrown and modelled porcelain, 2011. Diameter: 25 cm (10 in.); Miriam Hanid, silver bowl and spoon, 2011. *Photo: courtesy of Lisa Harrison, Miratis.*

2 China

Porcelain

The porcelain industry at Jingdezhen in southern China started over a thousand years ago during the Sung dynasty. There were specialists for each part of the production process: clay preparation, throwing, decoration and firing. The kilns could be as long as 50 m (164 ft) and could hold up to 20,000 pots. The highest-quality pots – fine white porcelain and celadon – were reserved for the imperial court. The Chinese potters reached a high standard of technical skill, making fine, thin-walled porcelain with perfectly applied glazes.

During the Ming dynasty (AD 1368–1644), a pure form of cobalt ore was imported from Persia to make a blue underglaze and by the 17th century large quantities of this blue and white porcelain were being exported to Europe. The porcelain shapes and decoration were tailored to meet European demand for dinner and tea sets. Chinese porcelain was greatly admired in Europe and enormous efforts were made to discover the secrets of producing it. At the same time, fine monochrome yellow porcelain was being made for the imperial court. This ware was bisque-fired to a high temperature, then glazed with a low-temperature lead glaze containing iron oxide.

Chinese influence on Europe

Chinese pots have influenced the shapes of pots being made in the West from the time they were first exported to Europe. In imperial China, shapes were usually symmetrical. Jars often had a high shoulder and a narrow base. Bowls were hemispherical, with a wide foot-ring and a fine, out-turned rim. Saucers were first imported to the West from China in the 17th century, together with small, handleless cups that originated in the formal tea ceremony of the Chinese court, where tea bowls were placed on decorative stands.

Teapots were first exported to Europe when tea drinking became popular there around 1650. Teapots had been made in China since the Ming dynasty in forms very similar to those used today. The red earthenware teapots made in Yixing were popular with Chinese intellectuals. They were small, holding only enough tea for one person, hand-moulded in natural forms and burnished. When they were exported to Europe, silver mounts were often added to the spout and handle, for connecting the lid by a chain. This style was imitated by the Elers brothers, two Dutch potters working in Staffordshire in 1690.

Teapots were also made in Dehua in China around 1650–1700 from a type of white porcelain called blanc de Chine. Dehua teapots were copied by porcelain factories across Europe and some look surprisingly modern today.

Yixing teapot, red earthenware, 2003. Height: 10 cm (4 in.). *Photo: Fay de Winter.*

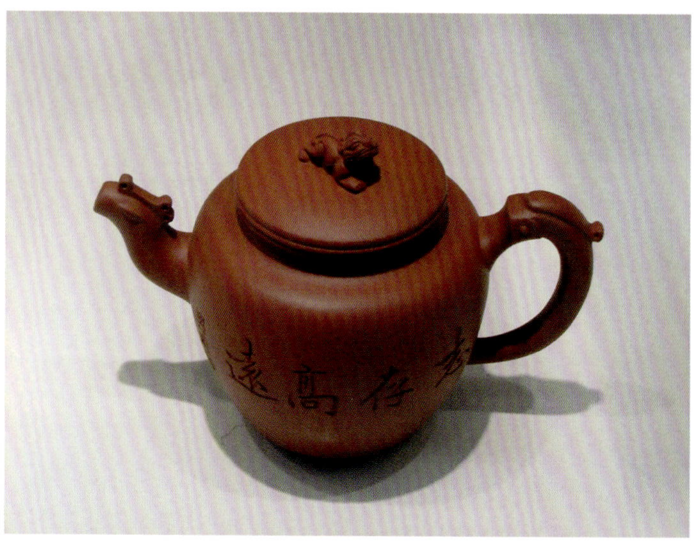

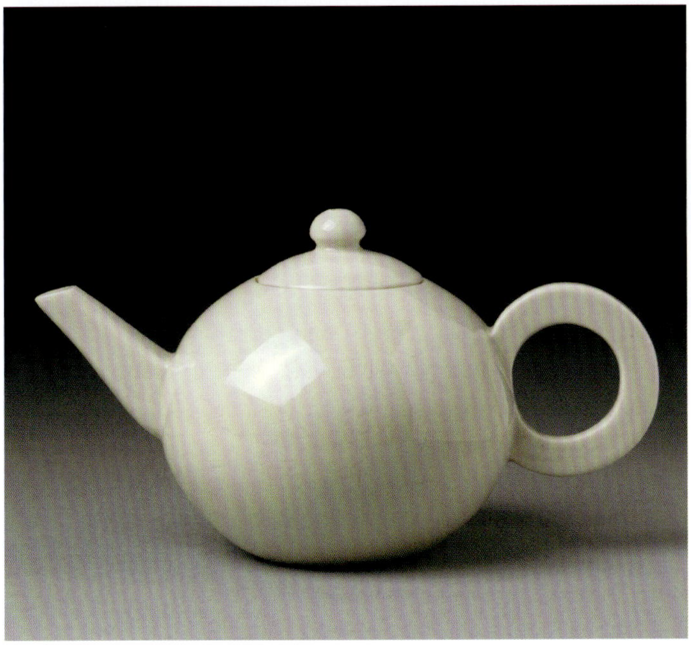

Dehua teapot, incised with poem, blanc de Chine porcelain, 1650–1700, height: 11 cm (4½ in.). *Photo: Victoria and Albert Museum, London.*

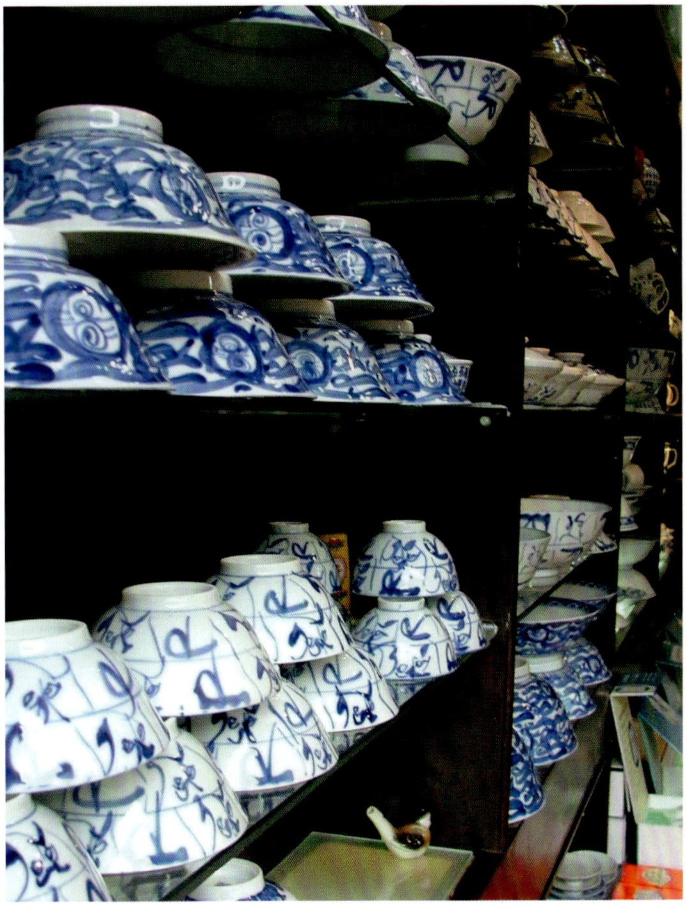

Blue and white porcelain bowls in Jingdezhen, China, 2003. *Photo: Fay de Winter.*

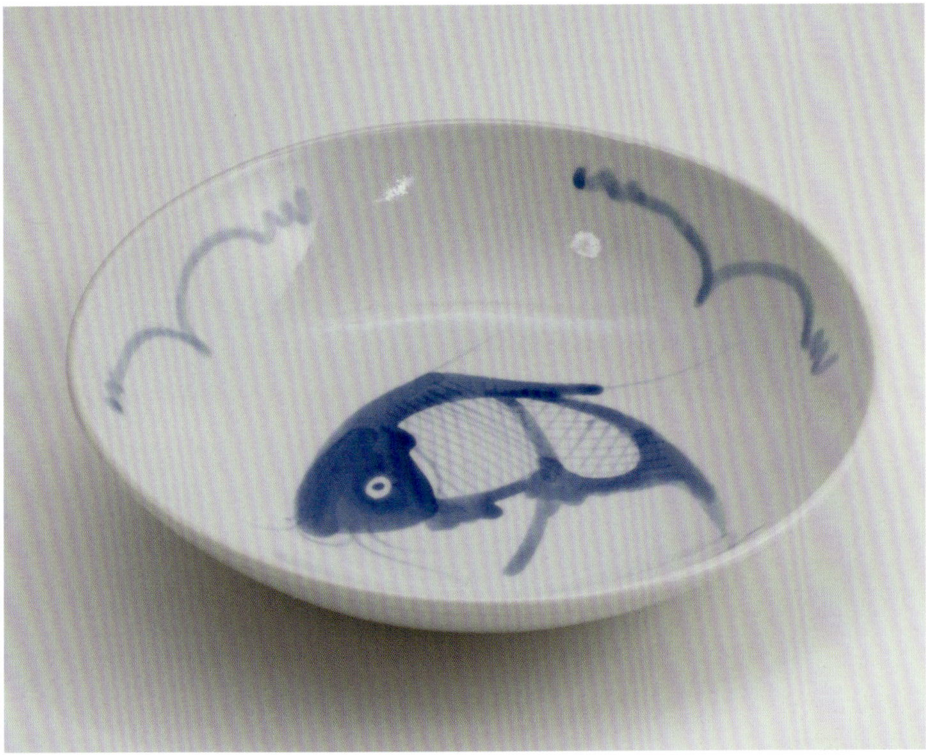

Blue and white porcelain bowl with hand-painted fish design, exported from China, 1990, diameter: 23 cm (9 in.). *Photo: Henry Bloomfield.*

3 Japan

Japanese tableware

In Japan, tableware has traditionally played an important part in enhancing the serving of food. Japanese meals often comprise small courses, each served on a separate dish. There is usually a small dish of pickled vegetables, a bowl of rice and a small, lidded lacquerware bowl of soup. Fish is often served on a flat dish and hot stews are cooked at the table in larger lidded bowls. Seasonal variations in food are reflected in the shape and decoration of the serving dishes; bowls decorated with plum blossom or maple leaves are used in the appropriate season. The bowls are often deeper in the winter to hold the heat, and shallower in summer when cold dishes are served. There can be several different cooking methods used in one meal, involving grilled, fried, boiled, steamed and raw food, each type served in its own bowl or dish.

There are many styles of pottery – some rustic, such as the unglazed, wood-fired Bizen ware, some highly decorated, such as Oribe, which has areas of copper-green glaze and iron-oxide brushwork. Each type of pottery comes from a different region and has its own special character. Great attention is paid to the presentation of food in Japan and handmade pottery is highly appreciated.

Tomoko Okuda, Oribe stoneware with red slip and green glaze, 2011. *Photo: Henry Bloomfield.*

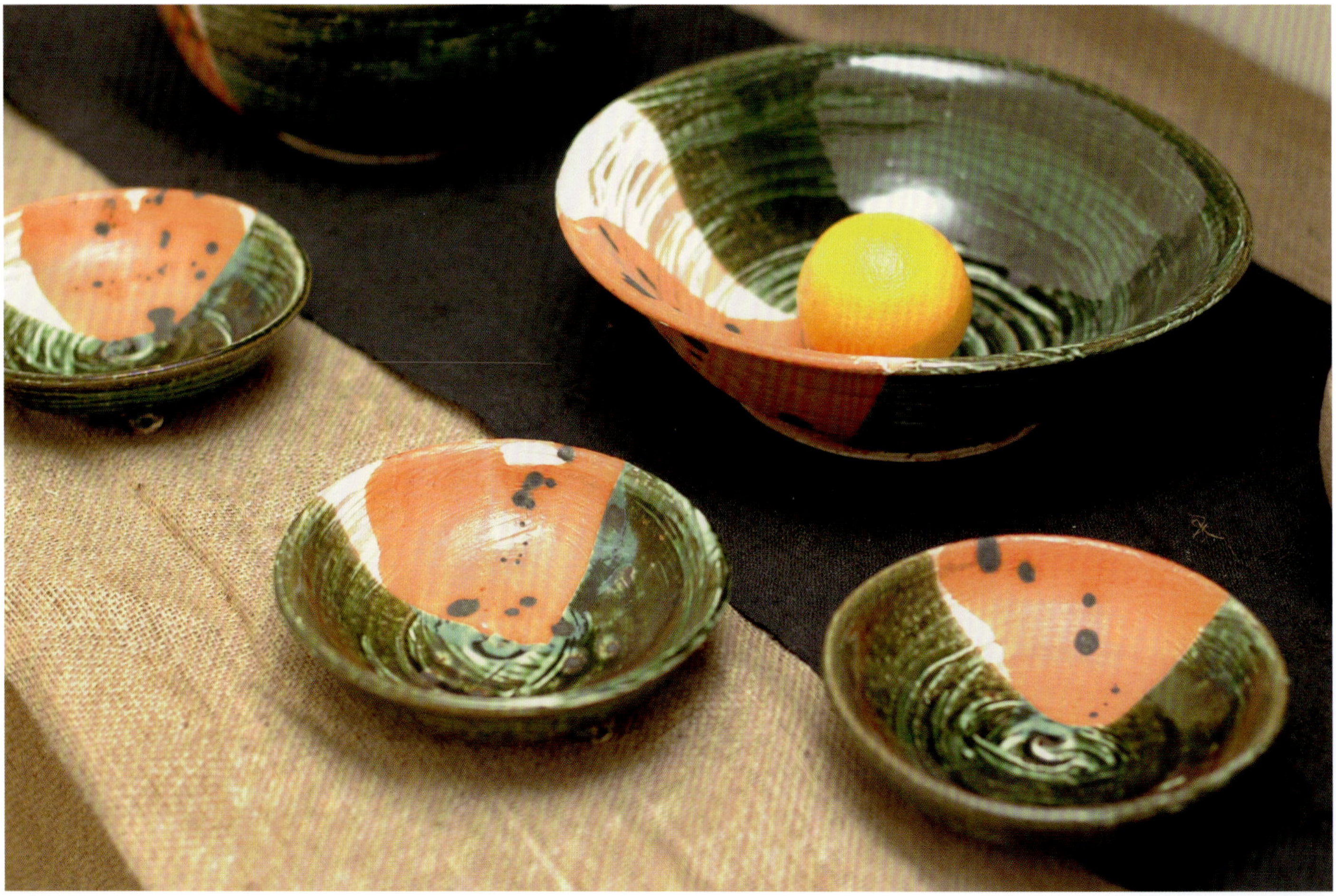

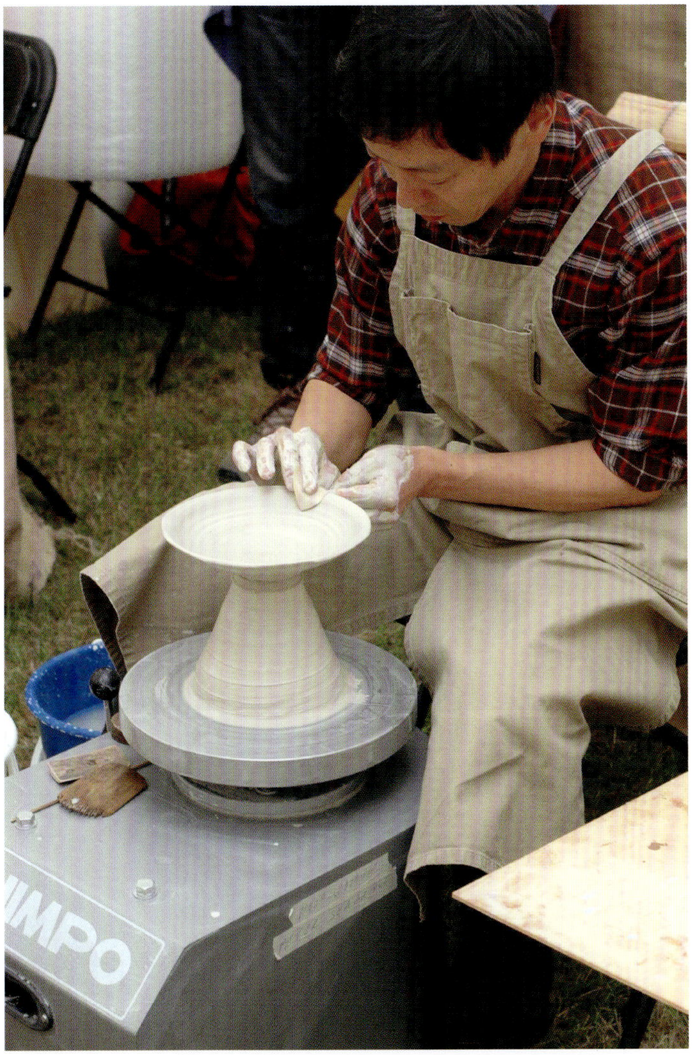

Japanese potter Masahiro Kumagae throwing a bowl on the wheel at Art in Action 2011. *Photo: Henry Bloomfield.*

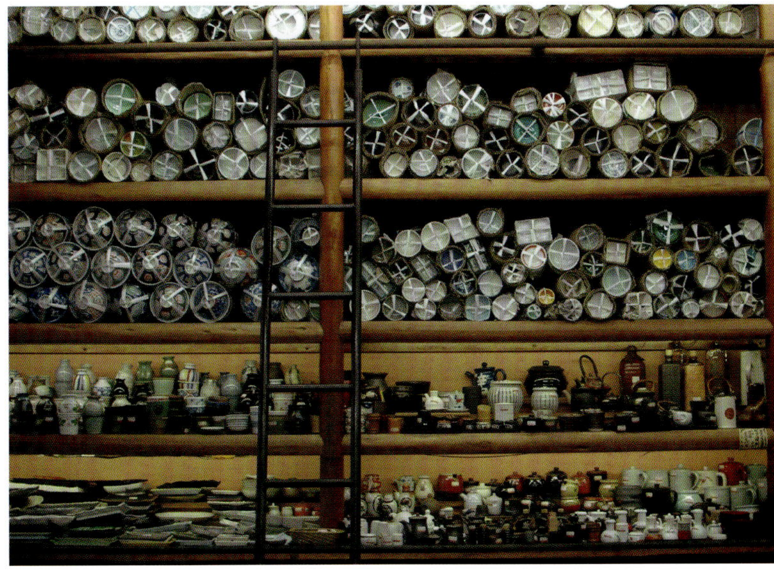

Interior of shop selling tableware to the restaurant trade in Kappabashi, Tokyo, 2011. *Photo: Henry Bloomfield.*

Japanese place setting with (clockwise from top left) rice bowl, fish plate, lidded soup bowl, side dish, chopstick rest and pickle dish. Soup is drunk from the bowl. *Photo: Henry Bloomfield.*

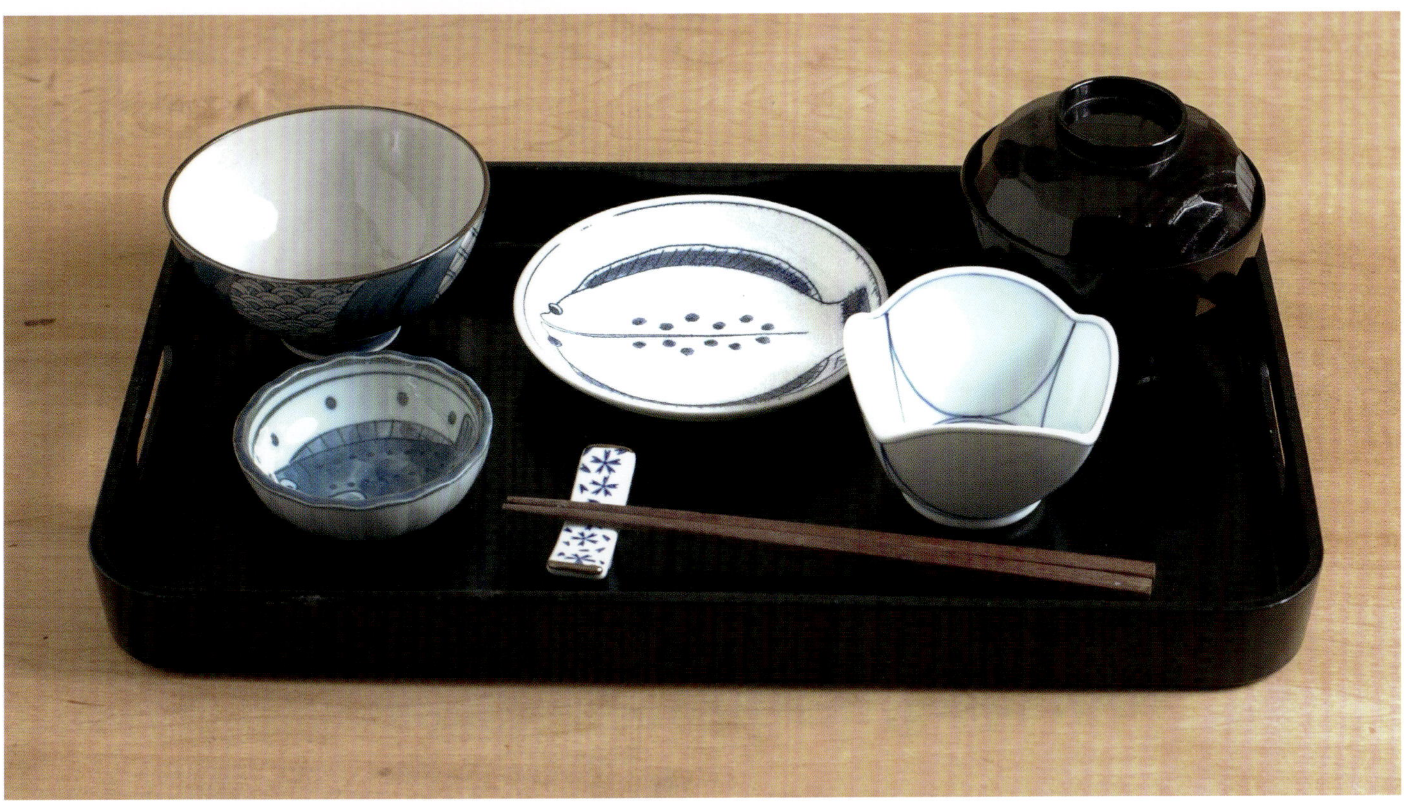

The tea ceremony

Tea was first brought to Japan from China in the 9th century by the Buddhist monk Eichu. The tea ceremony or 'way of tea' was developed in the 16th century by a Zen Buddhist, Sen Rikyu, who introduced the concept of wabi sabi, 'wabi' meaning austere simplicity and 'sabi' meaning weathered.

Beauty through use is an important concept in the Japanese tea ceremony, during which tea bowls and water jars are used. Tea bowls or *chawan* are often rustic in appearance, deep-sided in winter and shallower in summer. An aged, worn quality is valued, and sometimes old tea bowls can be purposely broken and repaired with gold lacquer to achieve that effect. Asymmetry of the form and imperfections in the glaze, such as pinholes, are

Hollis Engley, wood-fired thumb-hole tea bowls, Hatchville Pottery, Cape Cod, USA, 2011. Height: 10 cm (4 in.). *Photo: Hollis Engley.*

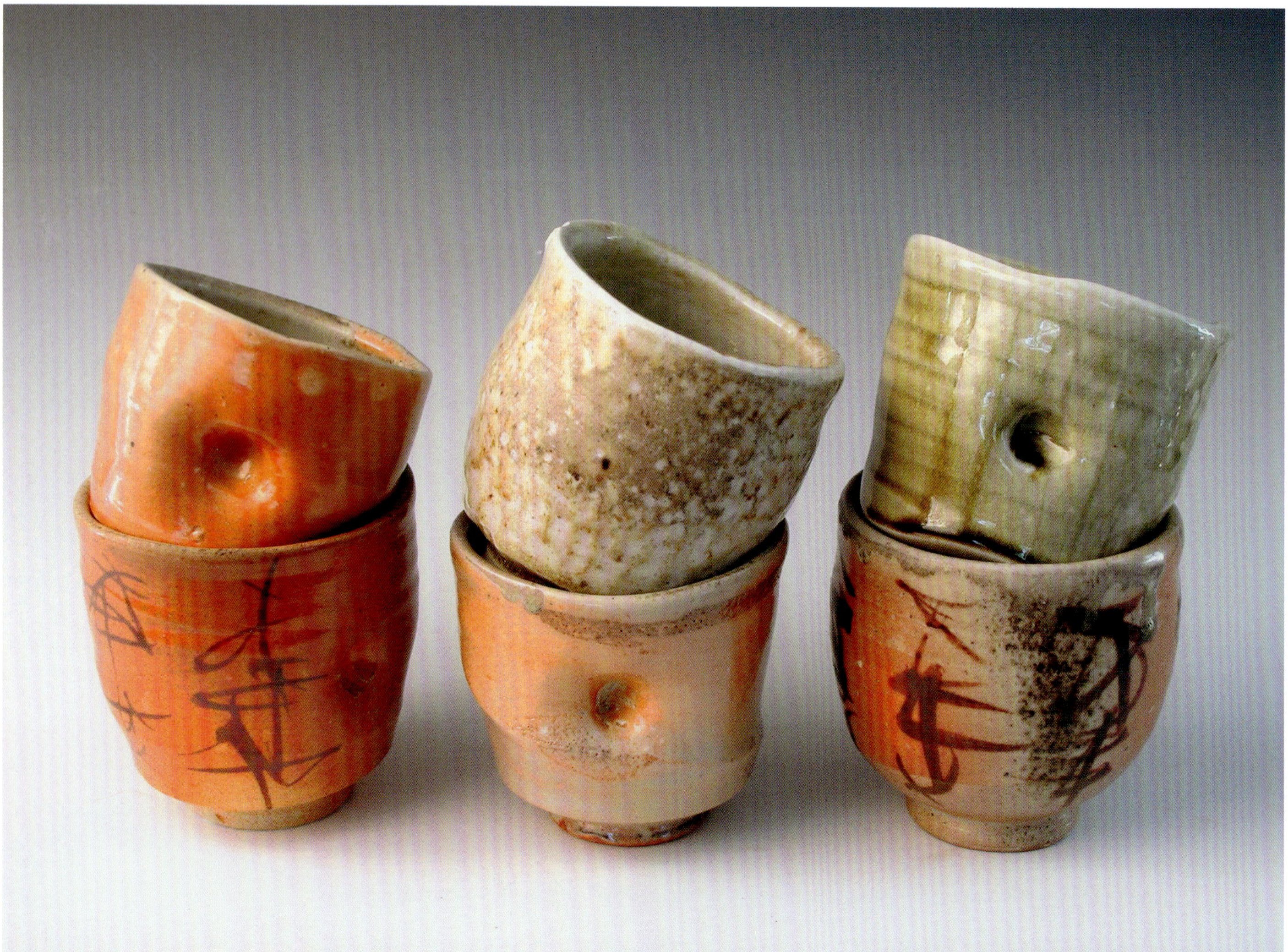

appreciated as qualities of the handmade, although many potters in the West would view them as faults. The tea used is *matcha*, powdered green tea, which is whisked with hot water to make a thick, foaming, bright green tea. Tea bowls are very expensive in Japan and are elevated to the status of art, as is the tea ceremony itself.

For everyday use, many Japanese people drink thin green tea from small cylindrical cups called *yunomi*. These have no handle and are held at the rim, with the other hand supporting the base. They are smaller than Western teacups or mugs and are filled frequently from a small teapot. In Japanese shops and department stores they are often sold in 'married couple' pairs, with a large size for men and a smaller one for women.

Cups and teapot, Shonzui pattern with kaki glaze on the rims, Japan, 1990. Shonzui was a potter who visited China during the Ming dynasty and returned to set up a pottery in Arita. The surface of the teapot is divided into separate areas, each with different geometric patterns. The *yunomi* have a textured surface and look handmade although they are in fact factory-made. *Photo: Henry Bloomfield.*

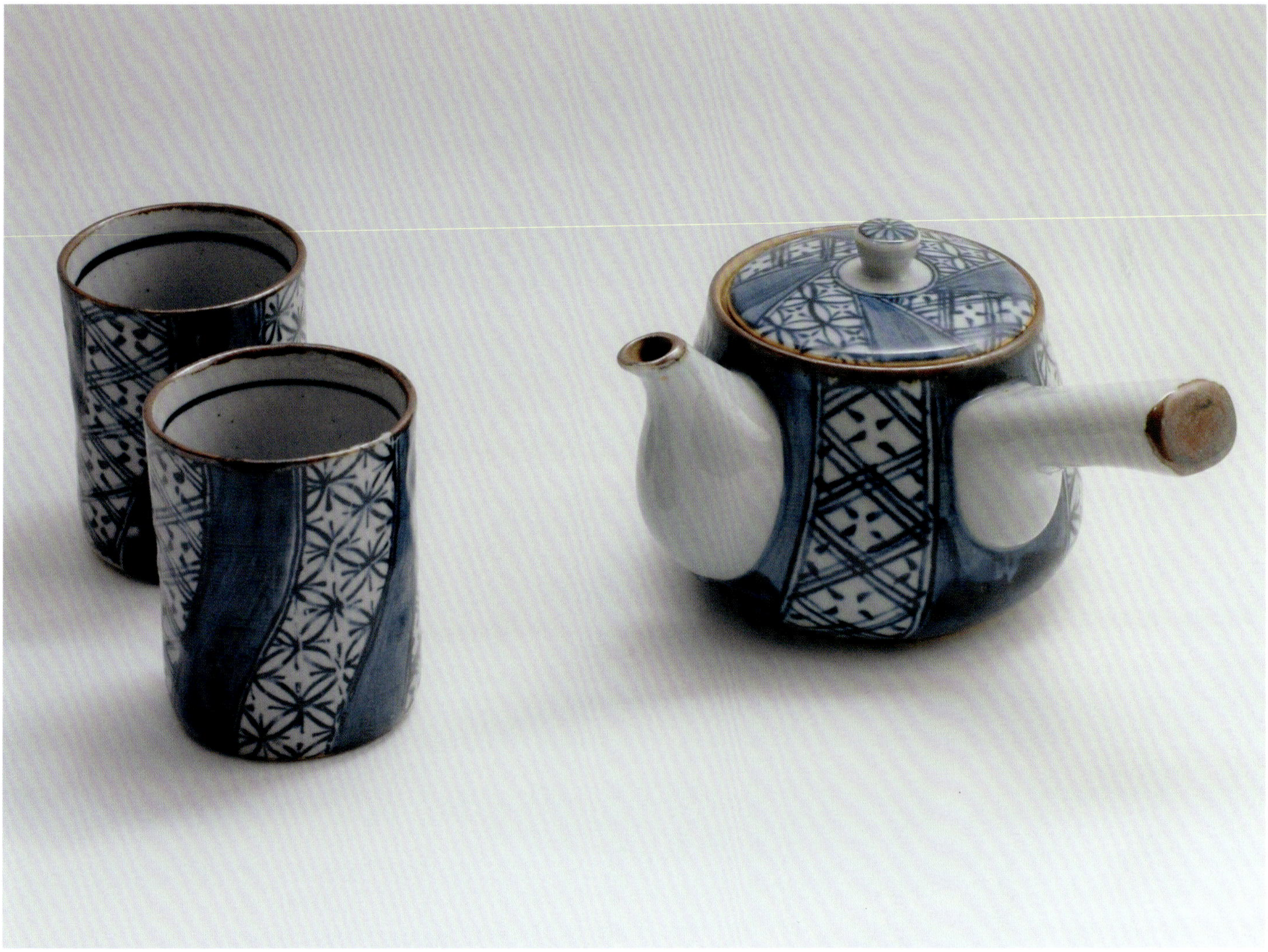

Japanese artists and designers

Kitaoji Rosanjin (1883–1959) was a famous Japanese potter, calligrapher and restaurateur who was interested in the harmony between food and vessel. He thought that tableware could enhance the presentation of Japanese cuisine and famously said 'the vessel is clothing for food'. He believed serving dishes and presentation could make food taste better; in his Tokyo restaurant, opened two years after the great Kanto earthquake of 1923, he served food on his own handmade tableware, often highly decorated and based on old Mino or Seto ware.

Rosanjin believed in surrounding himself with antique objects in order to learn about elegance and beauty. He made work in a wide range of styles and disciplines and was thought by many of his contemporaries to be eccentric and arrogant. He was not a supporter of Soetsu Yanagi's folk-craft movement, which was more concerned with beauty found in the humble wares of Japan's traditional artisans, as described in Yanagi's book *The Unknown Craftsman.* Instead, he preferred exquisite works of art. Japanese-American artist Isamu Noguchi (1904–88) lived on Rosanjin's estate during the early 1950s. Noguchi was a sculptor and designer inspired by ancient Japanese tomb figures. In 1952, he designed a cup with a pointed horn-like handle, modelled on an ancient earthenware cup he owned. His cup and two versions of a saucer were not put into production until 50 years later, when they attracted the attention of the Swiss design company Vitra.

Karin Eriksson, charcoal devil cup, 2000. Inspired by Japanese pottery, height: 6 cm (2¼ in.). *Photo: Karin Eriksson.*

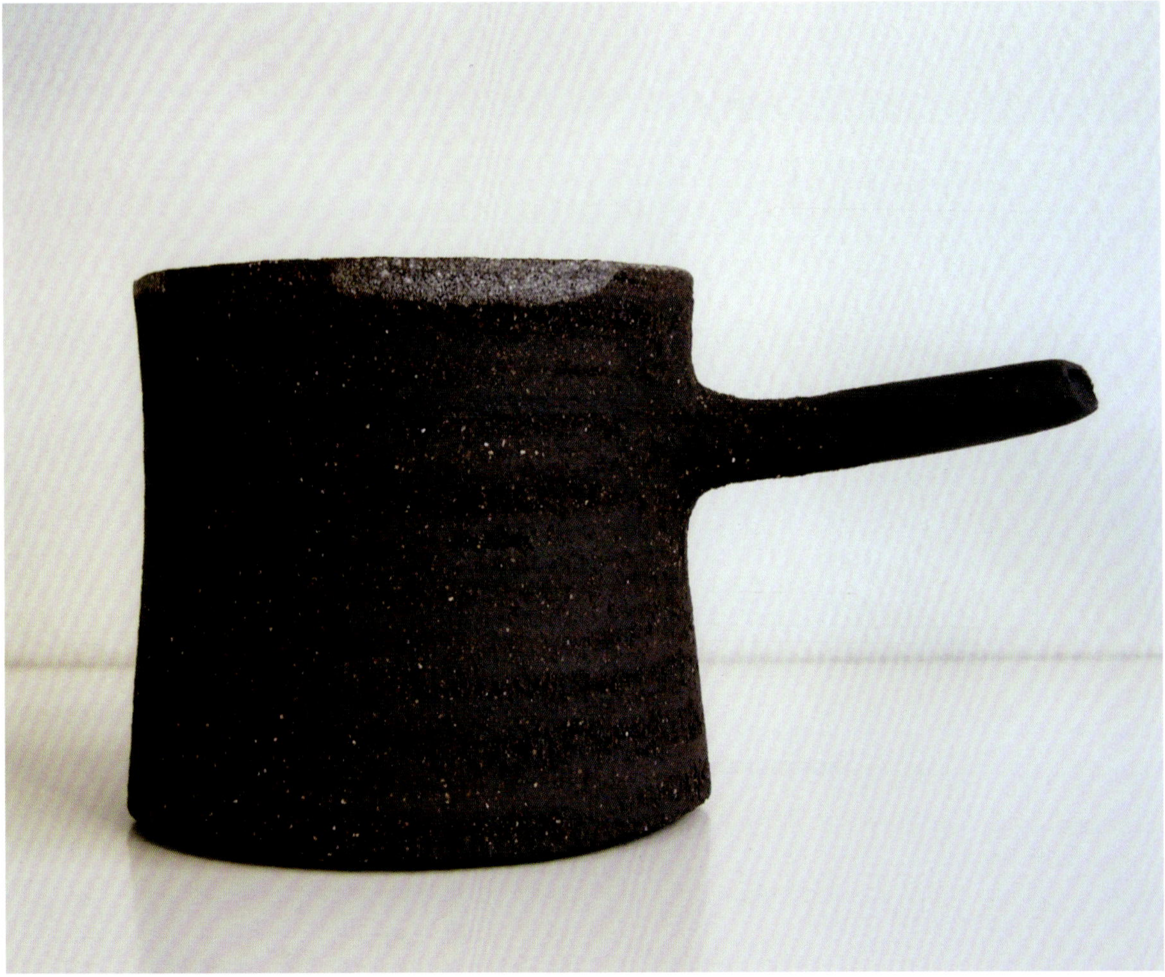

Sori Yanagi (1915–2011), son of Soetsu Yanagi, was also inspired by Japanese folk craft, but applied to modern materials and production methods. He designed several tableware ranges, including softly rounded square dishes, teapots and kettles. He also designed cutlery and furniture and was most famous for his 1956 Butterfly Stool, made from two curved pieces of moulded plywood. He often modelled his design prototypes in clay, and was able to combine the beauty of the handmade with the advantages of industrial production.

Pottery shop in Chawan-zaka, near Kiyomizu temple, Kyoto, 2011. *Photo: Henry Bloomfield.*

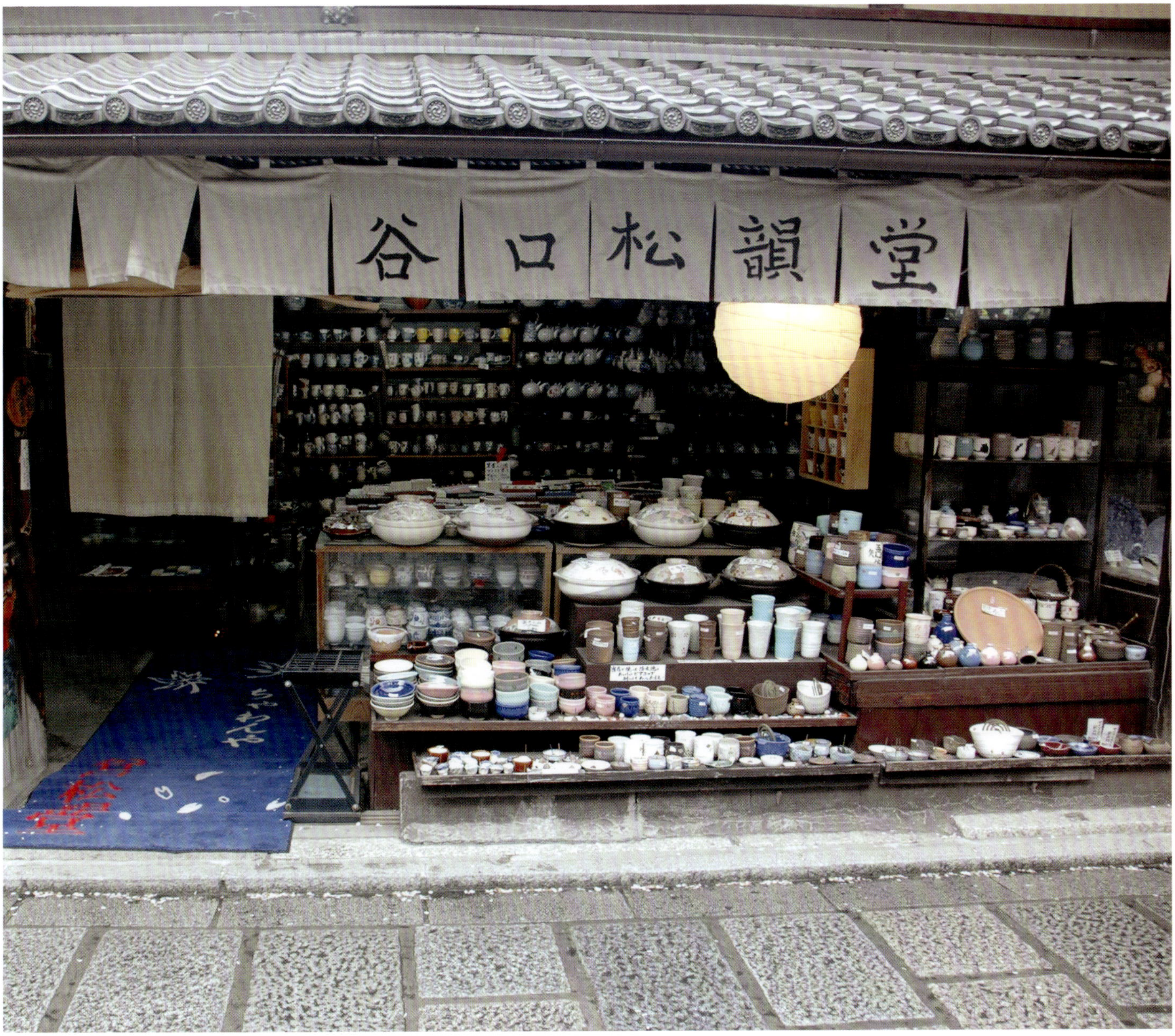

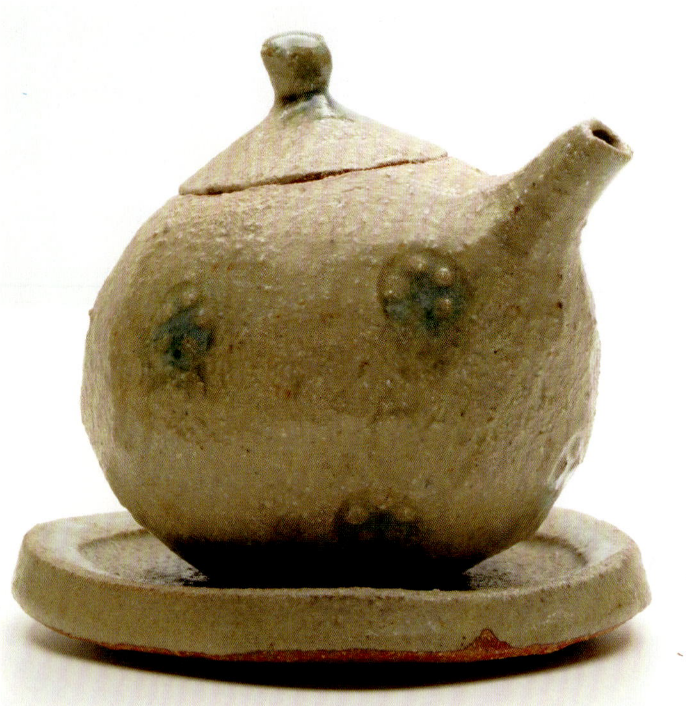

Yo Thom, soya sauce pourer, 2006. Thrown stoneware, height: 7 cm (2¾ in.). *Photo: Jonathan Thompson.*

The Japanese influence

Studio potters around the world are influenced by Japanese pottery, stemming from the legacy of Bernard Leach, Shōji Hamada and the studio pottery movement (see pp. 40–7). Industrially produced tableware in the West is also beginning to show a Japanese influence, with noodle bowls, soya sauce dishes and square plates increasingly being included in modern tableware collections.

Adrienne Baba, vegetable dishes on platter, 2010. Thrown and slabbed stoneware with matt glaze, fired to 1260°C (2300°F) in an electric kiln, 18 x 40 cm (7 x 15¾ in.). Adrienne makes tableware for several Japanese restaurants in London. *Photo: Keiko Oikawa.*

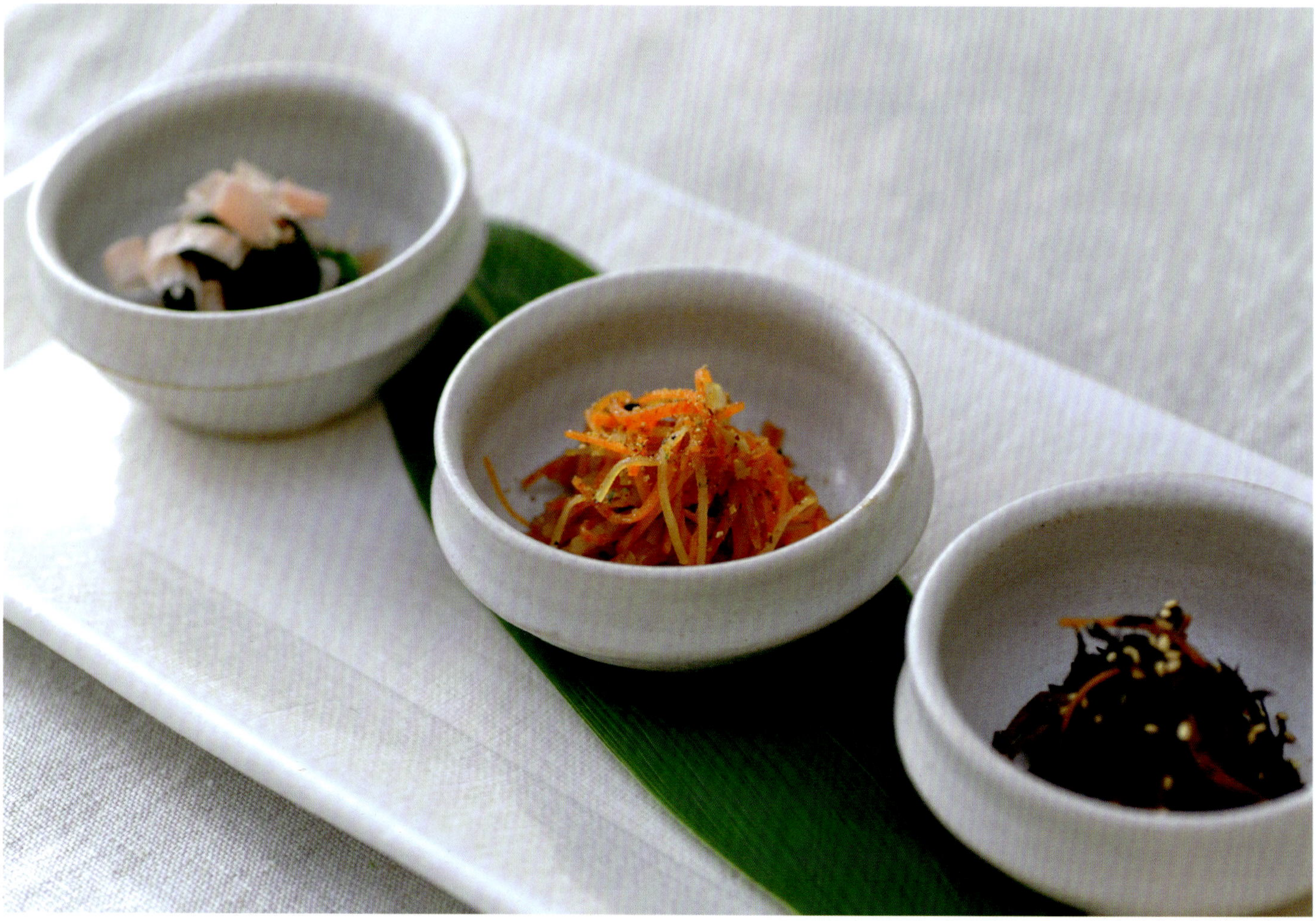

Kaori Tatebayashi, hump-moulded stoneware kurocha plate, kuro mini bowl, kohiki cup, 2008.
Photo: courtesy of the artist.

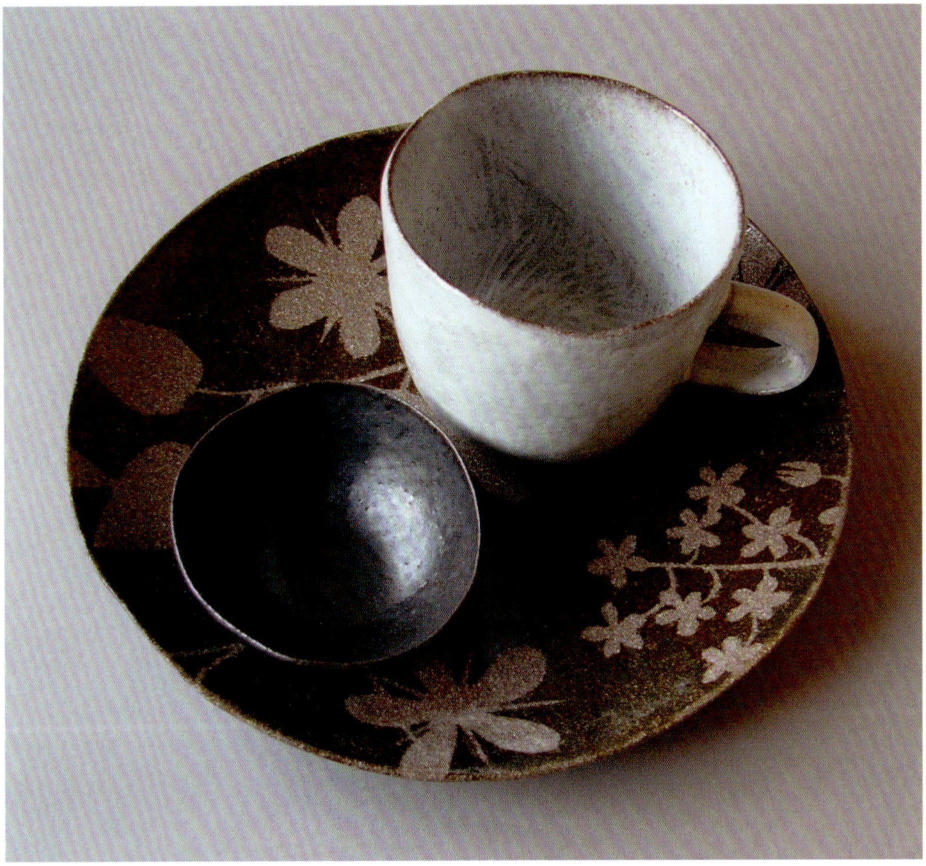

Yo Thom, rectangular plate with sushi, 2008. Wood-fired stoneware, 8 x 16 cm (3 x 6¼ in.).
Photo: courtesy of the artist.

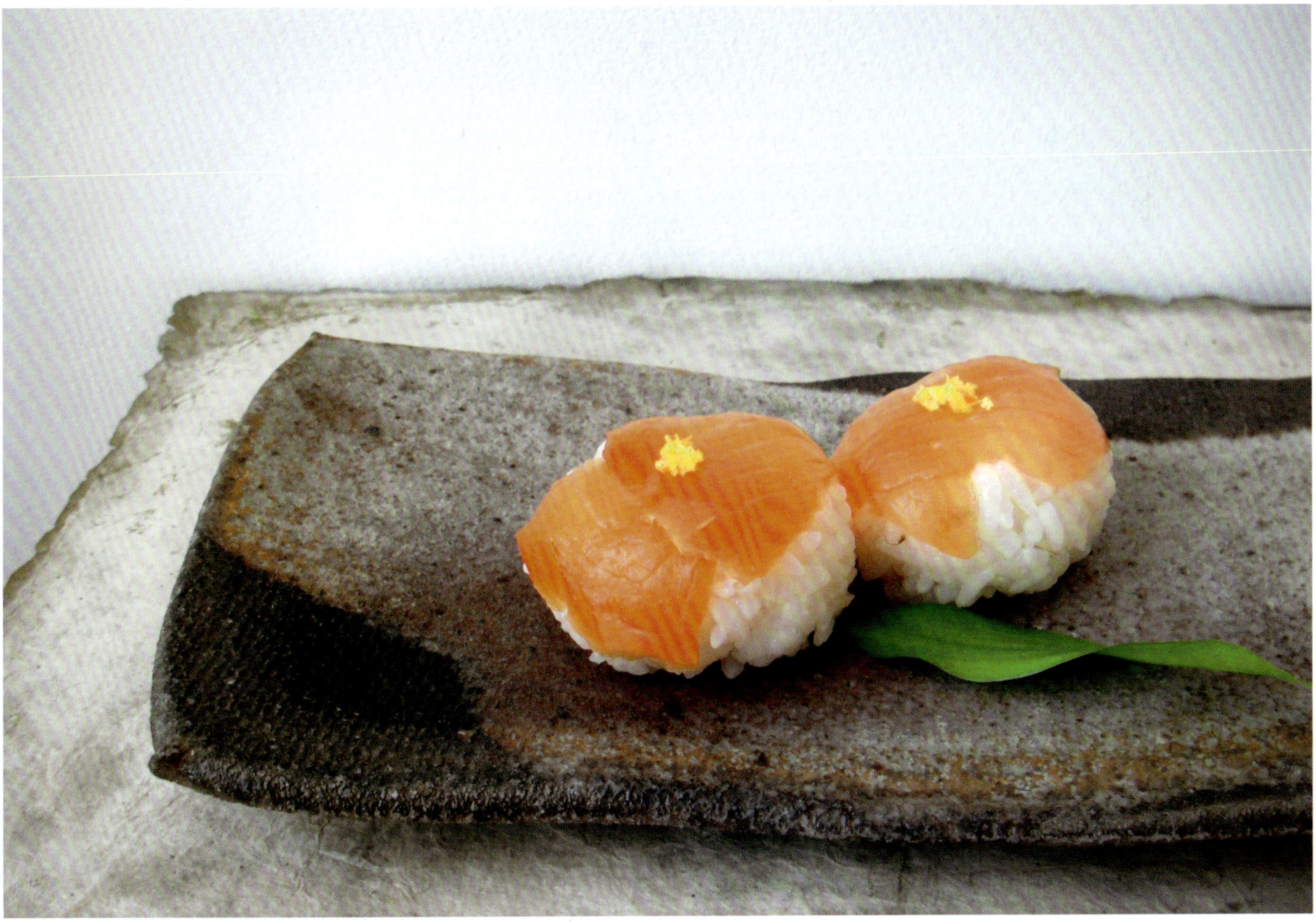

English country pottery

Medieval pots

Jugs have been made in England since medieval times. They were influenced by jugs imported from northern France, which were made of earthenware, thrown in a baluster shape (like the balusters in a balustrade) and decorated with red and white slips (coloured clays mixed with water). Medieval jugs were often decorated with thumb prints around the base and were sprinkled with galena (lead sulphide) and copper oxide to give a green glaze on the outside.

Pottery drinking vessels started to appear in the 15th century when stoneware jugs and tankards were imported from Rhineland Germany. These imports were copied by English potters, who made full-bellied earthenware jugs and mugs or tygs (three-handled cups), with several handles for shared drinking. Earlier mugs or tankards were made of wood, pitched leather or pewter. Silver or pewter platters and wooden trenchers were also used and dining was communal. The forms of pots were influenced, then as now, by the way we eat, whether communally or alone, and how food is served, either all at once or in courses.

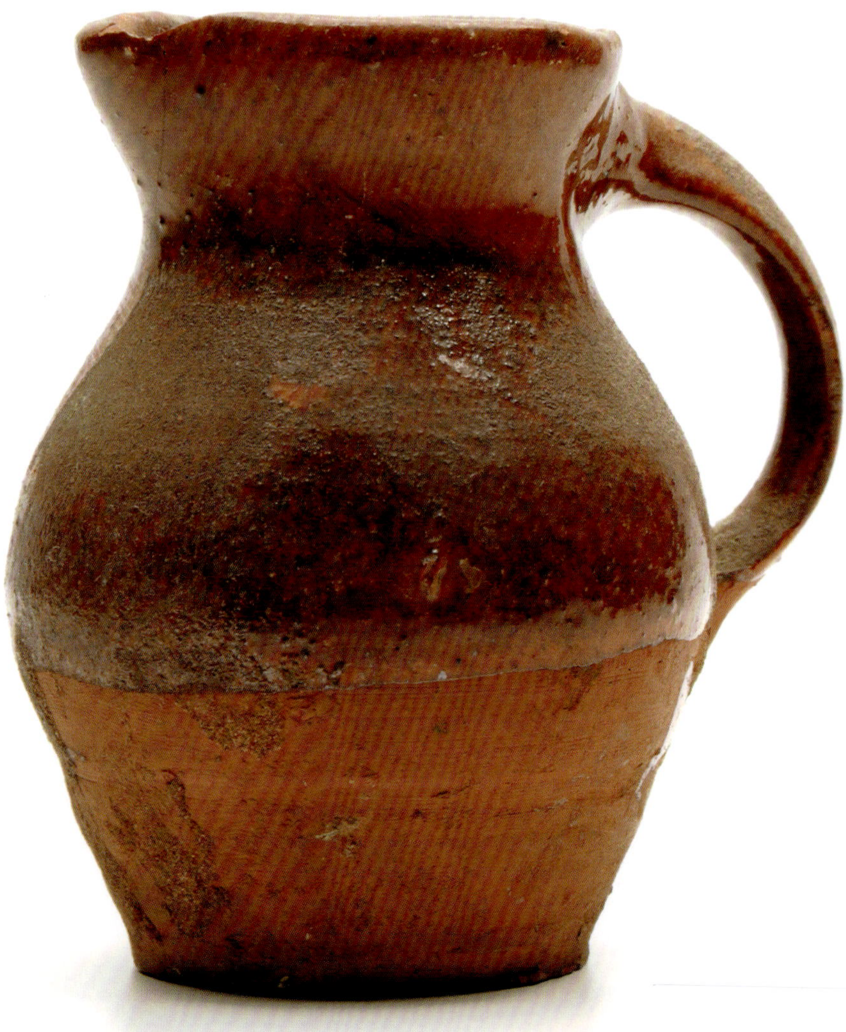

Devon earthenware jug with lead glaze from East-The-Water, Bideford, 19th century. Height: 10 cm (4 in.). Collection of Doug Fitch. *Photo: Jonathan Thompson.*

Svend Bayer, wood-fired stoneware jug, 1997. Height: 15 cm (6 in.). *Photo: Jonathan Thompson.*

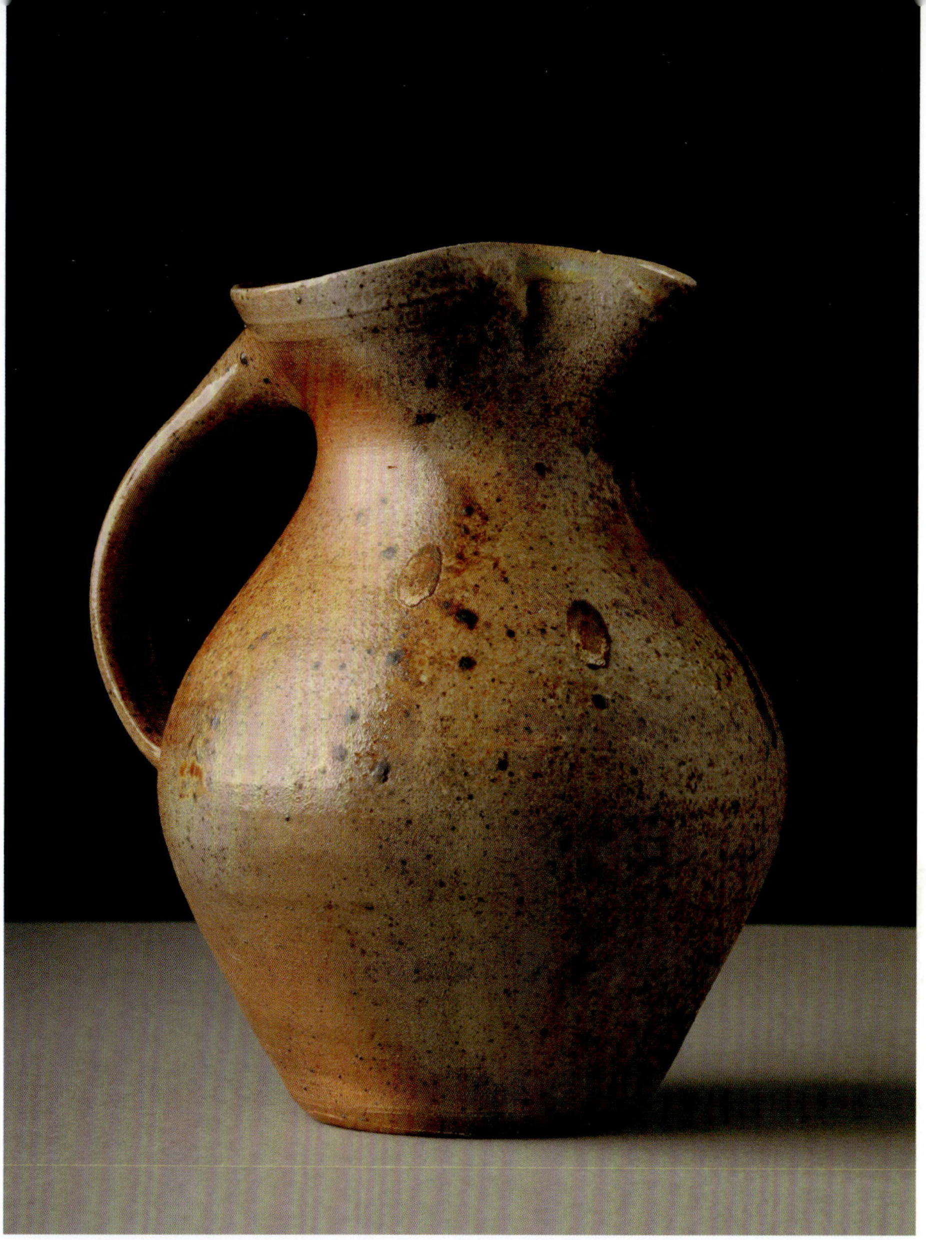

Doug Fitch, baluster jugs and watering can, red earthenware with sprigged decoration, slip and galena glaze, wood-fired, 2011. Height: 45 cm (18 in.). *Photo: Jonathan Thompson.*

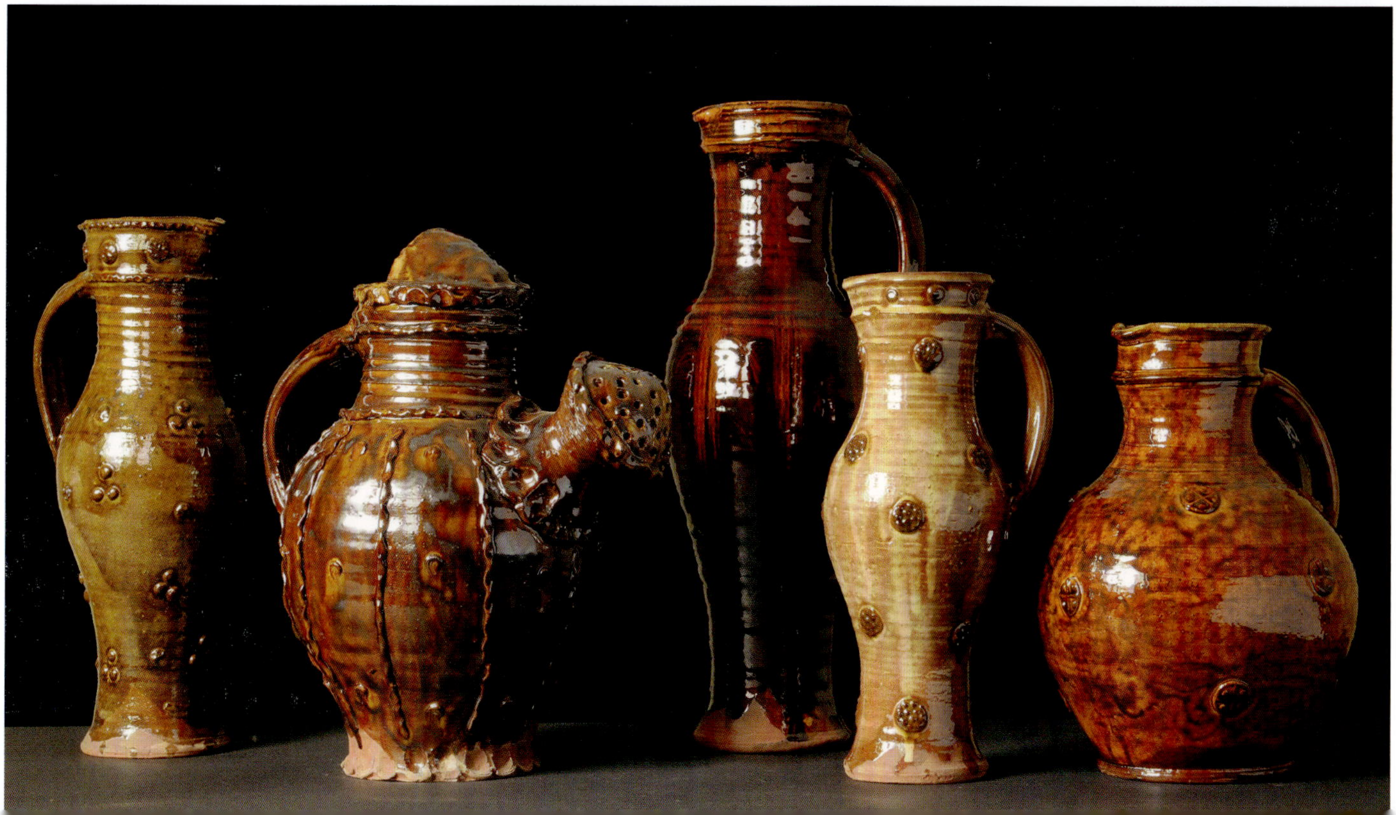

Slipware

At the end of the medieval period, there was a refinement in dining habits, with dining rooms separated from food preparation areas. Pots for the kitchen and the table became more specialised and began to include large jugs, smaller drinking vessels, baking dishes and pancheons (large kitchen bowls designed for settling milk, to remove the cream). Pots used in the kitchen were often purely functional while tableware could be more decorative. Commemorative pots were made for special occasions.

Doug Fitch, tyg (three-handled cup), red earthenware with sprigged decoration, white slip and galena glaze, wood-fired, 2011. Width: 18 cm (7 in.). *Photo: Jonathan Thompson.*

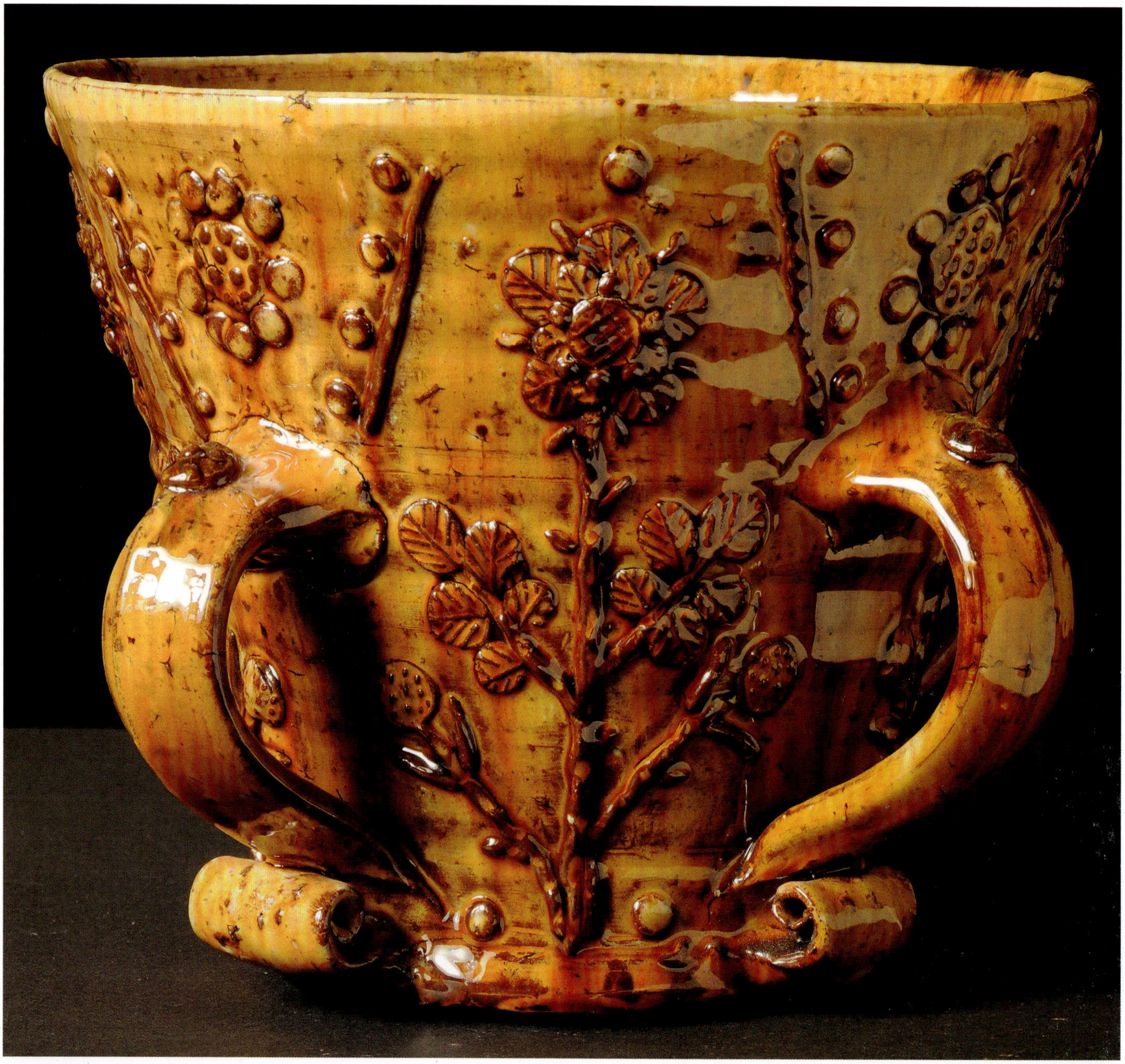

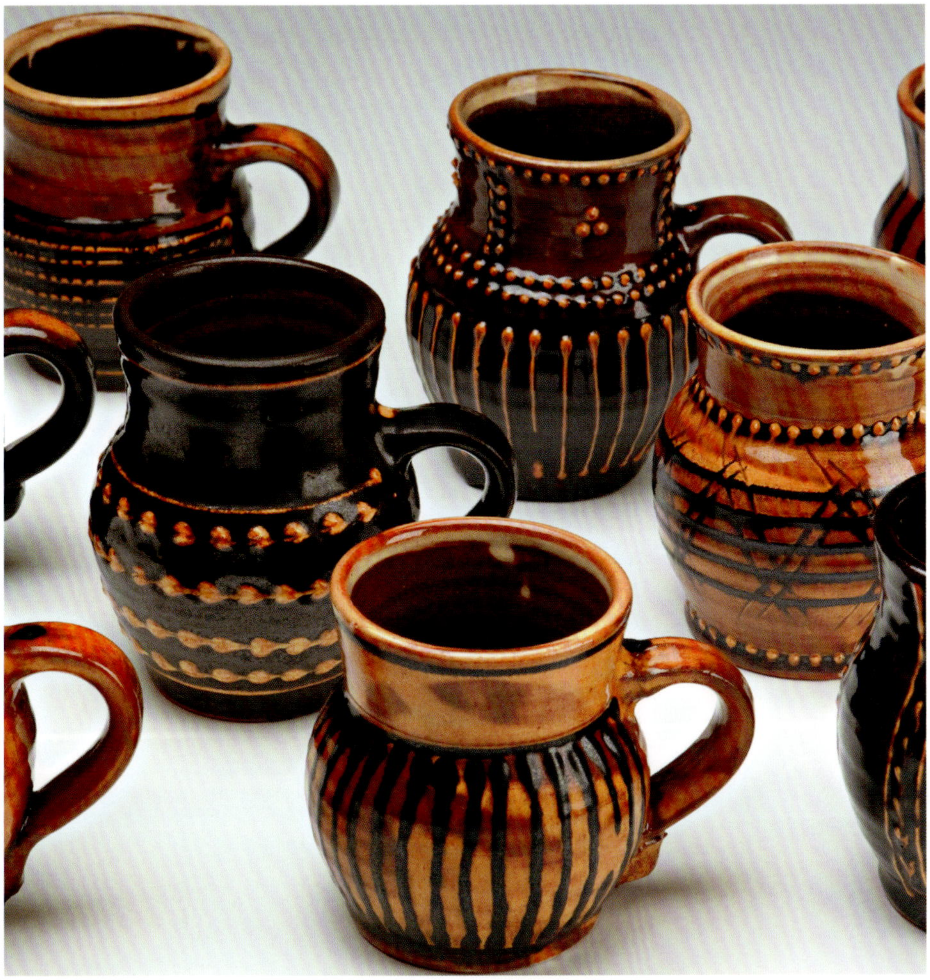

Hannah McAndrew, slip-trailed humbug mugs, 2010. Wood-fired red earthenware, height: 10 cm (4 in.). *Photo: Paul Adair.*

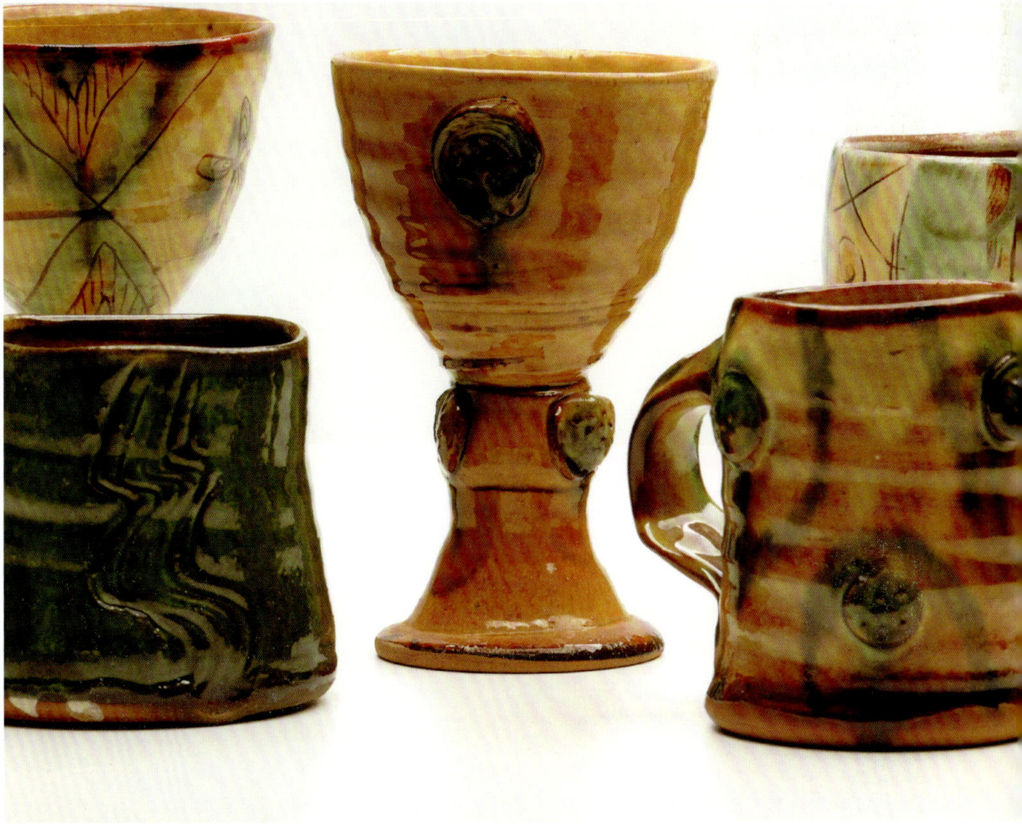

Svein Narum, Norway, mugs and goblets, 1993–2010. Earthenware, height: 14 cm (5½ in.). *Photo: Jonathan Thompson.*

Red earthenware pots decorated with white slip and covered with a lead glaze were made in North Devon and Staffordshire in large quantities. Harvest jugs, often elaborately decorated with sgraffito (drawings scratched through slip), were made to carry cider to the workers at harvest time. By the 17th century, large earthenware platters were in use, some of them elaborately slip-trailed.

Tin glaze

Tin-glazed earthenware, known as maiolica or Delftware, was imported to Britain from Spain, Italy and the Netherlands in the 16th century and was soon being made in London, Bristol and Liverpool. The coarse, buff clay body was covered in a smooth, white tin glaze superficially resembling imported Chinese porcelain. The ware was often decorated in cobalt blue, manganese purple, copper green and antimony yellow. The designs were initially copied from Chinese porcelain but soon included English

Paul Jessop, Barrington Pottery, Somerset, pancheon and jug, 2011. Smooth red clay with white slip decoration, simple finger swipe and light honey glaze, pancheon width: 38 cm (15 in.), jug height: 25 cm (10 in.). *Photo: Marion Lewis.*

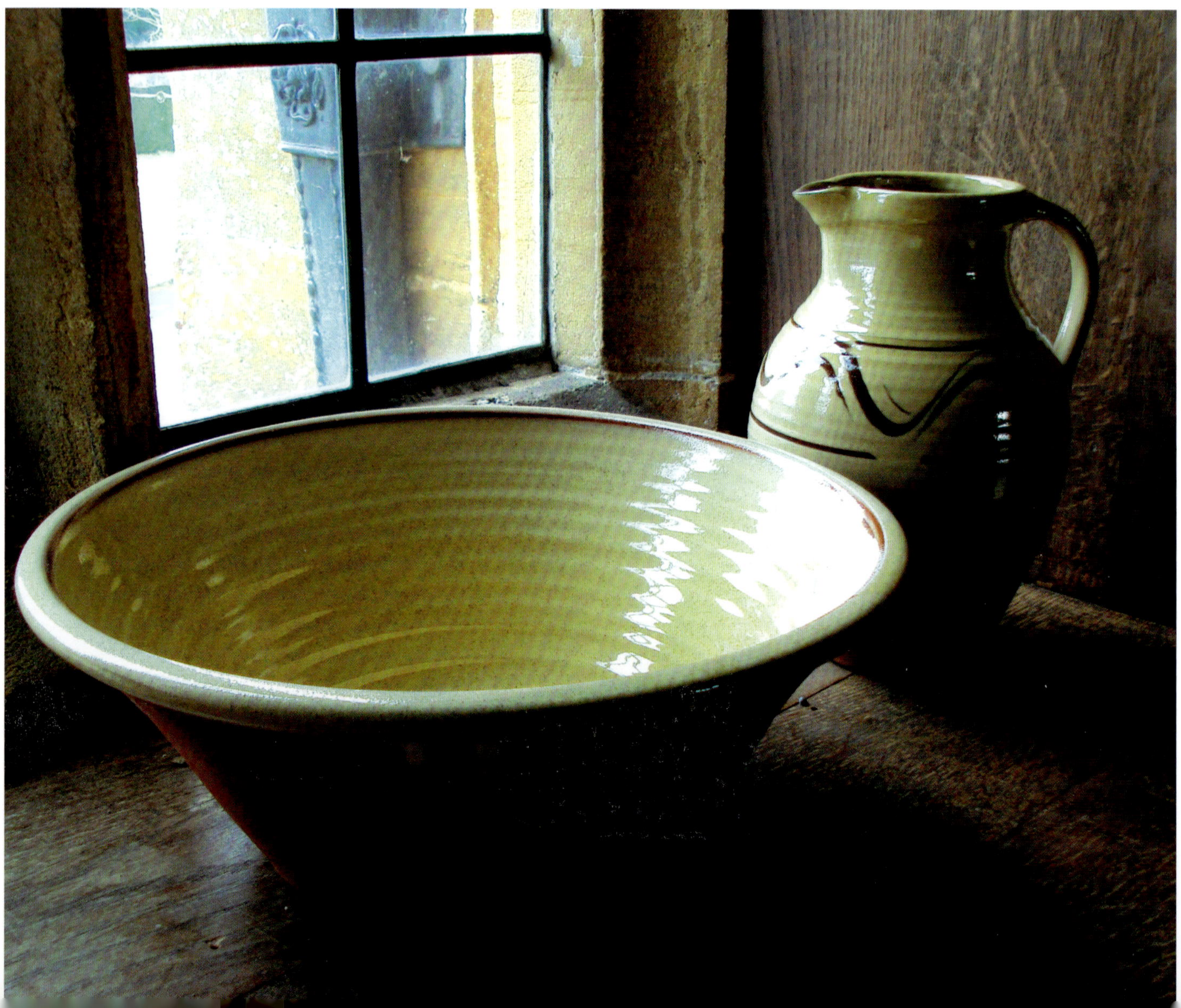

scenes. In the 17th century, large 'blue dash' chargers were decorated with portraits of King Charles II or Adam and Eve. Apothecary jars, posset pots and caudle cups were also made, the latter designed for serving hot drinks made from wine, milk and eggs.

Contemporary potters

Studio potters working today, such as Doug Fitch, are often inspired by the robust forms and decoration of jugs, dishes and platters made by early country potters. Other potters, such as Marshall Colman, work with earthenware in a more modern way, as can be seen in the images on the following page.

Kate Scott, thrown jugs, 2011. Tin-glazed red earthenware decorated with cobalt oxide using wax resist and sgraffito, height: 20.5 cm (8 in.). *Photo: Kate Scott.*

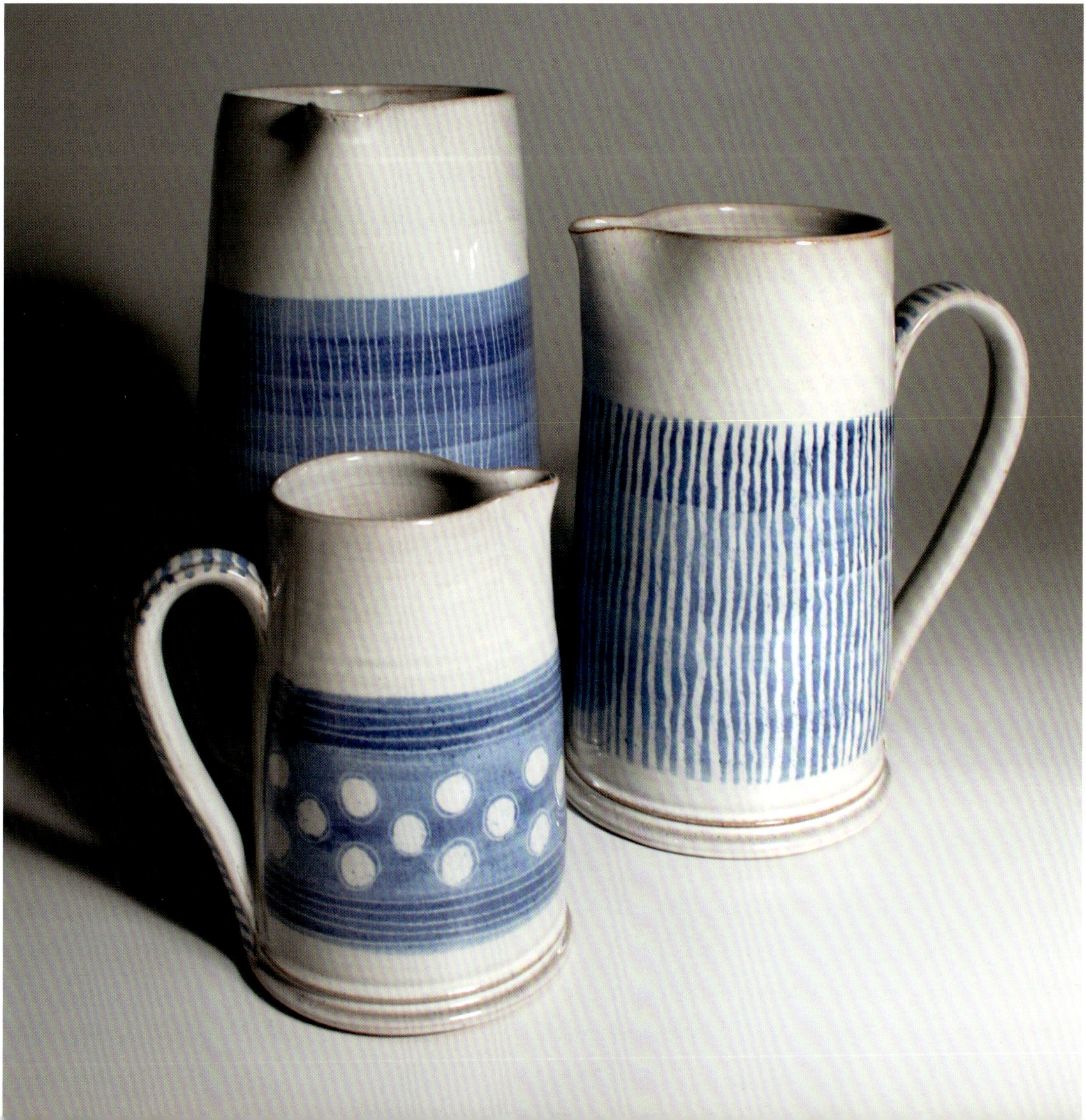

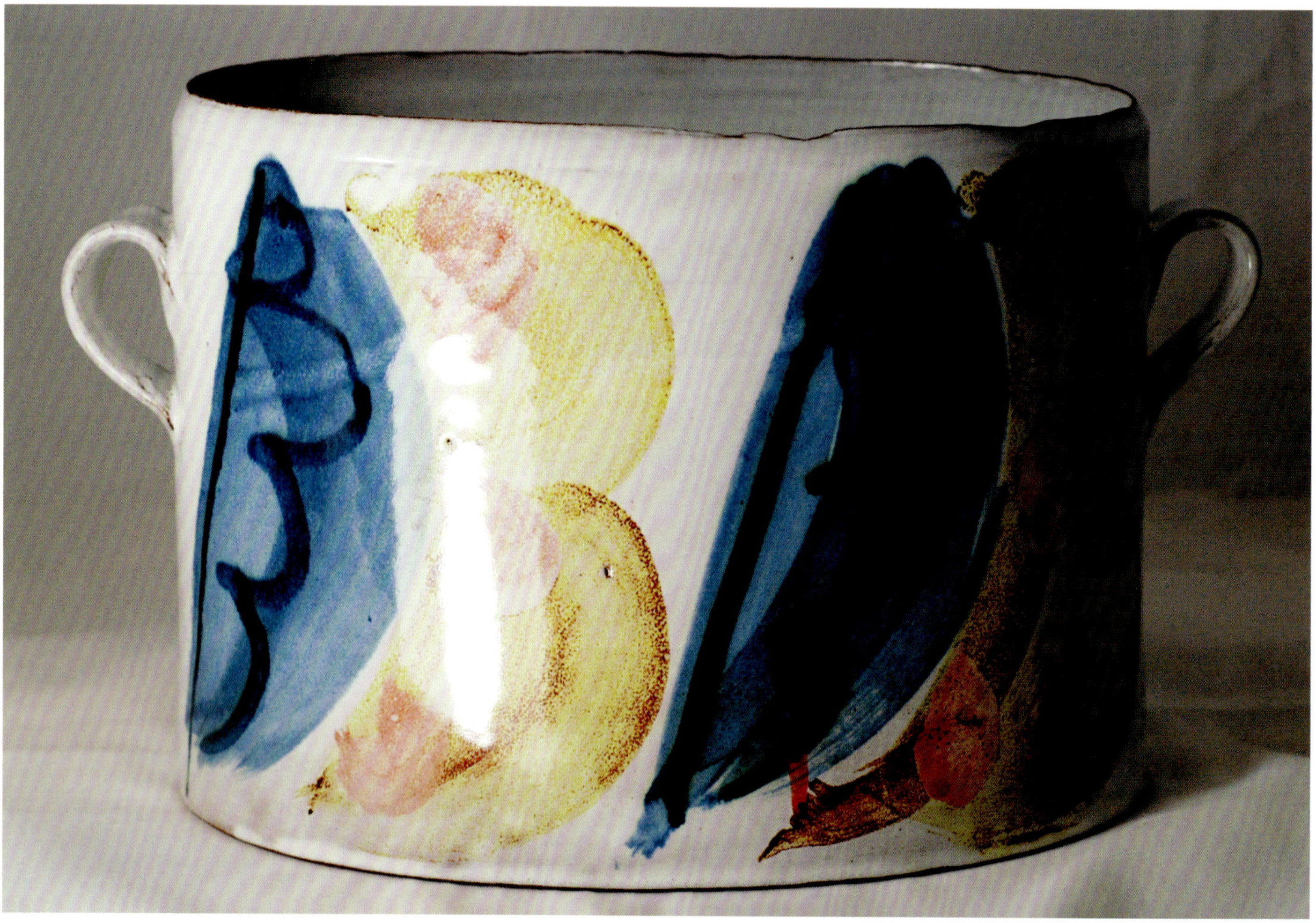

Marshall Colman, oval vessel, 2010. Tin-glazed earthenware with in-glaze decoration, 15 x 20 cm (6 x 8 in.). *Photo: by the artist.*

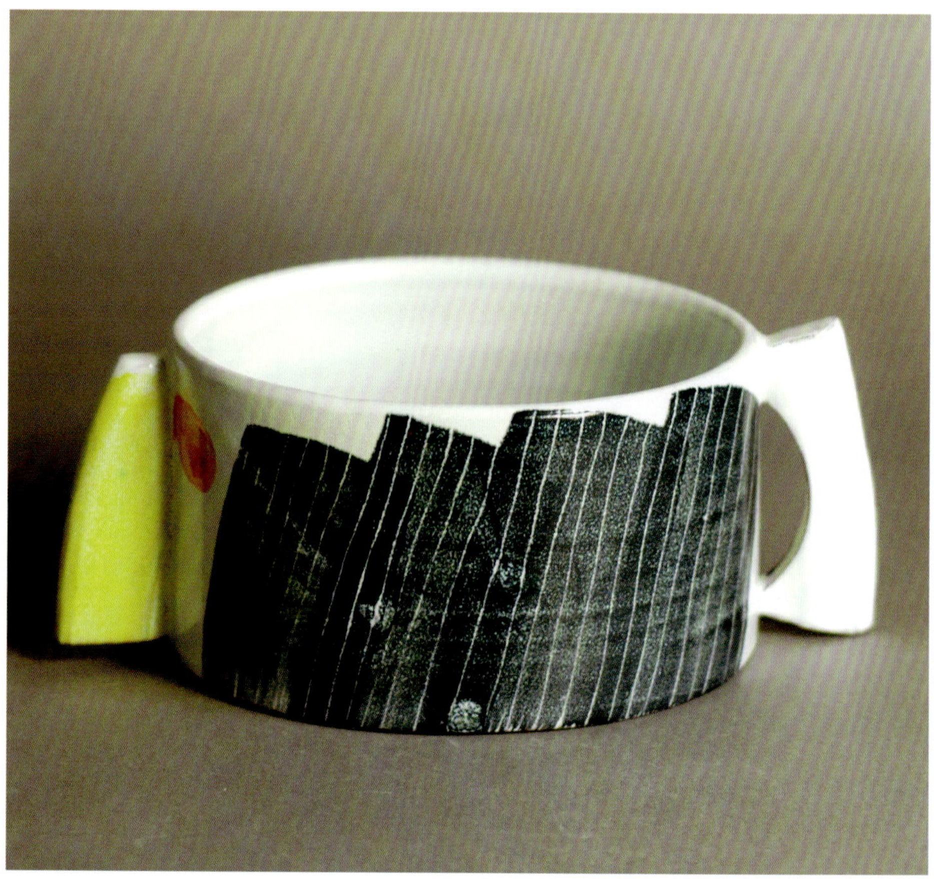

Marshall Colman, oval vessel, 2010. Tin-glazed earthenware with in-glaze decoration, 6 x 14 cm (2¼ x 5½ in.). *Photo: by the artist.*

Marshall Colman, straight-sided bowl, 2011. Tin-glazed earthenware with in-glaze decoration, diameter: 20 cm (8 in.). *Photo: by the artist.*

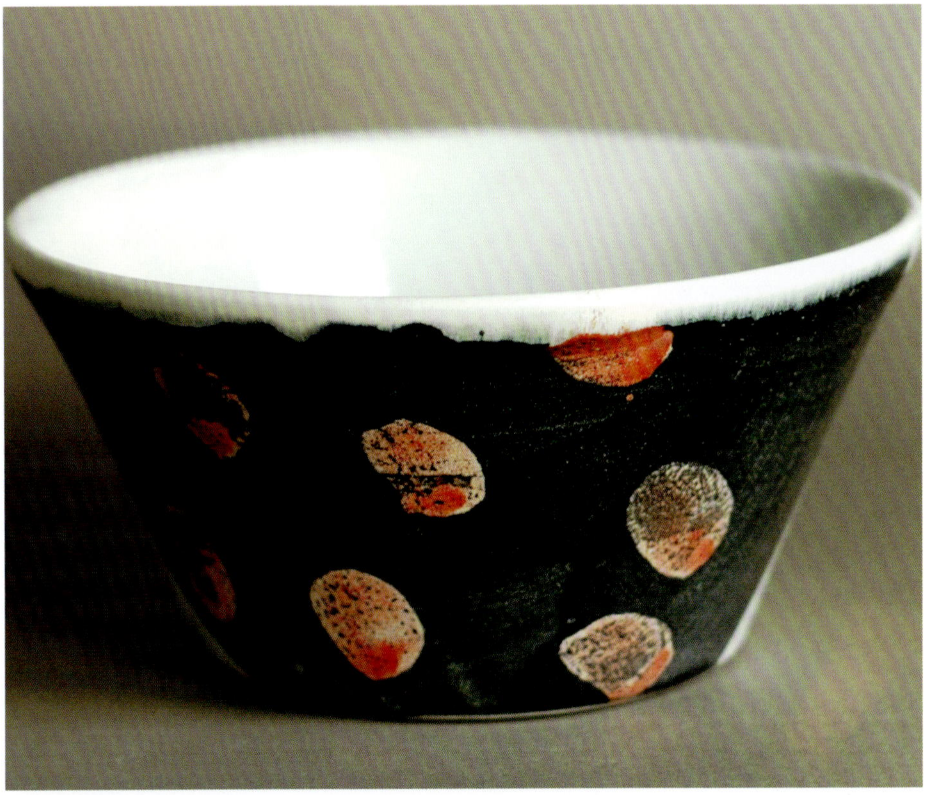

Marshall Colman, oval vessel, 2010. Tin-glazed earthenware with in-glaze decoration, 9 x 24 cm (3½ x 9½ in.). *Photo: by the artist.*

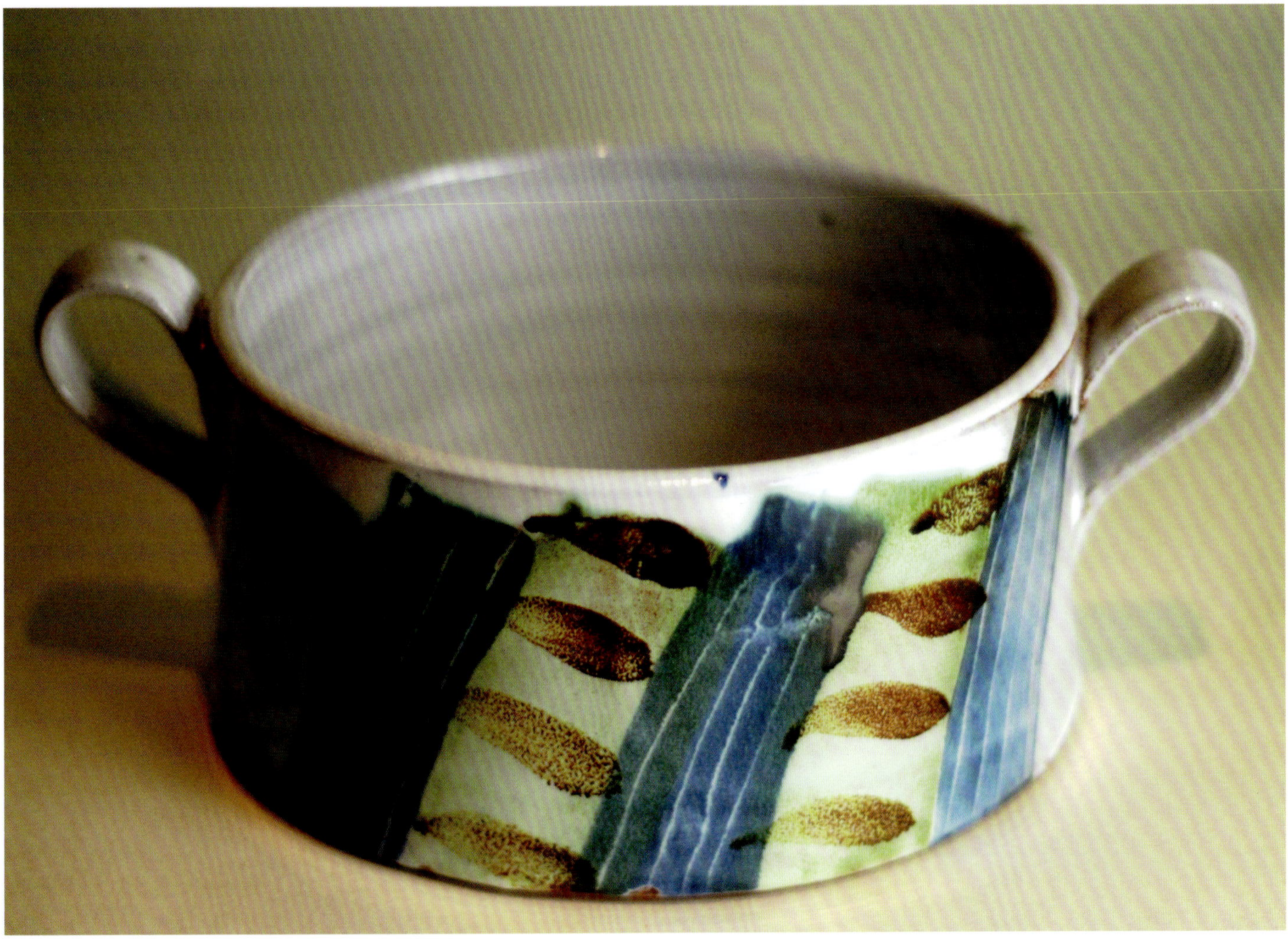

5 The Industrial Revolution

At the end of the 17th century, Stoke-on-Trent in Staffordshire, England, was home to a collection of small potteries making lead-glazed earthenware and salt-glazed stoneware pots to supply the local markets. Clay and coal for firing were locally available and pots were fired in brick bottle kilns. Over the next hundred years this cluster of six towns – Burslem, Hanley, Tunstall, Longton, Fenton and Stoke – was transformed into the world centre for mass production of pottery, with new materials and techniques in manufacturing and decoration and bold new designs.

Wedgwood's creamware

During the 18th century, Josiah Wedgwood (1730–1795) began mass-producing fine white earthenware in Stoke-on-Trent. The clay was whitened using light-coloured Devon ball clay and hardened by adding calcined flint. The use of plaster moulds made it possible to produce a large number of pieces either by slipcasting or jigger-jolley methods. The lead glaze contained a small amount of cobalt to counteract the yellow colour brought in by iron oxide impurities in the clay. Wedgwood's creamware was light, durable and more refined than earlier tableware. It was stronger than tin-glazed earthenware and cheaper than the European porcelain being made at Meissen and Sèvres. It was consequently very successful and was named Queen's Ware after being ordered by Queen Charlotte, the wife of King George III. Indeed, it seems to have been popular with royalty; Catherine the Great of Russia

Teapot with 'Abbey 1790' backstamp, height: 13.5 cm (5¼ in.), and semi-porcelain teacup, made by George Jones and sons in Stoke-on-Trent in the early 20th century as a copy of an earlier pattern. *Photo: Henry Bloomfield.*

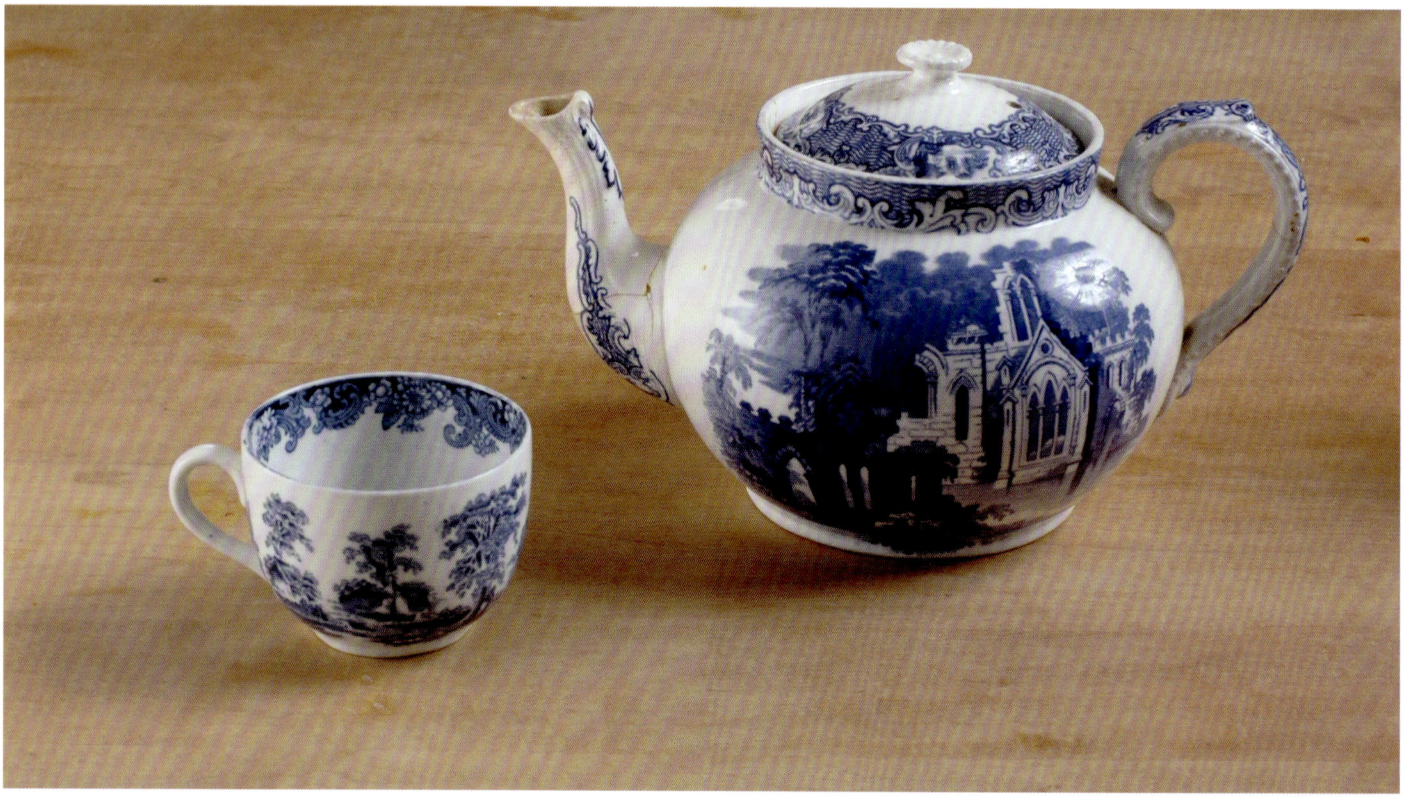

ordered a large dinner service of over 950 pieces. Wedgwood also made unglazed black basalt stoneware and coloured stoneware decorated with neoclassical designs in white relief, which he called Jasperware. He had a canal dug to transport his pottery and built a new factory, which he named the Etruria Works.

Bone china and the Willow pattern

In the late 18th century, deposits of china clay and Cornish stone, a feldspathic rock, were found by chemist William Cookworthy in southwest England. Josiah Spode invented bone china, a fine, translucent clay body made from china clay and Cornish stone with the addition of bone ash made from calcined cattle bones. Bone china was an English version of porcelain, the function of the bone ash being to flux and vitrify the china at a temperature achievable in a bottle kiln, around 1250°C (2282°F).

Transfer printing of cobalt blue underglaze was invented in the 1750s. This involved printing underglaze patterns onto paper from hand-engraved copper plates. The patterns were then transferred onto unglazed biscuit ware to produce blue and white china. One of the most popular prints was the Willow pattern, an English interpretation of a Chinese scene showing a willow tree by a lake with a bridge and a temple.

At the height of the area's production, there were several thousand coal-fired bottle kilns around Stoke-on-Trent, making vast quantities of pottery. For 200 years Stoke-on-Trent was the world leader in pottery production, but fell into decline at the end of the 20th century, unable to compete with cheaper foreign imports.

Wedgwood sauce boat, designed 1920, made in Stoke-on-Trent in the 1990s. White bone china, width: 22 cm (8¾ in.). *Photo: Henry Bloomfield.*

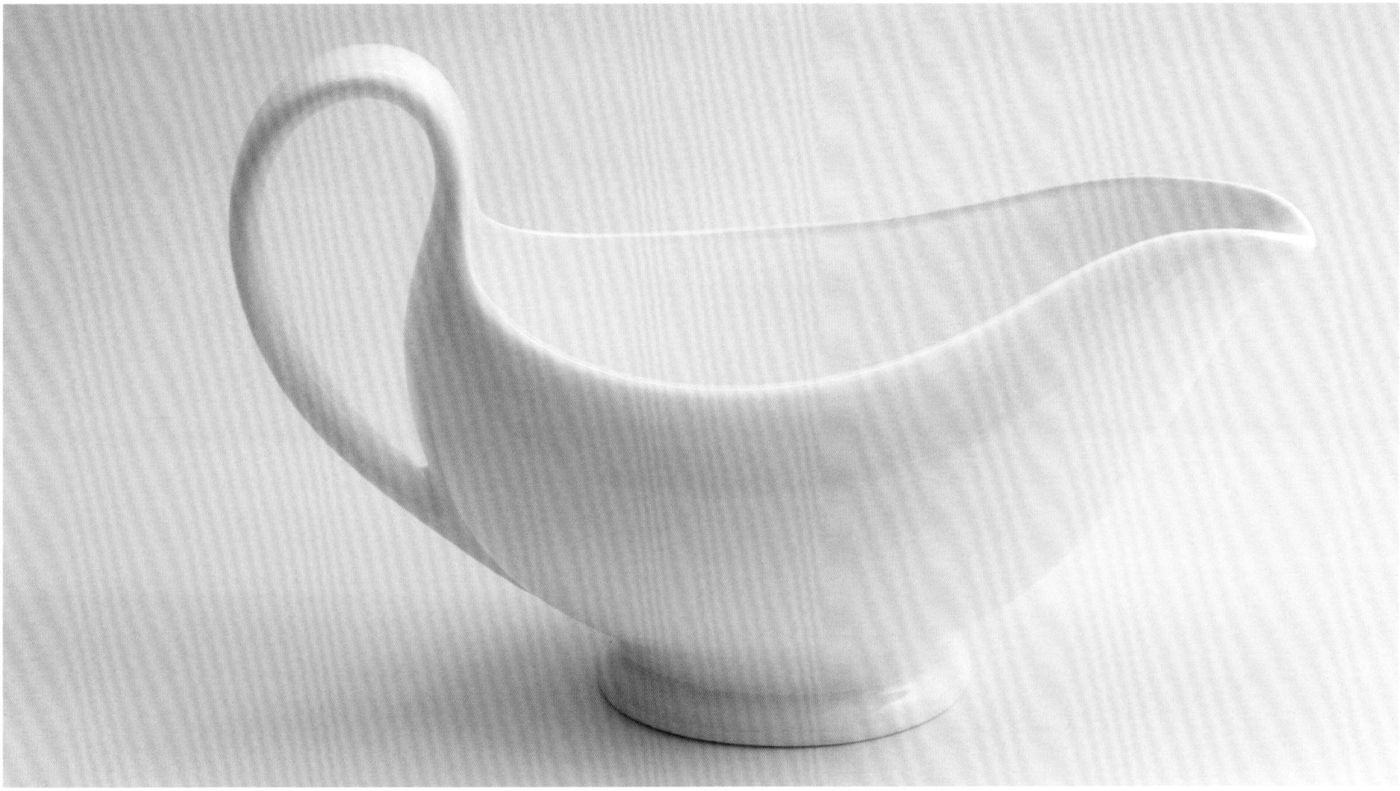

Stoke-on-Trent in the 20th century

In 1920 Wedgwood, the company established by Josiah Wedgwood in 1759 and run by his descendants, introduced their classic white bone china dinner service, which is still in production today. Wedgwood often employed artists to design and decorate their pots. In the 1930s architect Keith Murray designed vases, bowls and mugs for Wedgwood in the Art Deco style. His pots often had strong ribbing, inspired by Swedish designer Ewald Dahlskog, and were monochrome green, yellow or grey. He also designed a new, modern factory in Barlaston for Josiah Wedgwood, the great-great-grandson of the first Josiah. This burst of activity in Stoke, along with increasing demand, gave rise to influential new pottery companies and designers. Artists designing popular tableware ranges in the 1930s included Clarice Cliff and Susie Cooper. Their work was often highly decorated with flowers or stylised scenes and appealed to the fashion-conscious. In 1951, Wedgwood brought out commemorative pieces decorated by artists like Eric Ravilious and Norman Makinson for the Festival of Britain.

Mid-century potteries

Midwinter Pottery was founded in Stoke-on-Trent in 1910. During the 1950s the founder's son, Roy Midwinter, worked with artists and designers such as Jessie Tait and Terence Conran to produce decorated tableware ranges, including Salad Ware and Nature Study. He was influenced by organic American shapes (see p. 62) and in 1952 introduced the pottery's curvilinear Stylecraft range. Midwinter Pottery was eventually taken over by Wedgwood, which stopped making Midwinter designs in 1987.

Poole Pottery first originated in Poole, Dorset as Carter Stabler Adams, producing tiles and Art Deco pottery. From the 1930s they produced their Twintone tableware range, made from white earthenware with a soft matt glaze and contrasting colours on the inside and outside: sky blue and dove grey, pink and seagull (mottled grey and white), sepia and mushroom. The tableware was initially made in the flowing modernist Streamline shapes designed by John Adams in 1935. The range was updated in 1955 with round, flat knob shapes and coupe-shaped plates (without

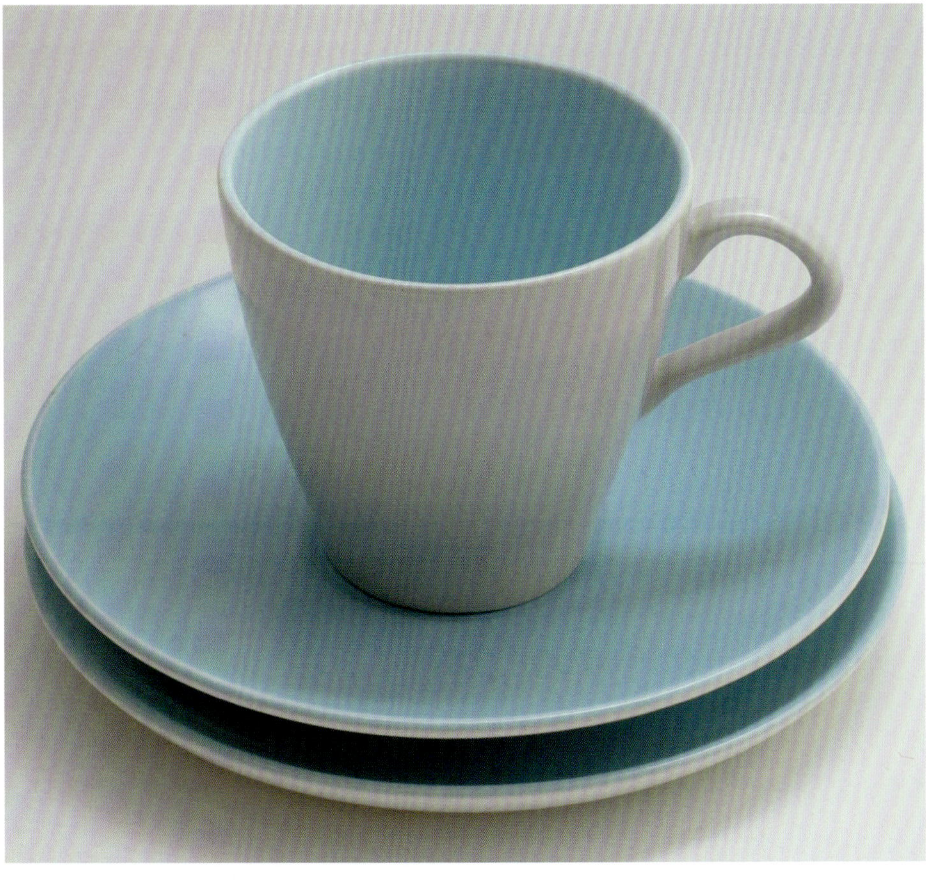

Poole Pottery, Twintone cup, saucer and plate, sky blue and dove grey, Contour shape. Produced 1958–81, saucer diameter: 15 cm (6 in.). *Photo: Henry Bloomfield.*

rims) by Alfred Read, and in 1959 Robert Jefferson designed stylish new Contour shapes with angled handles. Read also designed the hand-painted Freeform range in the 1950s, inspired by Scandinavian studio pottery (see pp. 56–61).

Production of the Twintone range stopped during the Second World War but then resumed and continued until 1981. Poole Pottery production has now moved to Stoke-on-Trent, where they make a range of art pottery.

Branksome China, breakfast cups and saucers, 2009. Cup diameter: 9 cm (3½ in.). *Photo: Tim Beddow.*

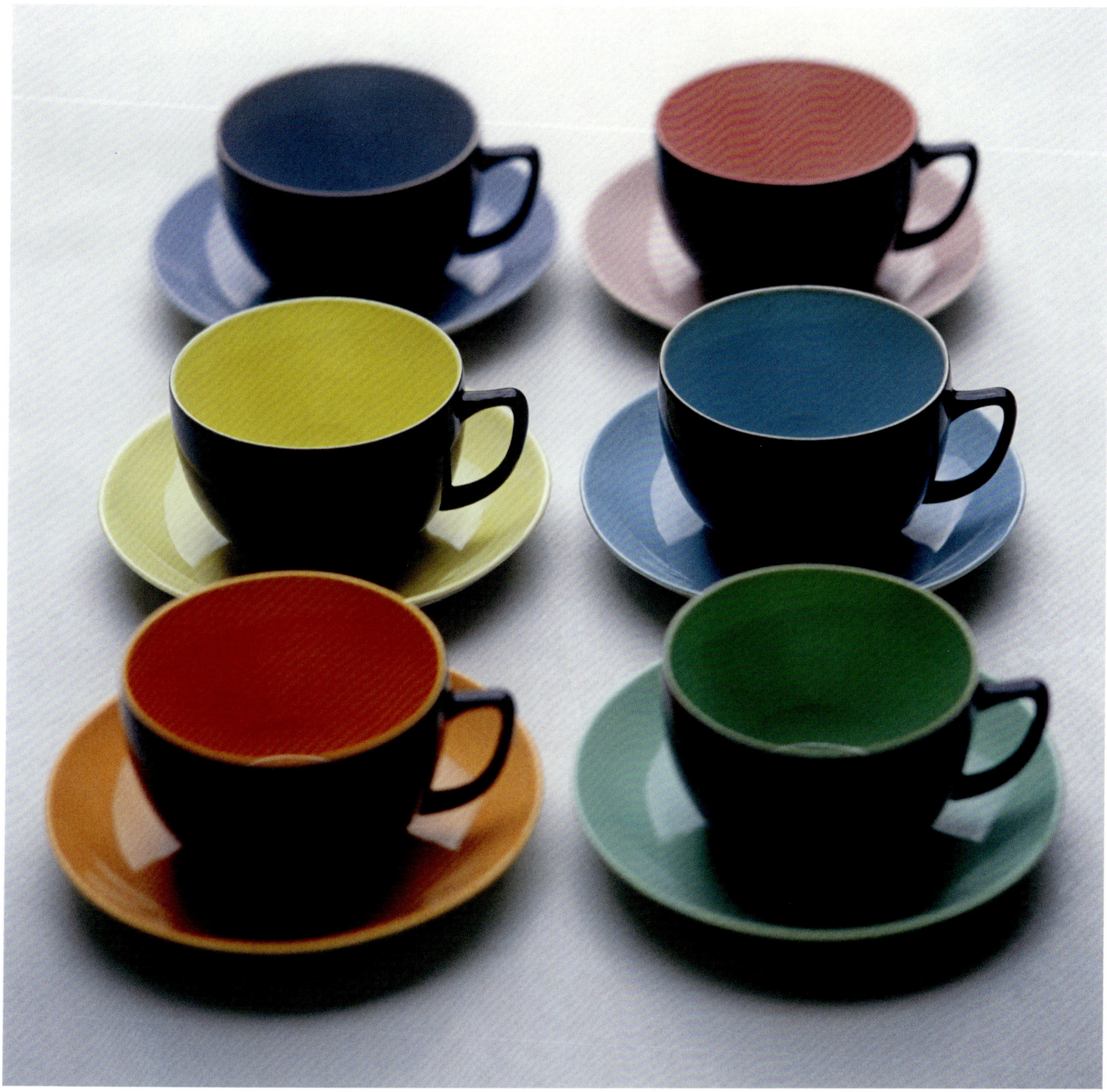

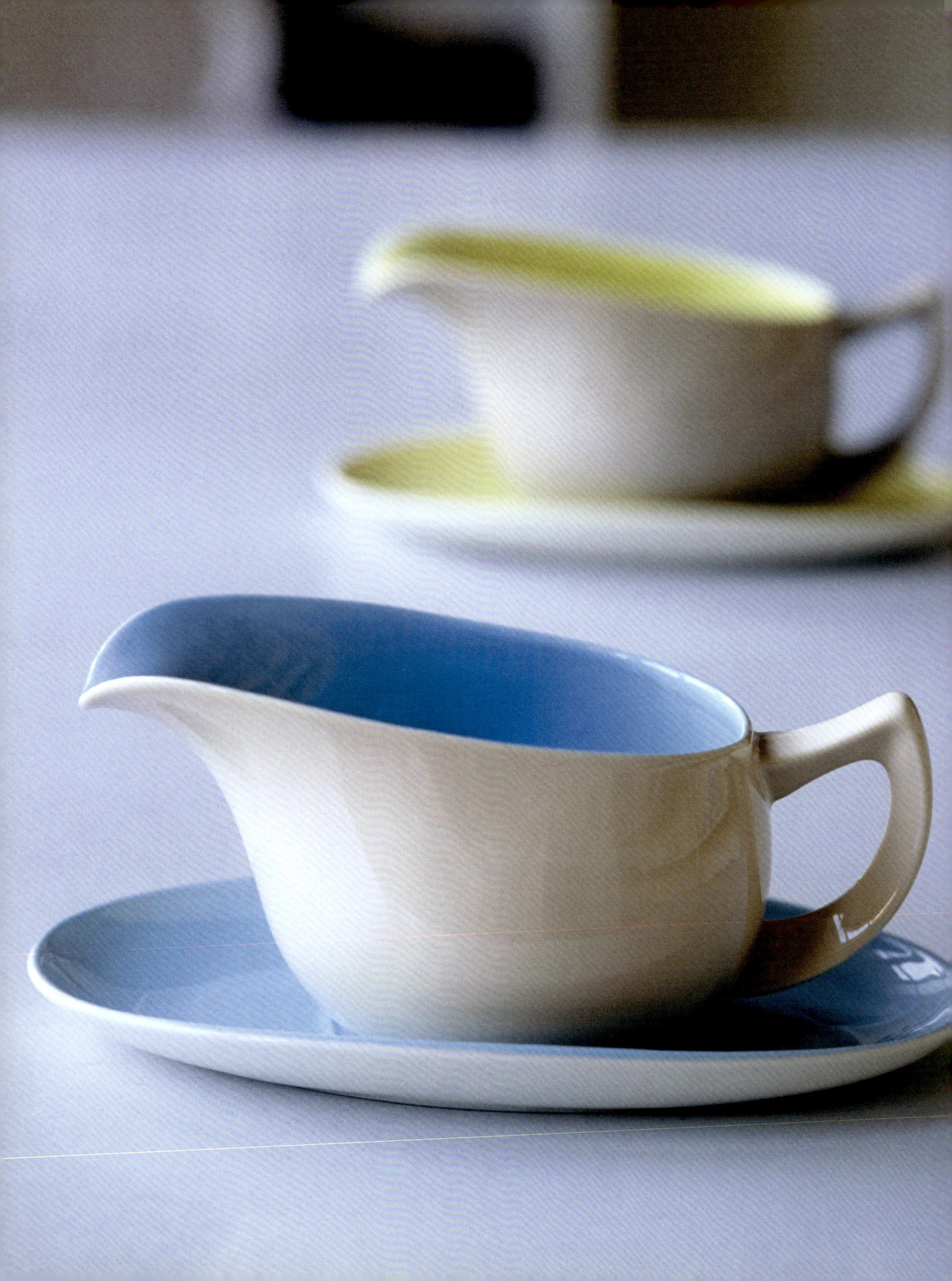

Branksome China was founded in Dorset in 1945 by Ernest Baggaley, who had worked in Stoke-on-Trent and at Poole Pottery, where he developed the two-colour glazes of the Twintone range. At Branksome, he developed his own white, high-firing porcelain clay body and made cups, plates and serving dishes glazed with pastel colours on the inside. The pieces were slipcast (or jollied) and fired to 1250°C (2282°F) before being spray-glazed and fired again to 1160°C (2120°F). The company was taken over by new owners in 2006, but ceased manufacture in 2012.

Stoke-on-Trent today

The pottery industry continues today in Stoke-on-Trent, though at a much reduced capacity, as there is now less demand for expensive formal dinnerware and more competition from cheaper imported ware.

There are a few small potteries in Stoke-on-Trent, such as Emma Bridgewater (founded in 1985), which produces sponge-printed earthenware; Burleigh (now owned by Denby), which makes traditional blue and white transfer-printed earthenware; and Repeat Repeat, which makes contemporary bone china. Larger potteries currently manufacturing in Stoke include Royal Stafford and Poole Pottery, both now owned by the Lifestyle Group. Tableware for hotels is produced in Stoke by several companies, including Dudson and Churchill China, which also makes tableware ranges for Jamie Oliver under the Queens brand. Portmeirion Pottery, which also owns Spode and Royal Worcester, has recently brought back some of its manufacturing from the Far East to Stoke-on-Trent, in particular Spode's Blue Italian range, decorated with pastoral scenes and Roman ruins and first launched in 1816. Wedgwood, as well as Royal Doulton and Waterford Crystal, are now owned by a New York investment firm that has moved most of the manufacturing to Indonesia, where they produce tableware ranges aimed at the wedding-gift market, designed by the likes of Jasper Conran and Vera Wang.

Emma Bridgewater, storage jar, made in Stoke-on-Trent, 1990. Cream earthenware, hand-sponged figs design, height 15.5 cm (6 in.). *Photo: Henry Bloomfield.*

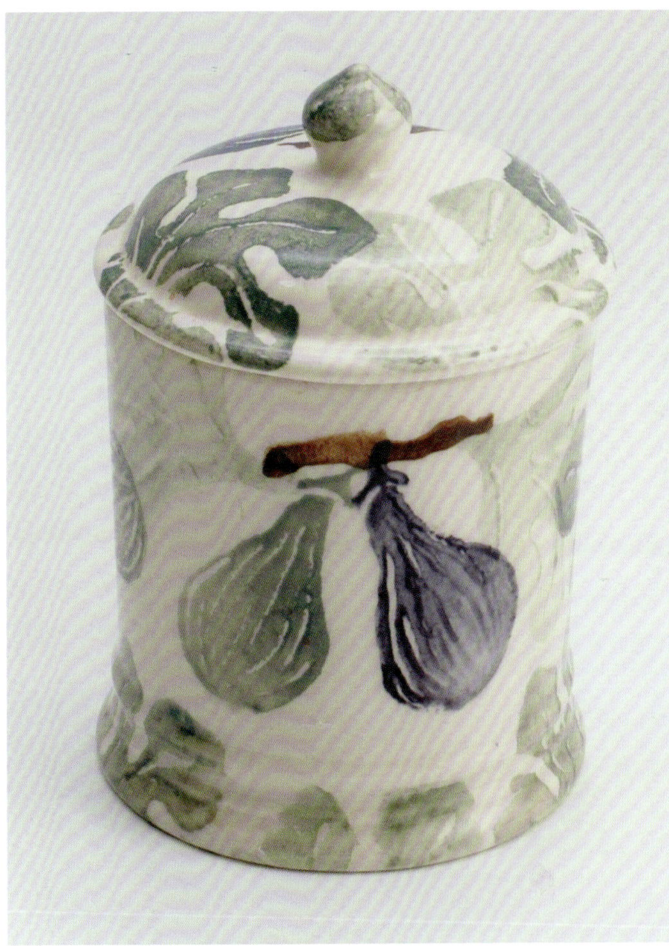

Branksome China, sauce boat and stand, 2009. Sahara and Arctic blue, Elephant grey and Evening primrose, height: 7.5 cm (3 in.). *Photo: Tim Beddow.*

The American market traditionally prefers high-quality British-made tableware to that manufactured in the Far East, and there are hopes that the potteries in Stoke-on-Trent will revive due to this demand. Stoke potteries are best at producing earthenware and bone china and have very high quality-control standards; porcelain, however, is usually manufactured in Europe or the Far East. Factories in the Far East have lower labour costs but also lower standards, and high percentages of seconds are often included in shipments.

There are several high-quality porcelain manufacturers in France, including Pillivuyt and Apilco, which makes sturdy white porcelain bistro ware including ramekins and soufflé dishes. German porcelain factories are often at the high end of the market and include Rosenthal, Nymphenburg, Arzberg and Villeroy & Boch.

One company based in Stoke-on-Trent that does make well-designed bone china tableware is Repeat Repeat, formed in 1984 by designers Gillian Naylor and Mark Faulkner. Here, Naylor explains the evolution of the company's designs and vision:

'Initially we produced surface-pattern designs for textiles and illustration for magazines, gift cards and wrap. Our design studio was based in Stoke-on-Trent, the heart of the pottery industry, which at that time was a hive of activity with factories of all types producing an amazing variety of ceramics, alongside mouldmakers, modellers, toolmakers, transfer printers, and colour and glaze manufacturers. Working within this bustling environment it was not long before we got involved and adapted our designs to work on bone china.

'In design terms we had a firm vision of what we wanted to achieve. We were surprised to find out that many potteries did not have any design input whatsoever. The norm was to use existing ceramic shapes and apply open stock ceramic transfers – mostly very traditional patterns – and subsequently different potteries would produce slight variations of the same patterns.

'We wanted a strong contemporary design element within our product range. Over time we developed a niche market for our designs and as sales gained momentum the time was right to get kilns and become more involved in our own production. We began designing and incorporating our own bone-china shapes into our collection.

'As the economy declined the larger factories began to close down or turned to outsourcing their manufacturing to China and Indonesia. Fashions and tastes changed. Formal dinnerware became less popular as fewer couples included a special dinner service on their wedding list – instead preferring cheaper and more disposable imported casual tableware. Sadly, a large number of the smaller factories fell by the wayside, as did their support industries, and skills developed over centuries began to wane.

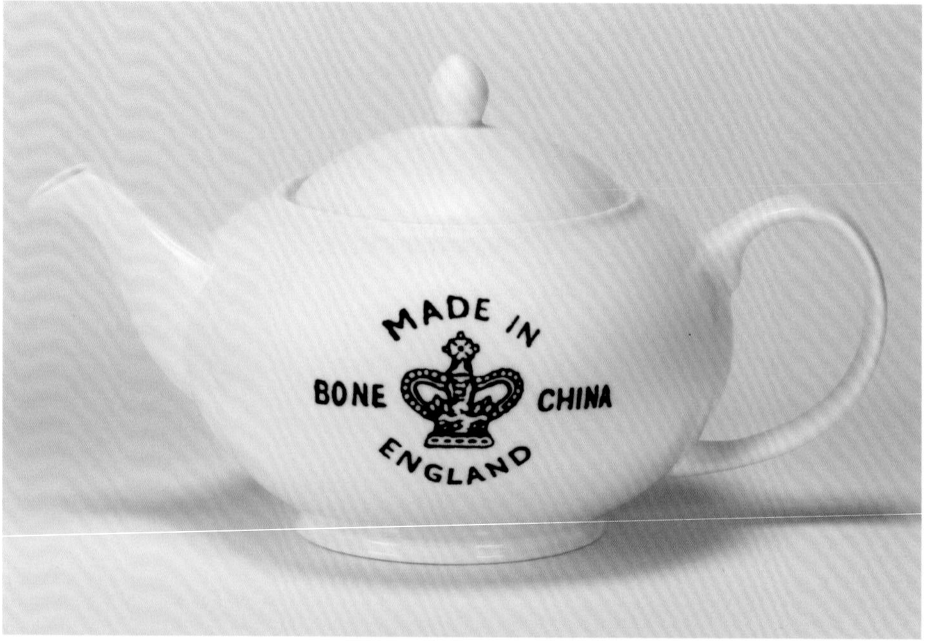

Britannia Backstamp teapot, 2009. Stoke-on-Trent bone china, height: 13.5 cm (5½ in.). *Photo: Repeat Repeat.*

'Ceramics made in Stoke-on-Trent, or anywhere in the UK, became more and more scarce and we wanted to shout from the rooftops that Repeat Repeat still produce bone china in England. This resulted in our Britannia range, most notably the Backstamp design. Traditionally, backstamps on the base of ceramics state where the product is made. We decided to celebrate that the piece is made in England by using a backstamp as a decorative motif, taking pride of place on the front of the bone china instead of being hidden away on the base.

'Despite the difficulties facing manufacturers in the current economic climate, we are finding that people are willing to pay a higher price for quality bone china, with the added bonus that it has been made in England.

'As a relatively small company we have the ability to adapt to market change. We have produced a range of tableware called Plum, pure white bone china with tactile raised patterns echoing the design styles of the mid-century. This is where we feel our strength lies: the ability to change and produce small-scale production runs to keep in line with, and also to play a part in, the ever-changing market trends.'

Britannia Backstamp mugs, 2009. Bone china, height: 8 cm (3¼ in.). *Photo: Repeat Repeat.*

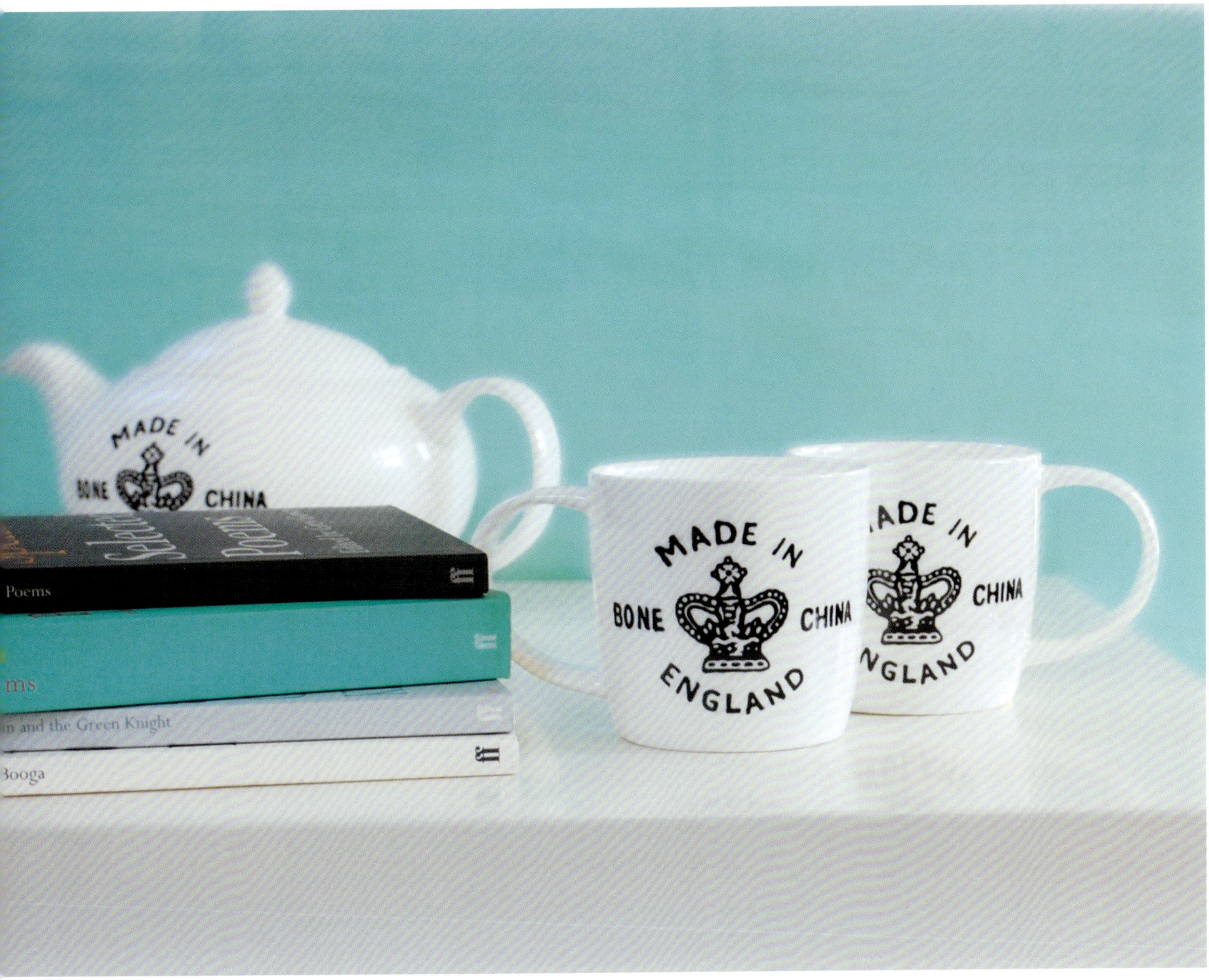

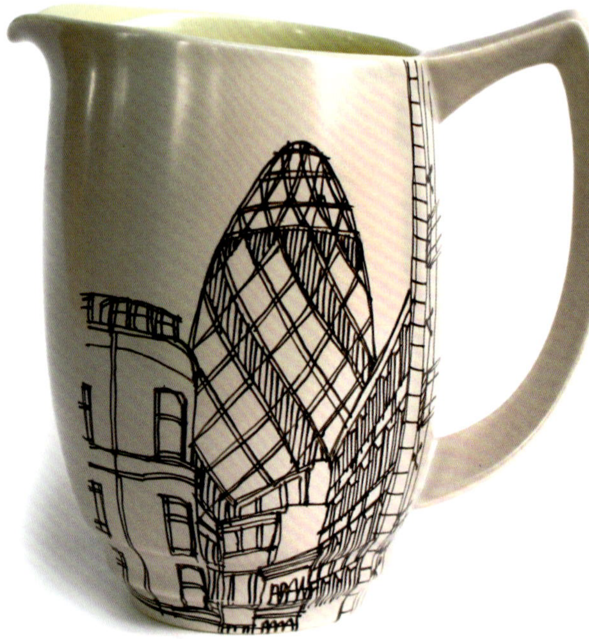

Esther Coombs, Branksome China jug, 2011. Features drawing of the Gherkin building in London, height: 12 cm (4¾ in.). *Photo: by the artist.*

Contemporary artists

Contemporary makers and designers have the freedom to find inspiration from a wide range of sources. May Luk is a contemporary artist who has been influenced by the designs of the English Industrial Revolution. She makes press-moulded stoneware plates and platters in her Brooklyn studio, sometimes covered with porcelain slip and designs, and screen-prints her own transfers in cobalt blue underglaze. Her Brooklyn Chinoiserie range includes the Manhattan Bridge and New York City water tower as well as elements from the traditional Willow pattern, while her Old Curiosity range incorporates Victorian engravings of pigeons, bicycles and hats.

Esther Coombs makes upcycled tableware. She finds vintage china at antique fairs and in charity shops and draws on it in black overglaze, refiring it in her oven. Her line drawings often feature urban and rural buildings. She also constructs cake stands by drawing on and assembling plates, upturned wineglasses, cups and saucers. She particularly likes decorating mid-century pieces from Poole Pottery and Branksome China.

Plum tableware group, 2011. Bone china made in Stoke-on-Trent, mug height: 8.5 cm (3½ in.). *Photo: Repeat Repeat.*

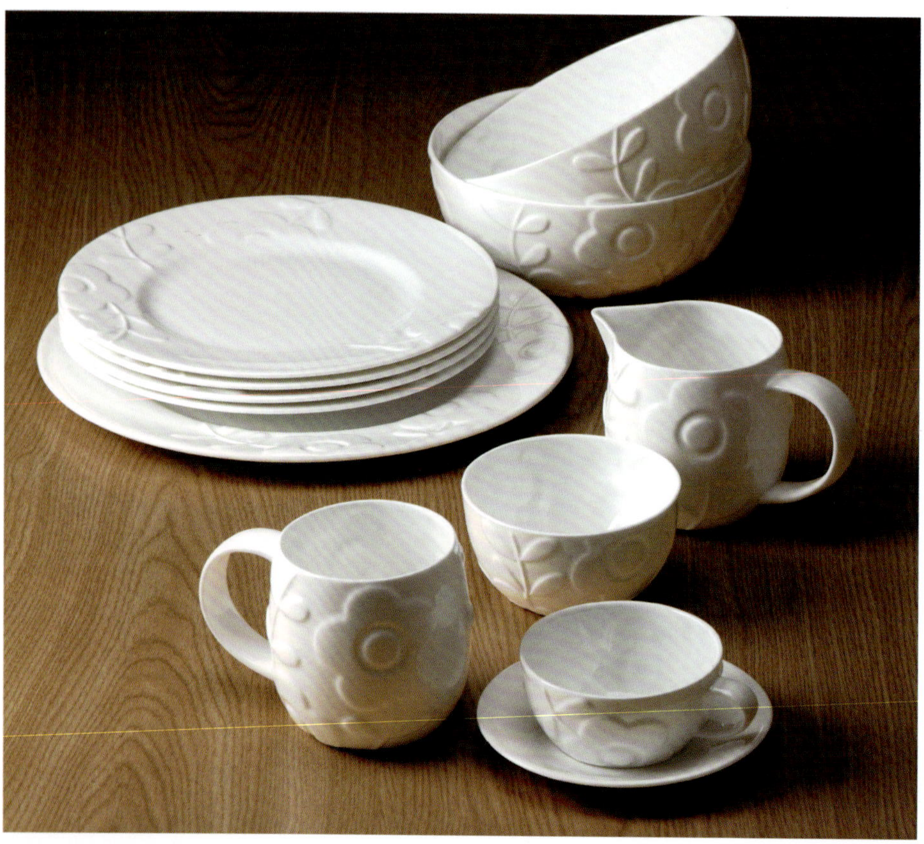

May Luk, Brooklyn Chinoiserie plates, 2010. Porcelain slip on stoneware, cobalt transfer print in underglaze, fired to cone 8 (1260°C/2300°F), platter width: 30 cm (12 in.). *Photo: Jessica Marquez.*

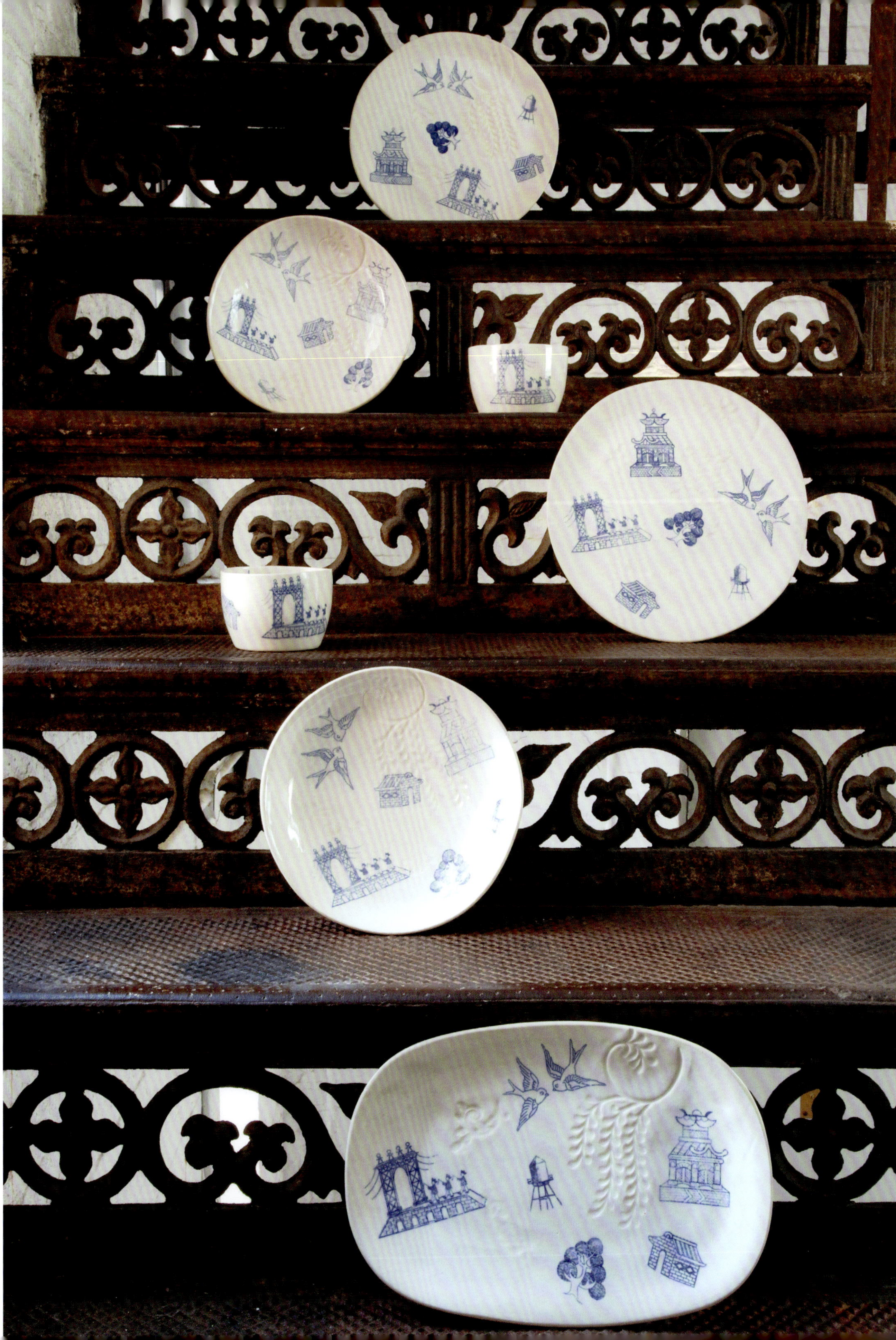

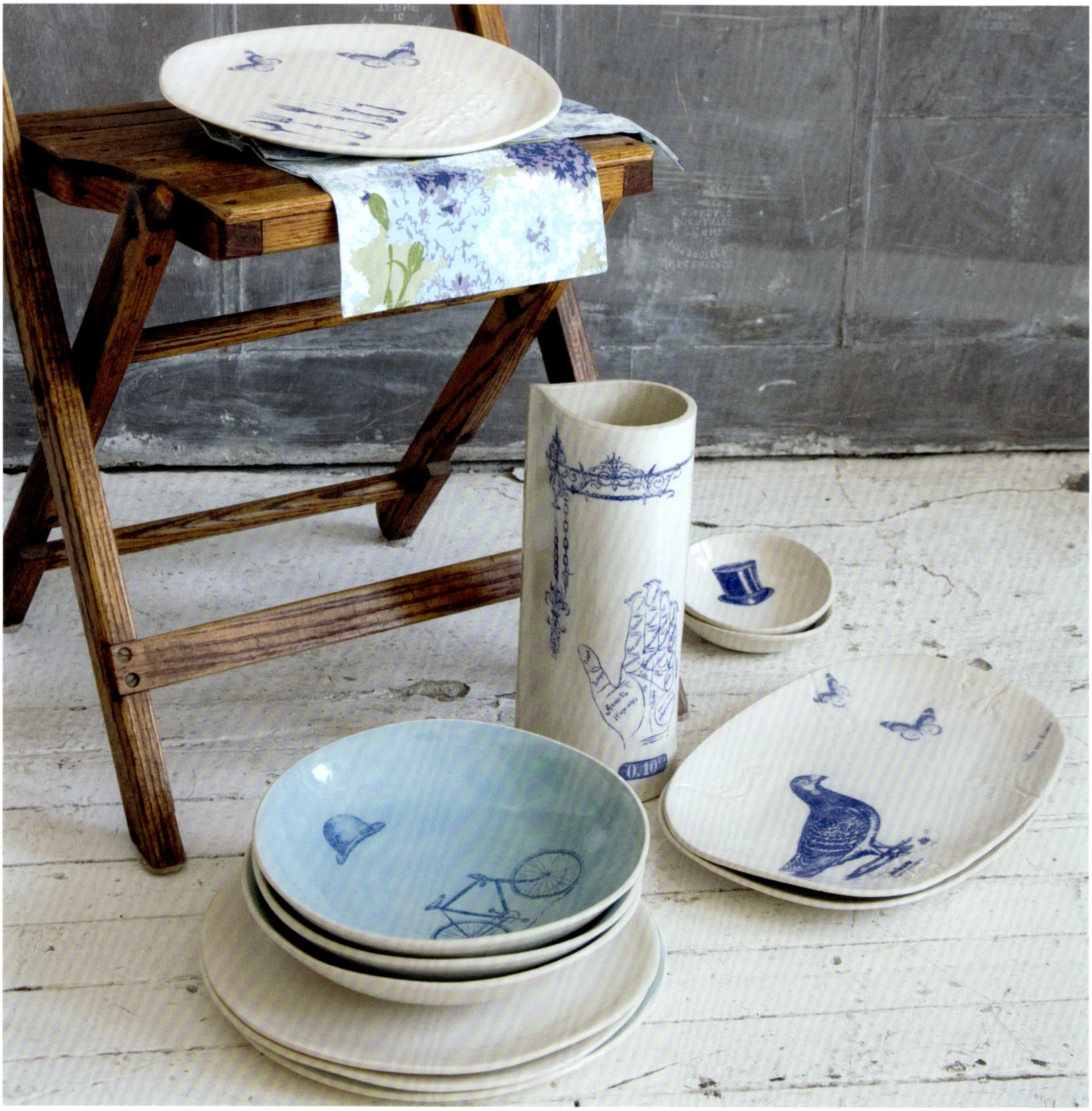

May Luk, Old Curiosity plates, bowls and Brighton vase, 2010. Porcelain slip on stoneware, cobalt transfer print in underglaze, fired to cone 8 (1260°C/2300°F), platter width: 30 cm (12 in.). *Photo: Jessica Marquez.*

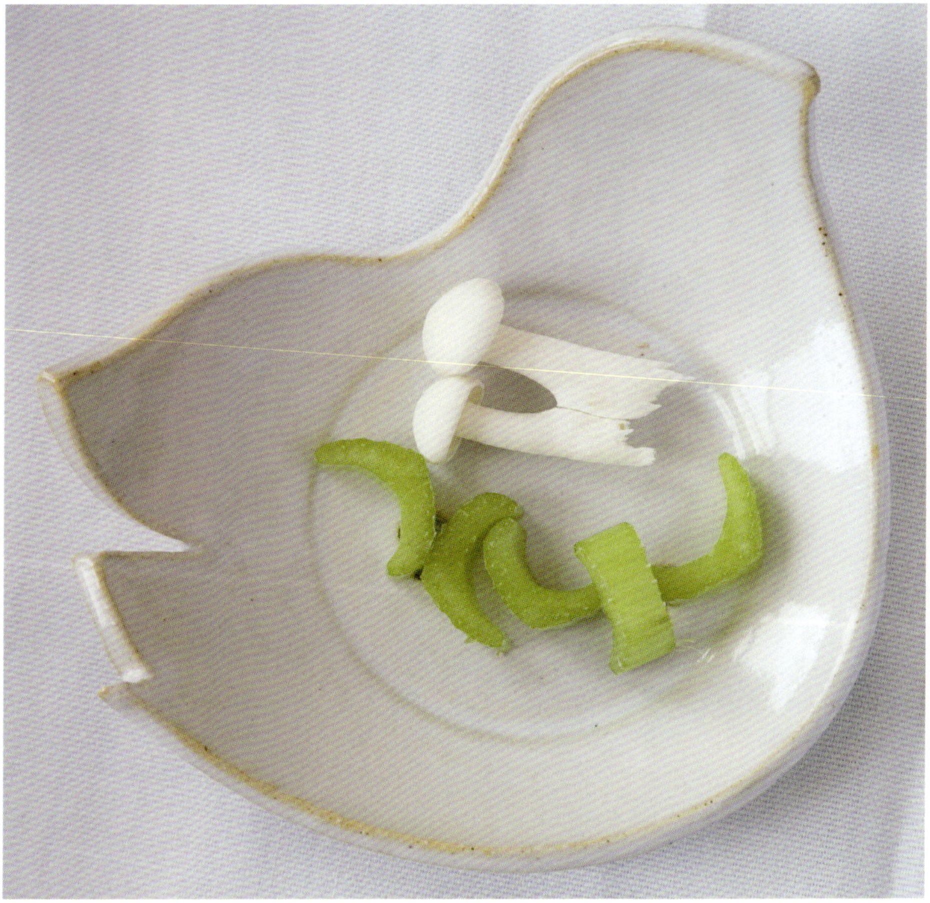

May Luk, Moon Glow dove dish, 2010. Stoneware, 18 x 15 x 4.5 cm (7 x 6 x 1¾ in). *Photo: Jessica Marquez.*

Esther Coombs, Poole Pottery earthenware coffee pot, 2011. Features drawings of beach huts, height: 22.5 cm (9 in.). *Photo: by the artist.*

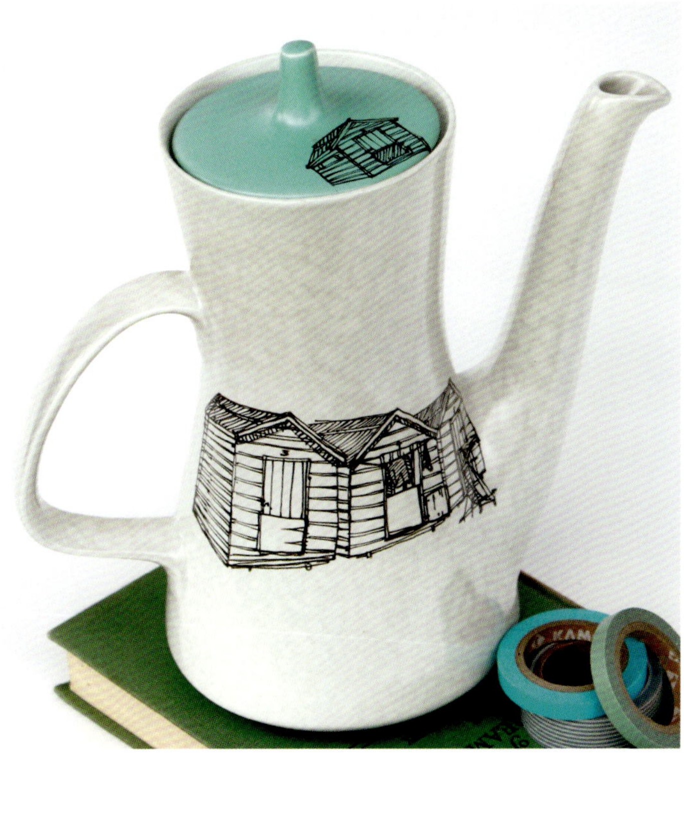

Esther Coombs, Poole Pottery earthenware cup and plate, 2010. Features drawing of the British Museum, diameter: 14 cm (5½ in.). *Photo: Charlotte Broster.*

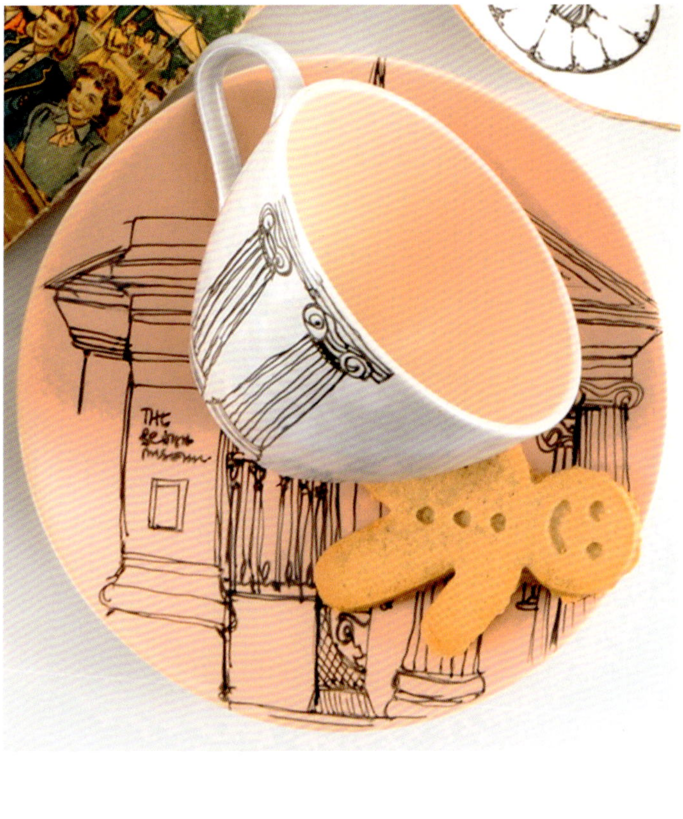

6 Studio pottery

Bernard Leach

In the 20th century, studio pottery was revived by Bernard Leach (1887–1979), a potter, writer and philosopher who had lived in the Far East and was interested in Chinese Sung pottery as well as traditional English slipware. He had a great deal of influence on the subsequent growth of studio pottery and established what has become the model for studio potters: the individual artist making pots in a small workshop or studio.

He set up a workshop in 1920 in St Ives, Cornwall, making one-off pieces for exhibition as well as a more affordable range of 'standard ware' for everyday use. He was assisted by Shōji Hamada from Japan, and later by his son, David Leach, who learned technical skills and management at Stoke-on-Trent. Bernard Leach trained a succession of apprentices, including Michael Cardew, who went on to establish several potteries making hand-thrown functional ware. Potters who trained at the Leach Pottery include Katherine Pleydell-Bouverie, Richard Batterham, Warren MacKenzie from the US and Harry and May Davis, who later emigrated to New Zealand. In this way, and through his book (*A Potter's Book*, 1940), the ideas of Bernard Leach spread throughout the world.

Leach standard-ware Z Bowls, 1968.
Thrown stoneware, diameter: 22 cm (8½ in.).
Photo: Henry Bloomfield.

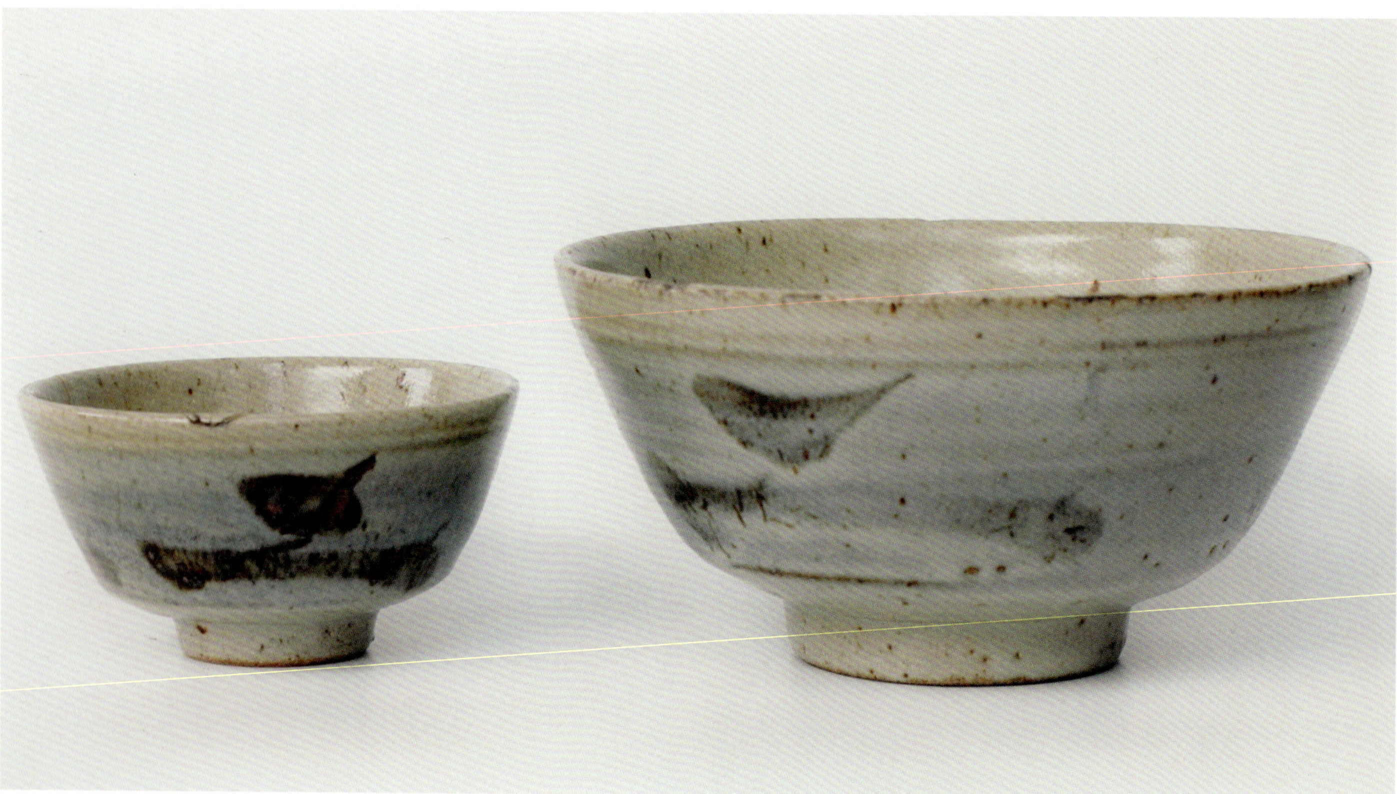

John Leach is the eldest son of David Leach and makes wood-fired stoneware pottery at Muchelney in Somerset. The pots are fired to 1320°C (2408°F) and decorated by the flames in the kiln, with glaze applied only on the inside. The three-chambered kiln can hold 2,000 pots and is fired six times a year. John Leach trained at the Leach Pottery in St Ives, at Aylesford Pottery in Kent and at Winchcombe Pottery in Gloucestershire.

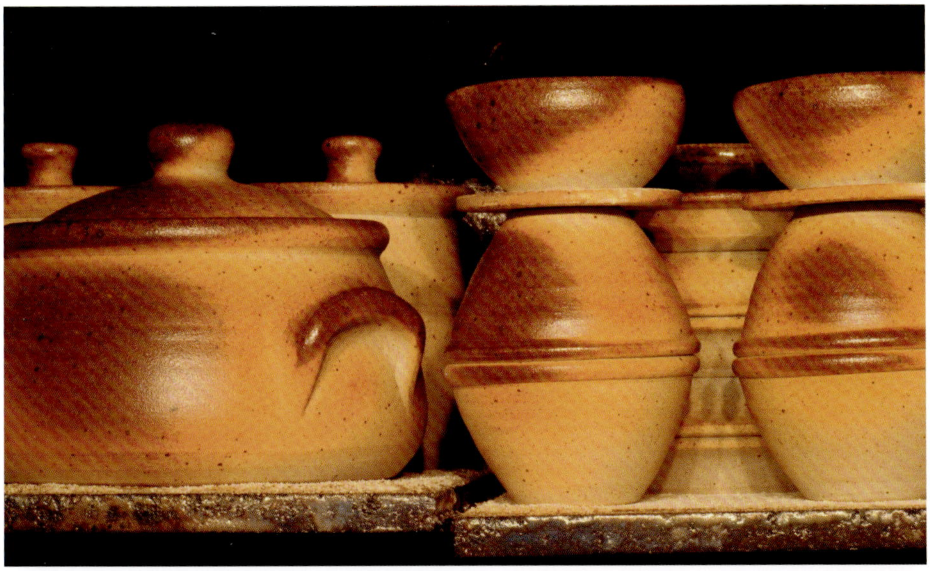

John Leach, Muchelney Pottery, stoneware casserole and bowls ready to be unpacked from the wood-fired kiln. *Photo: Carole Melbourne.*

John Leach pots being unpacked from the kiln, 2011. *Photo: Nick Fleming.*

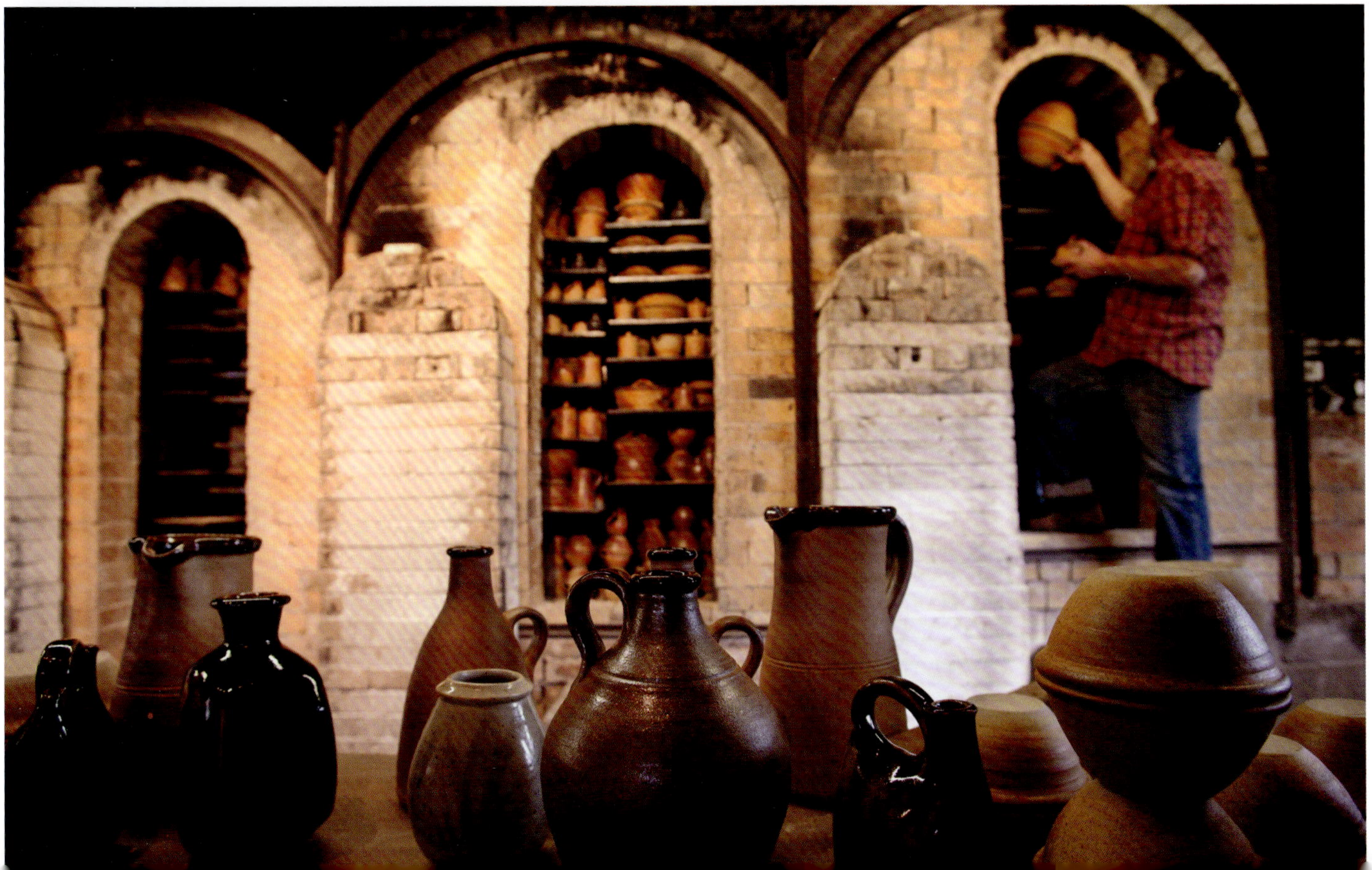

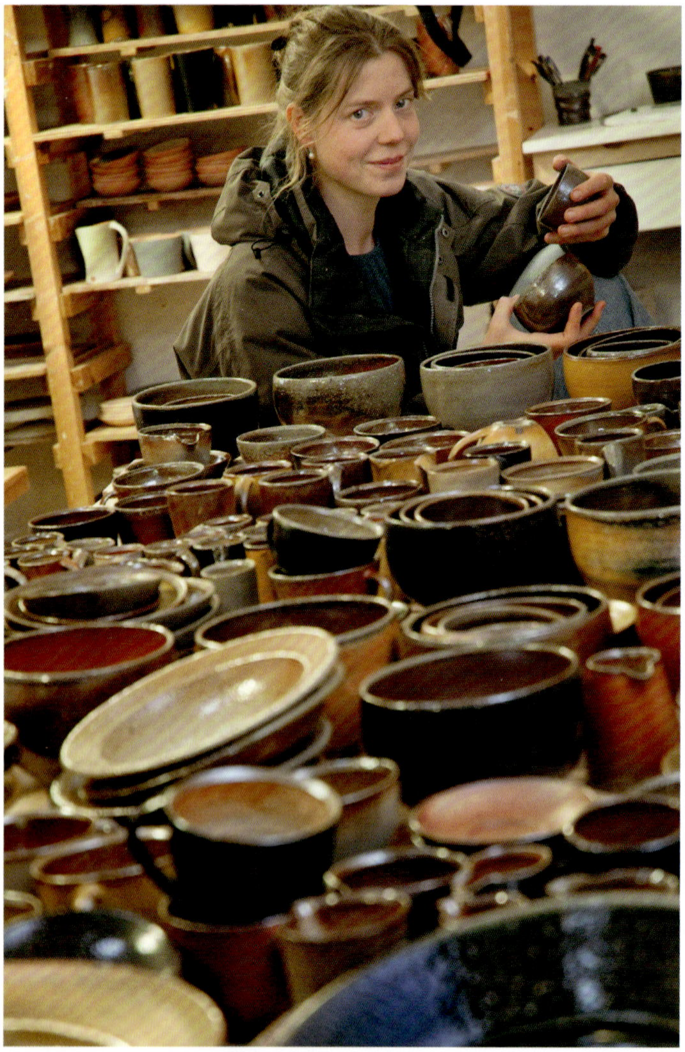

At the Leach Pottery today, a range of soda-fired tableware is being made by apprentice potters, who at the beginning of 2011 were Ella Phillips (UK) and Britta Wengeler (Germany). The range was designed by lead potter Jack Doherty and made using local stoneware clay from St Agnes, coloured with iron oxide. Like Bernard Leach, Doherty is keen to show the nature of the clay as well as traces of the firing process. Ware is fired in a soda kiln, which gives each pot an individual character. Inspired by the landscape of the Penwith peninsula in Cornwall, England, each piece is unique in colour and texture, united with the rest of the range through form and function.

Britta Wengeler, an apprentice potter at the Leach Pottery, in the studio with thrown soda-fired tableware designed by Jack Doherty. *Photo: Rebecca Peters.*

Espresso cups and saucers on Bernard Leach tiles, 2010. Leach Pottery soda-fired stoneware designed by Jack Doherty, height: 8 cm (3¼ in.). *Photo: Rebecca Peters.*

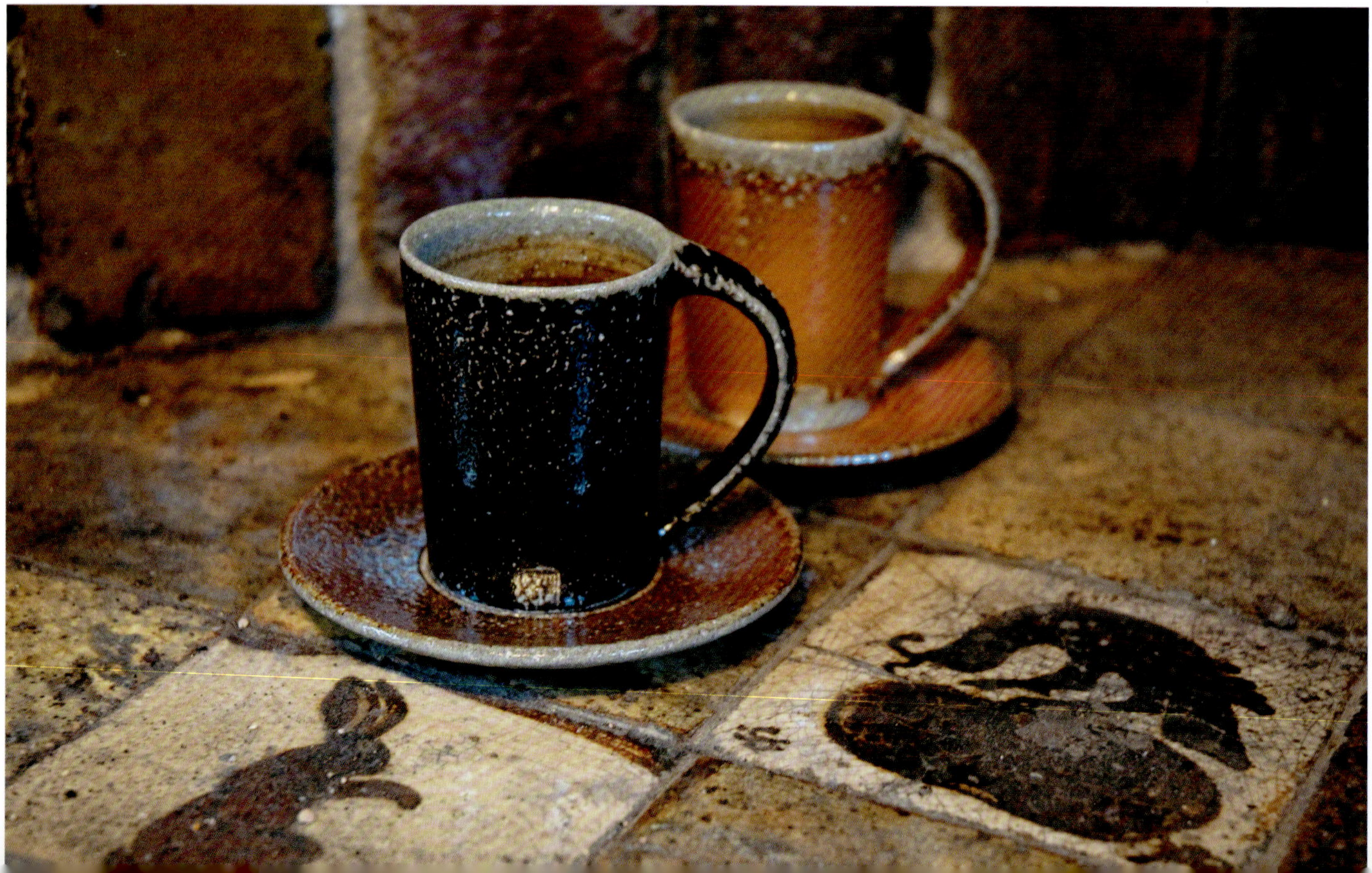

Michael Cardew and Winchcombe Pottery

In 1926, after training at the Leach Pottery, Michael Cardew rented the old pottery at Winchcombe in the Cotswolds. The pottery had previously produced a large output of washing pans, milk pans and flowerpots; closed since the First World War, the original chief thrower, Elijah Comfort, was able to help Cardew restart it. He was aided by the young Sidney Tustin, and later his brother Charlie Tustin and Ray Finch, who took over the pottery and whose son, Mike Finch, continues to run it today. Initially, Cardew made earthenware in the North Devon slipware style, single-fired with a galena glaze. The kiln was a large wood-fired updraught bottle kiln 3 metres (10 ft) in diameter. Cardew made slip-decorated pie dishes, sgraffito jugs, bowls and cider jars. At that time there were still a few country potteries in Cornwall and Devon, and Cardew had visited several of these, in particular the Fishleys of Fremington. Bernard Leach had also visited Lake's Pottery in Truro and was influenced by the country style.

Cardew had difficulties with the glaze and clay; the glaze crazed and the porous earthenware body allowed water to pass through. He tried firing to higher temperatures but this caused the pots to turn brown. The usual way to prevent crazing in earthenware is to fire the biscuit to a higher temperature, but Cardew didn't want to lose the beauty and spontaneity of the raw slip-decorated ware, so he later converted to stoneware.

In 1939, Cardew left Winchcombe and set up a pottery at Wenford Bridge in Cornwall, and later in Africa, making stoneware. Winchcombe Pottery was taken over by Ray Finch, who also converted to stoneware in the 1960s. This change meant less decoration, as slip is not generally used on stoneware. The pots were glazed with a speckled oatmeal or brown-black tenmoku glaze. The range appealed to wholefood restaurants such as Cranks, the David Mellor shop in Chelsea and the cookery writer Elizabeth David, and was consequently in great demand.

The influence of studio pottery

Potters inspired by Cardew to work in slipware include Clive Bowen and Doug Fitch. Many others who visited or worked at Winchcombe or Wenford Bridge have been inspired to make pots (including Dan Finnegan and Mark Hewitt, who both now live in America). Most studio potters make some tableware as well as more expensive one-off pieces and there are still a few small potteries producing impressively large quantities of tableware by hand.

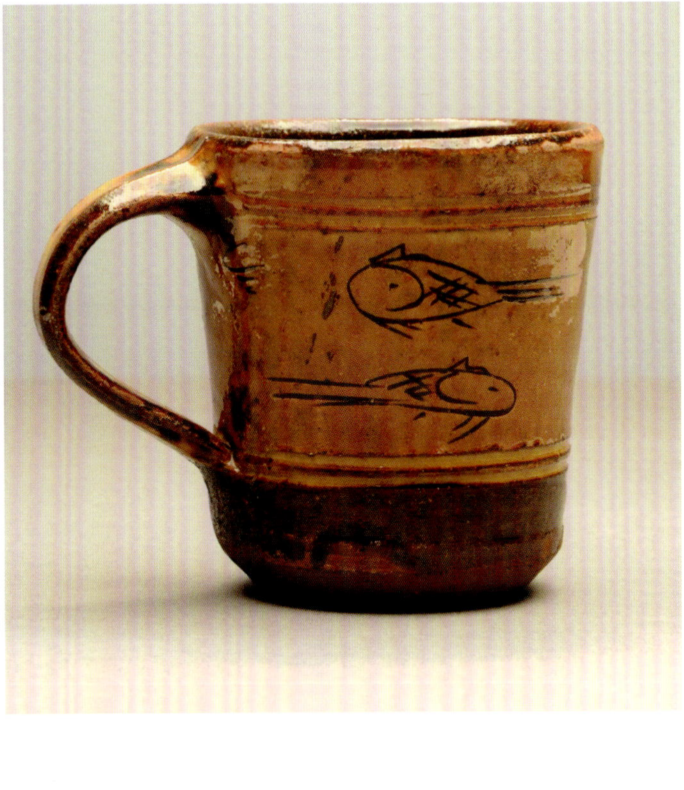

Michael Cardew, earthenware mug, 1930s. Sgraffito fish decoration and galena glaze, height: 10 cm (4 in.). *Photo: Jonathan Thompson.*

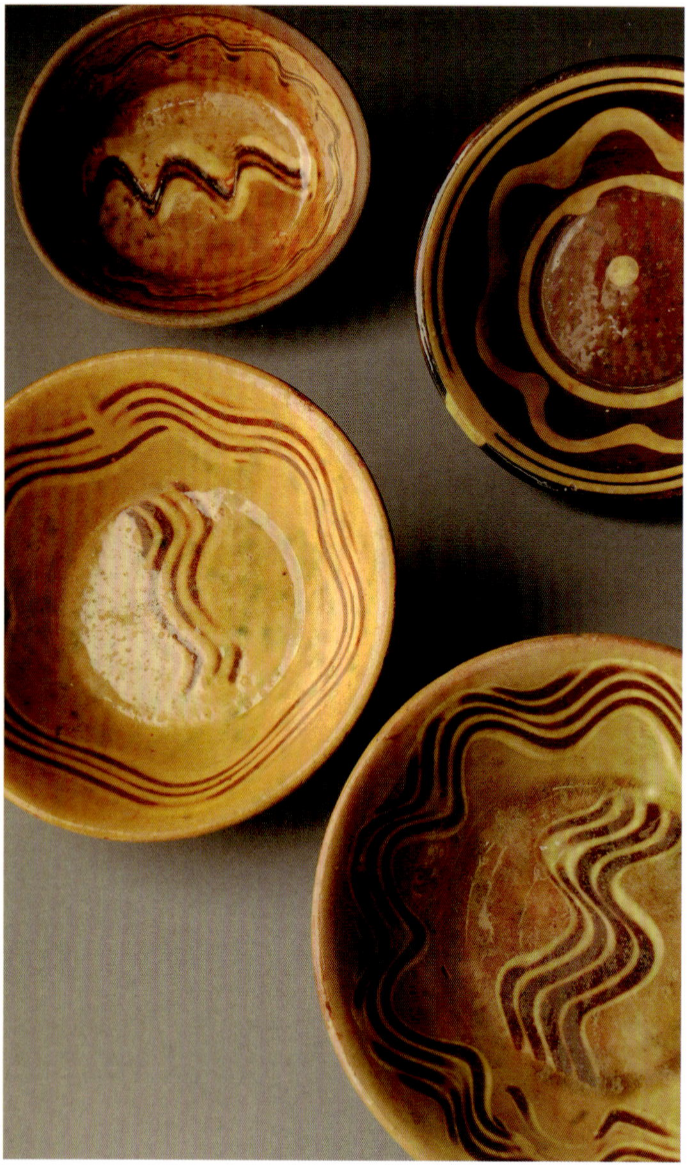

Winchcombe Pottery, earthenware baking dishes, 1930s. With combed slip decoration and galena glaze, width: 16 cm (6¼ in.). *Photo: Jonathan Thompson.*

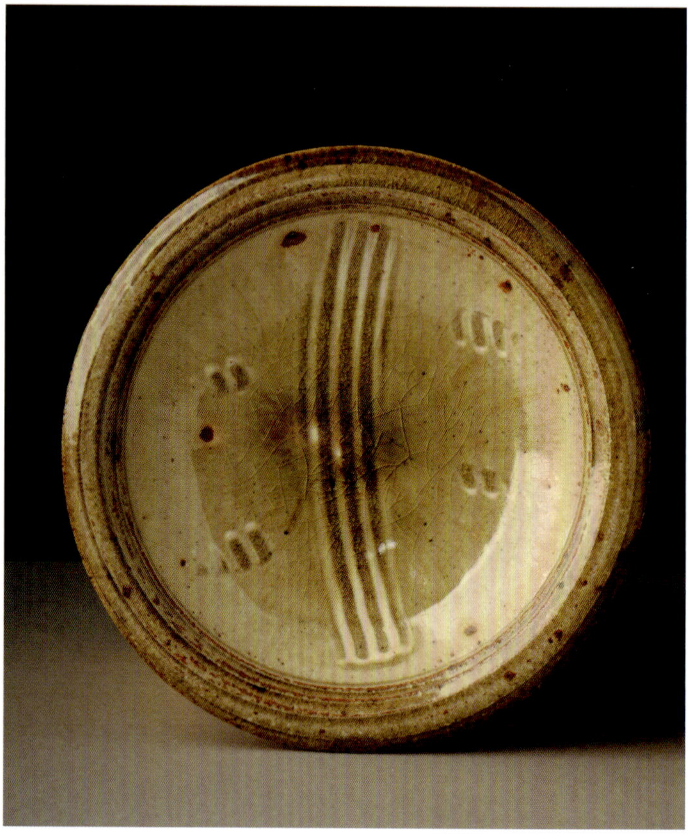

Alex McErlain, stoneware dish, 1990. *Photo: Jonathan Thompson.*

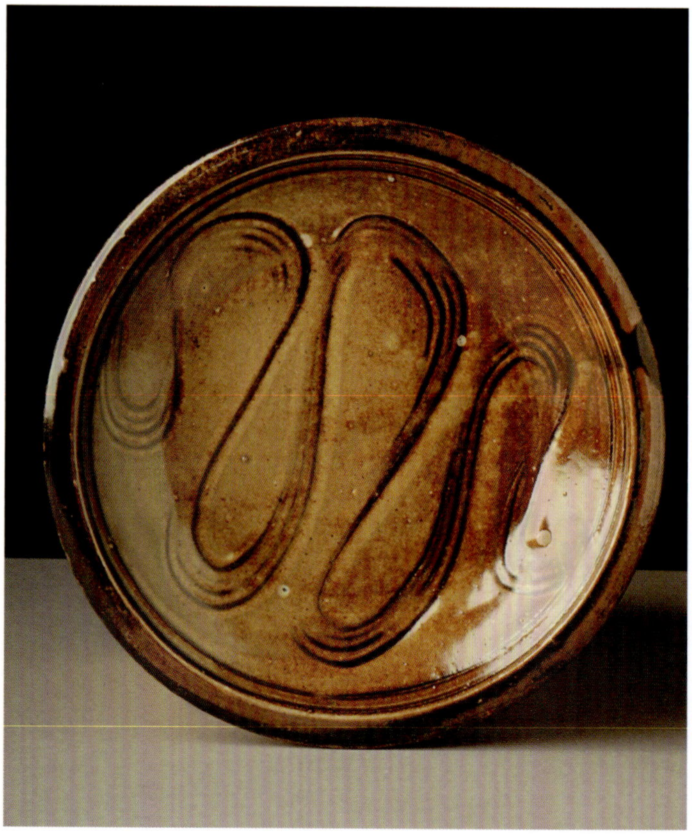

Mark Hewitt, stoneware plate with combed decoration, Wenford Bridge, 1970s. Diameter: 21 cm (8¼ in.). *Photo: Jonathan Thompson.*

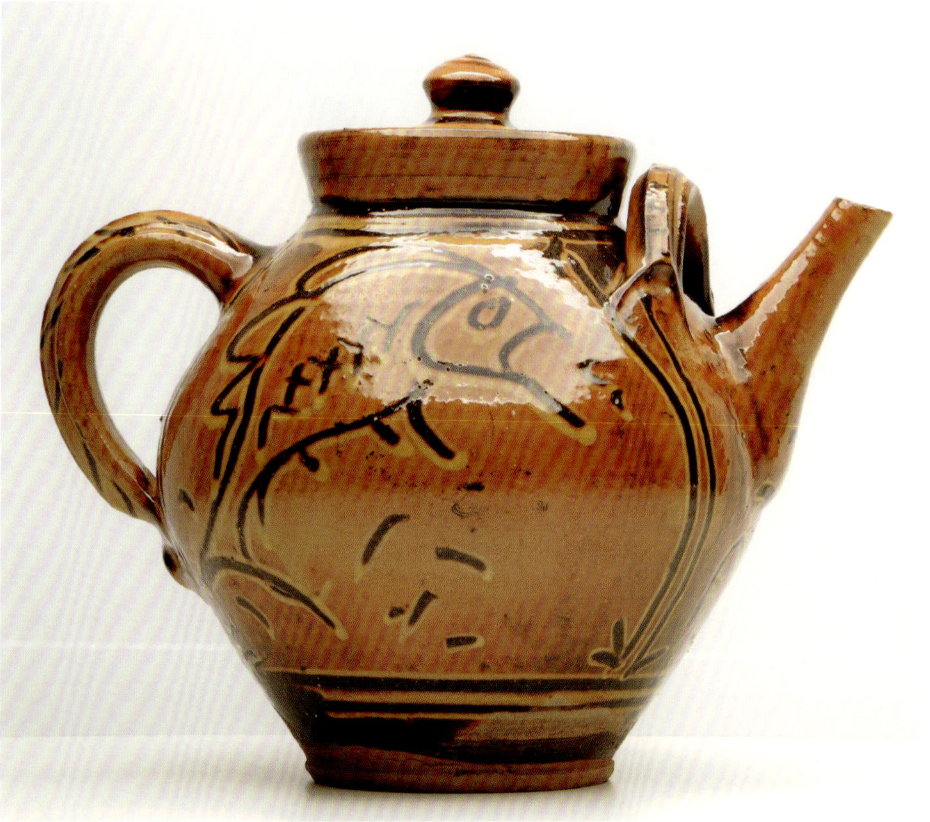

Clive Bowen, earthenware teapot decorated with a fish drawn through white slip, 1990s. The other side of the teapot has a lively drawing of a shrimp, height: 25.5 cm (10 in.). *Photo: Jonathan Thompson.*

Mark Hewitt, bowls, North Carolina, 2011. Wood-fired stoneware, diameter: 18 cm (7 in.). *Photo: Jason Dowdle.*

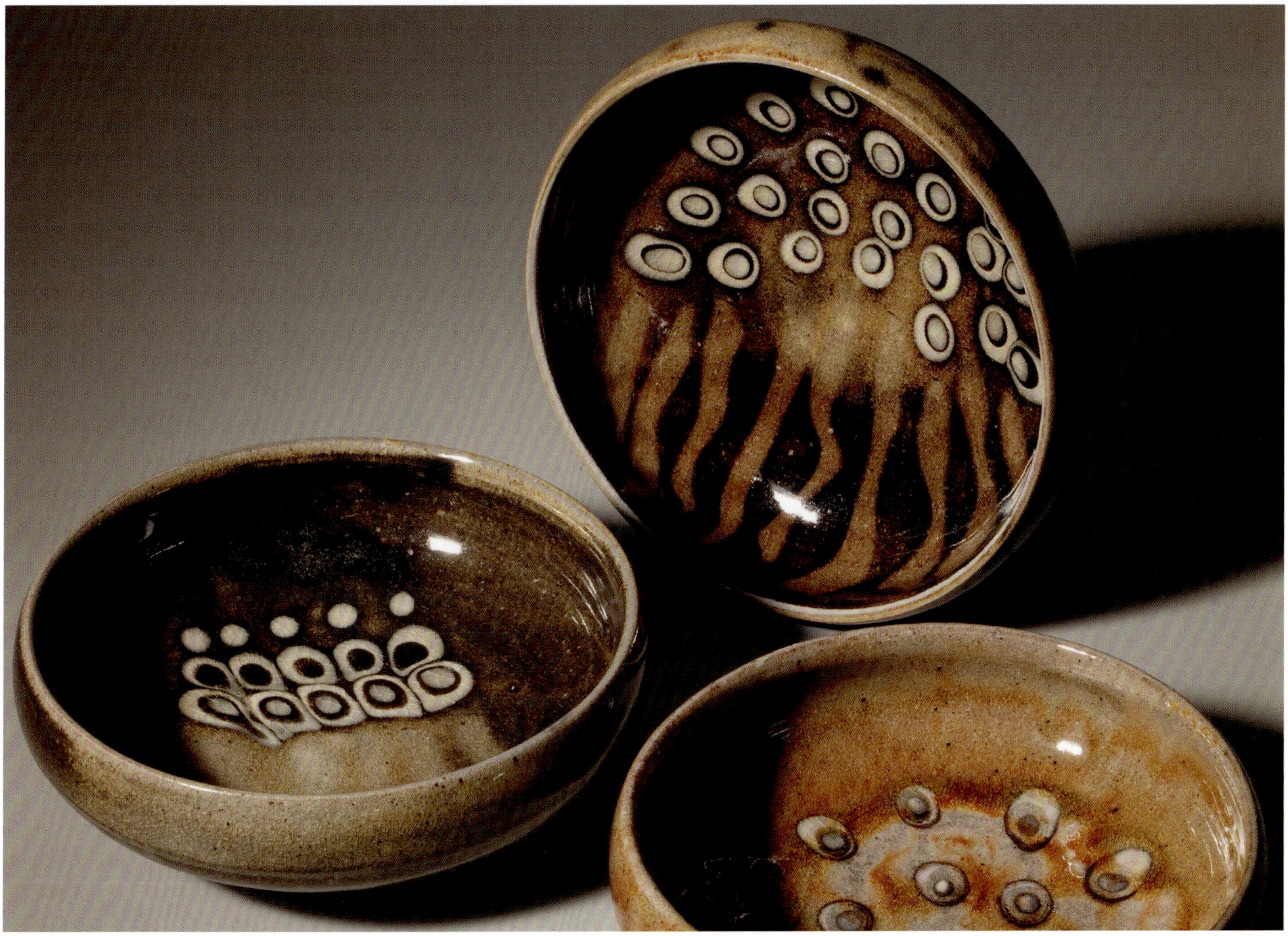

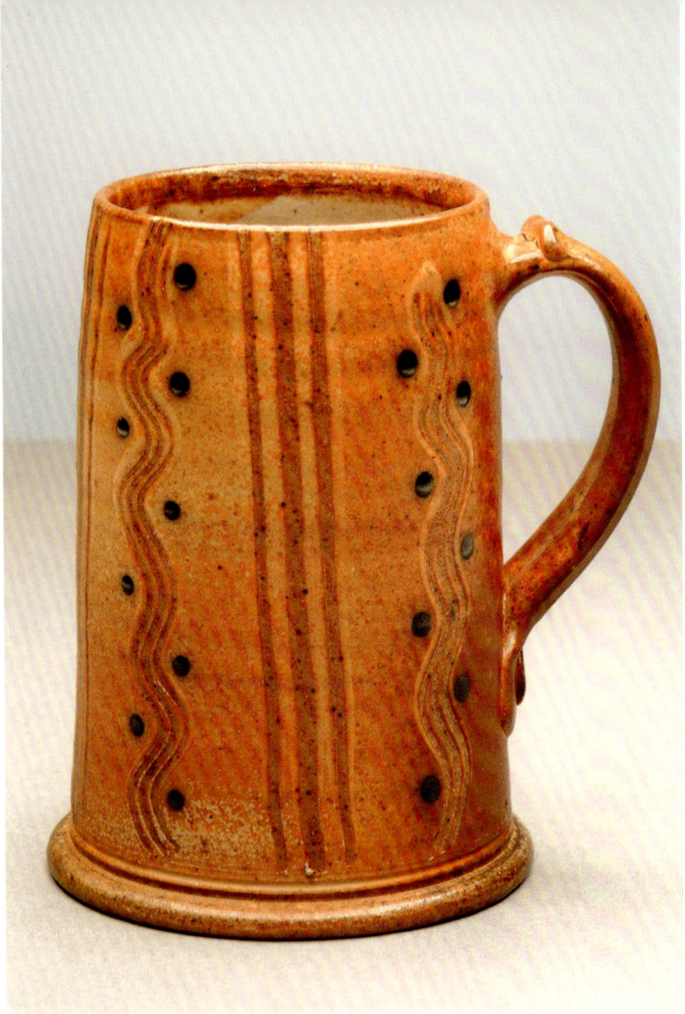

Dan Finnegan, Virginia, tankard, 2010.
Salt-fired stoneware, 15 cm (6 in.).
Photo: Jonathan Thompson.

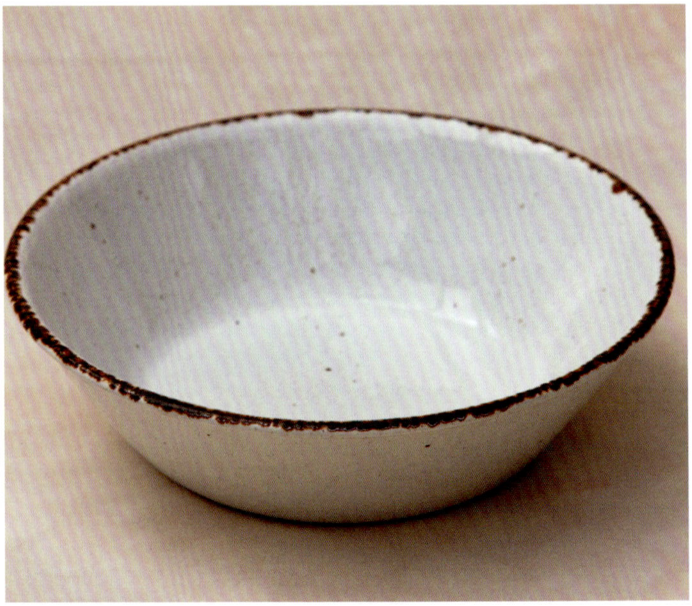

Stonehenge creation bowl, Midwinter Pottery, 1972. Stoneware, diameter: 16 cm (6¼ in.).
Photo: Nick Fleming.

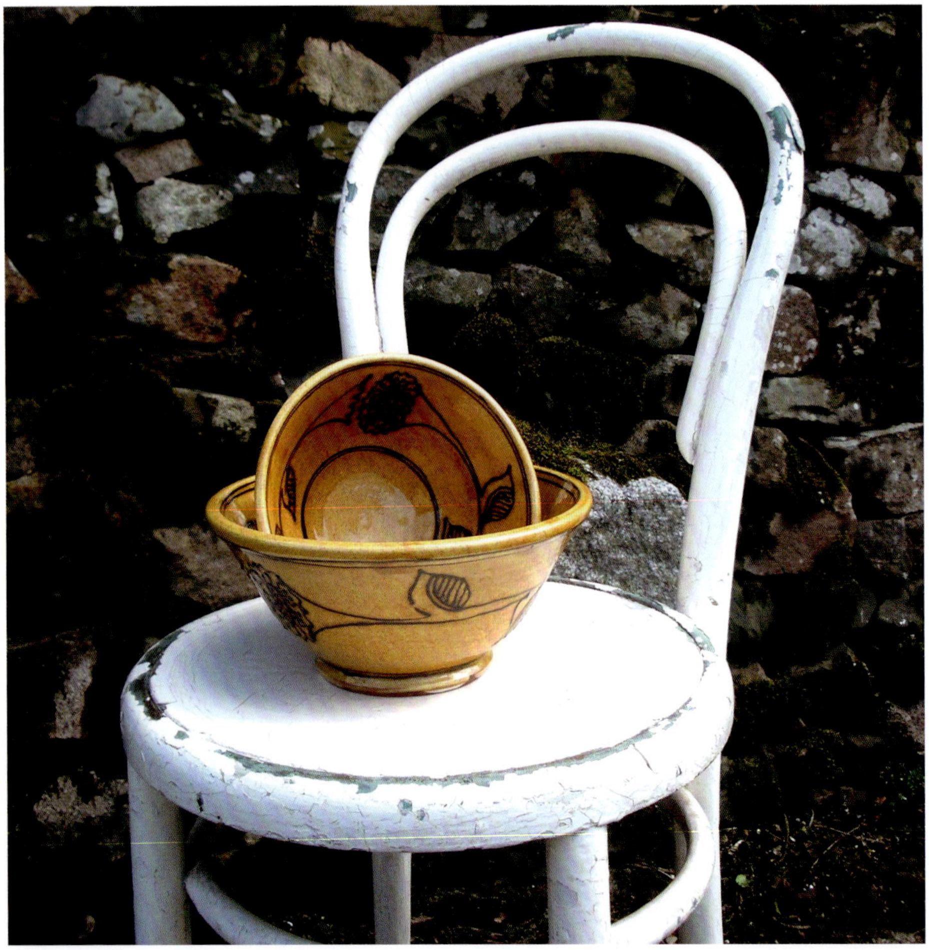

Hannah McAndrew, Daisy bowls, 2011. Honey-glazed earthenware with slip-trailed decoration, diameter: 18 cm (7 in.).
Photo: Hannah McAndrew.

Influence of studio pottery on manufactured ware

During the 1970s, some industrially produced pottery was influenced by studio pottery. Denby Pottery made a range called Potter's Wheel, designed by David Yorath in 1973. It was stoneware, glazed in a speckled oatmeal with concentric rings of iron oxide and a rust, yellow or blue circle in the centre. They al so produced oven-to-table ware, which could be used both to cook and serve food. Denby have continued to use rich, vibrant glazes like those used by studio potters.

In the same era, Midwinter Pottery produced its Stonehenge range, which had a speckled oatmeal glaze, iron oxide on the rims and, optionally, a large yellow and orange sun in the centre of the plates (there was also a blue moon and brown earth version).

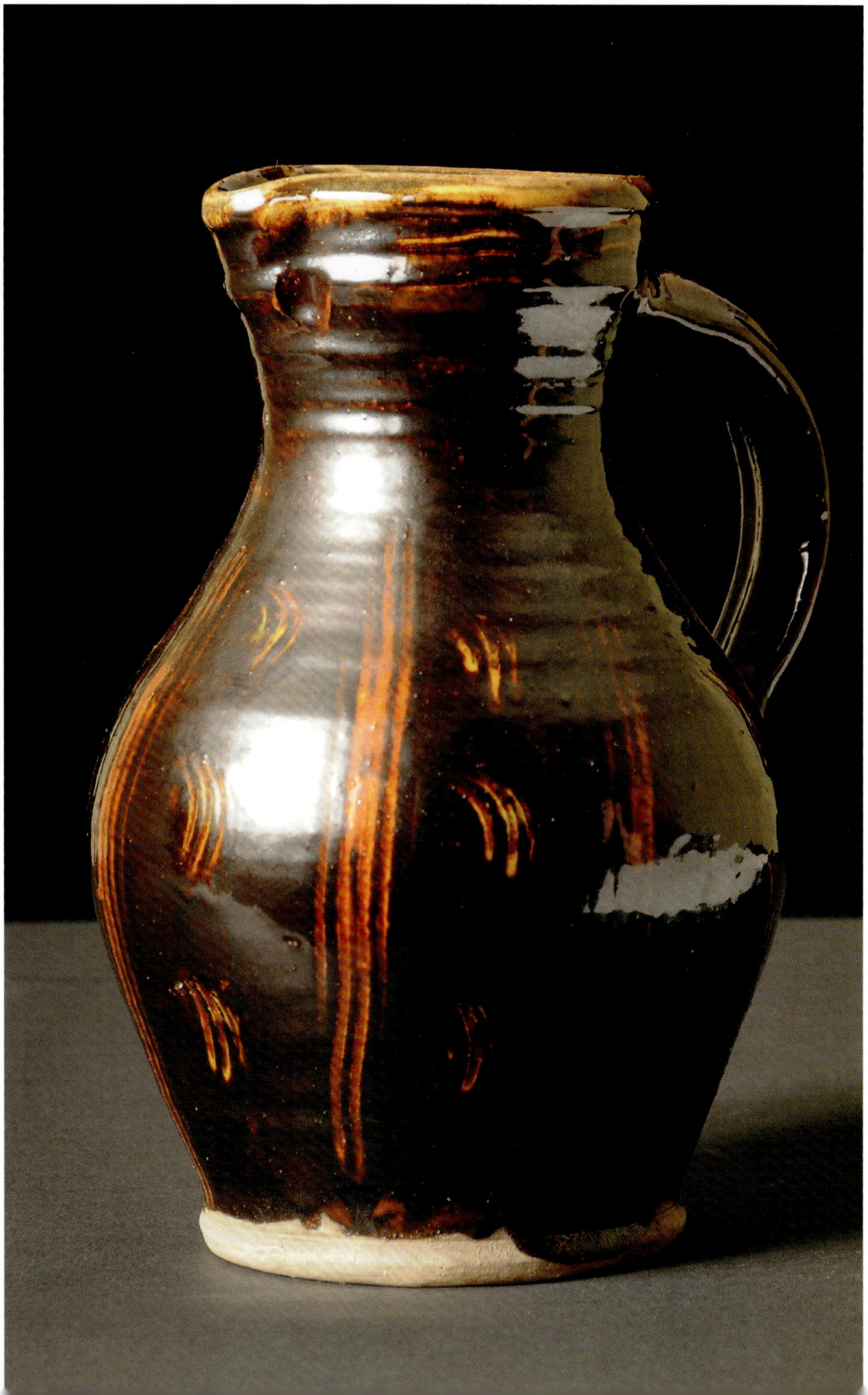

Doug Fitch, jug, 2011. Thrown red earthenware with combed decoration, black slip and galena glaze, wood-fired, 23 cm (9 in.). *Photo: Jonathan Thompson.*

7

The Bauhaus influence

Modernism

The influences of the Modernist movement in the early 20th century encouraged simplification of forms and the removal of unnecessary ornament. Also important was harmony between design and function. The Wiener Werkstätte (Vienna Workshop) was established in 1903 and aimed to unify art and craftsmanship in interior design. Ideally, everything in the home would be carefully designed as a whole, including the exterior, interior, furniture, textiles and tableware. Wiener Werkstätte members such as Jutta Sika designed modern porcelain tea sets to fit in with the modern interiors. Women in the Werkstätte usually trained in pottery or textiles as they were not permitted to do architecture or furniture design.

In 1913, Roger Fry and other members of the artistic Bloomsbury Group started the Omega Workshops in London, where they designed modernist tableware and other home furnishings. Some of the tableware was made at Poole Pottery (then known as Carter Stabler Adams) from earthenware with a tin glaze. They made bold, simplified forms which were not signed by the artist but marked with the Greek letter Ω (omega).

The Bauhaus school

The philosophy of the Modernist movement was established by the Bauhaus, a school founded by Walter Gropius in Weimar, Germany in 1919. Its ideals were 'form follows function', 'truth to materials' and the elimination of 'unnecessary detail'. Gropius was an architect but the aims of the school were initially to unify art, craft and design for industrial production. The Bauhaus school designed furniture, textiles, tableware and typography. In the pottery workshop in Dornburg, students were taught by sculptor Gerhard Marcks about line and form and by master potter Max Krehan on the technical skills of throwing, glazing

Lucie Rie, pourers with side handles, 1970s. Thrown stoneware, height: 12.5 cm (5 in.). Private collection. *Photo: Henry Bloomfield.*

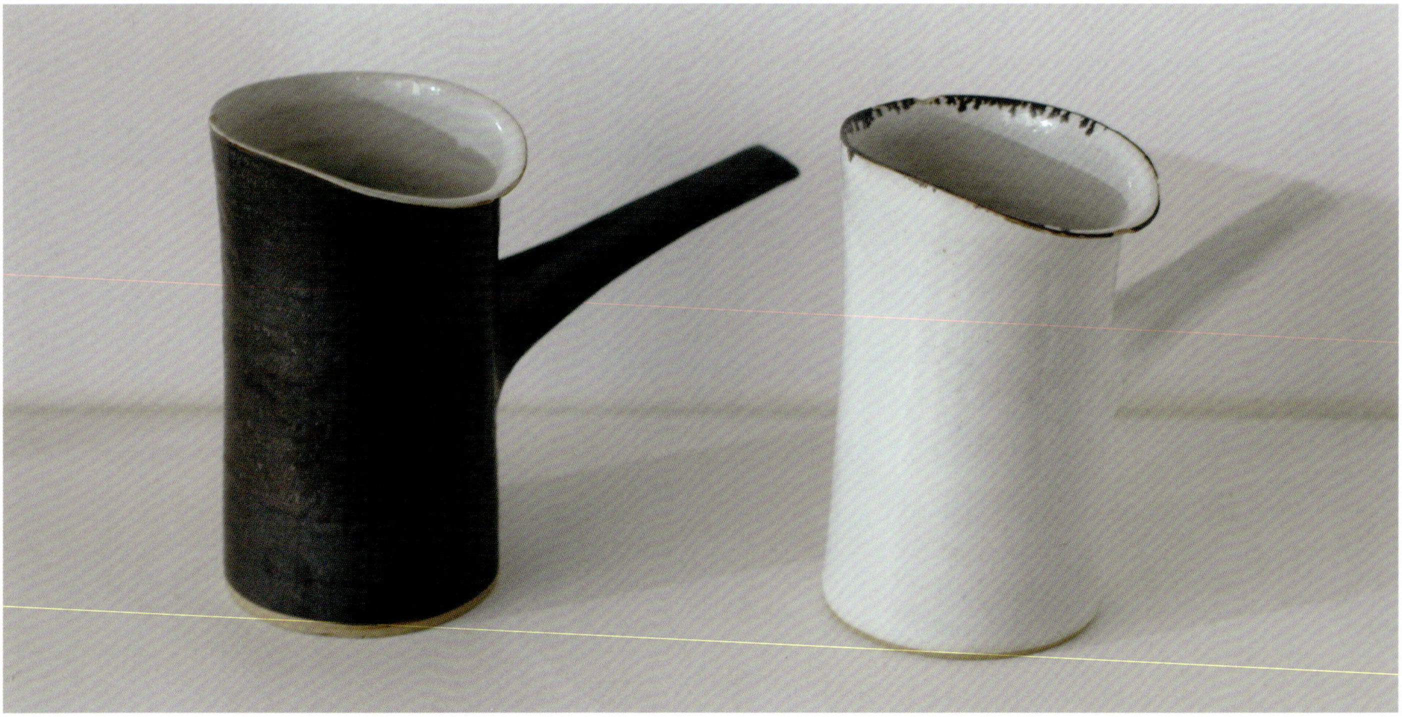

and firing. The pottery students included Otto Lindig and Theodor Bogler, whose pots were often geometric, cylindrical or straight-sided. Decoration was minimal and by the 1930s the first all-white porcelain tableware had been manufactured in Germany. Prior to this, white porcelain had only been used for industrial purposes.

KPM (Königliche Porzellan Manufaktur, known at the time as Staatliche Porzellan Manufaktur) in Berlin introduced a white dinner service called Urbino in 1931. Designed by Trude Petri, it had coupe-shaped plates without rims, inspired by plates from the Italian Renaissance. Also designing for KPM was former Bauhaus student Marguerite Friedländer Wildenhain, who later emigrated to the US and became a leading studio potter. Elsewhere in the country, the Arzberg factory in Bavaria commissioned a young architecture graduate from Stuttgart, Hermann Gretsch, to design a porcelain dinnerware service. The resulting range, called Form 1382, was launched in 1931 and has become a design classic. The teapot was almost spherical, with a distinctive knob on the lid in the shape of an inverted cone.

Lucie Rie

At the outbreak of the Second World War, potter Lucie Rie moved from Vienna to London where she made sophisticated, functional pots with her assistant Hans Coper, who went on to develop his own sculptural pots. Rie and Coper's pots were very different from the oriental-inspired pots being made by Leach at around the same time. They were modernist and urban, inspired by the Wiener Werkstätte and the Bauhaus school in Germany. The tableware was glazed with a white tin glaze and black manganese pigment and had little decoration except for sgraffito lines through the black.

Lucie Rie, thrown bowl, 1970s. Stoneware, diameter: 10 cm (4 in.). Private collection. *Photo: Henry Bloomfield.*

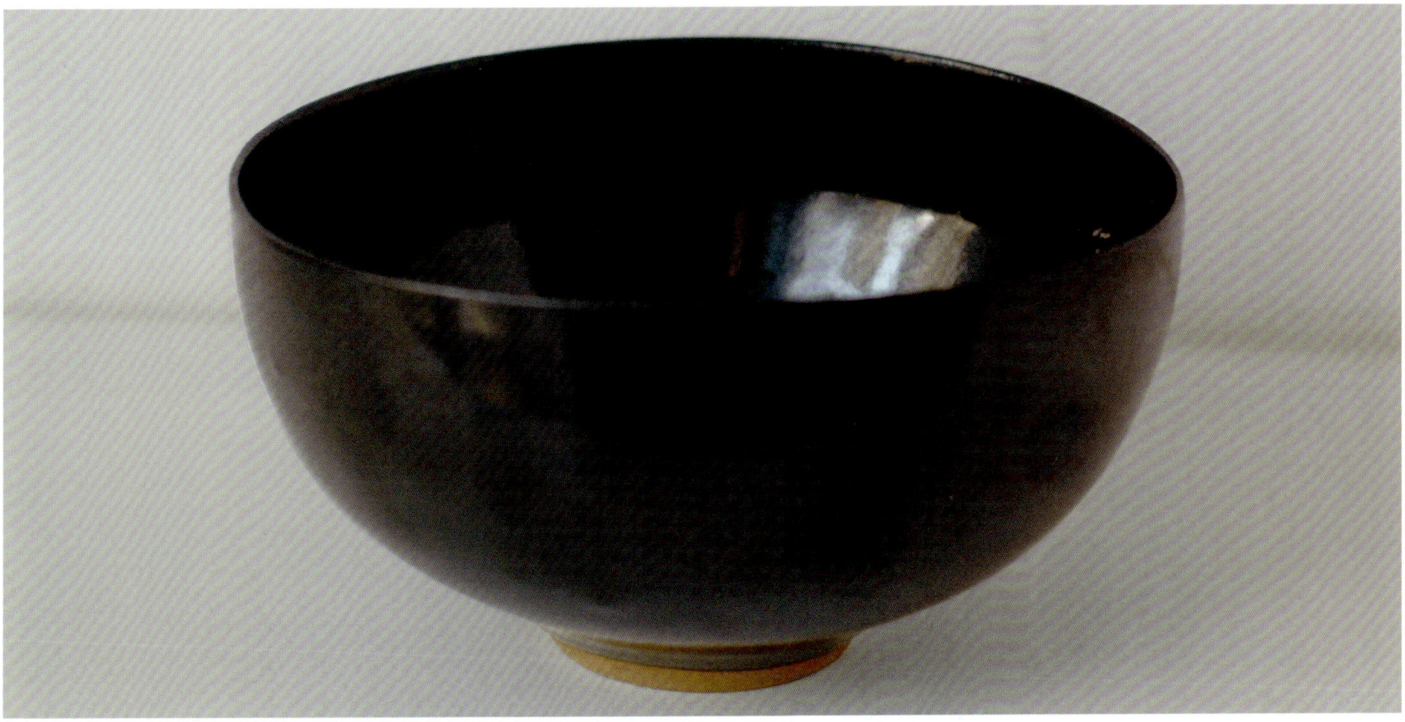

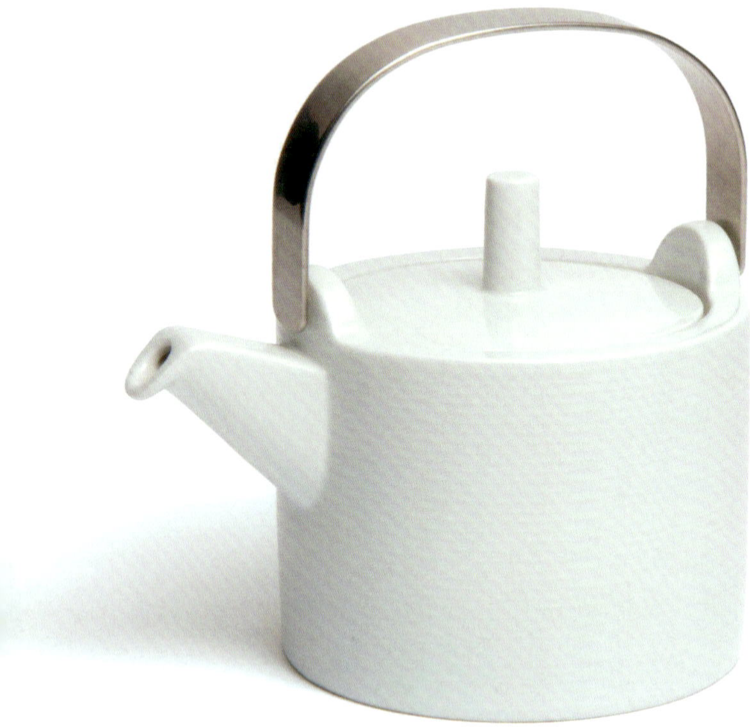

Loft teapot for Thomas, Rosenthal Group, designed by Martin Hunt, 2002. Height: 18.5 cm (7¼ in.). *Photo: David Mellor Design Ltd.*

Influence of the Bauhaus

Walter Gropius of the Bauhaus school moved to the United States in 1937 and in 1945 set up The Architects' Collaborative in Cambridge, Massachusetts. As well as teaching and practising as an architect, he designed a porcelain tea set for Rosenthal in 1969.

The influence of the Bauhaus school also continued in Germany. In the late 1950s Hans Nick Roericht designed a range of stackable porcelain tableware for use in cafeterias. A collar at the rim of each cup and bowl enabled the pieces to be stacked efficiently. Roericht was a student at the Hochschule für Gestaltung, a design college in Ulm, Germany run on Bauhaus principles. The range, called TC 100, was produced from 1962 until 2006 by Thomas for Rosenthal.

Walter Gropius TAC (The Architects' Collaborative) tea set, porcelain, 1969. Teapot: 11.5 x 23 cm (4½ x 9 in.). *Photo: David Mellor Design Ltd.*

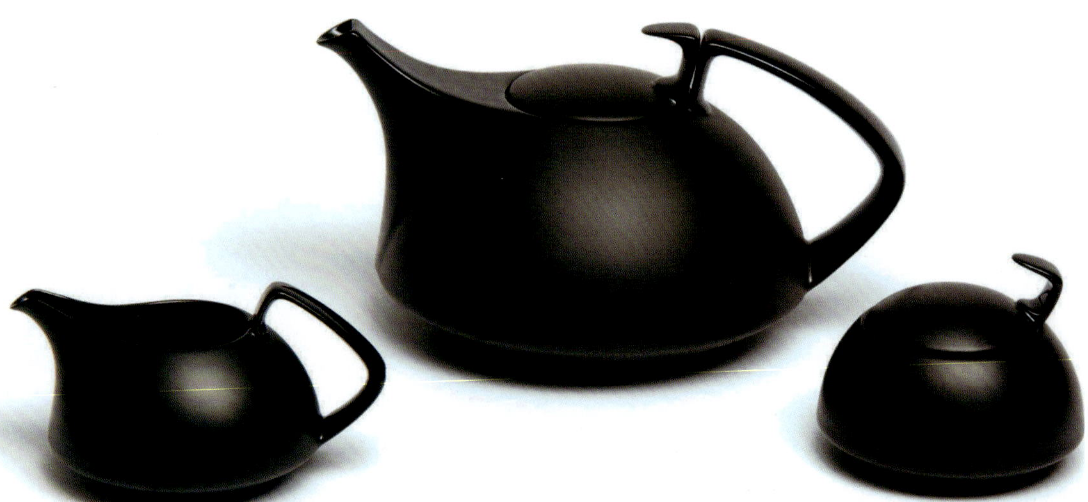

Contemporary designers

Designers for industry continue to be inspired by the Bauhaus. David Queensberry and Martin Hunt have designed a wide range of tableware since the start of their partnership in 1966, for an impressive list of clients including Hornsea Pottery, Habitat and John Lewis. Their aim is to make beautiful design with lasting value for the mass market. The porcelain Trend tableware was originally designed by Robin Levien in 1981 for Thomas, part of the Rosenthal Group in Germany. It was updated by Martin Hunt in 2001 and the new range was called Loft. It uses fine concentric lines and simple shapes with a range of round, oval or square plates to suit a range of world cuisines. The Loft teapot is beautifully designed – cylindrical with a straight spout and a curved steel handle.

Jiří Pelcl is a Czech designer who designs both one-off pieces and products for industry. Having studied architecture in Prague and furniture design at The Royal College of Art in London, he has now designed furniture, glass and ceramics, and feels that good design should be available to all at a reasonable price. Some of his work is organic but his Bohemia tableware is reminiscent of the Bauhaus – with a twist. The handles are double loops and some of the saucers have handles, while others have a side dish for a teabag. There are two versions, White and Cobalt, the latter decorated with motifs from the traditional Blue Onion pattern. The tableware is manufactured by Český Porcelán.

Jiří Pelcl, Bohemia White porcelain dining set for Český Porcelán, 2004. *Photo: Filip Slapal.*

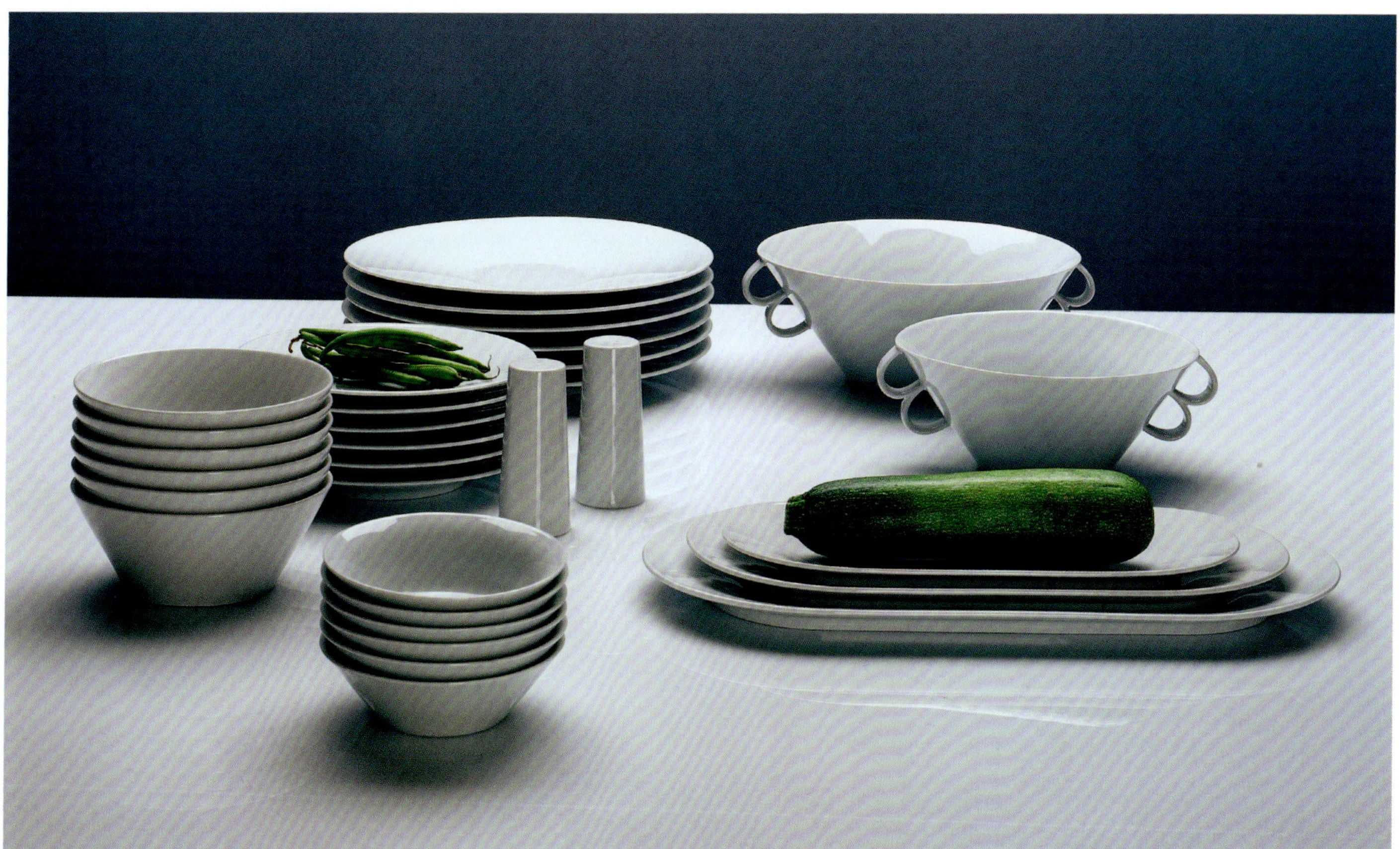

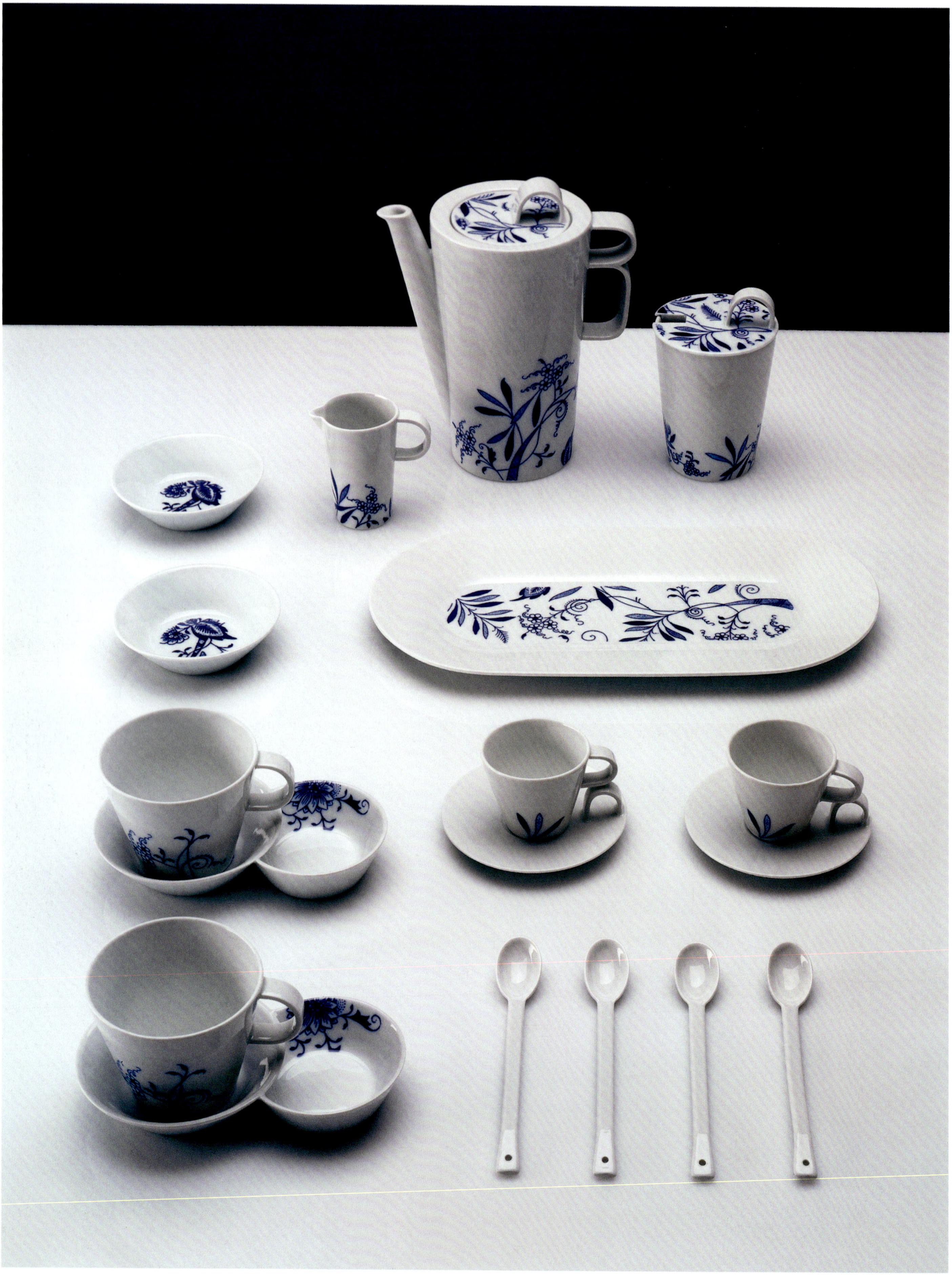

Jiří Pelcl, Bohemia Cobalt porcelain coffee set for Český Porcelán, 2004. *Photo: Filip Slapal.*

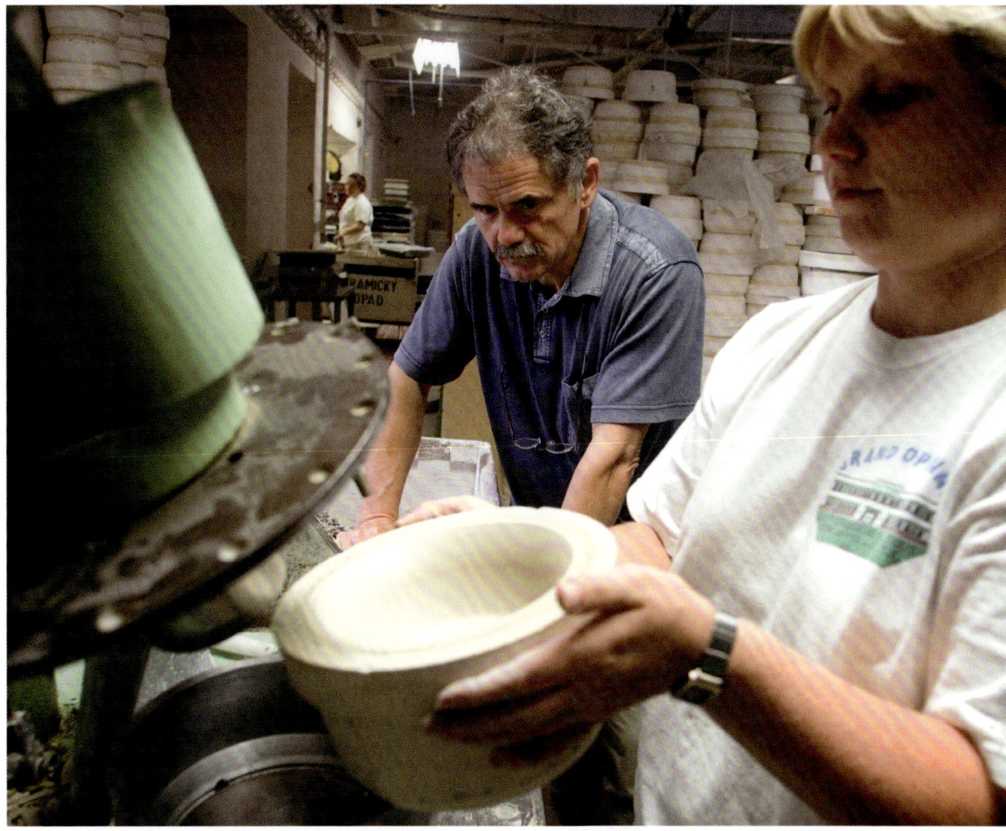

Jiří Pelcl, Bohemia bowl being made in Český Porcelán factory, Dubi, Czech Republic. *Photo: courtesy of Jiří Pelcl.*

Jiří Pelcl, Bohemia White porcelain being inspected in Český Porcelán factory. *Photo: courtesy of Jiří Pelcl.*

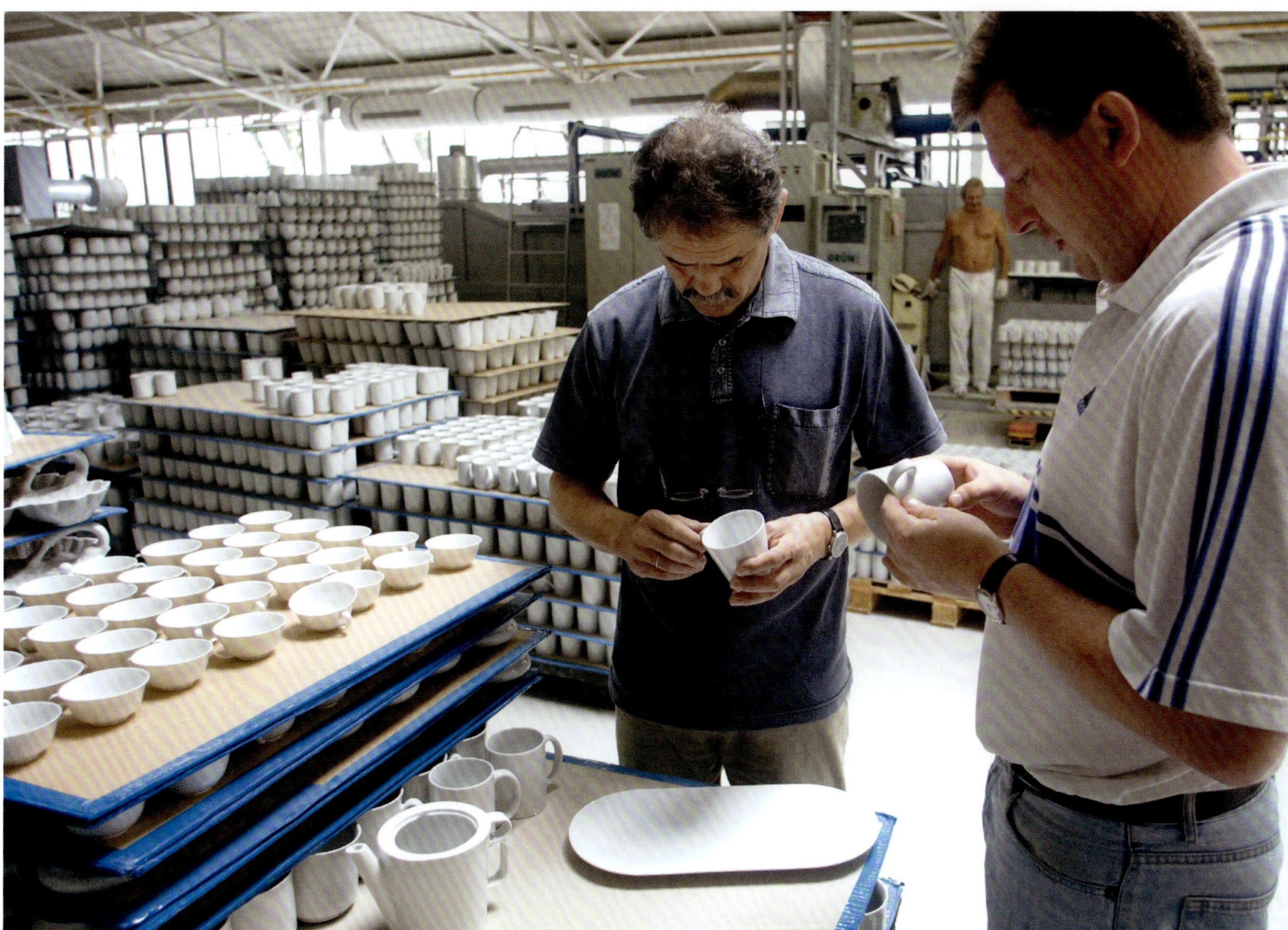

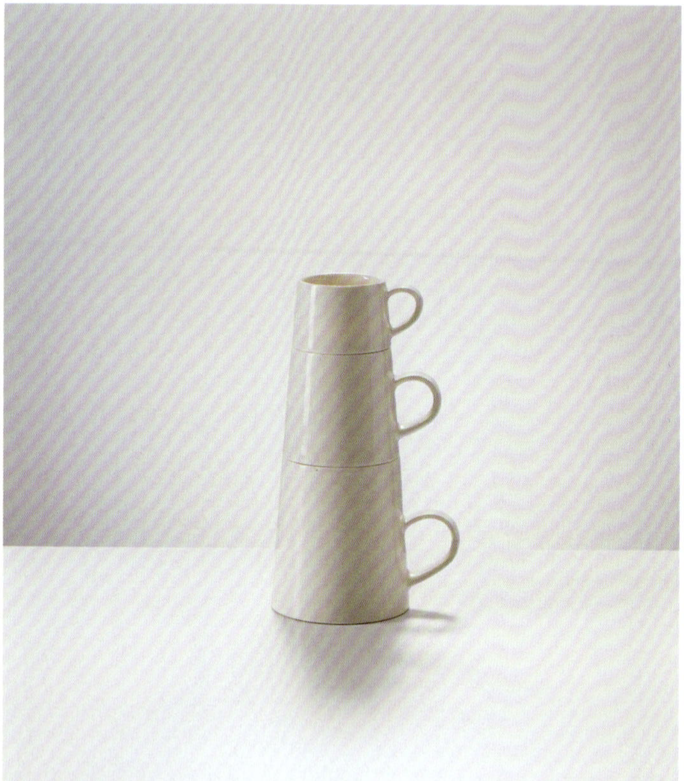

Billy Lloyd, stacking mugs, 2010.
Thrown porcelain, height: 20 cm (8 in.).
Photo: Michael Harvey.

Contemporary potters

There are several studio potters making Bauhaus-inspired minimalist pots in London. Two of these are Edmund de Waal and Julian Stair, who shared a studio in Camberwell in the 1990s and initially made tableware but now focus on installations. Many of their former apprentices are making tableware, including Chris Keenan and Billy Lloyd.

Lloyd studied ceramics at Camberwell College of Art and trained with Lisa Hammond and Julian Stair in London. He makes a range of porcelain tableware – jugs, teapots, stacking cups and dishes – from one conical form. His pieces are robustly functional and stripped of any superfluous detail.

Rupert Spira makes a range of fine stoneware, influenced by Far Eastern and modernist shapes. He trained with Michael Cardew at Wenford Bridge Pottery and now

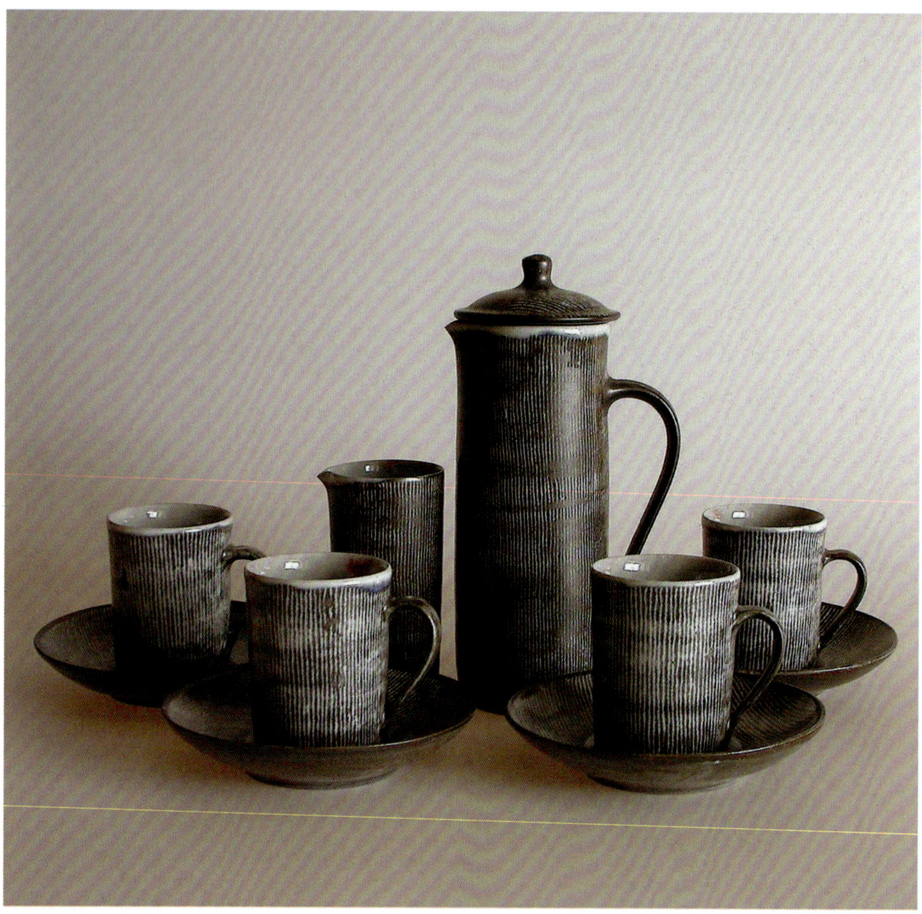

Rupert Spira, coffee set, thrown stoneware 2009. Fine lines incised through black pigment over white glaze, height: 25 cm (10 in.).
Photo: Ruth Middleton.

works from his studio in Shropshire making one-off pieces as well as tableware. Some of the tableware range is thrown by his assistant, and plates are made by the jigger-jolley method (see p. 77).

Derek Wilson's thrown functional ware is inspired by a diverse range of sources, including mid-century British Constructivism and the history of the ceramics industry in Europe and Asia. He trained at the Craft Council of Ireland's Ceramic Design and Skills course in Kilkenny, Ireland and the University of Ulster in Belfast.

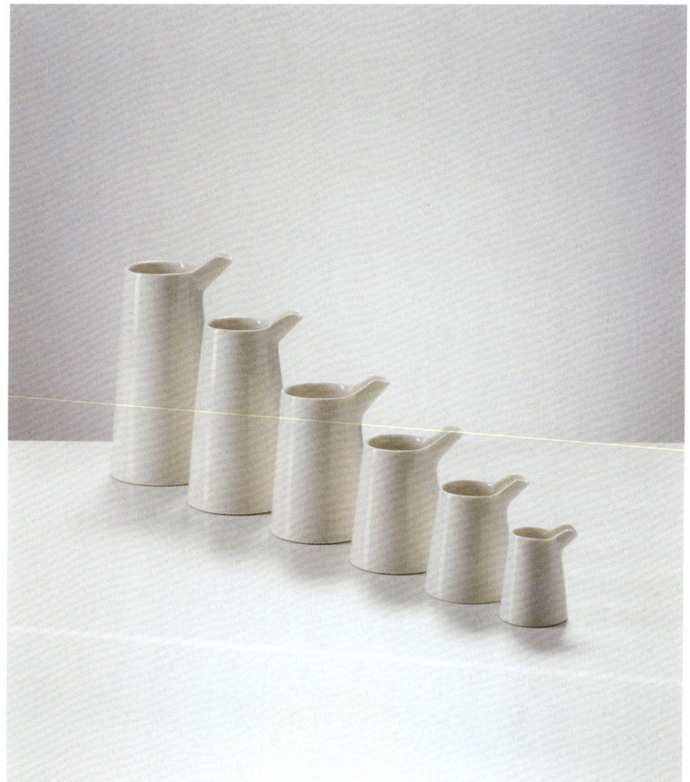

Billy Lloyd, trail of jugs, 2010. Thrown porcelain, height: 20 cm (8 in.). *Photo: Michael Harvey.*

Derek Wilson, four tall cups on oak tray, 2011. Porcelain. *Photo: Christopher Martin.*

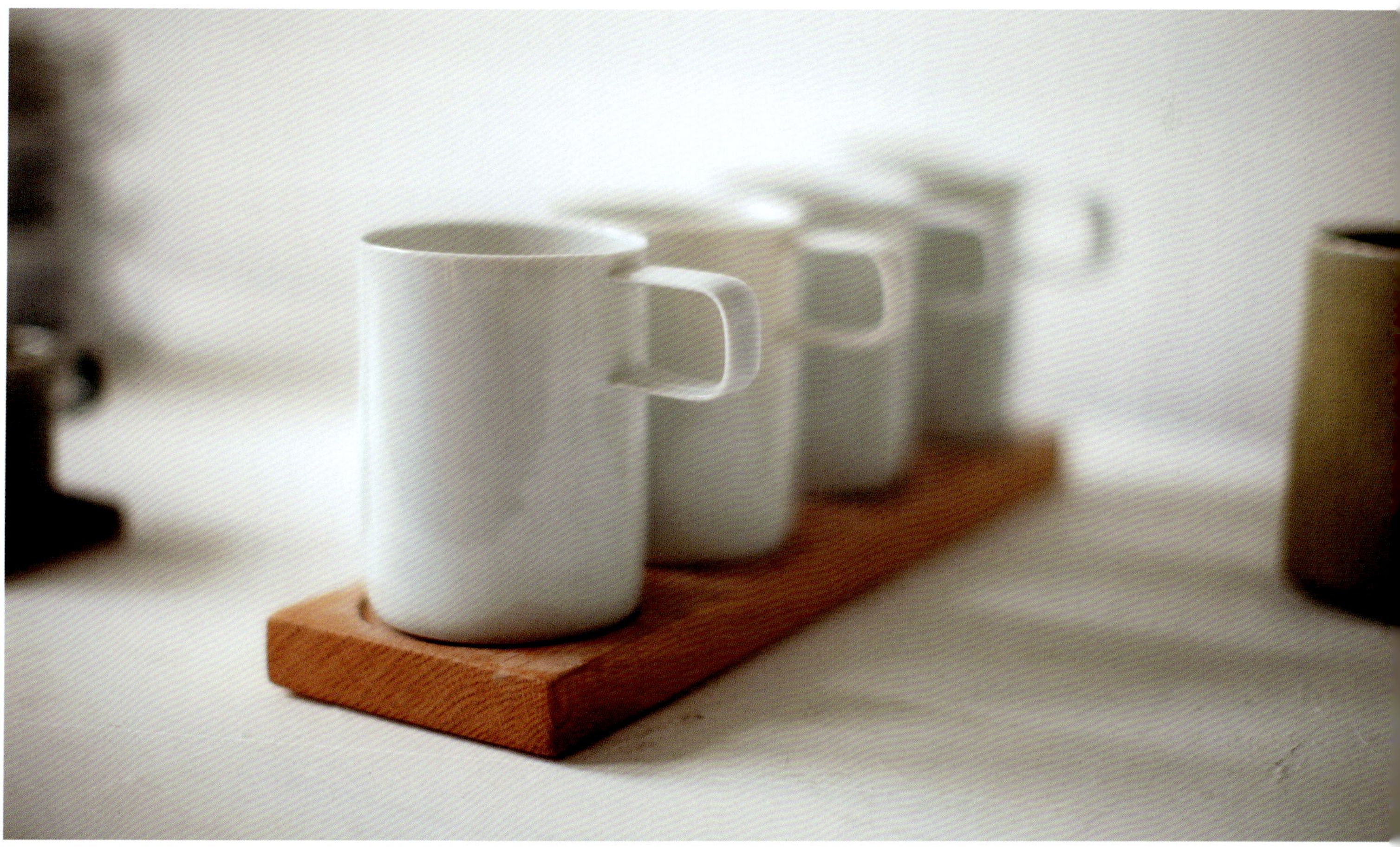

8 Scandinavia

The Nordic countries – Sweden, Finland, Norway and Denmark – have had a great deal of influence on design since the mid-20th century. Scandinavian design is often minimalist, functional and economically produced, following Swedish Design Council director Gregor Paulsson's 1919 plea for 'more beautiful things for everyday use'. In Scandinavia, manufacturing industries frequently employ artists and designers. Characteristic of Nordic tableware are bright colours and bold patterns, often influenced by textiles, such as those of the Finnish textile company Marimekko. Scandinavian folk art is also used to good effect as decoration on mass-produced tableware.

Sweden

Stig Lindberg (1916–82) was an artist-potter who collaborated with industry, working at the Gustavsberg ceramic factory near Stockholm, and becoming art director in 1949. He designed tableware ranges in the 1950s and 60s, often in tin-glazed earthenware decorated with stylised natural forms such as leaves and stripes. Studio potters like Lindberg often worked with industry, and mass-produced tableware benefited from these collaborations. Other Swedish tableware companies include Rörstrand (which set up the Arabia factory in Finland to access the Russian market) and Höganäs Keramik, both now part of Iittala (originally a Finnish glass company). Upsala-Ekeby was a Swedish tile company that employed artists and potters to design art pottery. In 1936 they took over the Gefle porcelain factory, where they made decorative tableware until the 1970s.

Finland

Famous designers from Finland include Kaj Franck and Tapio Wirkkala. Franck (1911–89) designed for Finland Arabia in Helsinki, which had an art department where ceramic artists designed ranges for manufacture as well as one-off pieces. Franck's Kilta tableware, designed in 1952 (and reintroduced in the eighties as Teema), was simple

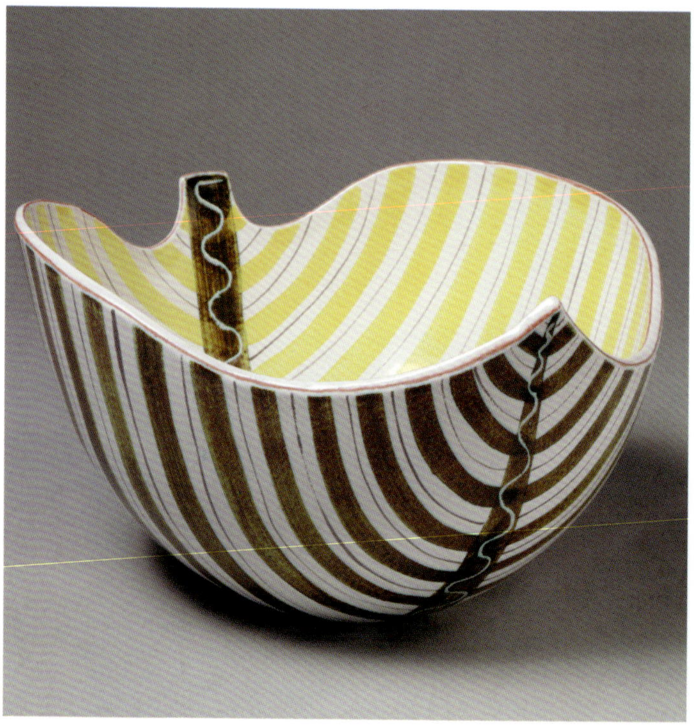

Stig Lindberg, salad bowl in the shape of a bowled leaf, Gustavsberg, Sweden, 1952. Earthenware with white tin glaze, length: 25 cm (10 in.). *Photo: Victoria and Albert Museum, London.*

and multifunctional, using only colour for decoration. The range was made from glazed earthenware, single-fired to save energy, and was heatproof. Ulla Procopé (1921–1968) was another designer who produced popular tableware ranges for Arabia, in particular the asymmetric wicker-handled GA teapot and the oven-to-table Ruska range in dark brown stoneware, first produced in 1961. She died at a relatively young age and is not as well-known as some of her contemporaries. Tapio Wirkkala (1915–85) designed sculptural organic vases and coffee sets for Rosenthal in Germany, as well as glassware for Iittala and furniture in wood and metal.

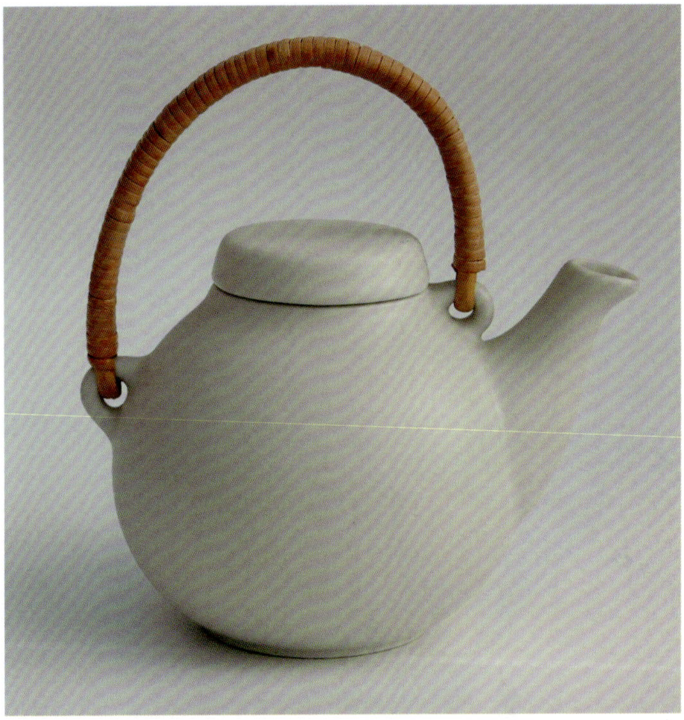

Ulla Procopé, GA teapot, Finland Arabia, 1953. Cane handle and semi-matt glaze, height: 15 cm (6 in.). *Photo: Henry Bloomfield.*

Kaj Franck, Kilta tableware, Finland Arabia, 1957. Single-fired earthenware with coloured glazes, white jug height: 6 cm (2½ in.). *Photo: Victoria and Albert Museum, London.*

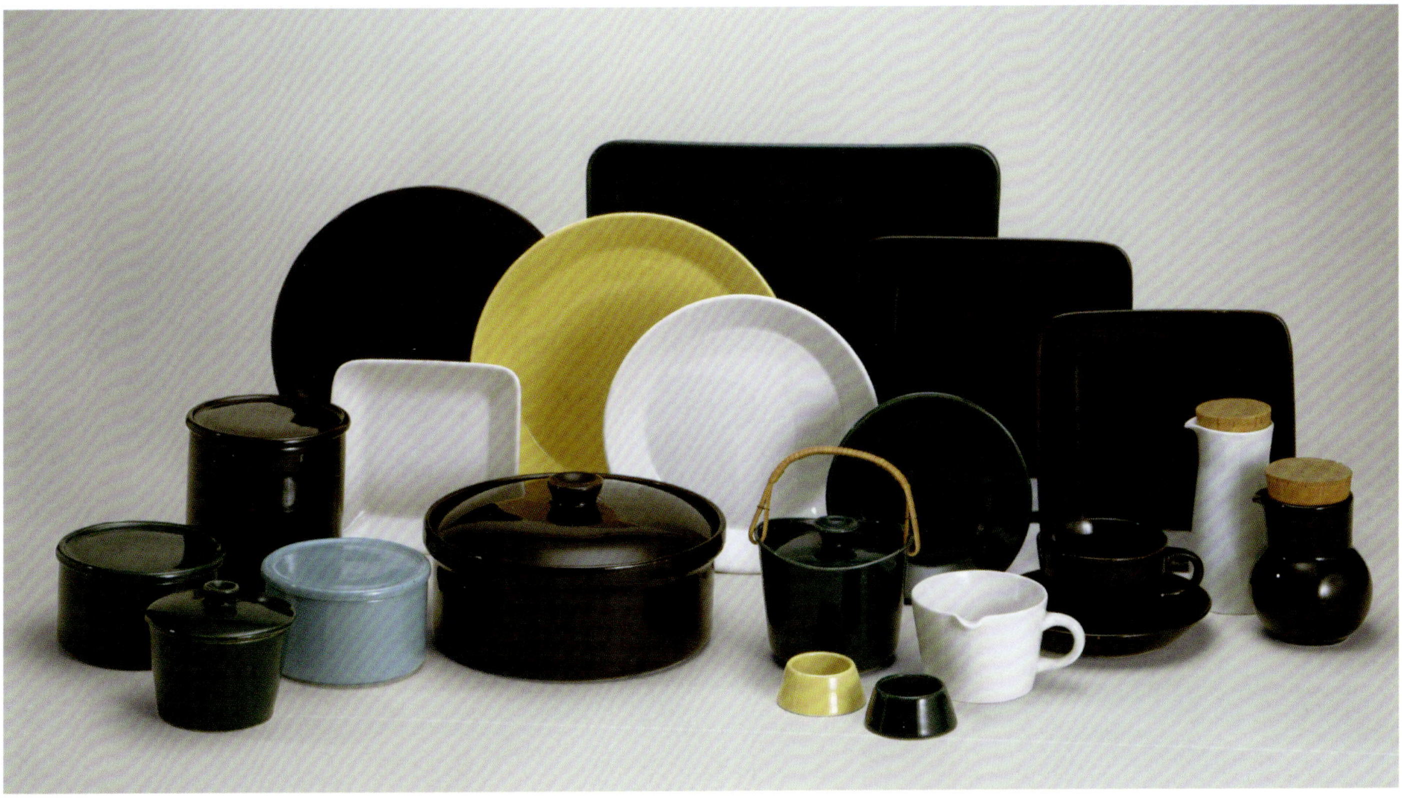

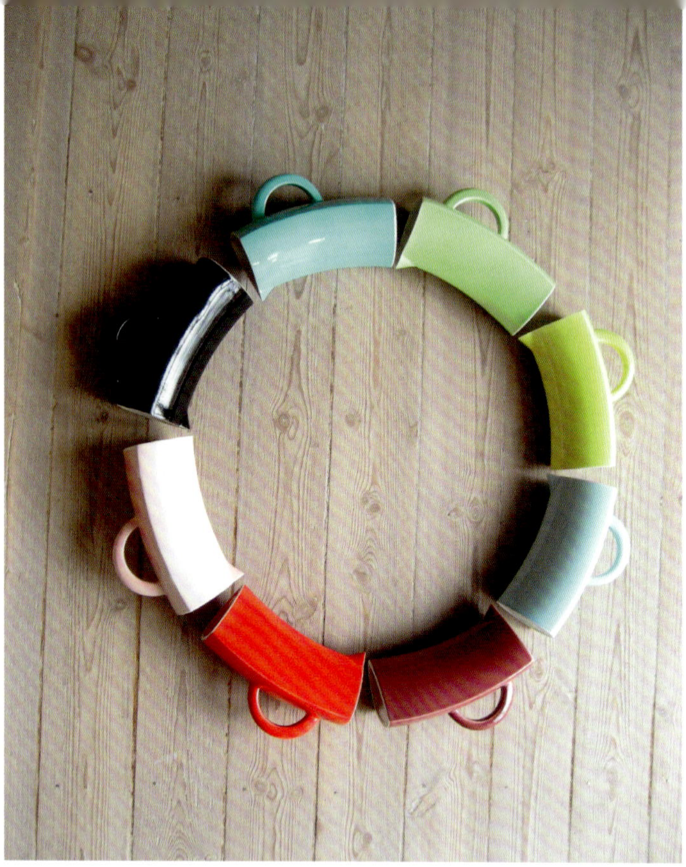

Rigmore Als, Copenhagen, Greeting jugs, 2008. Slipcast porcelain, 1-litre volume. *Photo: Rigmor Als.*

Norway and Denmark

There are several tableware manufacturers in Norway, including Porsgrund Porselen and Figgjo, which in the 1960s made quirky decorated ware with folk drawings of Norwegian life. Potteries in Denmark range from the Royal Copenhagen porcelain factory, famous for its Blue Fluted tableware, to smaller studio potteries like the Søholm Pottery, founded in 1835 on the island of Bornholm, initially producing utilitarian ware then moving on to art pottery in the 1950s and 60s.

Many Danish artist-potters worked as designers for industry. One of these was Gertrude Vasegaard (1913–2007), who designed tableware for Bing & Grøndahl and Royal Copenhagen. She had her own studio and made thrown prototypes for her mass-produced designs. Other 20th-century Danish studio potters include Axel Salto and Eva Staehr-Nielsen, who worked at the influential Saxbo art-pottery studio and designed for Royal Copenhagen. Saxbo Pottery, established in 1930 by chemist Nathalie Krebs, produced oriental-glazed organic forms in stoneware.

Marimekko Räsymatto, porcelain teapot with rubberwood handle and knob, and mugs. Designed by Sami Ruotsalainen, pattern by Maija Louekari, height: 9 cm (3½ in.). *Photo: courtesy of David Mellor Design Ltd.*

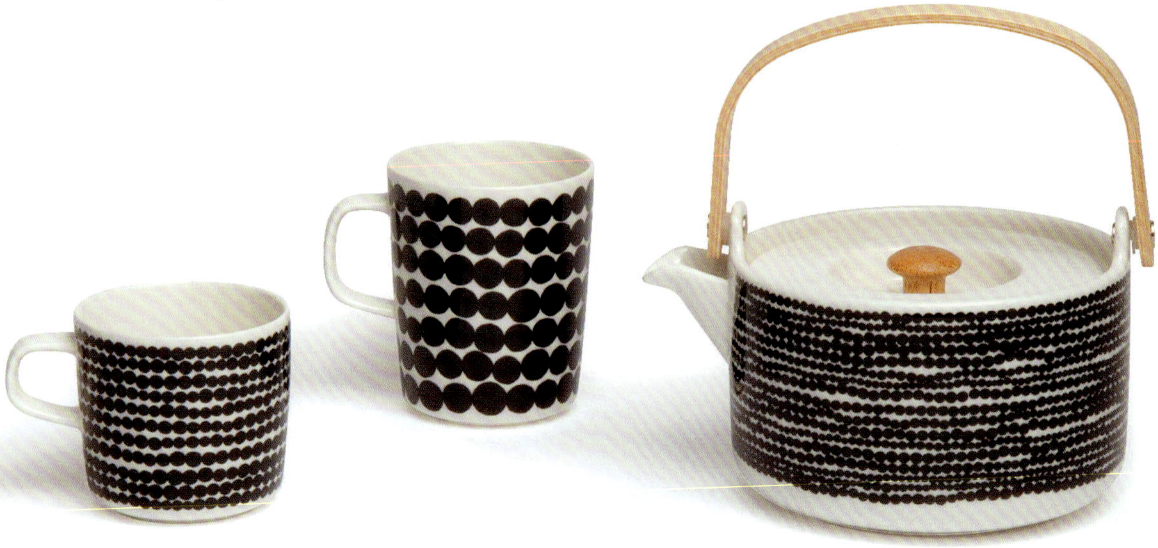

Scandinavian-influenced potteries in England

Several potteries in England made Scandinavian-influenced tin-glazed earthenware after the Second World War. Briglin Pottery was set up in a basement in the West End of London in 1948 by Brigitte Appleby and Eileen Lewenstein. They produced handmade Scandinavian-style earthenware decorated with swirling patterns in wax resist and manganese dioxide, covered with a white tin glaze. Eileen left Briglin in 1956 and later became co-editor of *Ceramic Review* magazine with Emmanuel Cooper. Brigitte moved to a larger basement and expanded the pottery. At the height of its production during the 1960s and 70s, Briglin Pottery had a staff of 15 and could make more than 3,000 pieces a week.

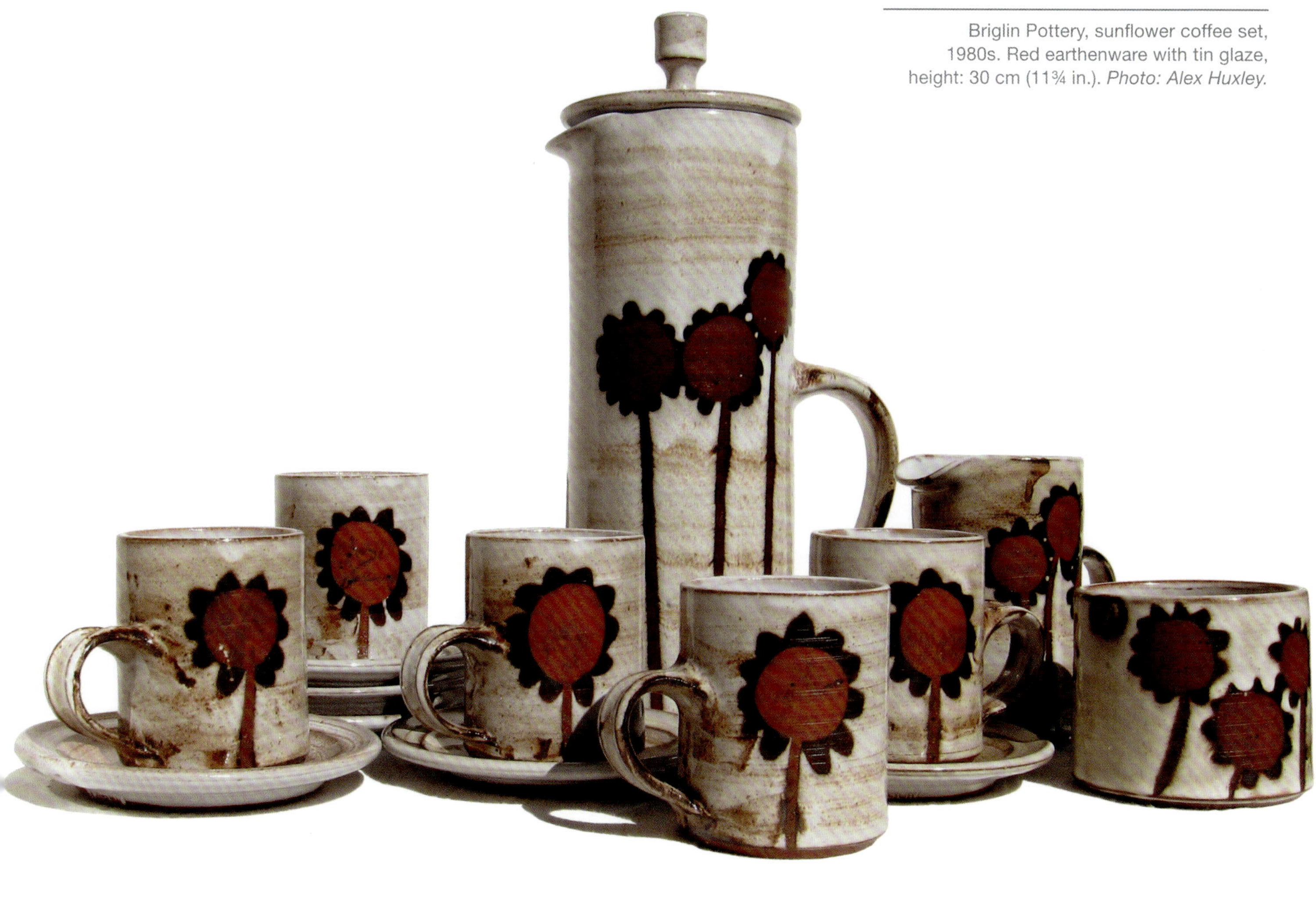

Briglin Pottery, sunflower coffee set, 1980s. Red earthenware with tin glaze, height: 30 cm (11¾ in.). *Photo: Alex Huxley.*

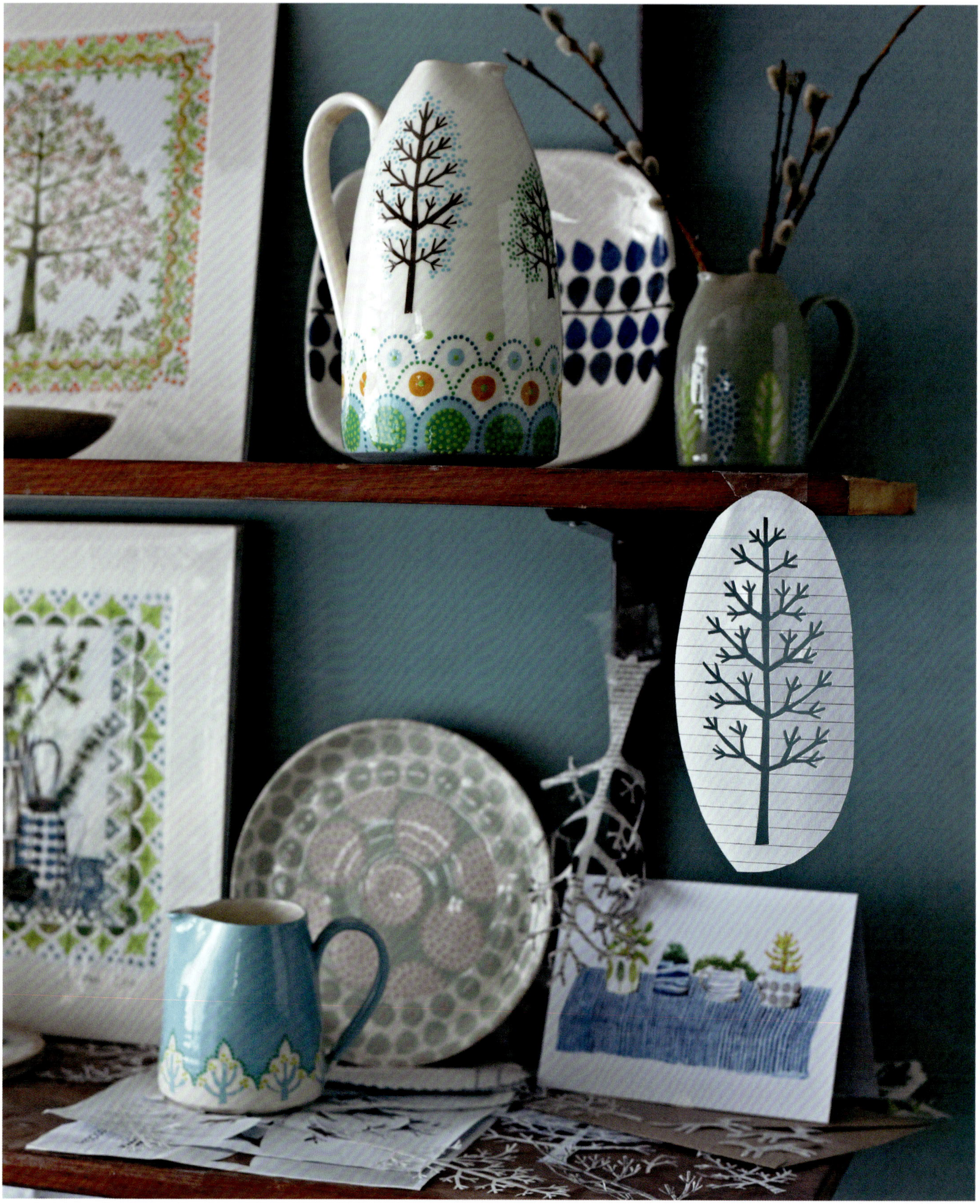

Katrin Moye, watercolours, jugs and plates, 2012. Thrown white earthenware, papercut decoration, clear leadless glaze, fired to 1100°C (2012°F). *Photo: Katrin Moye.*

Marianne de Trey ran a pottery at Shinners Bridge, Dartington in Devon and made a range of earthenware with decorative brushwork from 1949. Her husband, potter Sam Haile had died tragically in a road accident the previous year, leaving de Trey to run the pottery alone, managing a staff of up to five. Decorated tableware was in demand after the Second World War as only plain utility ware had been produced during the period of the conflict. De Trey had studied textile design at the Royal College of Art and loved pattern. She converted to stoneware in 1960 and used techniques including throwing and jigger-jolley methods. Decoration was carried out using slips, wax resist and brushed-on oxides.

The Scandinavian influence continues to be found in tableware today. Contemporary potter Katrin Moye makes slip-decorated earthenware in the Scandinavian style. Having a German textile-artist mother, she was surrounded by patterned textiles as a child and is influenced by Scandinavian folk art. Many of her ranges are inspired by patterns she loved growing up and some are named after members of her family. She uses earthenware clay, thrown and turned on the wheel, and decorates with coloured slips and underglazes using techniques including sponging, trailing and paper resist. Moye has also designed a range for English Country Pottery, which is slipcast in stoneware and hand-decorated with leaves and dots using engobes. The pattern is based on the leaves of the birch tree in her garden.

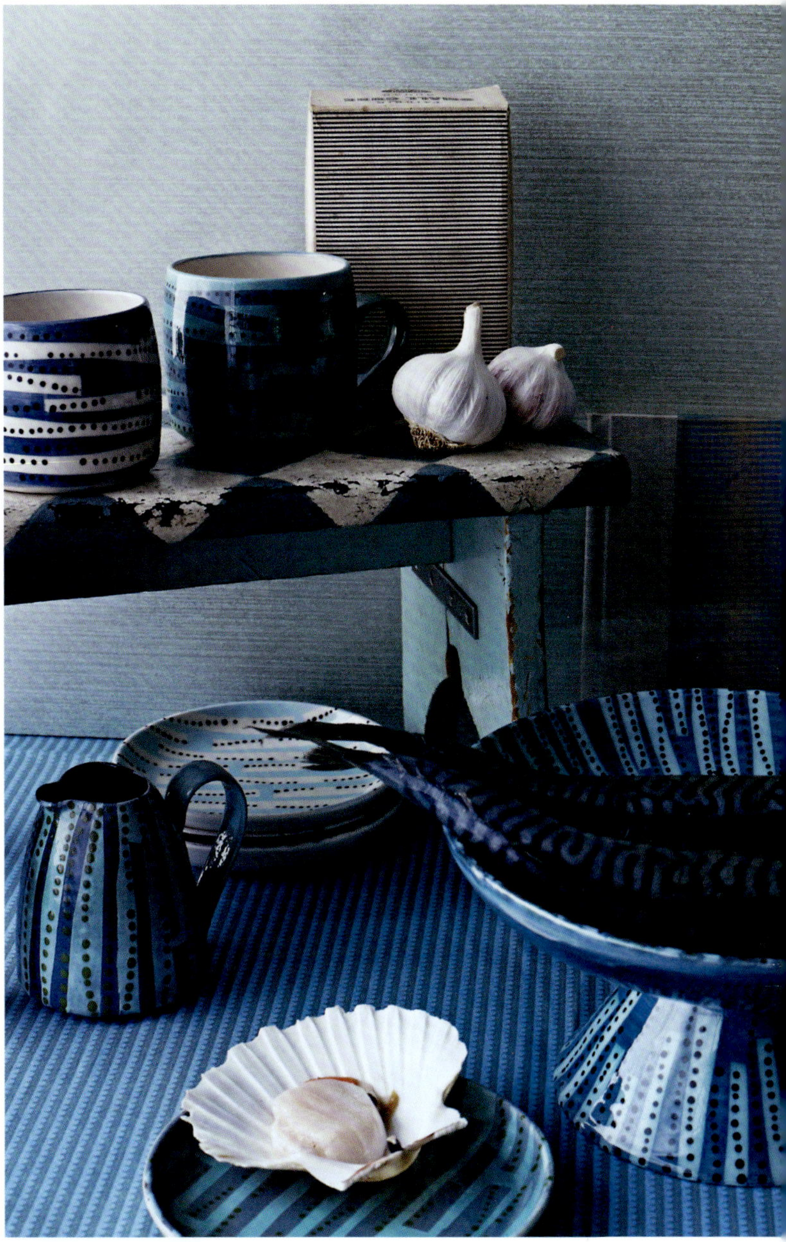

Katrin Moye, dotted stripe tableware, 2010. Thrown red earthenware, slip decoration. *Photo: Iwan Essery.*

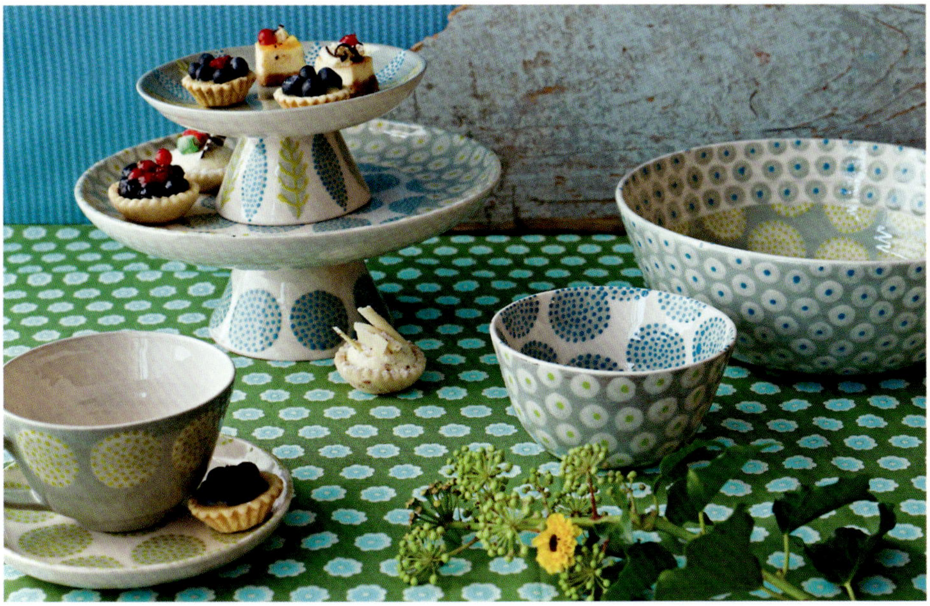

Katrin Moye, Tiny Hoops and Dandelions tableware collections, 2010. Thrown red earthenware, slip decoration, diameter: 30 cm (12 in.). *Photo: Iwan Essery.*

9 America

Biomorphic design

Biomorphism in art and design involves the use of organic shapes based on natural forms. The term was first used in 1936 by the director of the Museum of Modern Art in New York to describe the organic art of Jean Arp (also known as Hans Arp), which was a reaction against Cubism and Constructivism. American designers such as Russel Wright, Eva Zeisel and Edith Heath had a great influence on British designers in the mid-20th century, producing organic forms with flowing curves. Russel Wright designed a very successful tableware range in 1937 called American Modern, originally made by Steubenville Pottery in Ohio. It had biomorphic shapes and bright colours including chartreuse and coral, and is currently manufactured by Bauer Pottery in California.

Eva Zeisel

Another designer who utilised biomorphic shapes to great effect was Eva Zeisel (1906–2011). She was originally from Hungary and worked in the German and Soviet ceramics industries before being imprisoned in Russia for sixteen months and then emigrating to New York at the outbreak of the Second World War. She was almost immediately successful in America, designing the first all-white dinner service in the US, which was exhibited at the Museum of Modern Art in New York in 1946. Her forms

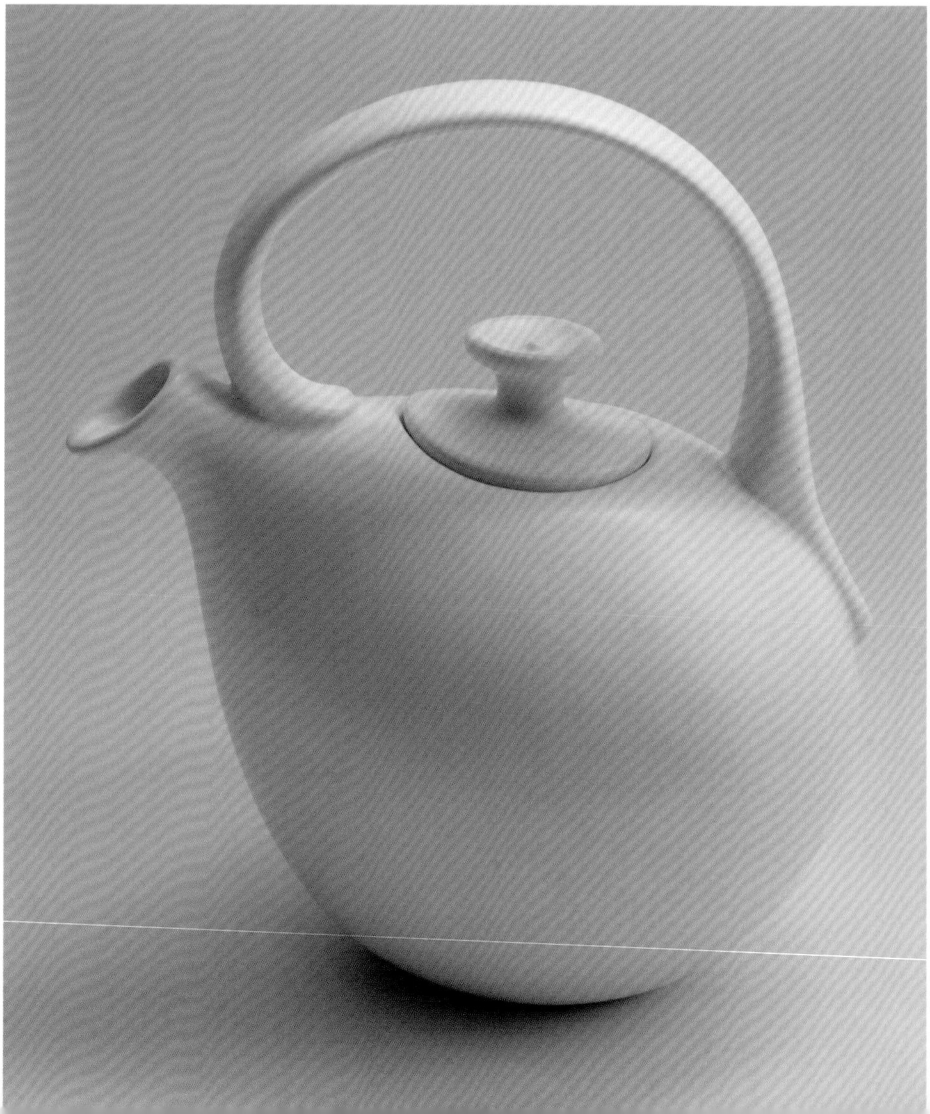

Eva Zeisel, Granit teapot, designed in 1983, produced by Design Within Reach in 2009. Stoneware, height: 18 cm (7 in.). *Photo: Henry Bloomfield.*

were organic with a playful nature, characteristic of mid-20th-century modern design. Avoiding angular shapes, she preferred rounded and voluptuous forms, often with exaggerated handles. Her most popular dinnerware ranges were Hallcraft Tomorrow's Classic (1952) and Hallcraft Century (1957), originally made by Hall China in Ohio and now (since 2004) made in earthenware by Royal Stafford in Stoke-on-Trent and sold in the US by Crate and Barrel. The original pieces from the 1950s sometimes had patterns but the current Classic Century range is made only in plain white or black. The new range includes the addition of a mug and slightly larger dinner plates to adapt to current dining habits.

Heath Ceramics

Edith Heath (1911–2005) designed for Heath Ceramics, a small company she founded in 1948 in Sausalito, California, which still produces plain, functional vitreous ware (fired to 1150°C/2100°F) in a range of colours. Edith adapted shapes from her thrown pieces to be made using moulds, either by jigger-jolley methods or by slipcasting

Heath Ceramics, teapot with wrapped copper handle, designed 1947. Designed by Edith Heath, diameter: 19 cm (7½ in.). *Photo: Jeffery Cross.*

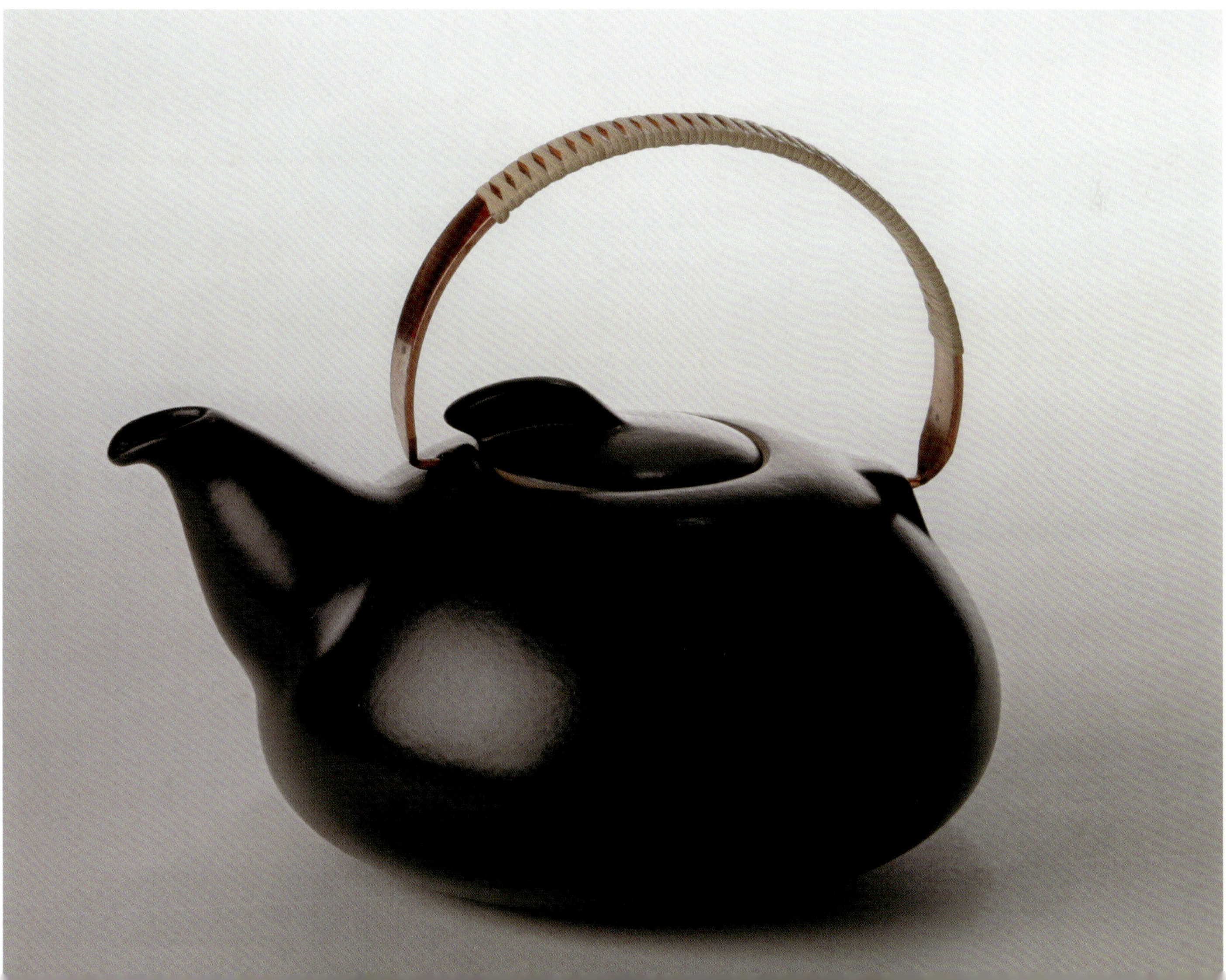

(see pp. 77, 80). She developed her own clay body using locally available clays. It can be fired to earthenware temperatures but is non-porous and vitrified like a stoneware clay body. The glaze is wiped from the rims of the ware so that the warm-coloured clay body can be seen.

Edith designed a range of plates and bowls called Coupe, and later a range named Rim, which could be stacked efficiently for use in restaurants. She was influenced by Bauhaus ideas as well as her Danish heritage, but in the 1980s she designed a range of Asian-inspired square dishes and platters. Heath Ceramics is now run by new owners, a husband-and-wife team who still use the same clay body and shapes and have brought out new ranges of dinnerware and seasonal colours.

Heath Ceramics, four mugs on a square tray, 2010. Diameter: 30 cm (11¾ in.). *Photo: Jeffery Cross.*

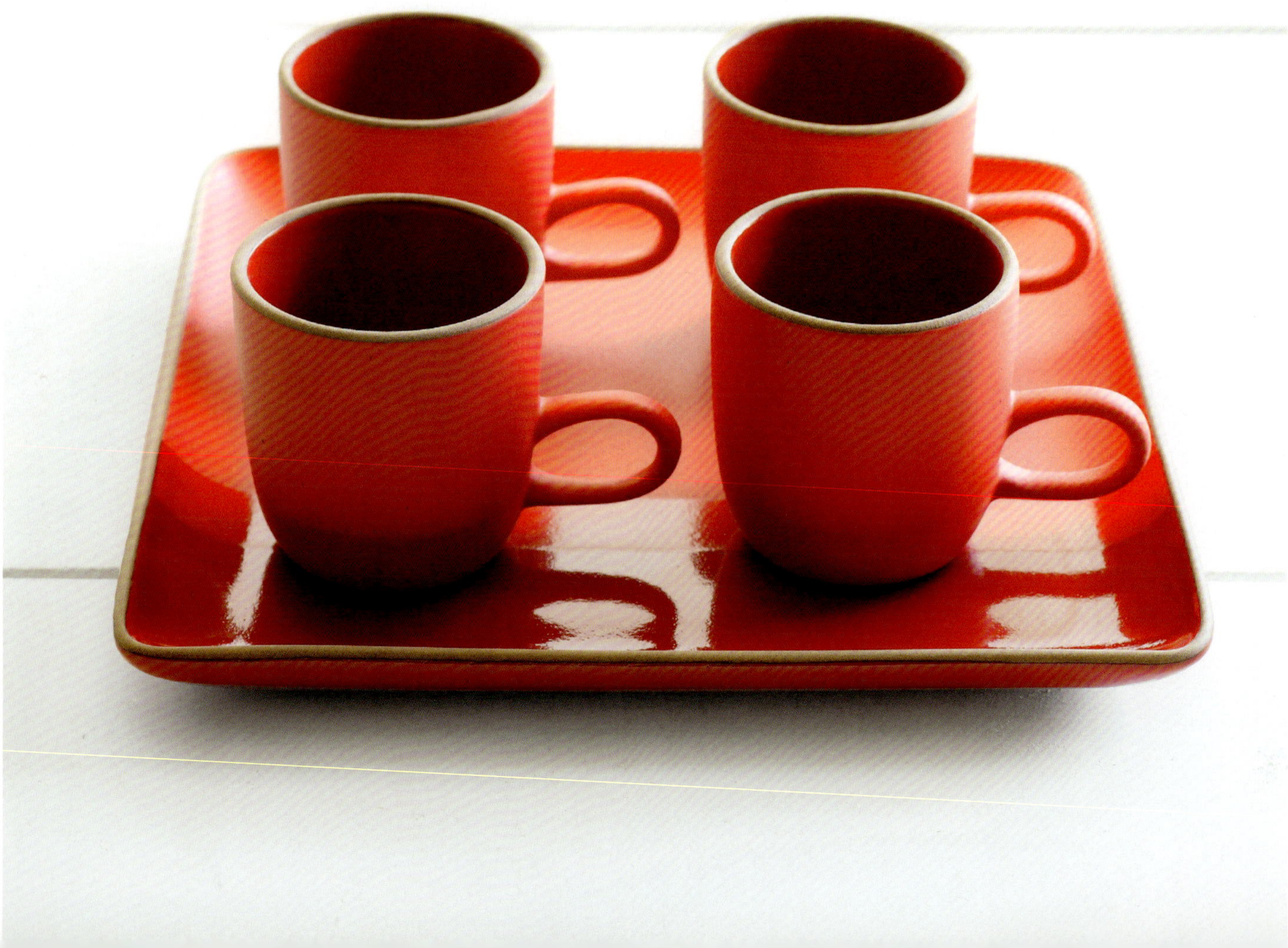

Contemporary biomorphism

Many potters in the US make tableware in the studio pottery tradition begun by Bernard Leach and continued by American potters such as Warren MacKenzie. Other potters are more influenced by the Bauhaus style, led in America by studio potters Marguerite Wildenhain, who attended the Bauhaus school and designed tableware for industrial production in Berlin, and Gertrud and Otto Nazler, who emigrated from Vienna. However, there are also contemporary American potters who are inspired by biomorphic design.

One such designer-maker is David Pier, who has designed an oval ergonomic cup with an undulating rim and recessed handle. The cup is unusual in that its design is not constrained by the manufacturing process. The saucers can also be used as lids or to facilitate stacking of the cups. Pier has researched the use of rare earth oxides in his transparent glazes and uses a range of colours on his work.

David Pier, Lux-Delux Ultimate 8 oz (230 ml) coffee cups, 2007. Slipcast porcelain, height: 9.5 cm (3¾ in.). *Photo: David Pier.*

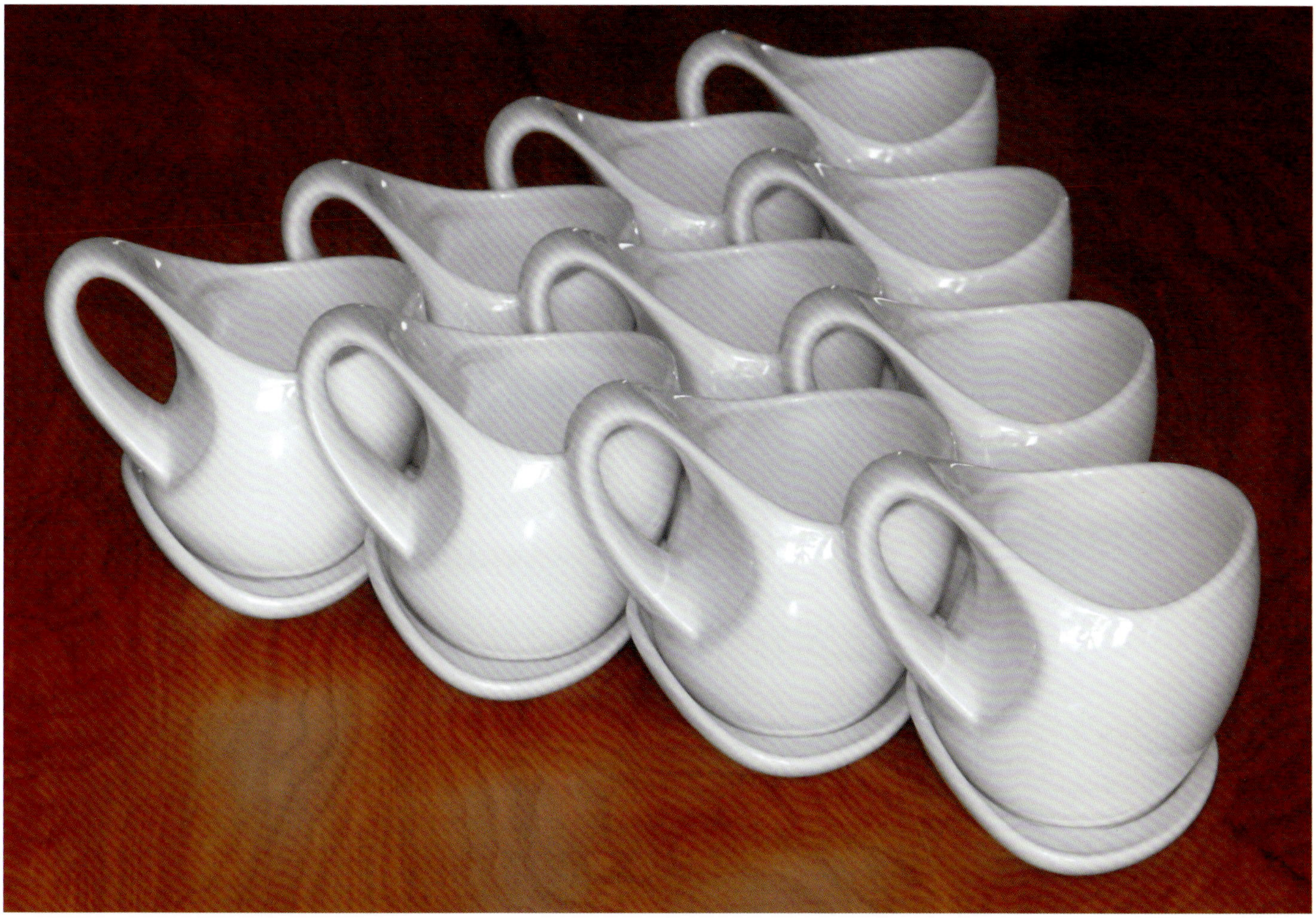

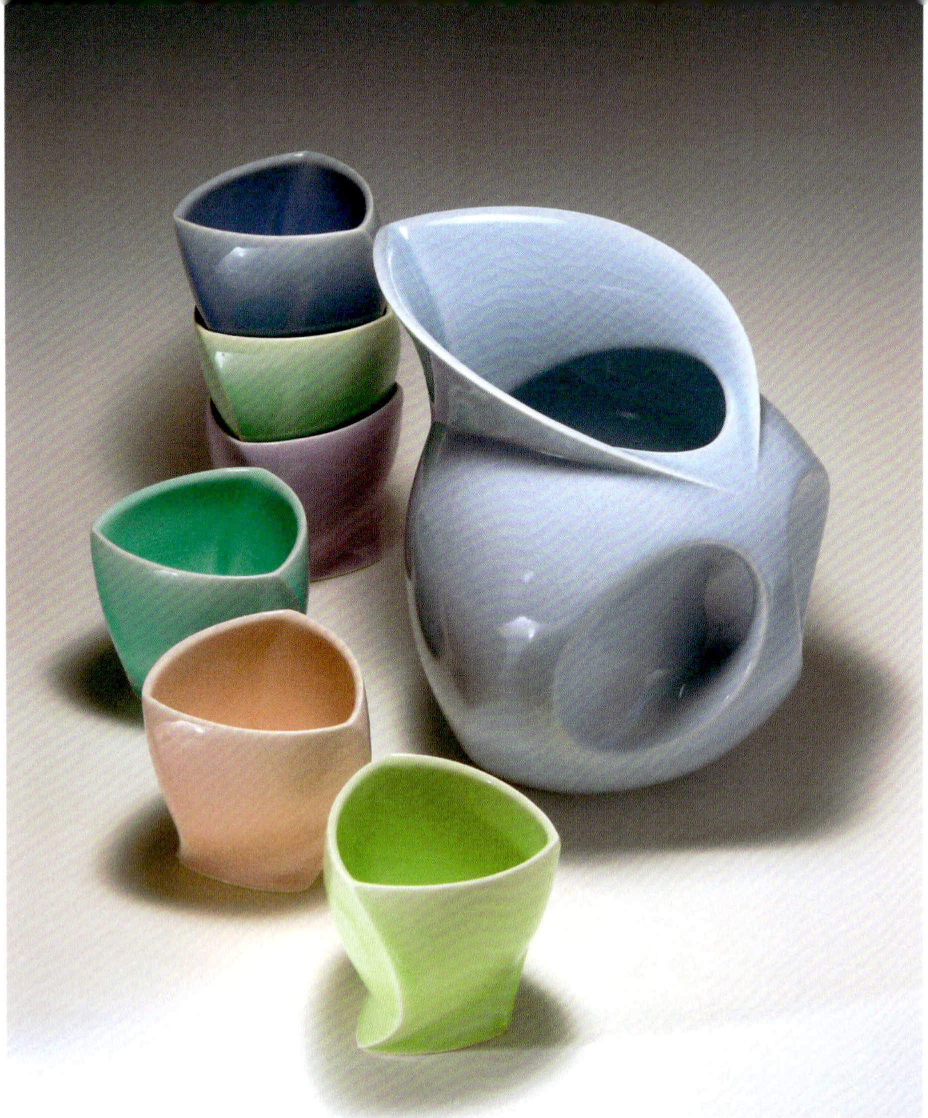

David Pier, pitcher with six cups, 2005. Slipcast porcelain, rare earth glazes, height: 23 cm (9 in.). *Photo: David Pier.*

Peter Saenger, sugar and creamer on tray, designed 1980, produced 2011. Design models created by filling balloons with plaster and nestling them together. Porcelain, 12.5 x 15 x 23 cm (9 x 6 x 5 in.). *Photo: Peter Saenger.*

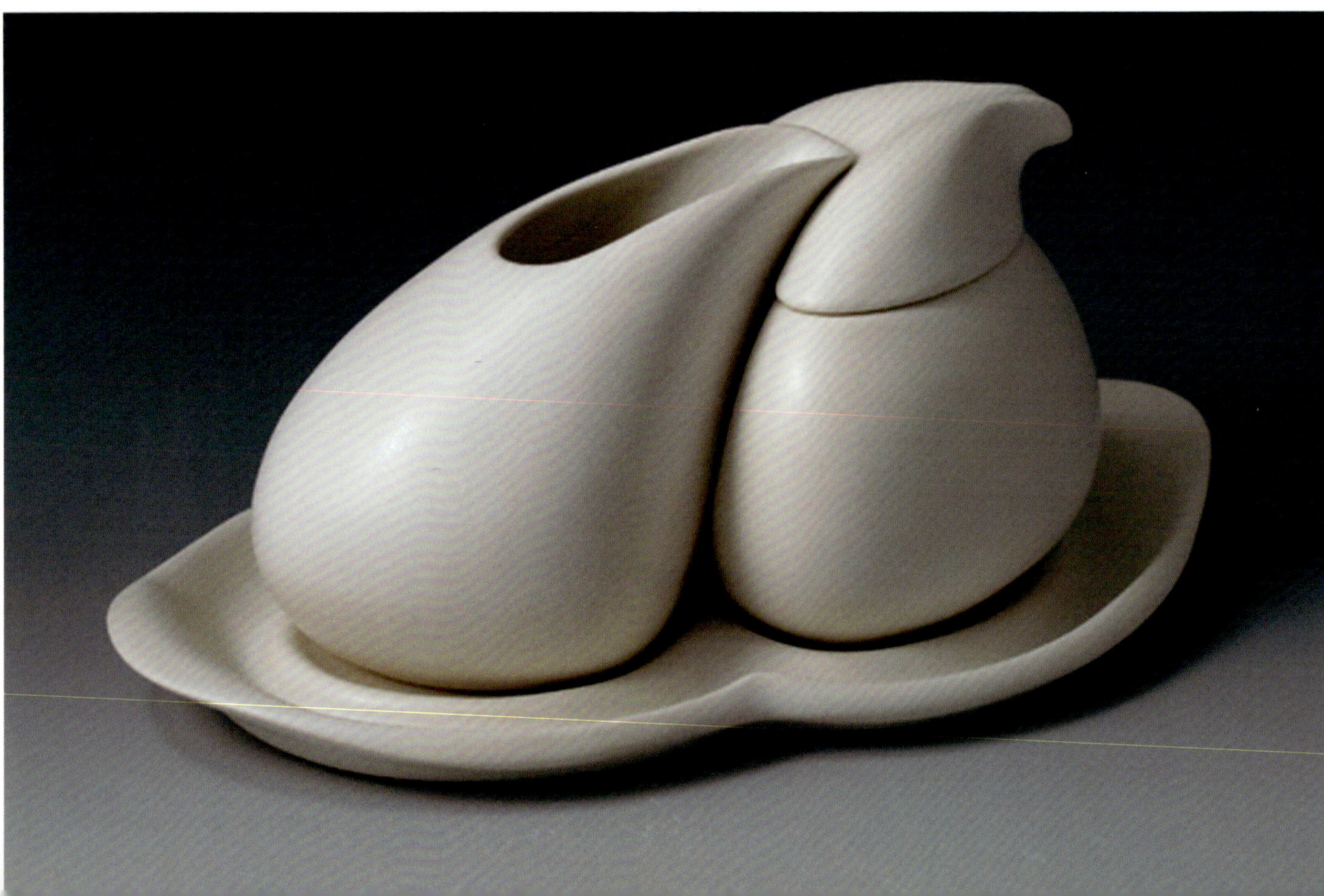

Another potter influenced by biomorphism is Judi Tavill, who makes thrown, cut and reassembled functional ware. Her previous career in fashion and textiles has led her to reference fabric, draping and wrapping in her ceramic work. Her pieces have beautiful sculptural form and movement while remaining within the confines of functional ceramics.

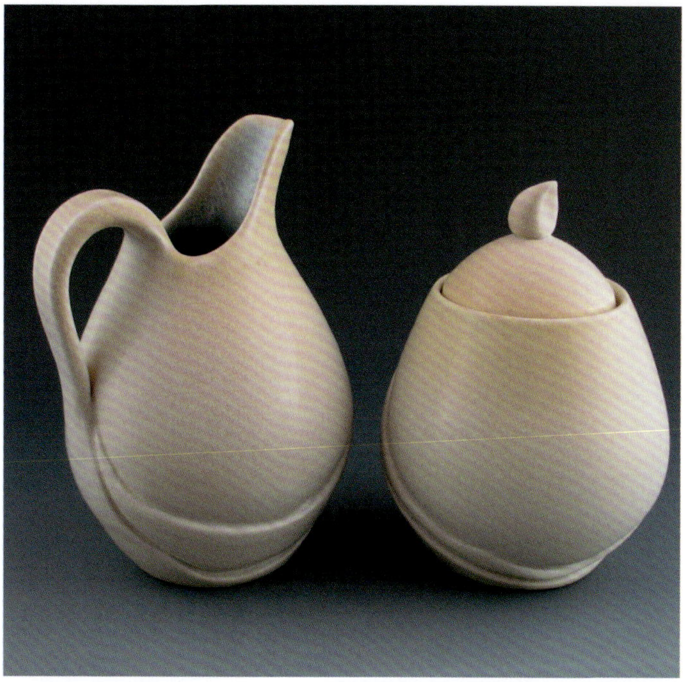

Judi Tavill, sugar and creamer, 2009. Thrown and carved porcelain, fired to cone 5-6 (1240°C/2264°F), height: 13 cm (5¼ in.). *Photo: Judi Tavill.*

Judi Tavill, grey-blue chip and dip bowl, 2010. Thrown and carved porcelain, fired to cone 5-6 (1240°C/2264°F), diameter: 28 cm (11 in.). *Photo: Judi Tavill.*

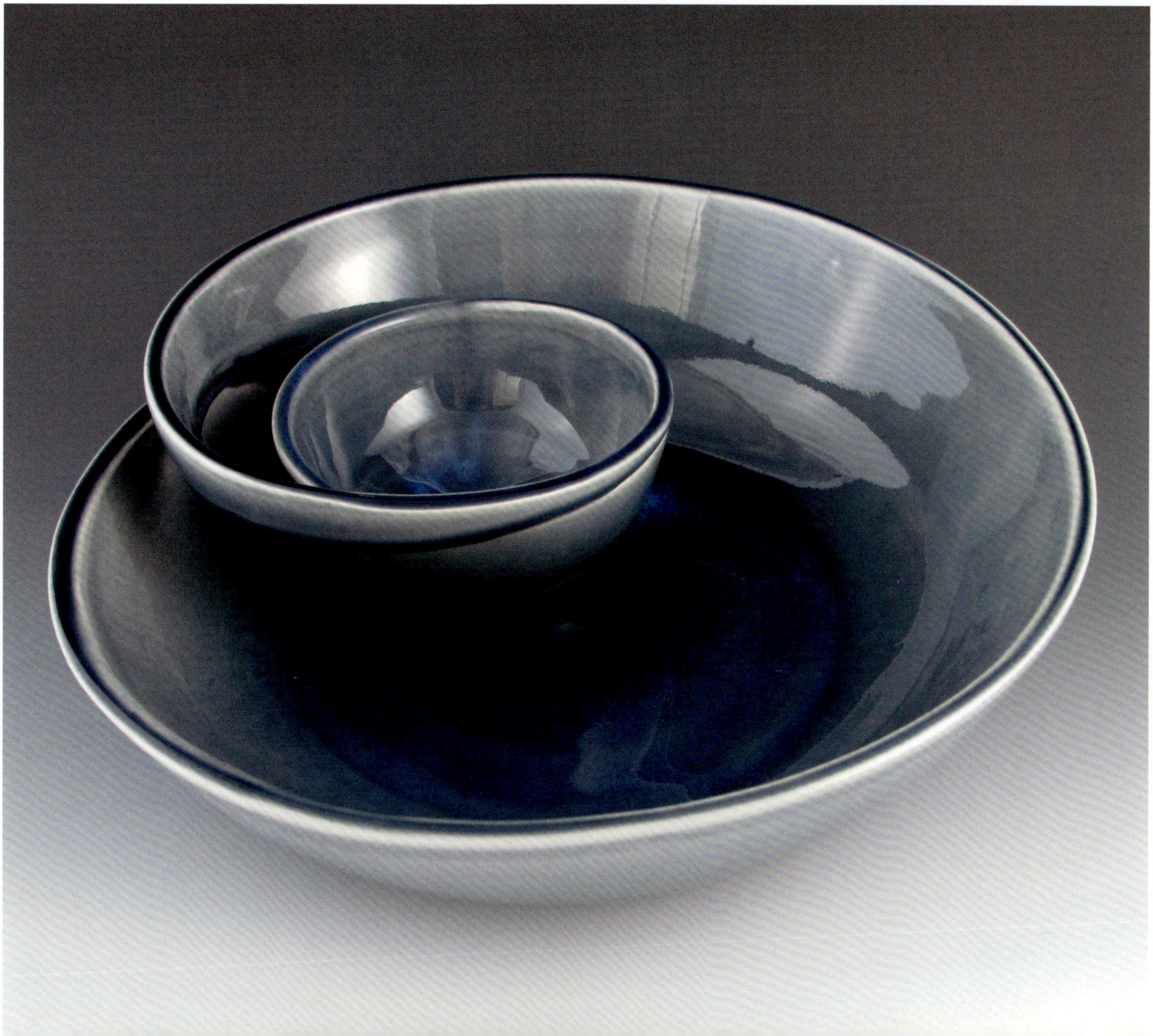

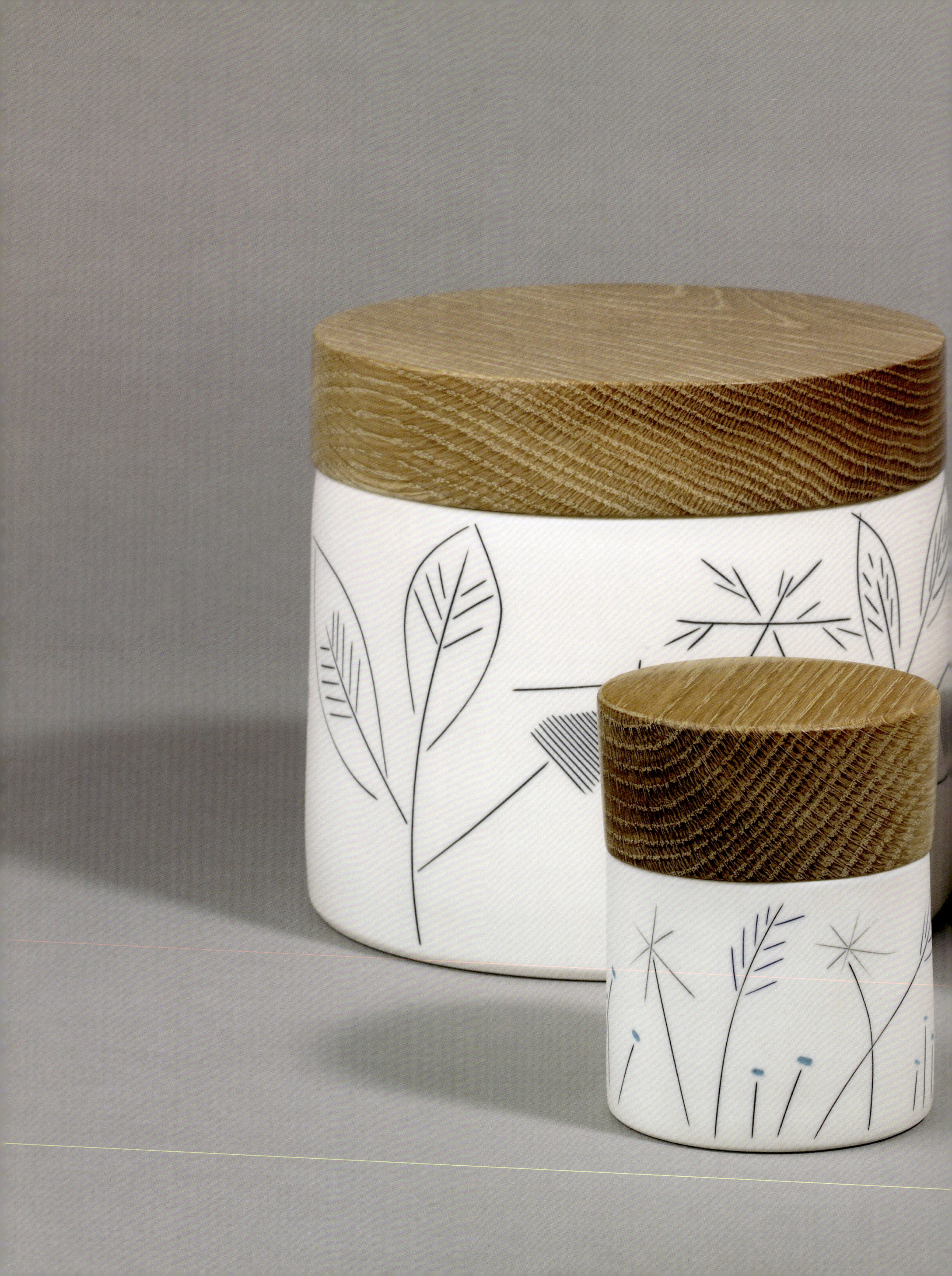

Part 2

DESIGN AND FORM

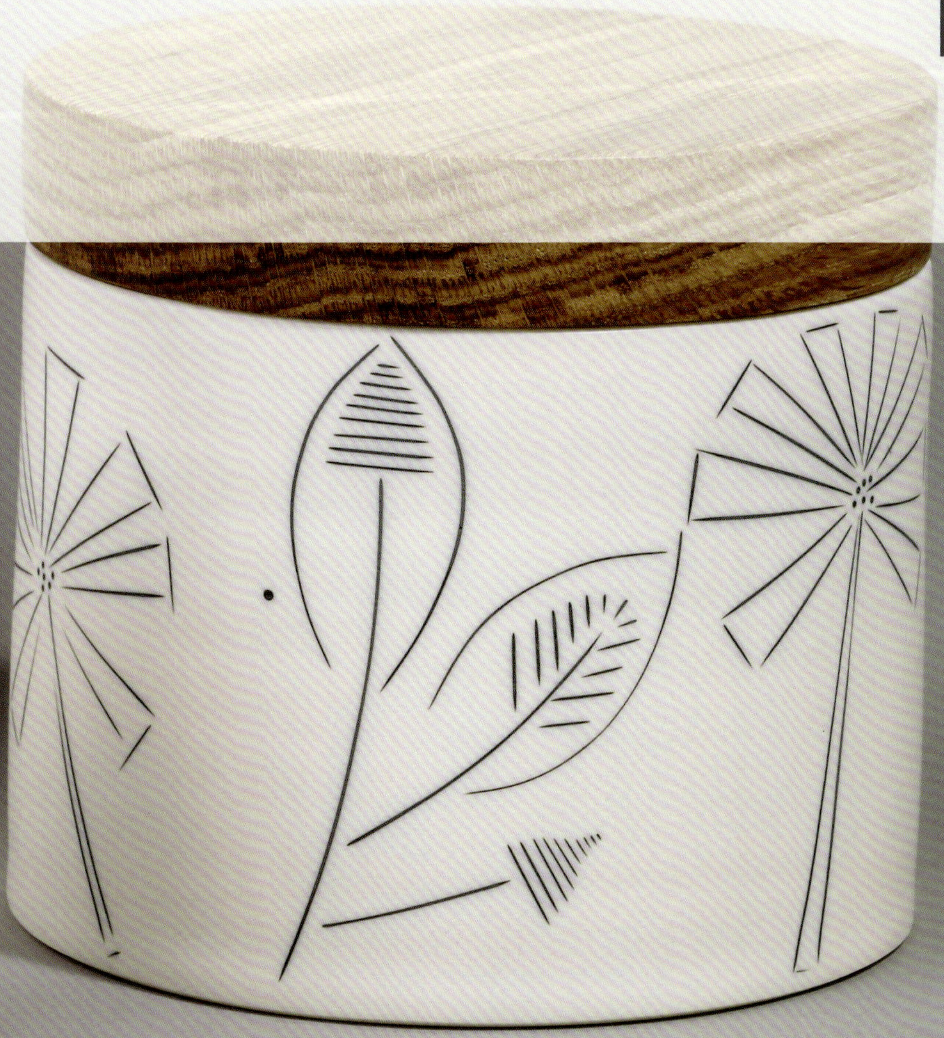

10 Contemporary design

Inspiration

There are many sources of inspiration for tableware design. Traditionally, pottery forms were handed down from master to apprentice. When new forms were imported from the East, they were copied and adapted for use. Also, design of tableware often follows design concepts seen in architecture. In the 18th century the architecture of the classical world was rediscovered, and inspired the use of Greek cameos on Wedgwood's jasperware. Modernist ceramics in the early 20th century were geometric and functional, like the architecture of the Bauhaus movement, and a reaction to strict minimalism was to introduce humour through form or decoration. Natural forms and patterns often provided inspiration, with biomorphism and stylised patterns from nature becoming popular in the 1950s.

Jiří Pelcl with technical drawing of Bohemia White teapot in Český Porcelán factory, Dubi. *Photo: courtesy of Jiří Pelcl.*

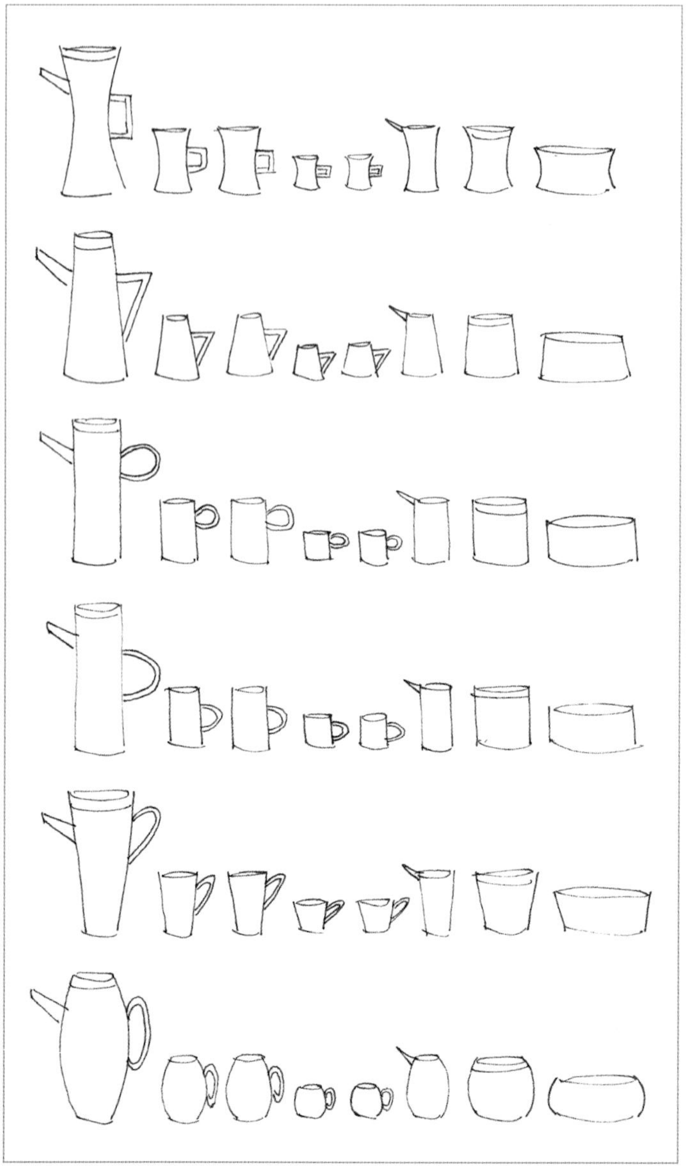

Billy Lloyd, drawings for tea/coffee sets, teapot, mugs, espresso cups, milk jug, sugar jar, bowl, 2012. *Photo: Billy Lloyd.*

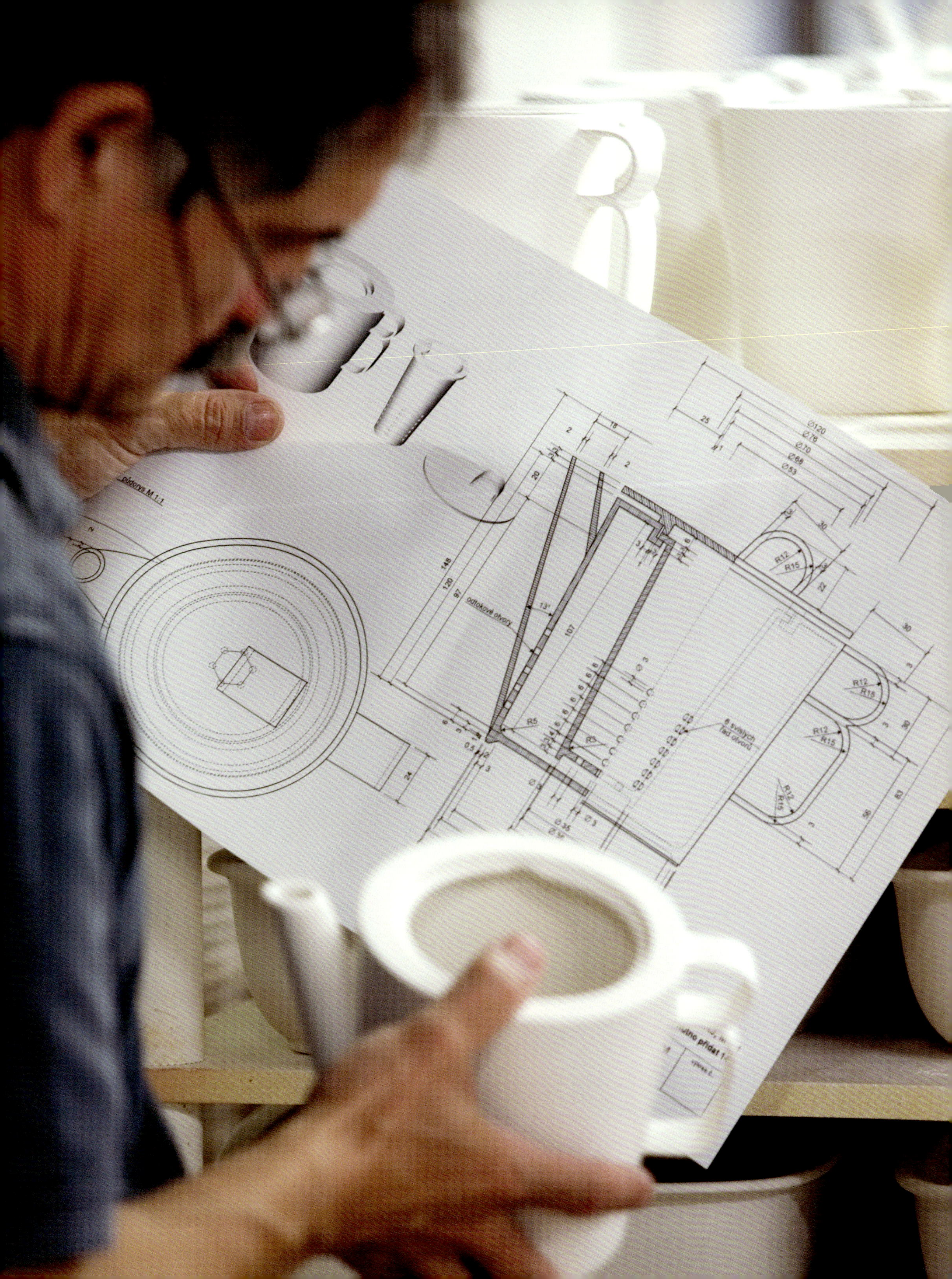

Design

Design usually starts with drawing, either by hand or aided by a computer, although some potters prefer to design as they make. When designing tableware, the making process must be taken into account as well as the type of clay used. For example, when using one-piece moulds, to enable the piece to drop out of the mould easily bowl and beaker shapes must be made with no undercuts. Cups and bowls are stronger and cheaper if made by jolleying rather than slipcasting. Bowls with a slightly out-turned rim are less likely to warp during making and firing than those with straight rims. More complex shapes like teapots can only be made by slipcasting or assembling several thrown pieces. When throwing on the wheel, it is very difficult to make spherical or teardrop shapes, as they slump easily. All these manufacturing considerations influence the design of traditional and modern pottery.

When designing a range of tableware, the maker should ensure that all the pieces work well together and have a unifying theme in form, colour or pattern. For example, a single shape such as a cylinder, cone or sphere could be used for all the pieces in a tea set. The handles on the cups, milk jug and teapot could all be the same shape but different sizes in proportion to the size of the pot. Dinnerware sets usually include a minimum of a dinner plate, side plate, bowl and mug, and these should all have the same style. Colour and pattern can be varied across a number of different pieces that work together in harmony; see, for example, Courtney Murphy's maiolica-decorated earthenware (below).

Courtney Murphy, tableware, 2011. Maiolica-decorated earthenware, fired to cone 02 (1120°C/2048°F), mug height: 9 cm (3½ in.). *Photo: by the artist.*

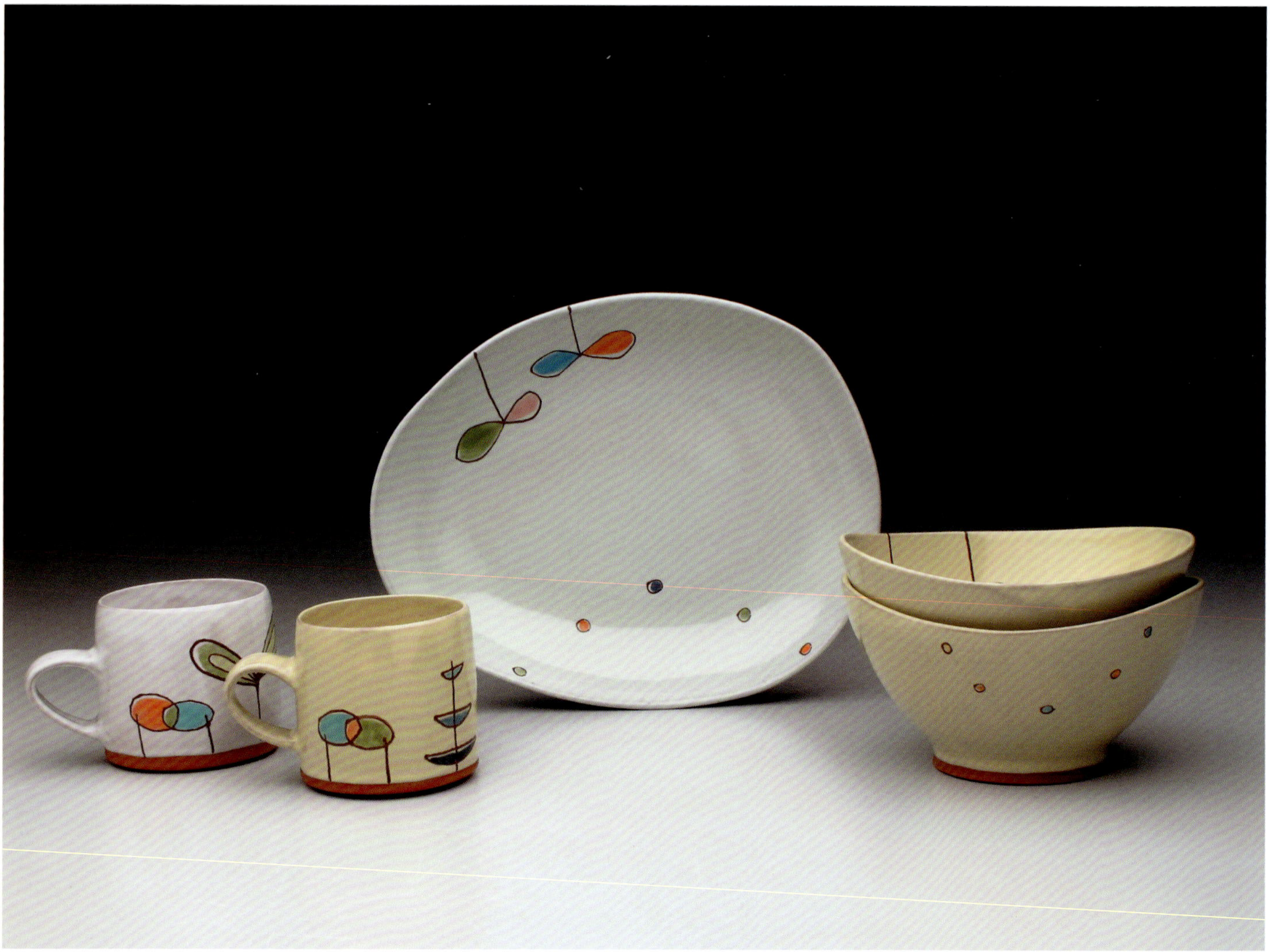

Types of clay

There are three basic types of clay: earthenware, stoneware and porcelain. Earthenware is fired up to 1150°C (2102°F) and remains relatively soft and porous after firing. It is available in several colours including red terracotta, which contains iron oxide, and cream earthenware, which is made from lighter-coloured ball clays. Red earthenware is the most plastic clay for throwing. It is a secondary clay, transported from its place of origin by river or glacier. During transport, the clay particles are abraded and broken up, resulting in a very small particle size and high plasticity. Some types of earthenware can be fired to a slightly higher temperature so that they begin to vitrify and become less porous.

Stoneware is fired to around 1250°C (2282°F) and becomes hard, vitrified and non-porous. It is less liable to chip or crack than earthenware and can be used for oven-to-table ware. It usually fires to a buff or grey colour, but white-firing stoneware clay bodies containing ball clay and china clay are also available.

Porcelain is fired to a similar temperature to stoneware but is very white, translucent and vitrified. It is made from china clay, feldspar and flint. Bone china is similar to porcelain but contains up to 50% bone ash, which makes it more translucent when fired. It has low plasticity and is most suitable for industrial making methods using moulds, such as slipcasting. Porcelain and bone china are much stronger than earthenware and last longer without chipping or cracking. Their strength means that tableware made from porcelain or bone china can be much thinner and lighter.

Making methods

Using moulds

Moulds are used in mass production to produce large numbers of identical pieces. They are usually made of Plaster of Paris, which is very absorbent, but can also be made from biscuit-fired clay. Plaster of Paris was used in Staffordshire from the mid-18th century and enabled the beginnings of mass production. Plaster moulds will deteriorate through use but new ones can be made from the original master model.

Handmade plates and dishes are often made by rolling out a slab of clay and pressing it into a mould. Alternatively, the clay slab can be draped over a hump mould.

Juliet Walters pressing a slab of clay into a plaster mould. *Photo: Henry Bloomfield.*

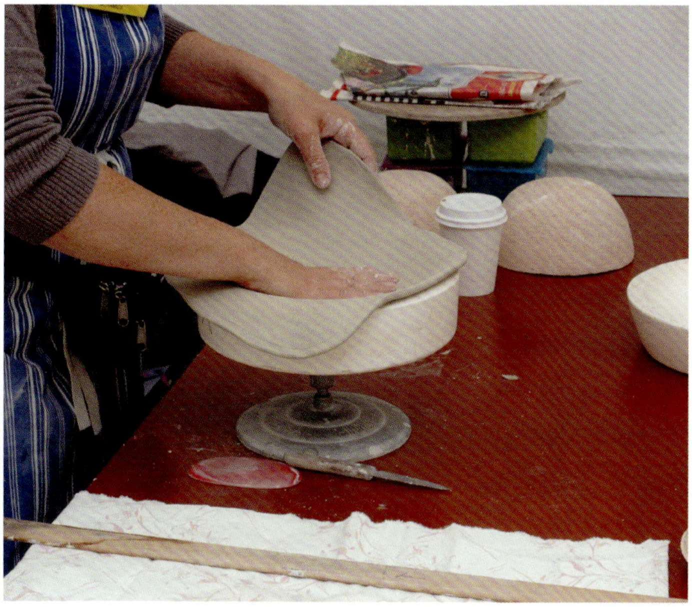

Trimming off the edges of the slab. *Photo: Henry Bloomfield.*

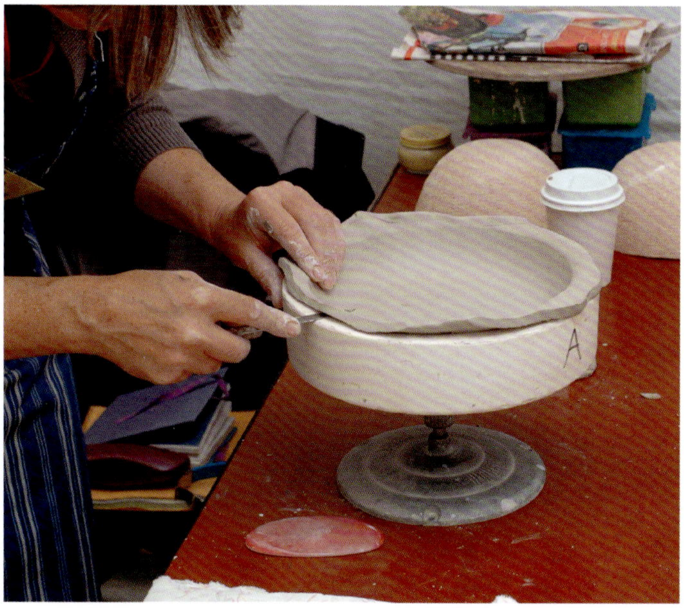

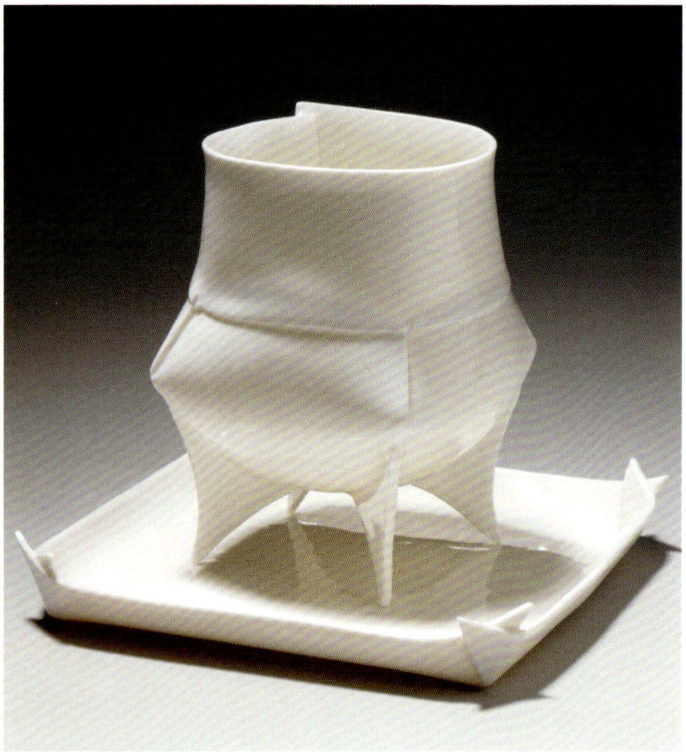

Ann Van Hoey makes folded bowls and cups in earthenware and porcelain. Her work was spotted by the Belgian company Serax Maison d'être in the Flanders Expo in 2008 and her tableware was put into production. Her Étude Géométrique bowls with folded corners were inspired by Japanese origami and won a bronze medal at the Ceramic Biennale in Korea in 2009. The large bowls are press-moulded in chocolate-coloured earthenware clay, inspiring the panel at the International Biennale of Contemporary Ceramics in Vallauris in the South of France to name her 'Madame Chocolat'. She has experimented with folding different numbers of corners to give a series of round, square, triangle, eye-shaped and teardrop-shaped bowls.

Ann Van Hoey, handmade cup on a tray, 2008. Flax porcelain, height: 8.5 cm (3½ in.). *Photo: Dries van den Brande.*

Ann Van Hoey, Étude Géométrique, 2008. Unglazed earthenware, 17 x 30 x 30 cm (6¾ x 12 x 12 in.). *Photo: courtesy of Ann Van Hoey.*

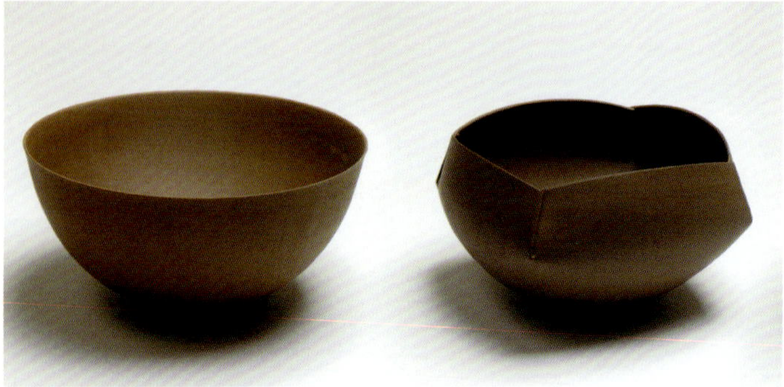

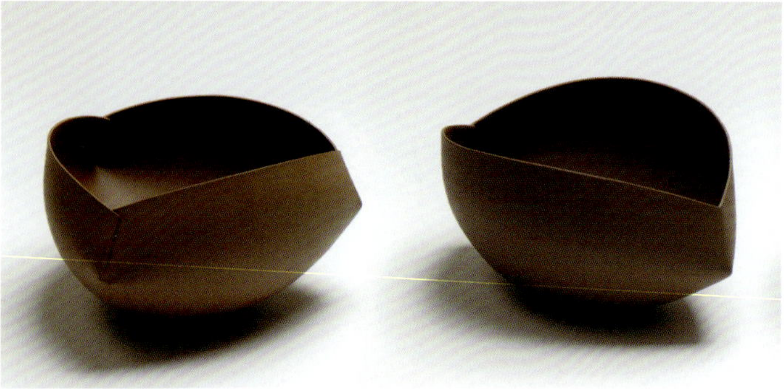

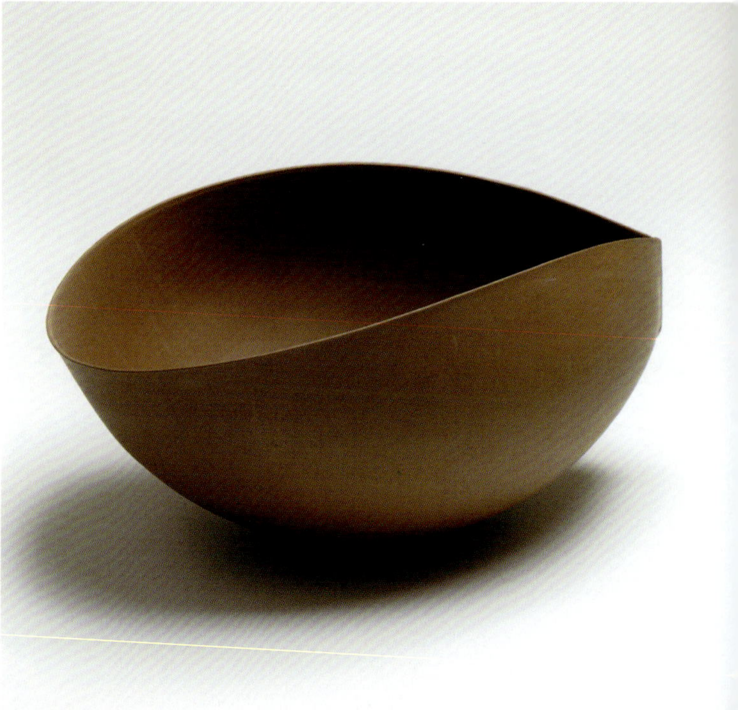

Van Hoey cuts slabs of clay using wedge-shaped paper templates and presses them into a bowl-shaped mould. When these are leatherhard, she removes them from the mould, then makes cuts with a large pair of scissors and overlaps the edges. Her range of tableware, handmade from Scarva flax porcelain, includes bowls, cups, jugs and plates. To prevent the cups from warping, she adds a slabbed collar around the rim of each one. Many of her handmade tableware pieces have a ribbed or knobbled texture and some stand on four feet. The mass-produced cups and bowls are slipcast in bone china and are less fragile than Van Hoey's handmade porcelain pieces.

Ann Van Hoey, handmade cups and bowls, 2008. Flax porcelain, height: 8.5 cm (3½ in.). *Photo: Dries Van den Brande.*

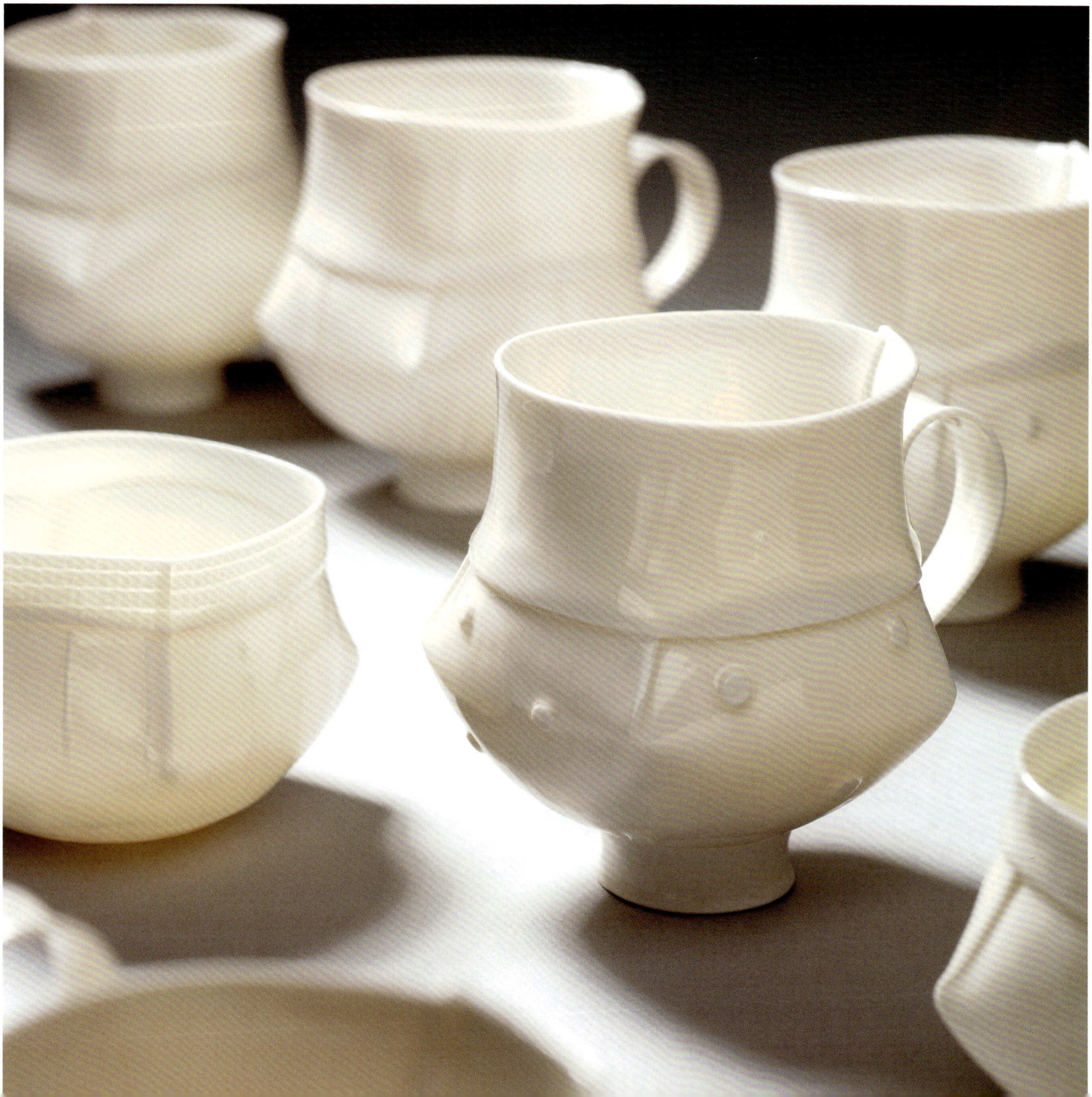

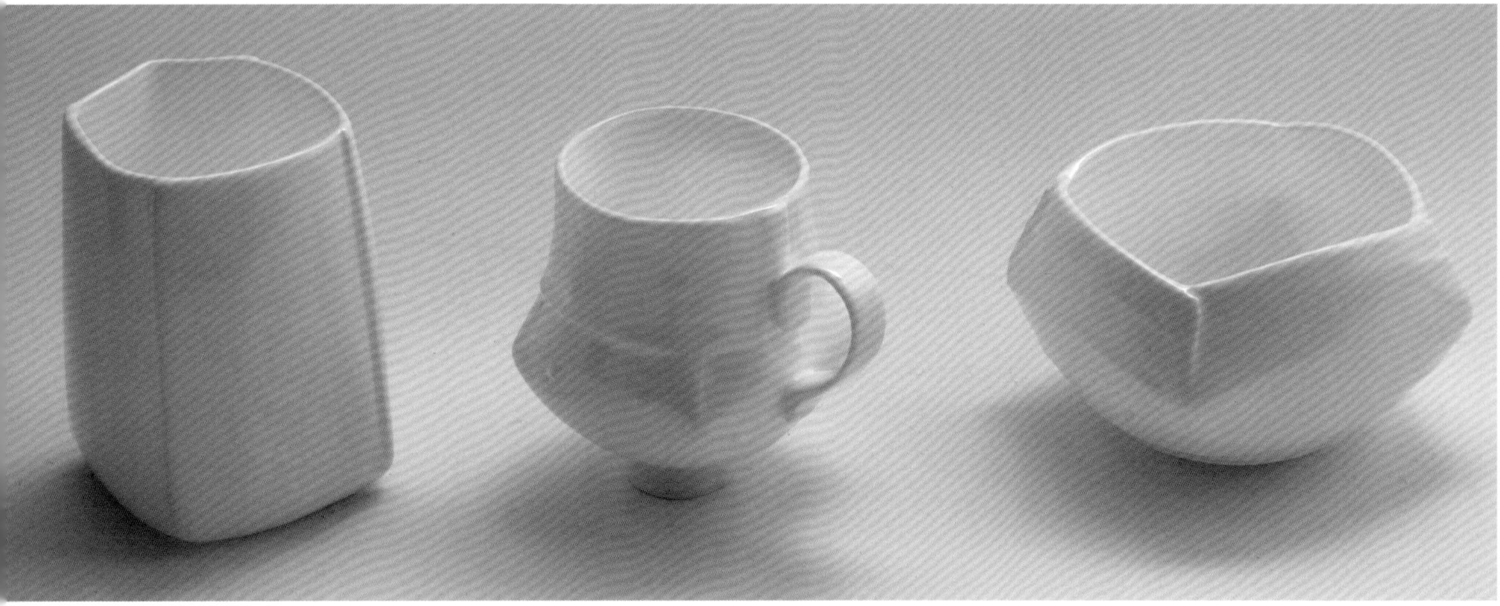

Ann Van Hoey, Enchanting Geometry tableware, 2010. Slipcast bone china, manufactured by Serax, Belgium, height: 8 cm (3 in.). *Photo: Henry Bloomfield.*

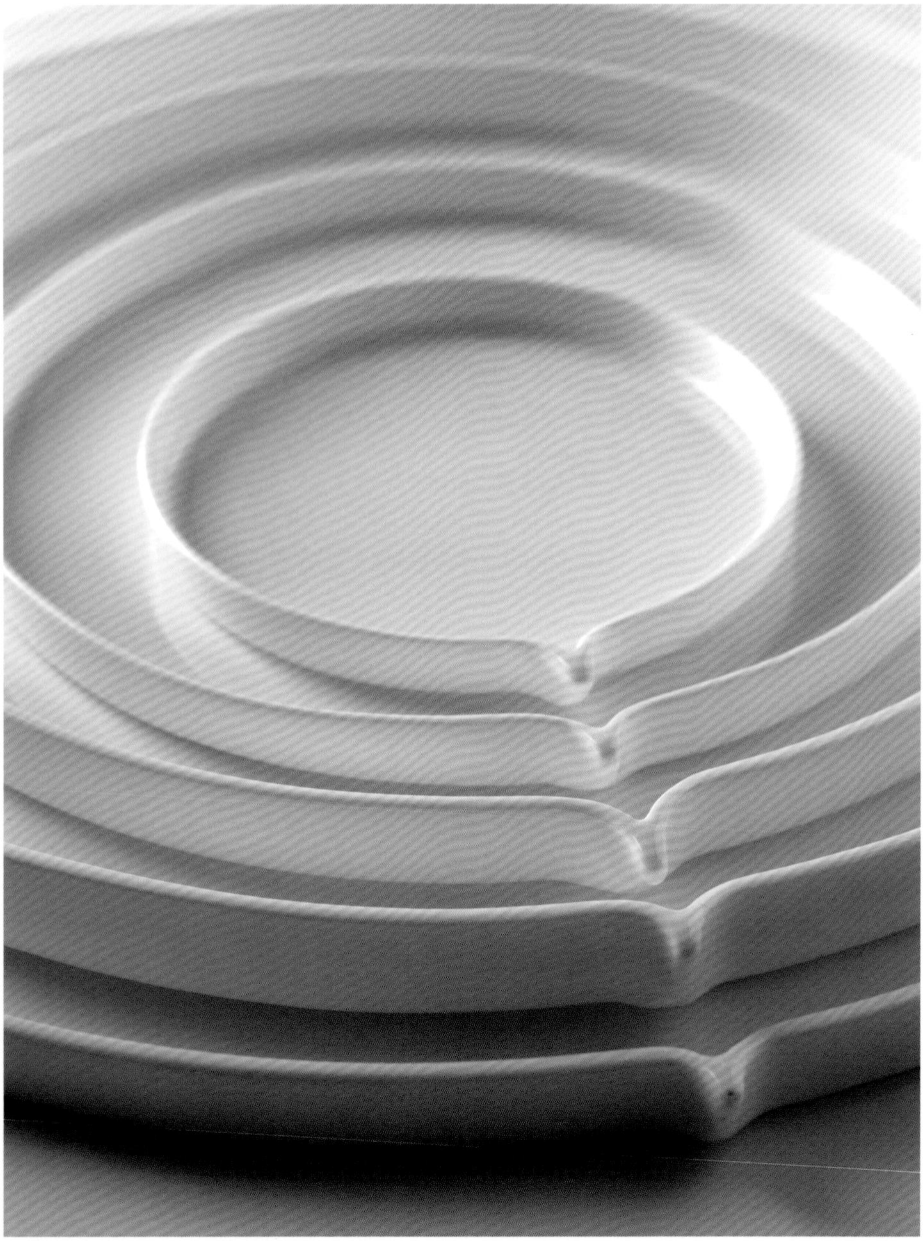

Ann Van Hoey, Geometry plates, designed for chef Peter Goossens, 2011. Porcelain, manufactured by Serax, Belgium, maximum diameter: 30 cm (11¾ in.). *Photo: courtesy of Serax.*

Jolleying

Moulds are also used in a mechanised version of throwing called jolleying, a method used since the Industrial Revolution. A lump or slab of clay is placed in a plaster mould and a profile is pressed down into the rotating mould to form bowl or cup shapes. An alternative method called jiggering is used to produce plates. The mould used in this case is a hump mould and the profile forms the back of the plate and foot-ring. Small potteries often use jiggering to produce plates, which are difficult to make in quantity by throwing on the wheel. Roller-head jigger-jolley machines used in industry have a rotating three-dimensional former, instead of a two-dimensional profile, to form the back of the plate. Jigger-jolley methods are similar to throwing in that the clay particles are compressed and become aligned in one direction, giving strength to the finished piece. The disadvantage of this method is that only round shapes can be made.

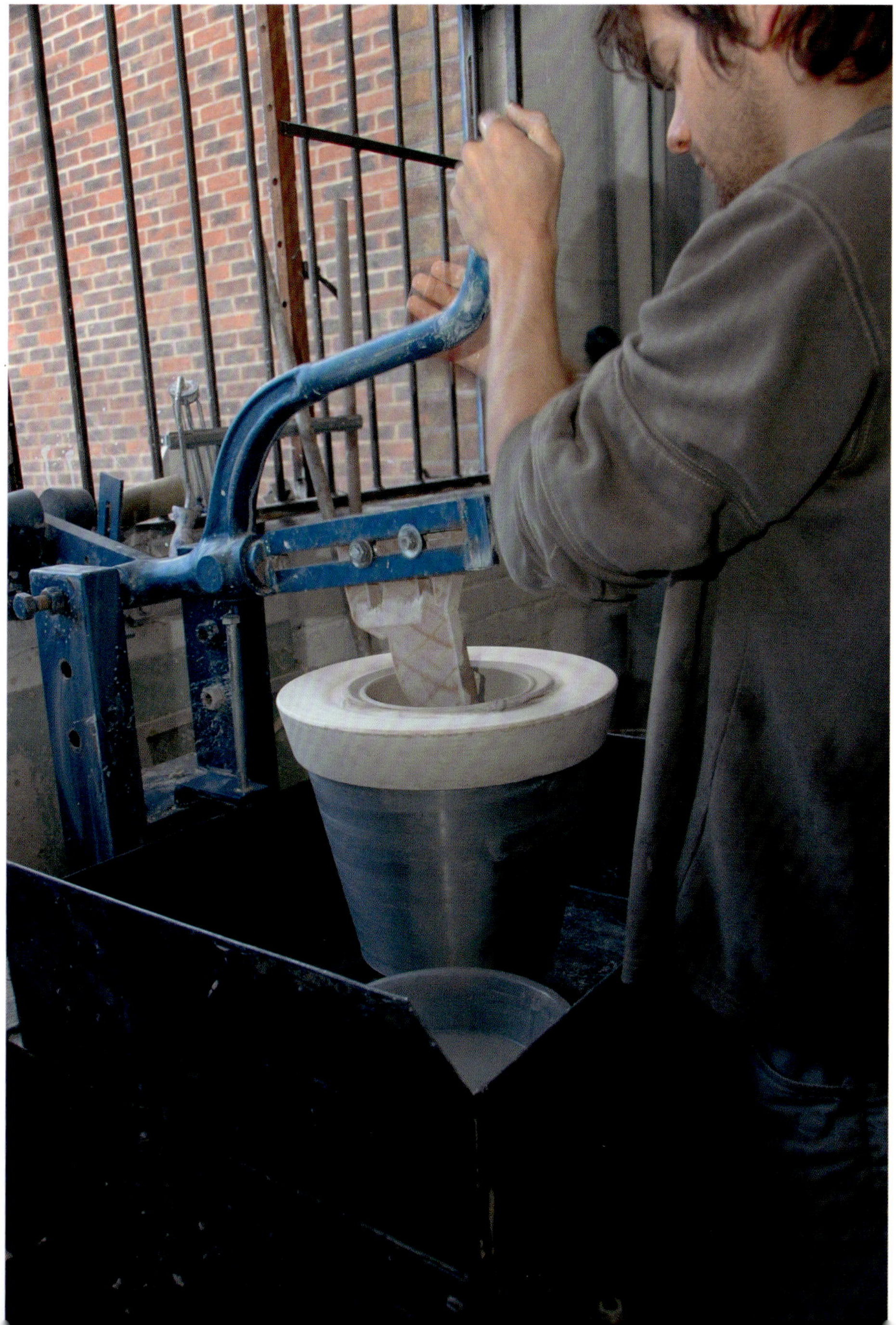

Owen Wall making a bowl in a jolley mould. *Photo: Linda Bloomfield.*

Linda Bloomfield: Manufacturing

As well as being the author of several books, I make a range of hand-thrown porcelain tableware with coloured glazes on the inside and a tactile satin matt white on the outside. Finding it difficult to keep up with demand in a one-person studio, I decided to have some of my range mass-produced. I wanted to use porcelain for its whiteness, strength and density, preferring it to bone china, which is very thin, light and fragile-looking. The idea was to retain the hand-thrown look while making the mugs using industrial methods. The mugs were made in jolley moulds with subtle ribbing to give a hand-thrown feel. The roller head used to shape the inside of the mugs also had fine ribbing. The handles were slipcast separately and attached to the mugs. The mugs were then spray-glazed, fired to 1250°C (2282°F) in a continuous kiln, and a logo was applied to the base using a printed transfer before the mugs were refired to a lower temperature. Using this method, a large number of mugs was made, glazed and fired in a short time, with each process being carried out by a different specialist worker.

Linda Bloomfield, hand-thrown mugs, 2011. Porcelain, height: 11 cm (4¼ in.). Stylist: Twig Hutchinson. *Photo: Emma Lee.*

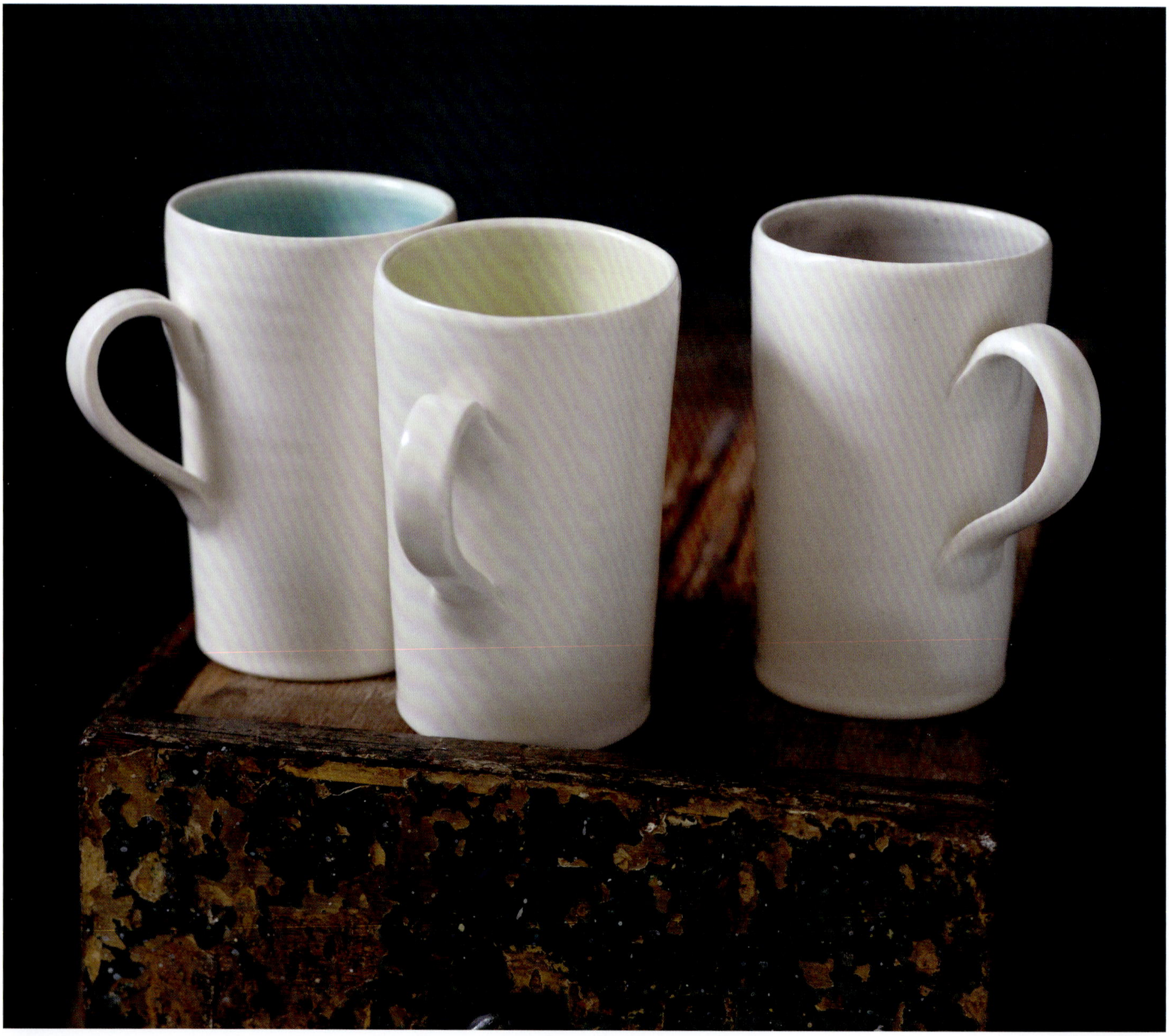

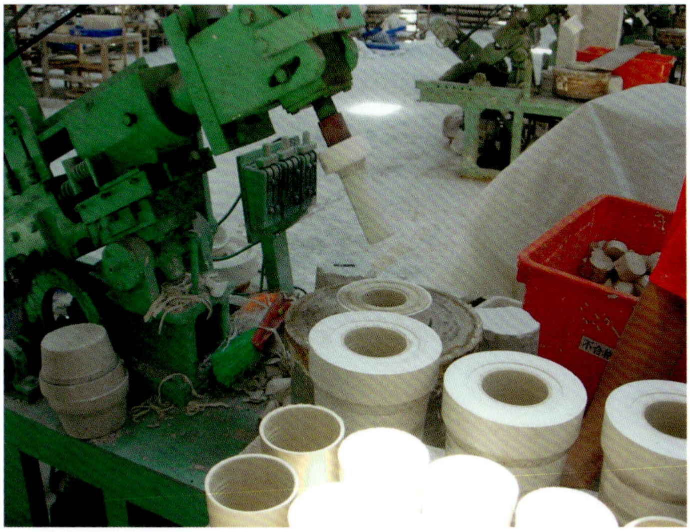

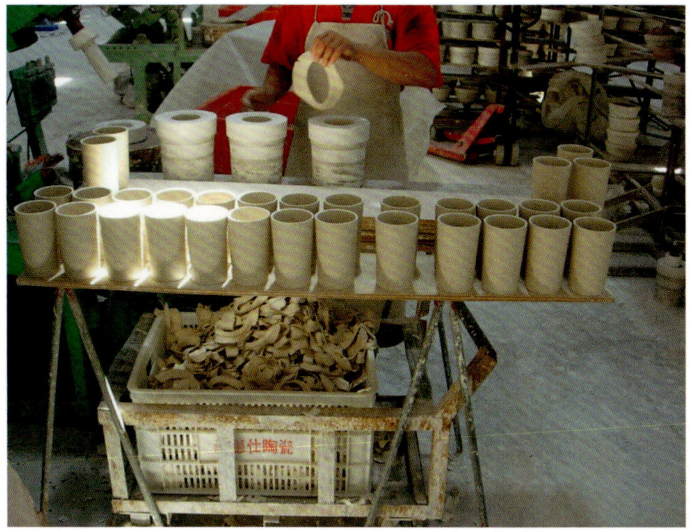

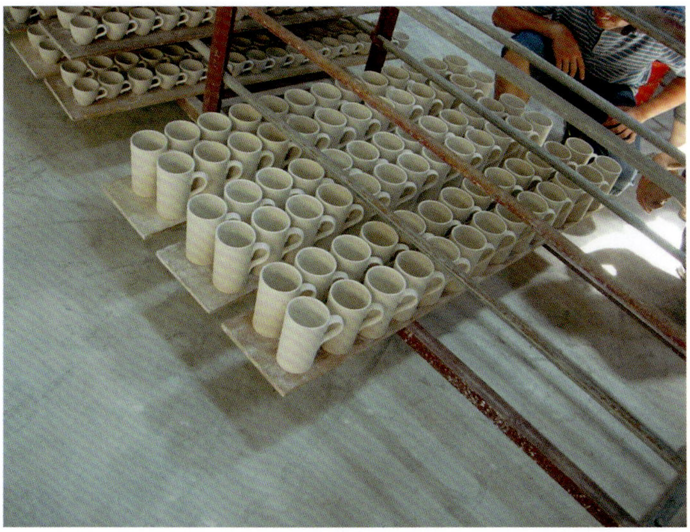

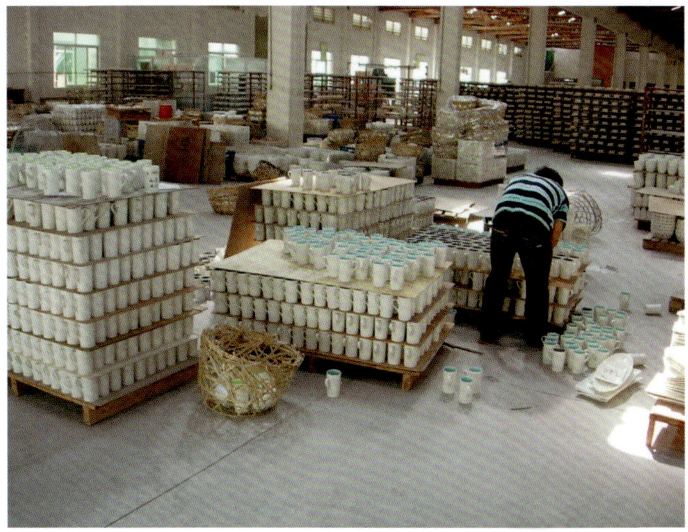

Top row: Mugs being made in jolley moulds in a factory in China. They are ribbed both inside and outside to give a handmade look. The image right shows excess clay being removed from the top of the mould. Bottom row: Porcelain mugs dry on a rack, and the finished mugs are checked. *Photos: Charles Randall.*

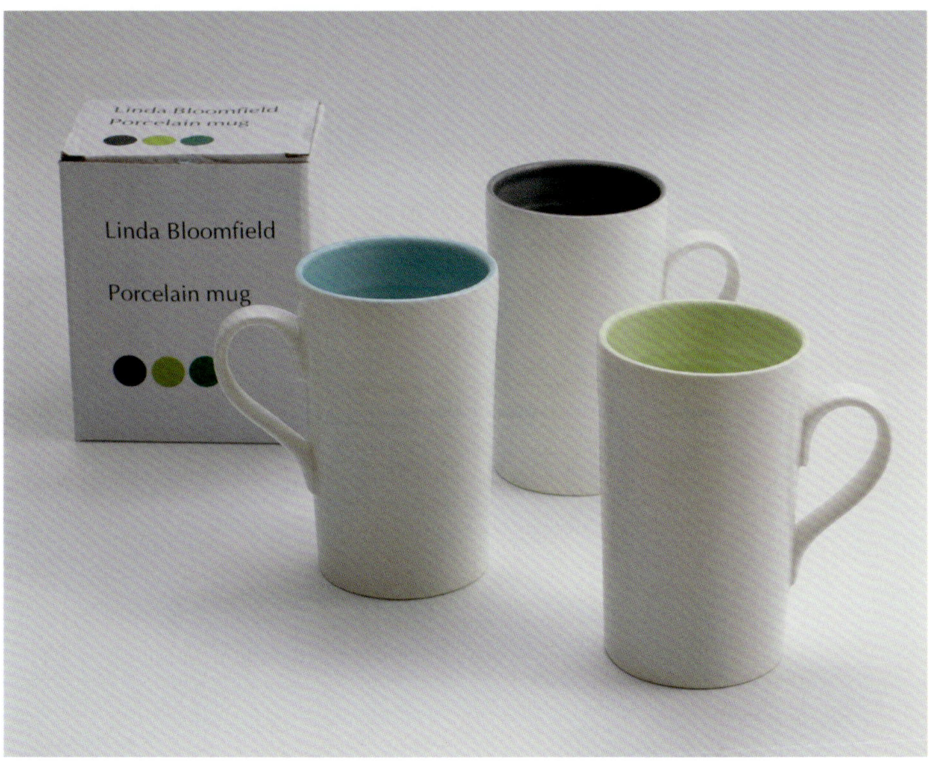

Linda Bloomfield Design, mugs, 2011. Porcelain, height: 12 cm (4¾ in.). *Photo: Henry Bloomfield.*

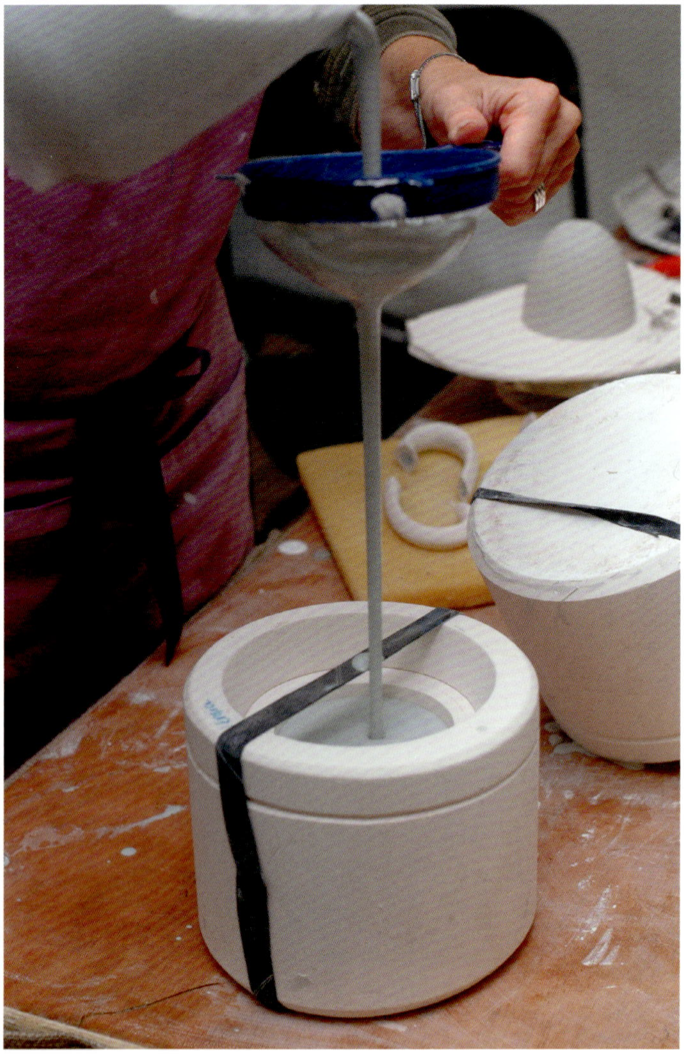

Sasha Wardell pouring slip into a bowl mould.
Photo: Henry Bloomfield.

Slipcasting

Complex hollow shapes like teapots are cast from multi-piece moulds into which slip is poured. The walls of the plaster mould soak up the water in the slip and a skin forms. The excess slip is poured out and the pot can be removed from the mould and trimmed as soon as it has dried. Slipcasting has been possible since Plaster of Paris came into use during the Industrial Revolution and is the preferred method in industry when a shape is too complex to be made by jigger-jolley methods. It has the advantage that asymmetric shapes can be made.

Handles are often cast separately as it can be difficult to force the slip into the extremities of the mould. They are joined onto the pot when firm enough to handle, using slip as a glue. The pot and handle should be at the same state of dryness so that they shrink at the same rate, to ensure the handle does not fall off.

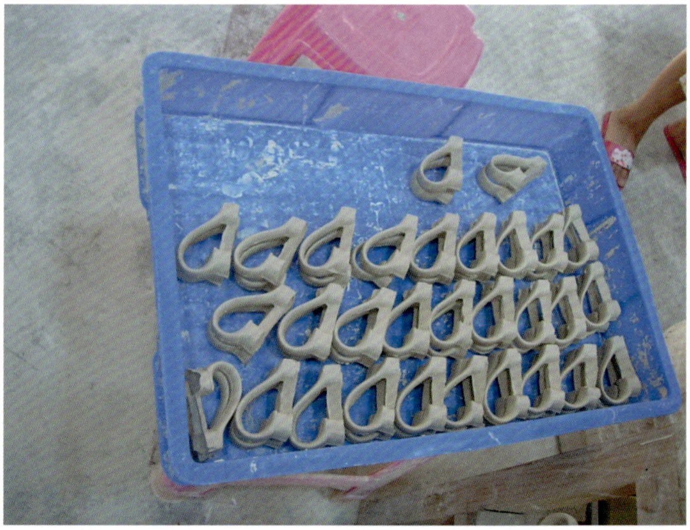

Mug handles made by slipcasting. The plugs left from casting are removed before the handles are applied to the mugs.
Photo: Charles Randall.

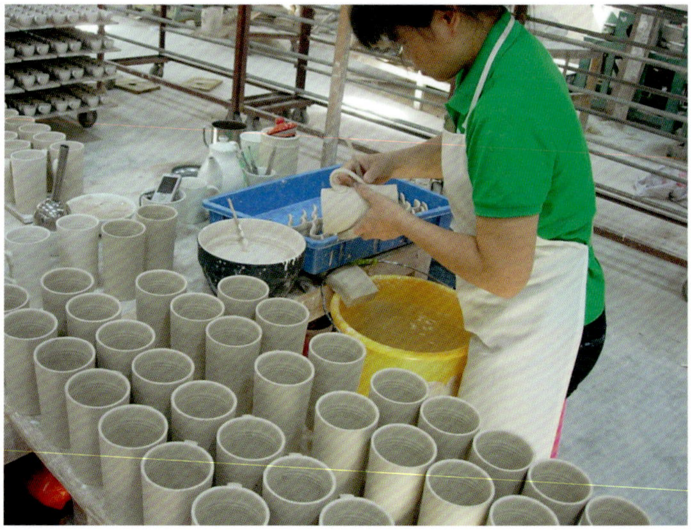

Applying handles to porcelain mugs.
Photo: Charles Randall.

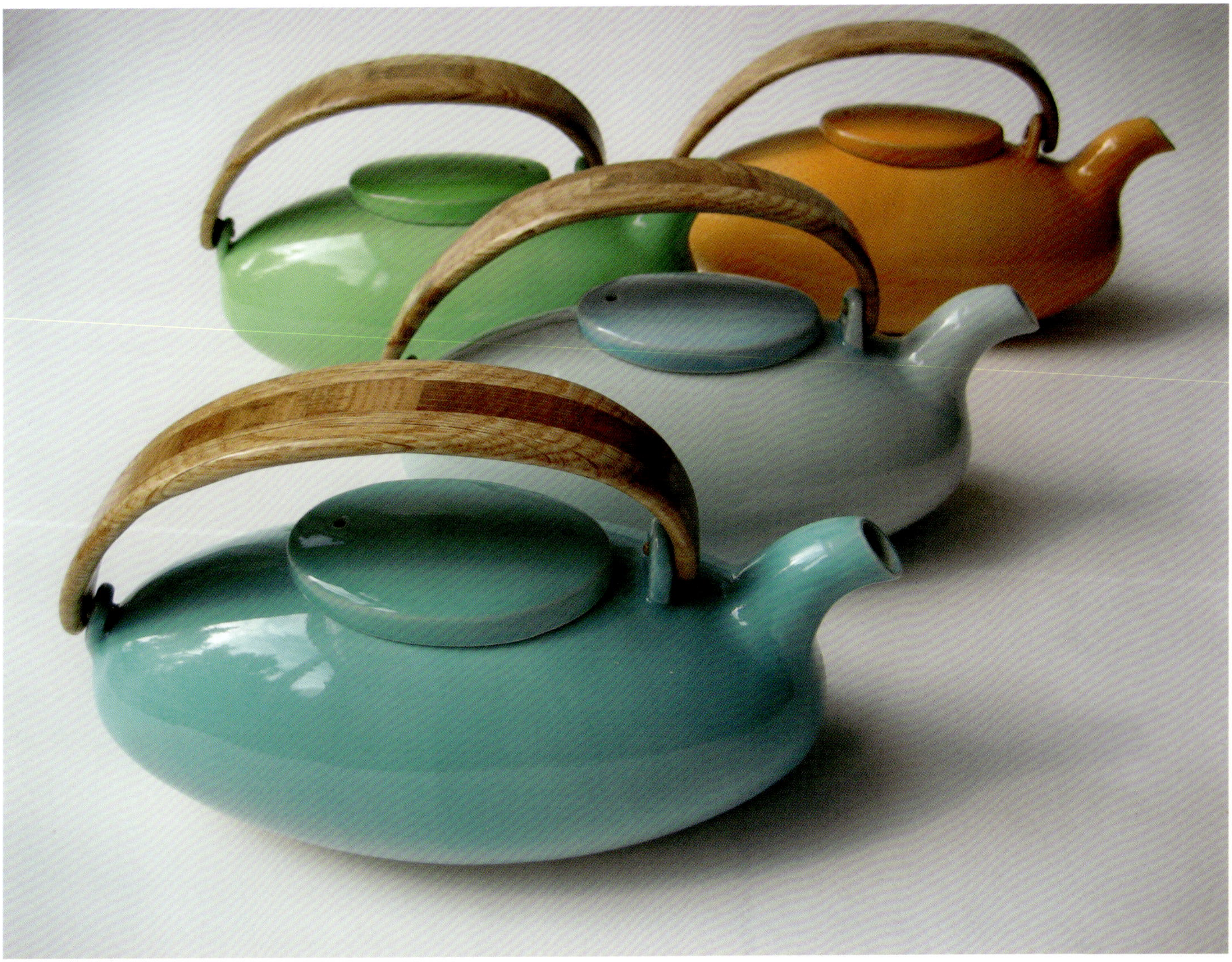

Rigmor Als, Denmark, Theo teapots, 2008. Slipcast porcelain, 1.5-litre (3 pints) capacity, height: 16 cm (6¼ in.). *Photo: courtesy of the artist.*

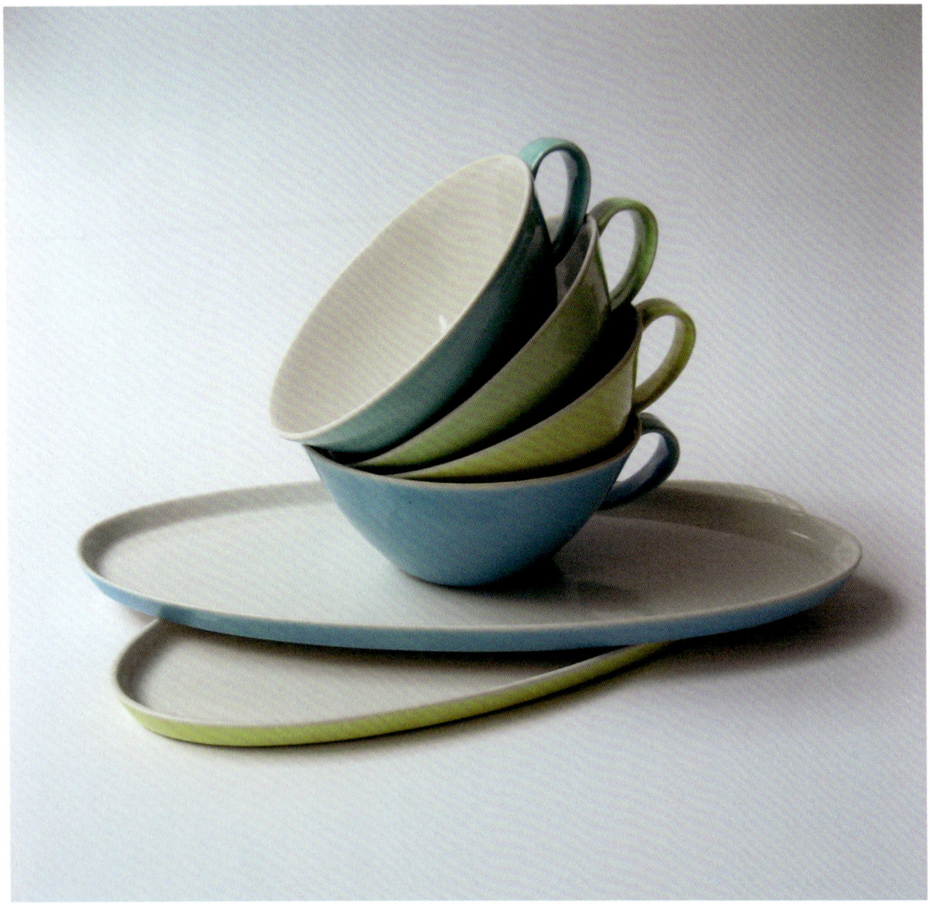

Rigmor Als, Denmark, Summer cups and plates, 2010. Slipcast porcelain, 32.5 x 15 cm (12¾ x 6 in.). *Photo: courtesy of the artist.*

Aiga Siceva-Sattler, Boxing Hare bowls, 2010. Slipcast white Limoges earthenware, tin glaze with black transfers, height: 12.5 cm (5 in.). *Photo: Jacqui Hurst.*

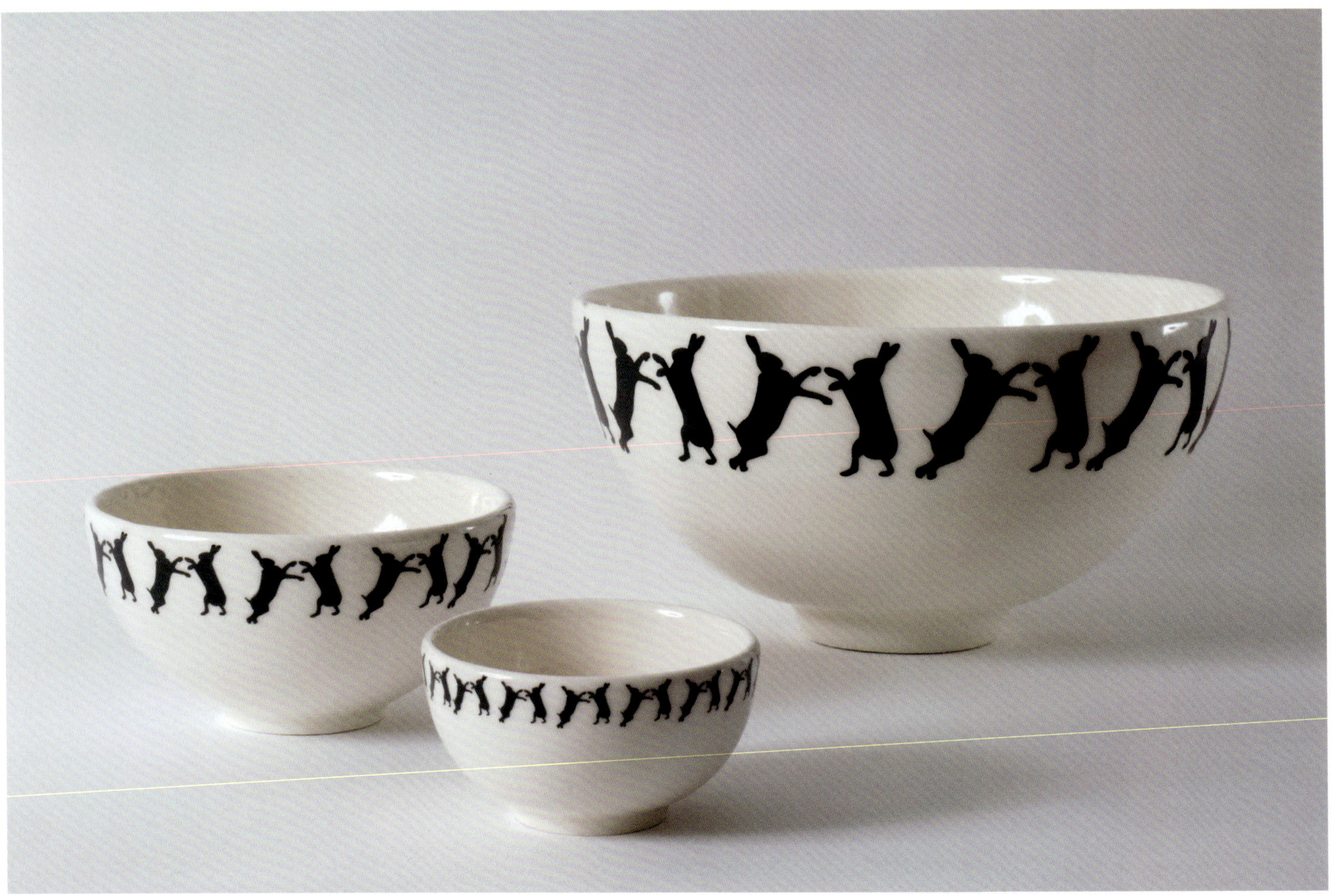

Aiga Siceva-Sattler, selection of mugs, 2011. Slipcast earthenware, height: 9.5 cm (3¾ in.). *Photo: Valts Kleins.*

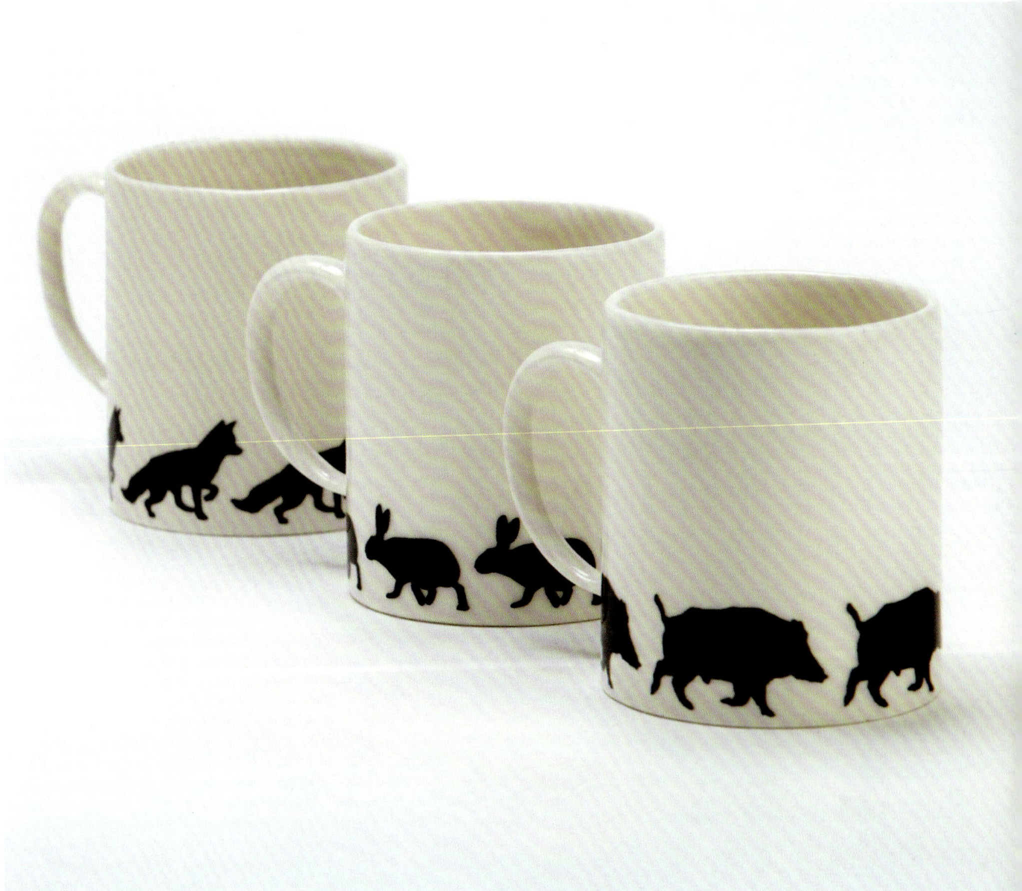

Aiga Siceva-Sattler, Gone Hunting salt and pepper pots, 2011. Slipcast white Limoges earthenware, tin glaze with black transfers, height: 9.5 cm (3¾ in.). *Photo: Valts Kleins.*

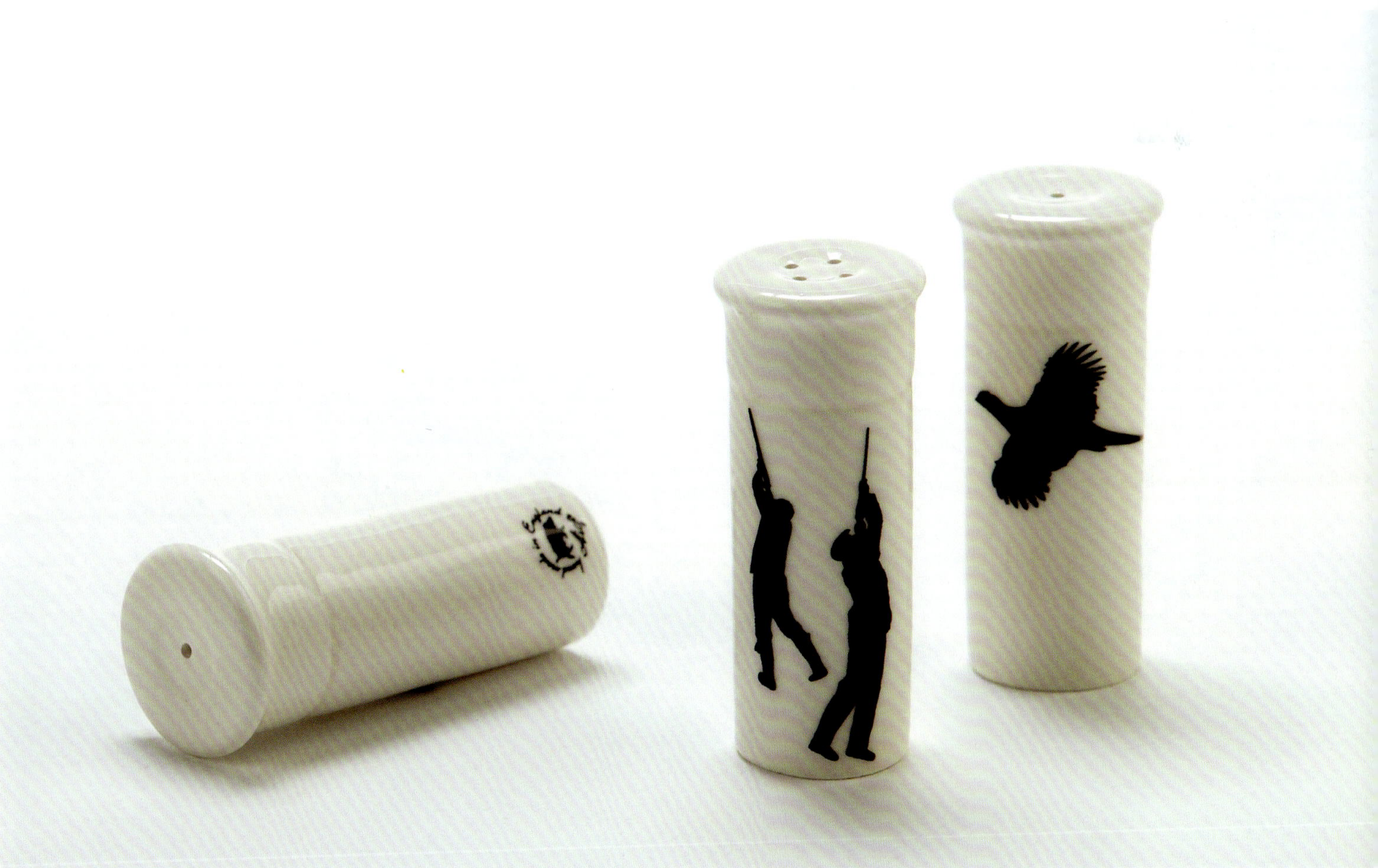

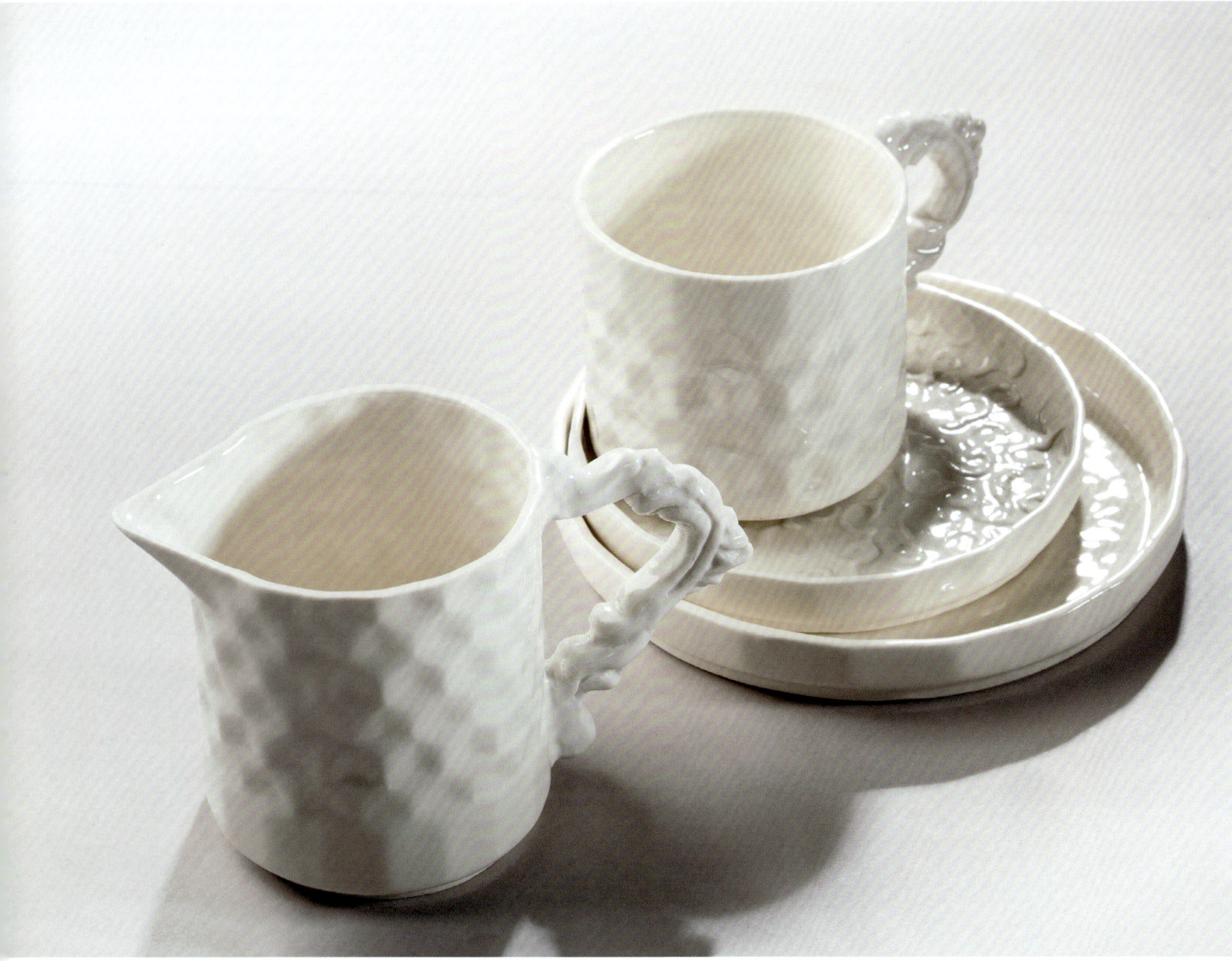

Piret Kändler, Estonia, Aino cup and jug, 2011. Slipcast porcelain, height: 8 cm (3¼ in.). *Photo: Priit Grepp.*

Slipcasting can be used to show the hand of the maker in mass-produced tableware. In 1990 Linda Styles and Sue Ward enrolled on a foundation course at Falmouth School of Art. Subsequent progression to a BA (Hons) in Studio Ceramics provided an opportunity for them to explore the traditional concept of functional studio pottery as a 'craft' on the one hand, and ceramics as a unique 'art' object on the other, in an environment which appeared to reinforce that divide.

They initiated a self-guided joint assignment to explore and challenge the nature of the art-versus-craft object, laying particular emphasis on status, display, context, desirability and related cost. The aim of Styles and Ward was to clone the mark of the hand by using industrial process in the form of mould/slipcasting production.

'We felt that our ceramic 'art' could be viewed as sculpture, painting, installation or tea set, mass-produced at affordable unit price,' says Styles.

'Preliminary solid shapes were crudely handmade in clay, from which plaster moulds were taken. White earthenware slip was then used to produce a variety of vessels, including a teapot, which acted as blank canvases on which to explore and develop decoration and embellishment.

'Months of extensive experimentation followed with different slips, glazes, firing times and temperatures, and all results were carefully and methodically recorded.'

At this point a combination of Styles's extremely colourful, flamboyant style and Ward's considered, minimal approach could have proved a sticking point. But this was not the

Piret Kändler, Eerik slipcast porcelain cups with lids, 2011. Enamel transfers designed with Eerik Kändler, height: 10 cm (4 in.). *Photo: Priit Grepp.*

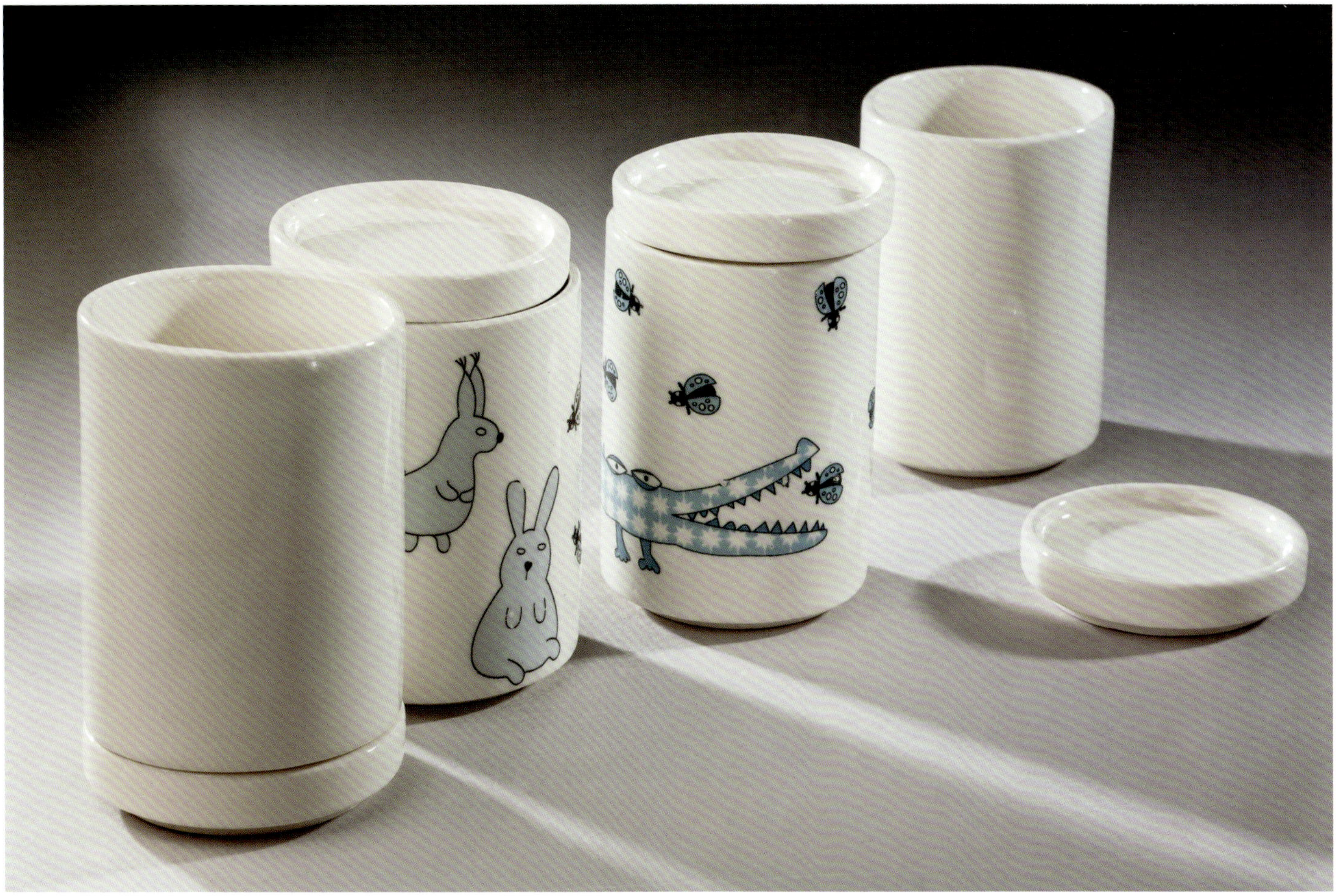

case; the striking, freely applied black line on white was given greater impact by the application of one other single bright colour, carefully placed.

Anxious to determine whether they had an ugly duckling or a swan, and keen for an expert opinion, a single red-handled mug was selected, carefully packed in a small box, and sent off to Sir Terence Conran with a note asking him simply to judge it on its merits – no explanation, no justification, no provenance. After two or three weeks a phone call summoned the pair to London with a selection of work for the Conran Shop buying team to examine. This resulted in several orders. The rubber-spouted teapots went on to be shown at Ceramic Contemporaries 2 at the Victoria and Albert Museum in 1995, and the mugs

Styles and Ward, rubber-spouted teapot with neoprene finger rest, 1995. Earthenware, height: 11 cm (4¼ in.). *Photo: Linda Styles.*

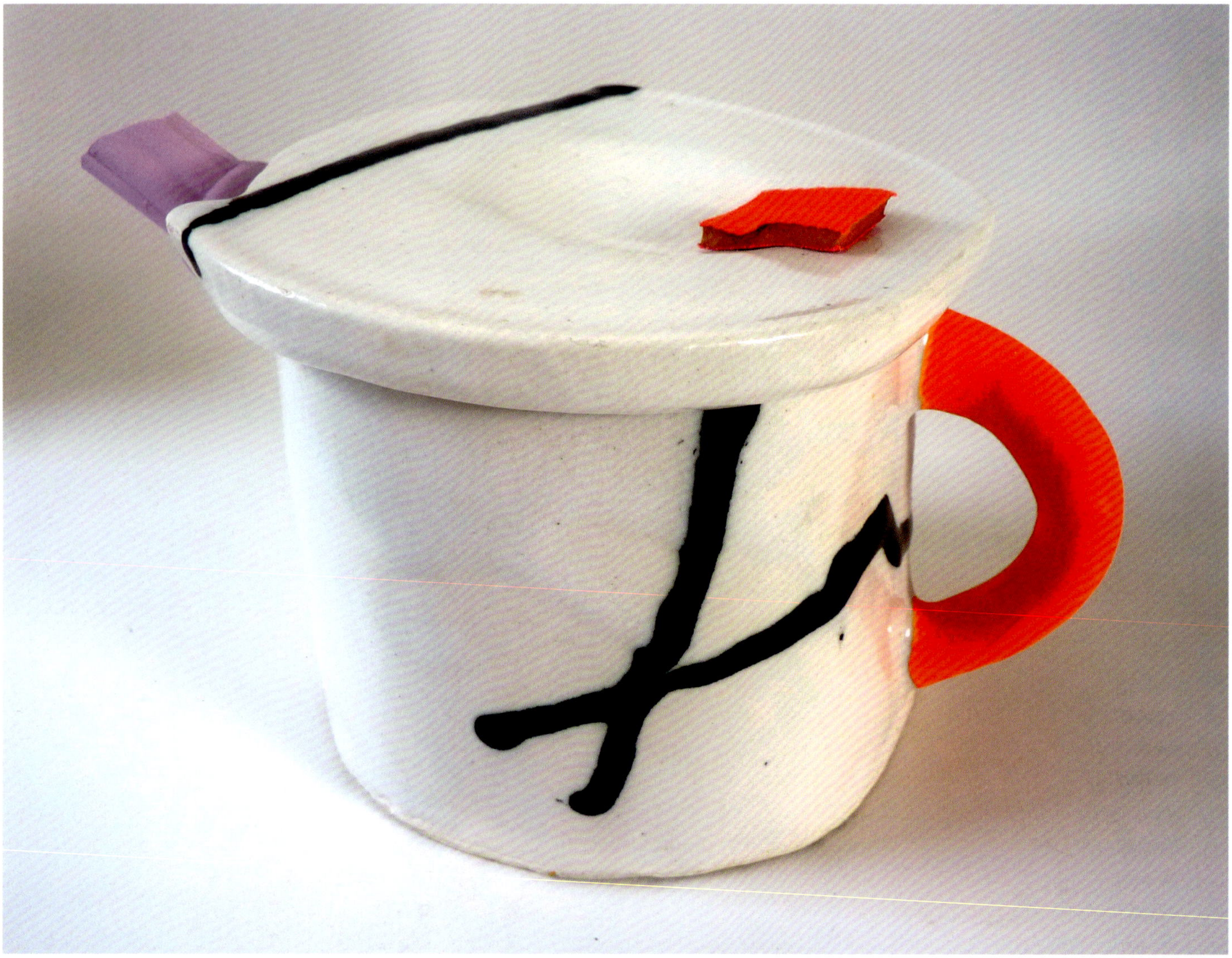

appeared at the Craftsman Potters' Association's 'Setting Out' show in 1996.

In contrast to the prevailing trends in postmodern society, where technology encourages and increases isolation, and the fragmentation and alienation of communities is commonplace, Styles and Ward have worked together successfully in a spirit of joint endeavour and mutual support. 'We still believe wholeheartedly that the sharing of skills and pooling of resources is the way forward,' says Styles.

Styles and Ward, slipcast mugs made for the Conran Shop, 1995. Earthenware, height: 7 cm (2¾ in.). *Photo: Linda Styles.*

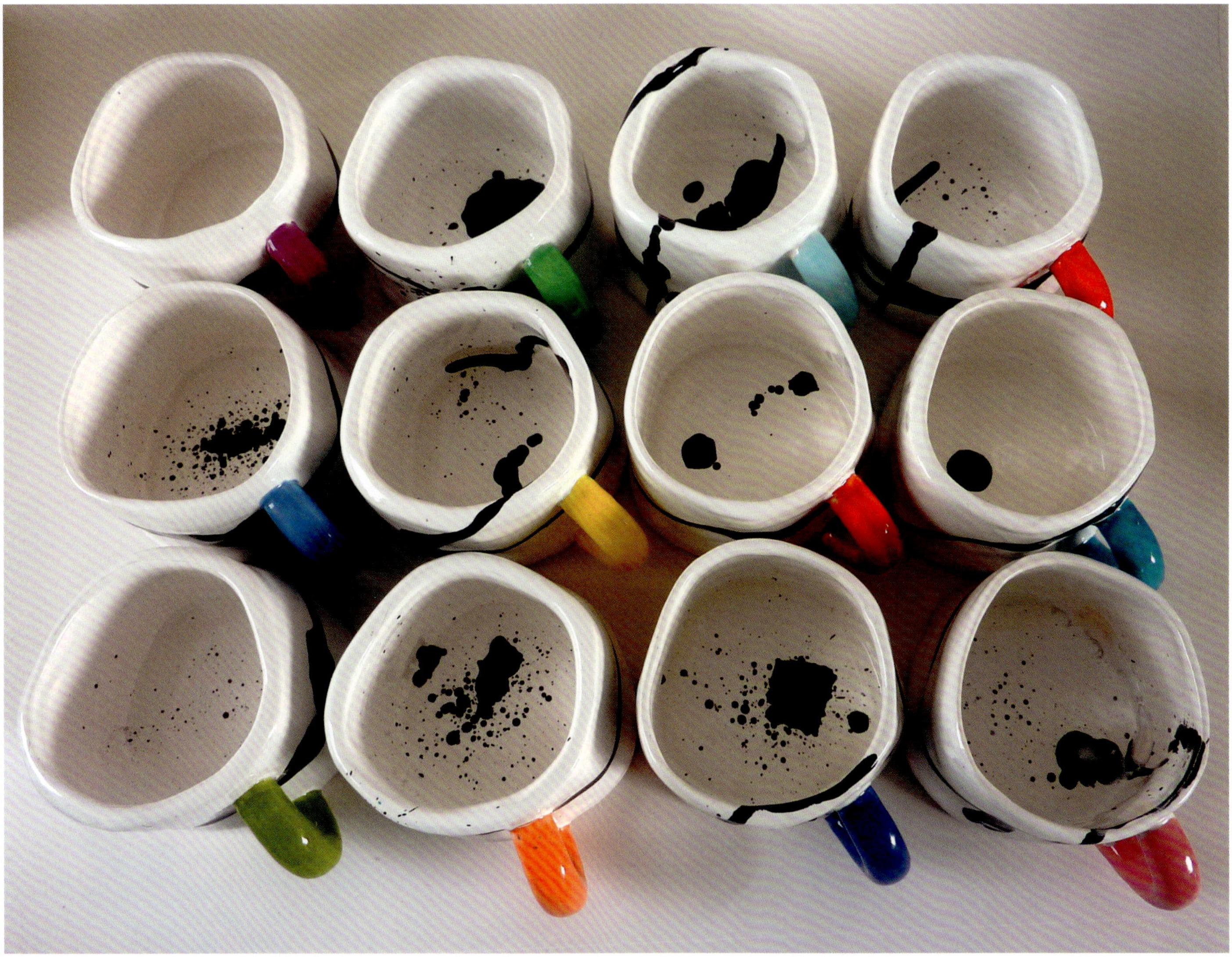

Throwing

Throwing can be used to produce tableware, but nowadays it is mostly used in small studios and workshops or to make prototypes for slipcasting. Throwing originated with the invention of the potter's wheel in Mesopotamia around 5,000 years ago and remained the fastest way to make pots until plaster moulds came into use during the Industrial Revolution. Country potters such as Isaac Button, who worked at Soil Hill in Yorkshire until the 1960s, were able to throw hundreds of pots in a day. This requires a lot of practice, to the extent that it generally takes about seven years to become a production thrower. It is hard work to make a living throwing tableware alone, so some potters train assistants to help throw their tableware, allowing them more time to make higher-priced individual pots.

The basic technique involves putting a lump of clay on a potter's wheel and forming it into a pot, using the wheel's momentum and one's hands to pull the form up or out, and lubricating where necessary with water. A batch of pots will usually have slight variations in the throwing lines left by the potter's fingers spiralling up the pot, although some potters choose to remove them. These variations typically distinguish hand-thrown pots from those made in a mould, but some mass-produced ranges are now being slipcast from handmade pieces.

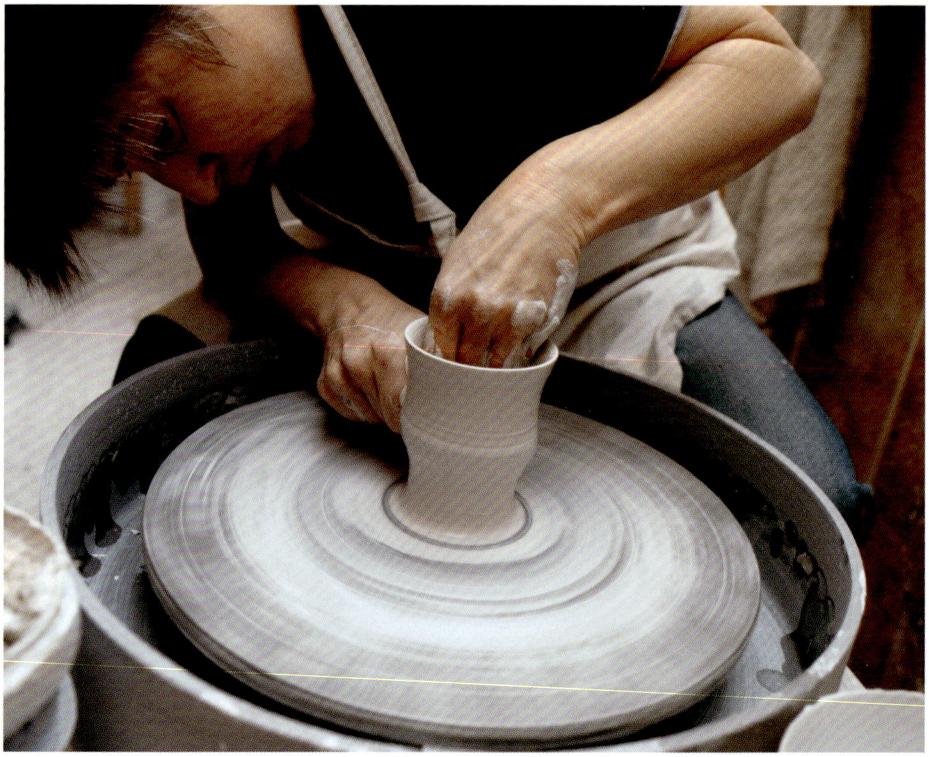

Linda Bloomfield throwing a cup, 2011. *Photo: Nick Hand for the Balvenie Masters of Craft Awards.*

Adding a dimple to a cup, 2011. *Photo: Nick Hand for the Balvenie Masters of Craft Awards.*

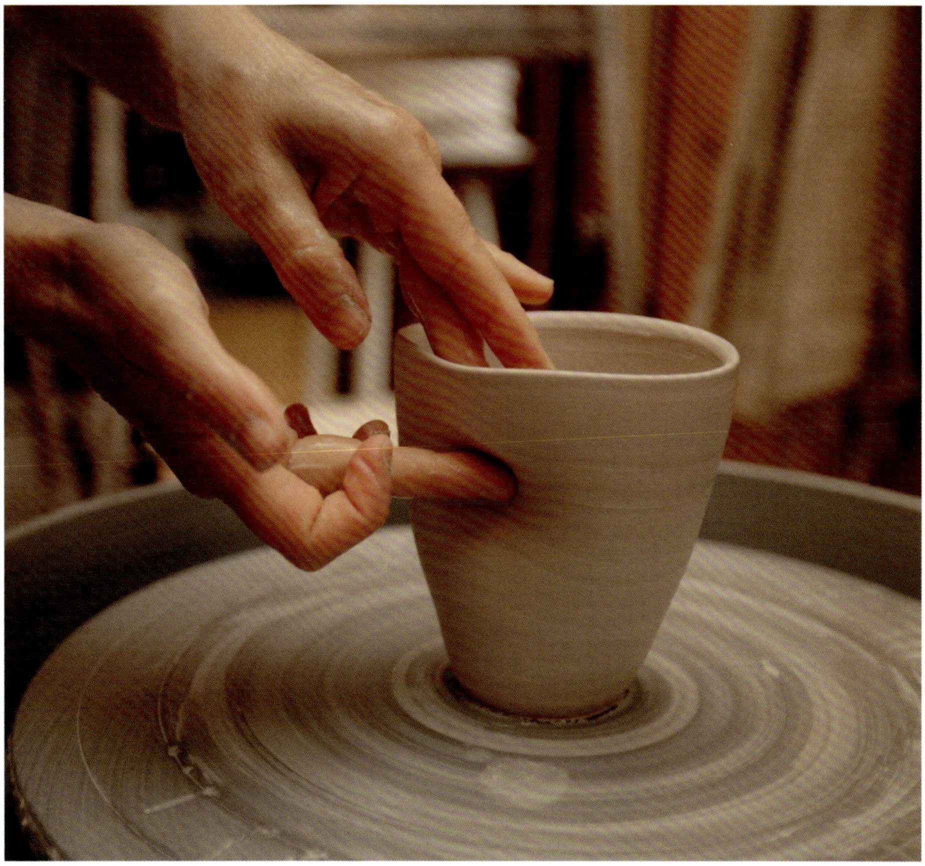

Linda Bloomfield, dimpled cups and bowl, 2007. Thrown porcelain, coloured glazes, height: 9 cm (3½ in.). *Photo: Jacqui Hurst.*

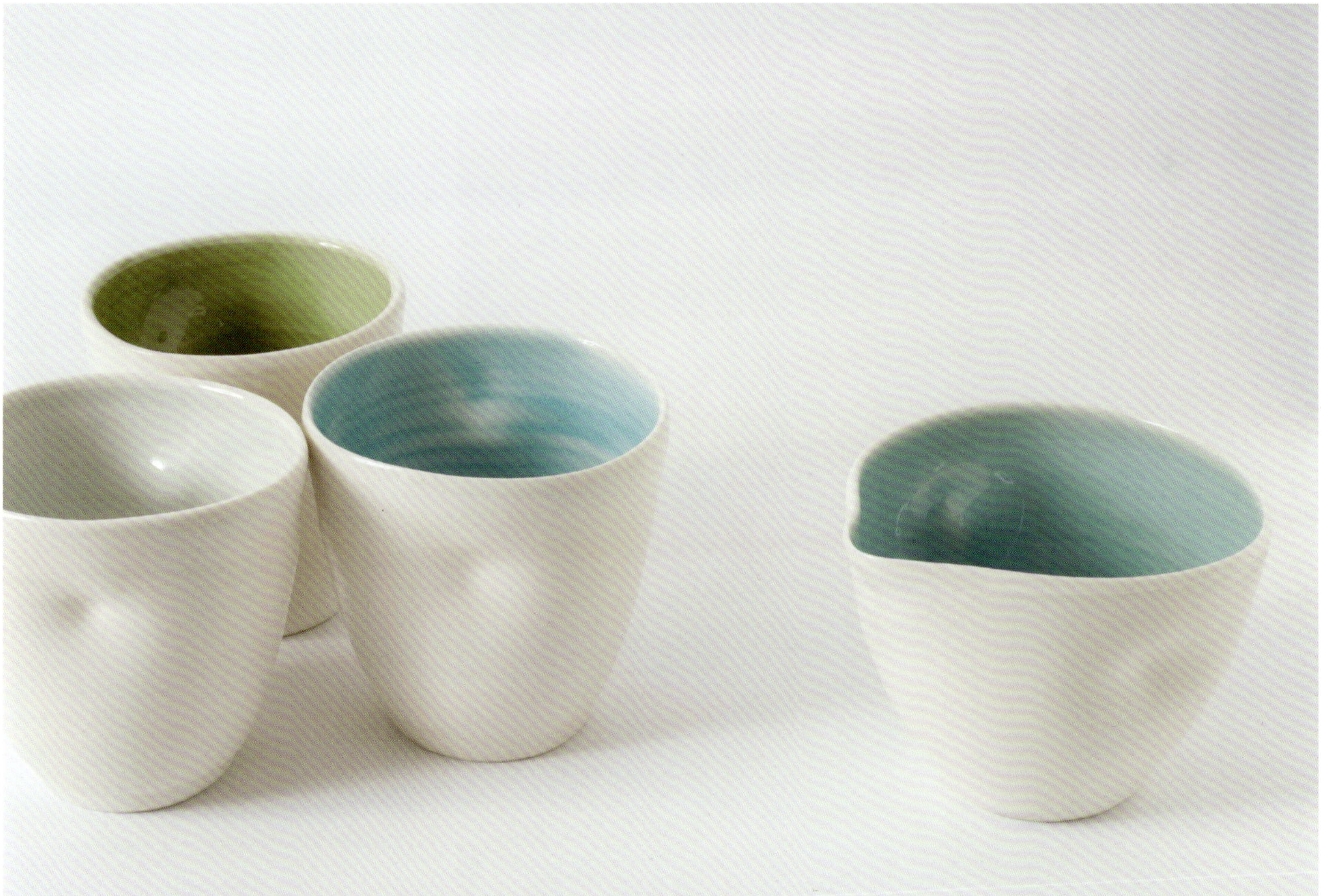

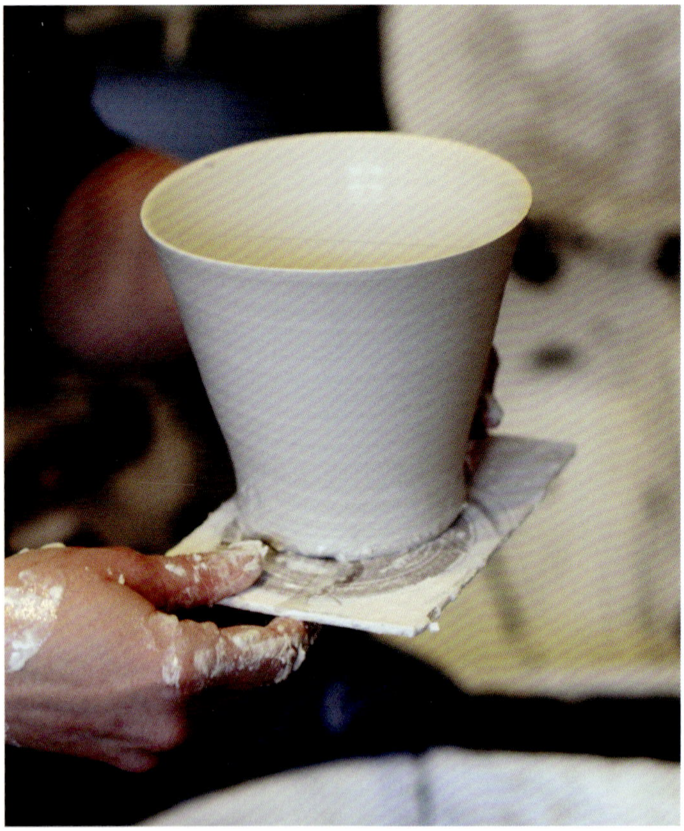

Rachel Dormor throws porcelain in her Cambridge studio, where she also makes her slipcast porcelain Mid-century Modern tea set. In 2009 she completed an MA in ceramic design at Staffordshire University. Her range includes colanders, jugs, cups and saucers in white or pale blue, some with botanic line drawings printed on them. She stocks a range of outlets in the UK, Europe and the US.

Rachel Dormor, cup, 2009. Freshly thrown porcelain, diameter: 14 cm (5½ in.), 2009. *Photo: Dan Logan.*

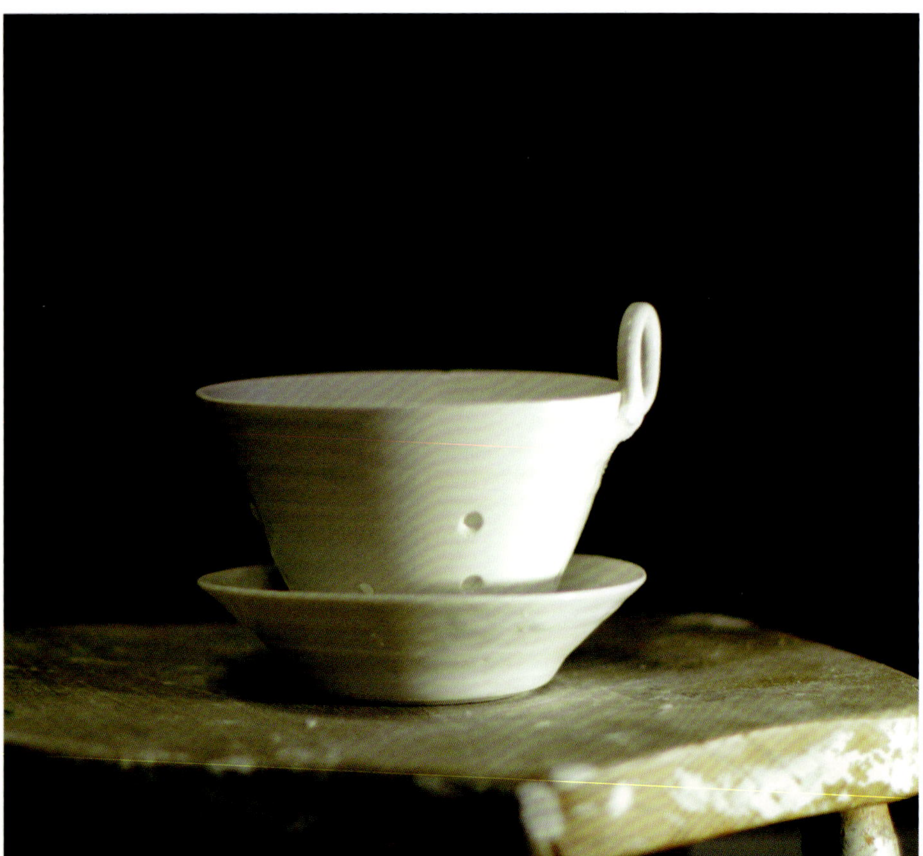

Rachel Dormor, small colander, 2009. Thrown porcelain, diameter: 13.5 cm (5¼ in.). *Photo: Dan Logan.*

Rachel Dormor, tableware, 2010. Top shelf: thrown porcelain jugs, height 14–16 cm (5½–6¼ in.); middle shelf: slipcast porcelain Mid-century Modern tea set: bottom shelf: thrown porcelain teapot, cups and colanders; dresser: thrown porcelain bowls and dishes, black Wedgwood jasper cup and saucer. *Photo: Dan Logan.*

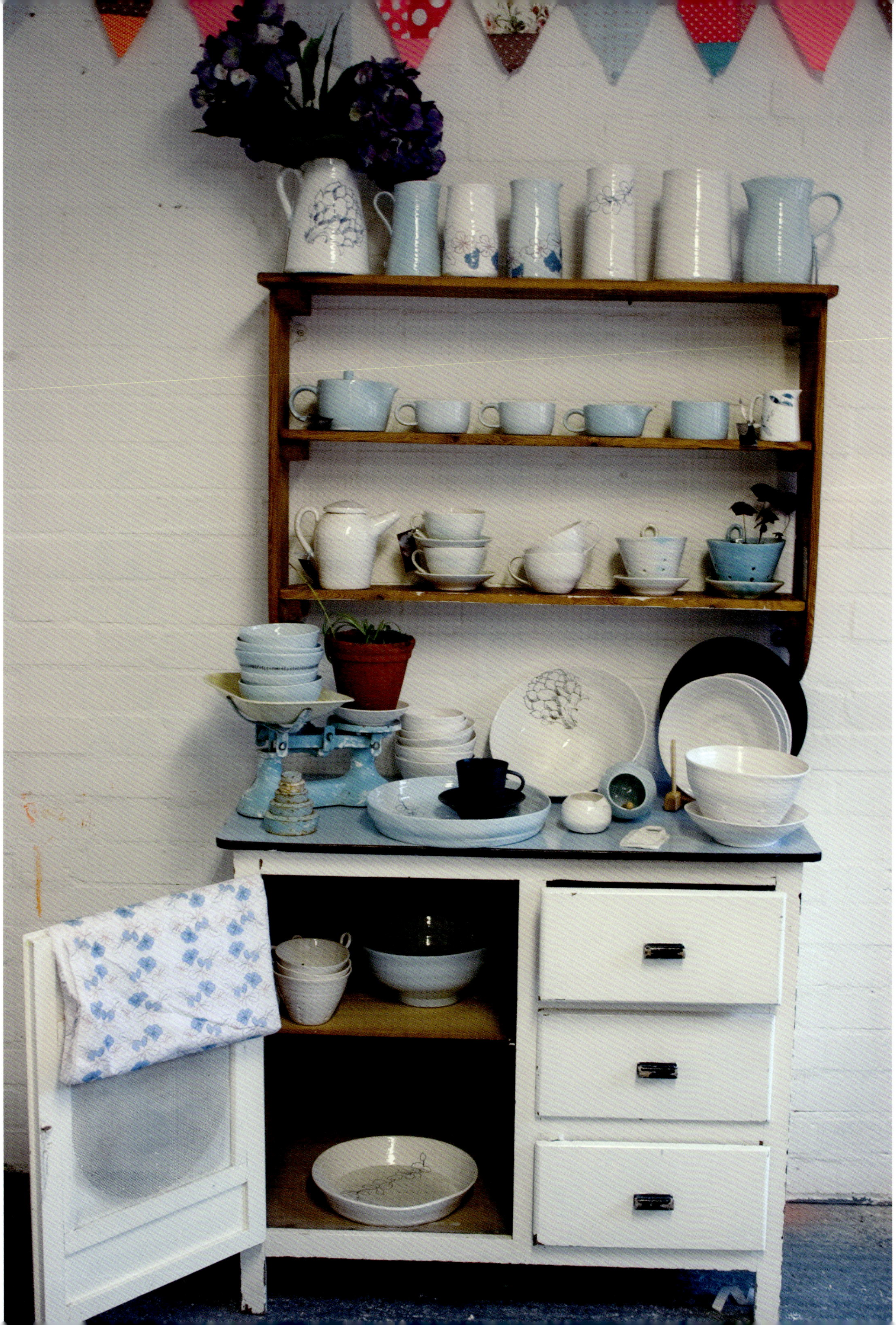

Glazing and firing

Pottery is usually fired twice. The first firing, called the biscuit firing, is to a relatively low temperature, around 1000°C (1832°F). The biscuit firing strengthens the ware so that it can be handled during glazing.

Glaze is a suspension of powdered materials in water. It contains silica, fluxes like sodium and calcium, and is similar to glass, with the addition of clay to make it more viscous when molten so that it does not run off the pot. Glaze can be applied by dipping, pouring or spraying, while colour can either be mixed into it or applied by brushing, sponging or transfer printing onto the biscuit ware. After the glaze has been applied, the pots are fired again, usually to a higher temperature than the biscuit firing. The glaze melts during firing into a smooth, hard coating.

In industry, in the UK, the biscuit firing is often to a higher temperature than the glaze firing. The ware can be supported on racks during the biscuit firing to avoid warping and slumping. As the glaze firing is to a lower temperature, no further warping takes place and only minimal support is needed for the glazed ware. There is also sometimes a third, low-temperature firing where applied transfers, or decals, are fired onto the surface of the glaze.

Glazing a plate. The glaze is poured onto the biscuit-fired plate, then swirled around and poured off. *Photo: Henry Bloomfield.*

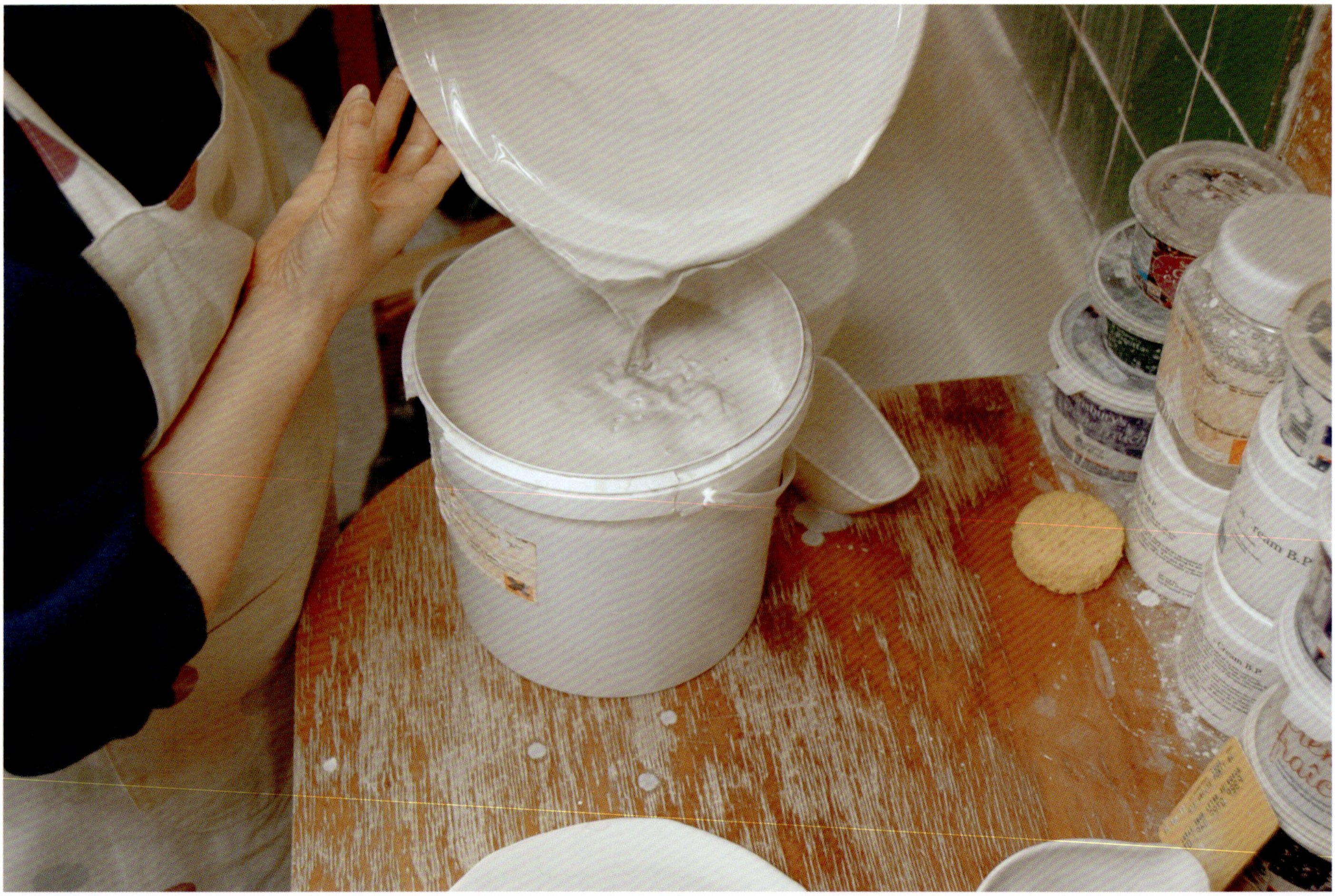

There is a wide variety of kilns available, fired using wood, oil, gas or electricity. In industry, continuous tunnel kilns are used, in which the ware moves slowly through the kiln on trolleys. Smaller potteries have kilns that may take a few weeks or months of work to fill, and that are fired a number of times a year. Many studio potters prefer fuel-burning kilns, which give rich but unpredictable glaze effects. In a gas or wood kiln, the air intake can be restricted to give a reducing atmosphere, where oxygen for combustion is drawn from the glaze and clay body. Certain types of glaze such as celadon, a grey-green oriental glaze, can only be fired in reduction. In industry, electric kilns are usually preferred as they produce cleaner, more repeatable results. In the oxidising atmosphere of an electric kiln, glaze colours are generally brighter.

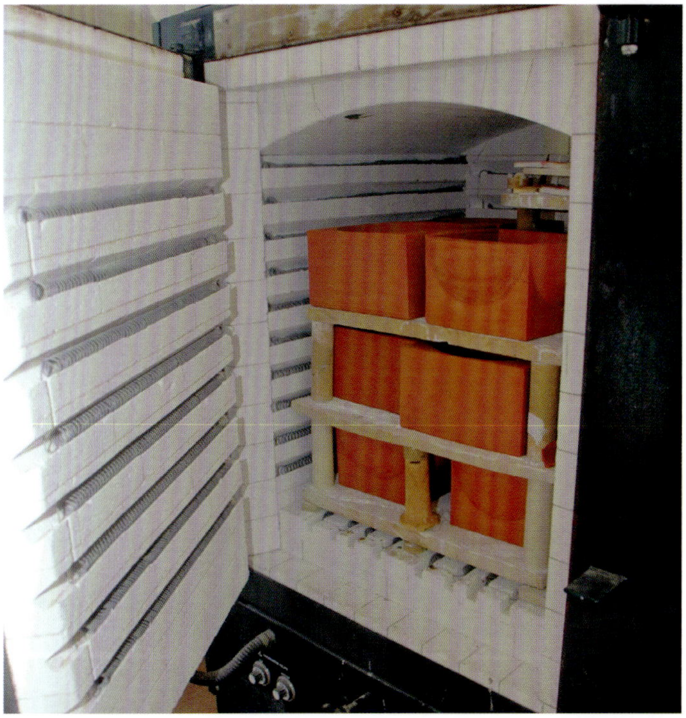

Front loader electric kiln at Glebe Road studios, London.

The wood-fired kiln at John Leach's Muchelney Pottery. Nick Rees and Mark Melbourne are unpacking the kiln. The kiln is three-chambered, can hold up to 2,000 pots and is fired around six times a year. *Photo: Nick Fleming.*

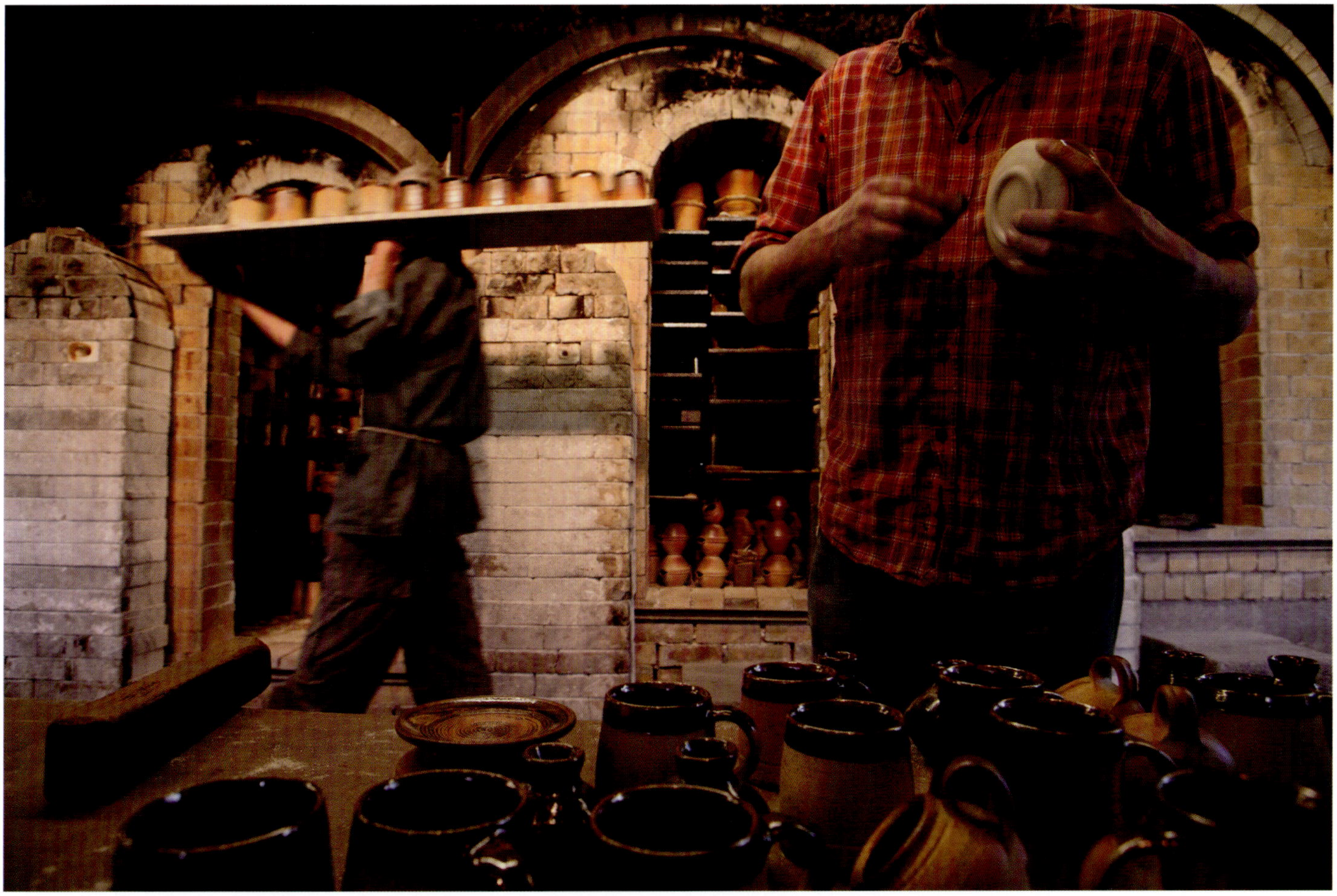

11 Manufactured tableware

Some potters design ranges for industrial production. This involves collaboration with industry and designing and throwing prototypes to specification. The pieces must not only fit the design brief and size requirements but must also be possible to reproduce using industrial methods. Tableware mass-produced in this way can reach a much larger number of people than most handmade ware.

Kevin Millward for Portmeirion

As well as making his own work, Kevin Millward has made prototypes for tableware ranges by Portmeirion, Spode and Wedgwood. One of the best-selling ranges is the Sophie Conran range, designed in 2005 in collaboration with Julian Teed of Portmeirion and Sophie Conran herself. Sophie is the daughter of Sir Terence Conran and cookery writer Caroline Conran, and brings her cooking skills and design heritage to the collaboration, while Julian uses his knowledge of the industrial manufacturing process to design the pieces. The tableware has strong throwing lines and looks handmade, although it is slipcast in porcelain from moulds of Millward's thrown prototypes.

Another of Millward's Portmeirion ranges was the Liquid range (now discontinued), which had handles that sprung organically from the body as well as asymmetric rims on plates and bowls, reminiscent of designs of the 1950s. He also designed a teapot and egg cup for the Toast tableware range in earthenware. Millward has worked in the ceramics industry in Stoke-on-Trent and understands the mould-making process, as well as being a skilled thrower. He works predominantly in low-fired white earthenware and also uses a higher-firing super-white earthenware for some prototypes. He is currently making his individual hand-thrown work in high-fired cream earthenware marbled with a black clay body, inspired by thrown and turned industrial creamware from the mid-18th century. The cream earthenware is difficult to throw so he has to work quickly and precisely, aiming to retain the vitality of the thrown form in the finished piece.

He often alters his forms while they are still on the wheel, giving gentle modulation to the rim and enhancing tensions in the thrown form. He turns the base to give the illusion that the piece floats free from the surface on which it is placed. He uses a lead-based glaze to give a high level of shine and also to enhance the smoothness and freshness of the pot. Millward lectured at Buckinghamshire New University and the University of Westminster in Harrow until the closure of the Ceramics course in 2012.

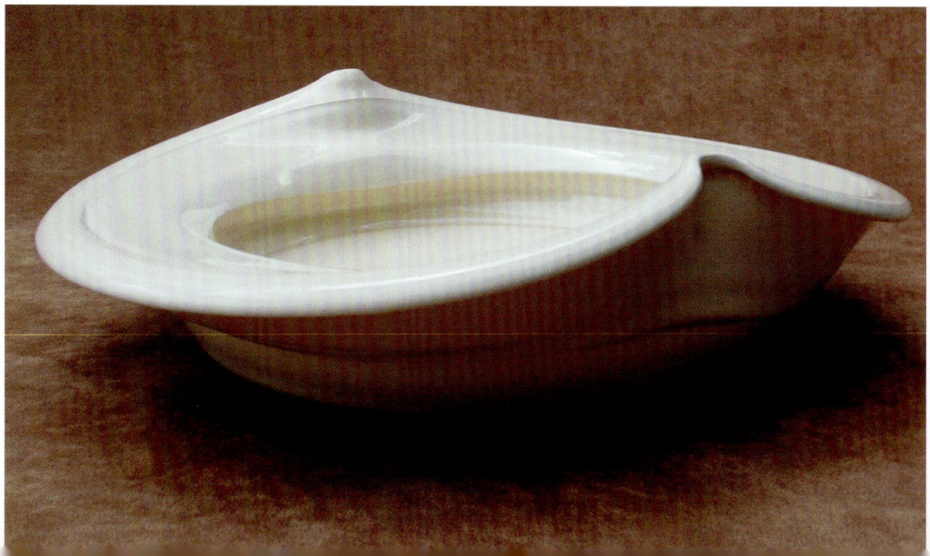

Kevin Millward, thrown dish, 2005. White earthenware, 35 x 9 cm (13¾ x 3½ in.). *Photo: courtesy of the artist.*

Sophie Conran for Portmeirion, Storage jars and set of ramekins, 2011. Porcelain, diameter: 9 cm (3½ in.). *Photo: Dominic Blackmore.*

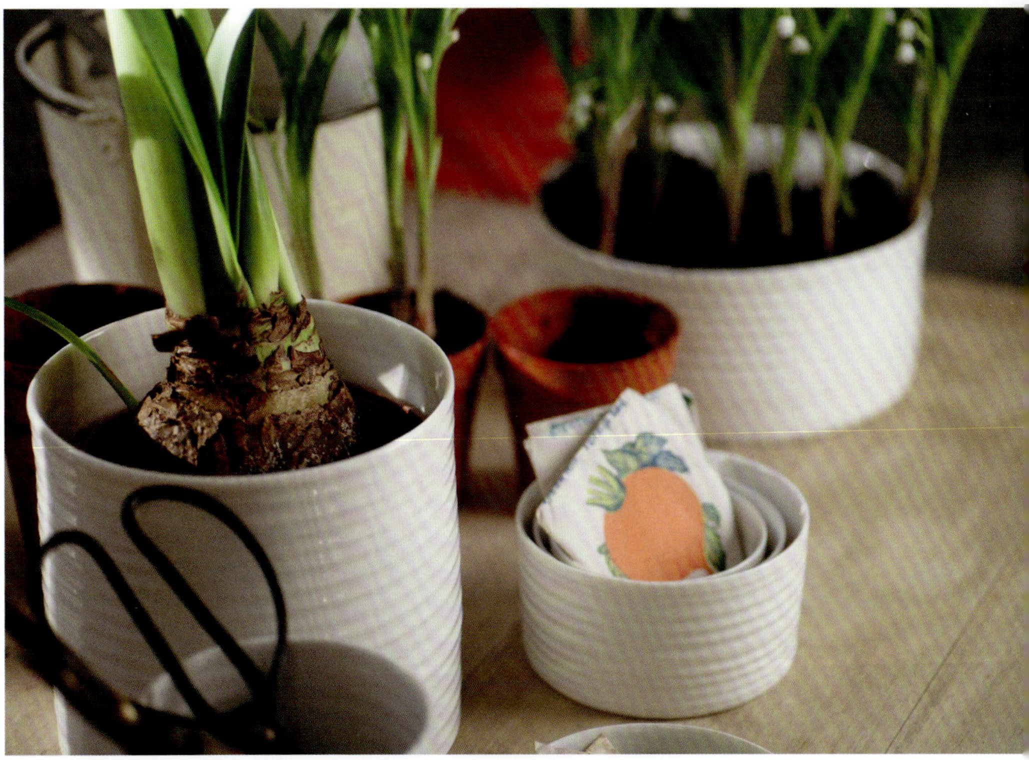

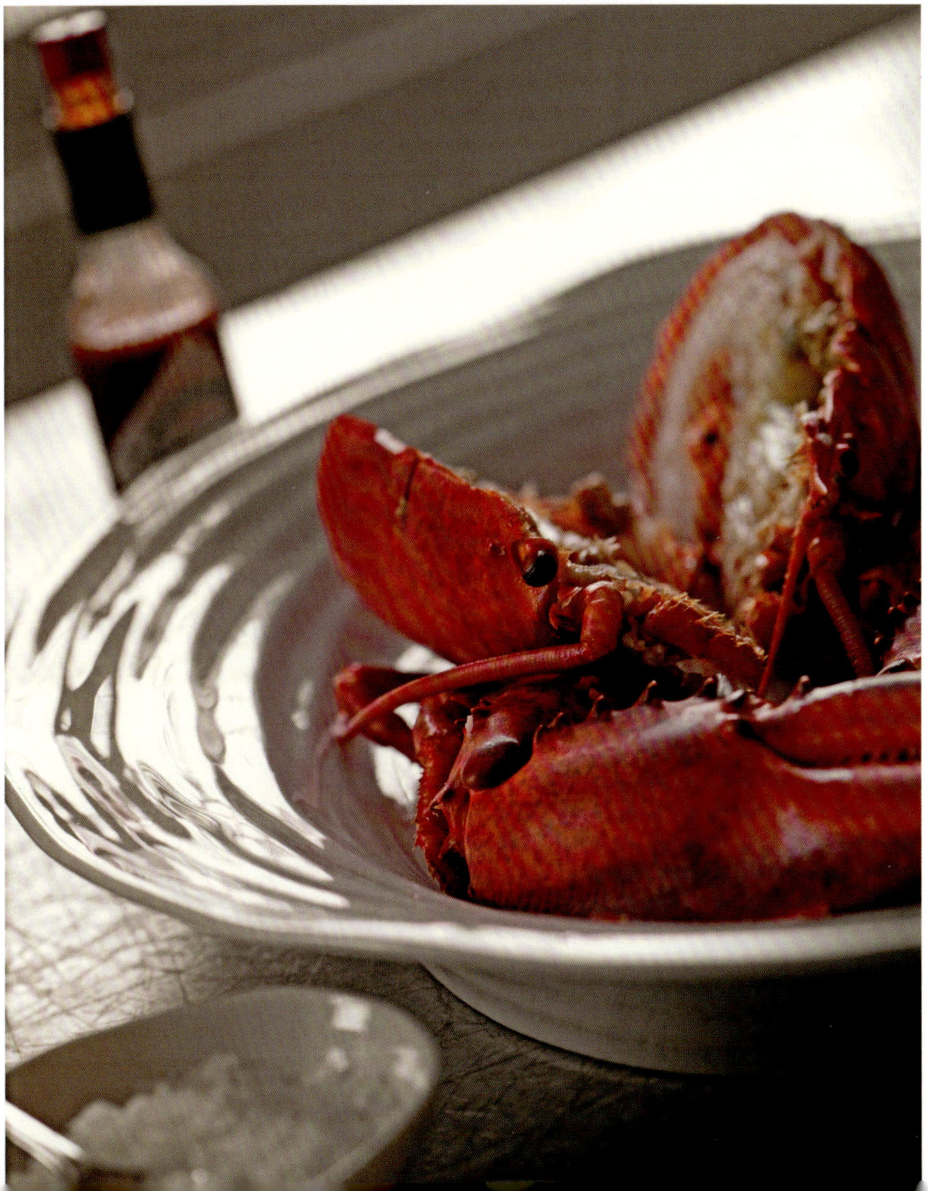

Sophie Conran for Portmeirion, round white platter, 2011. Porcelain, diameter: 26.5 cm (10½ in.). *Photo: Dominic Blackmore.*

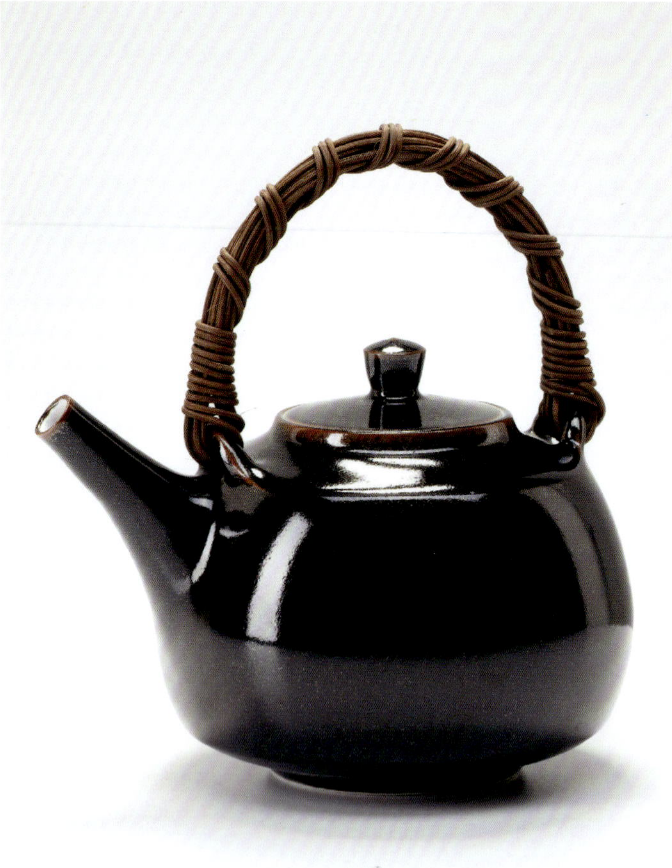

Chris Keenan for Habitat

Studio potter Chris Keenan was asked to design a Japanese-inspired range for Habitat in 2004. He trained with Edmund de Waal and now works from his own studio in south London, making porcelain bowls, cups and teapots. Keenan uses blue celadon and black tenmoku glazes on his thrown porcelain, so his idea for the range was to combine the colours of the day and night sky. Sky is 'sora' in Japanese, hence the name given to this range. The shapes were based on his thrown work, including a black teapot, footed cups, and bowls in celadon and black. Patterns of sgraffito lines and stamped dots were used on the cups, bowls and plates. The tableware was influenced by Japanese forms, with square plates for sushi and small bowls for soy sauce, as well as bowls for noodles or pasta. The range was manufactured in Japan in a factory outside Nagoya.

Chris Keenan, teapot, 2010. Thrown porcelain with tenmoku glaze, height: 24 cm (9½ in.). *Photo: Michael Harvey.*

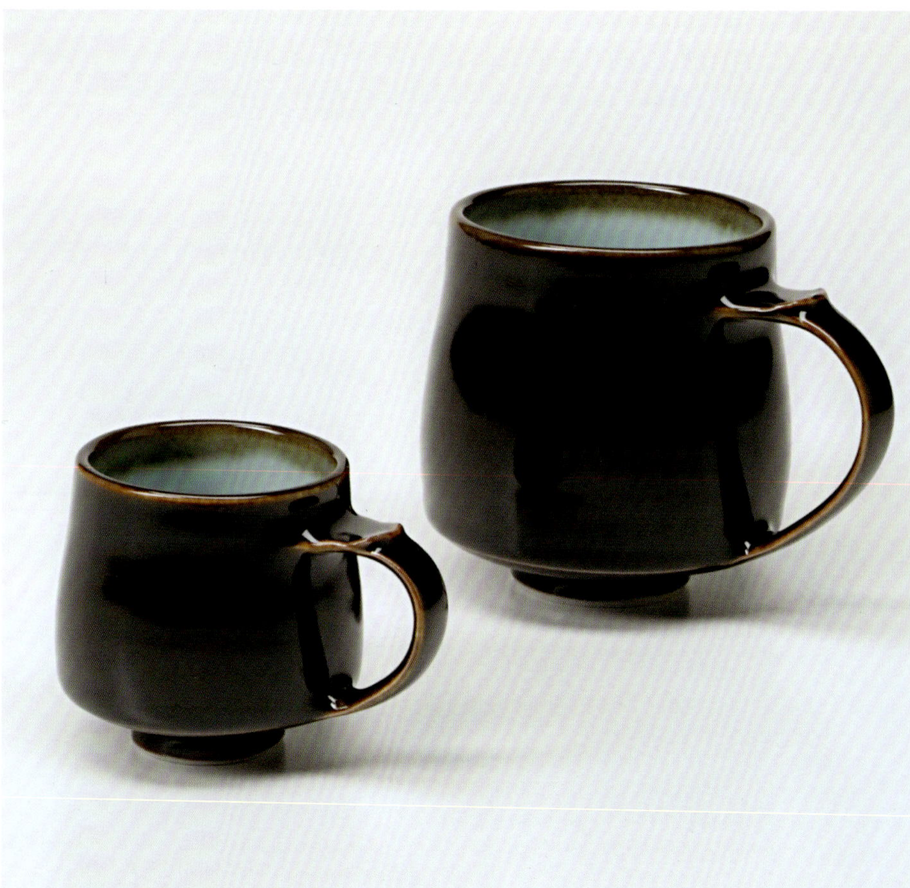

Chris Keenan, cups, 2010. Thrown porcelain with tenmoku and celadon glazes, heights: 5–10 cm (2–4 in.). *Photo: Michael Harvey.*

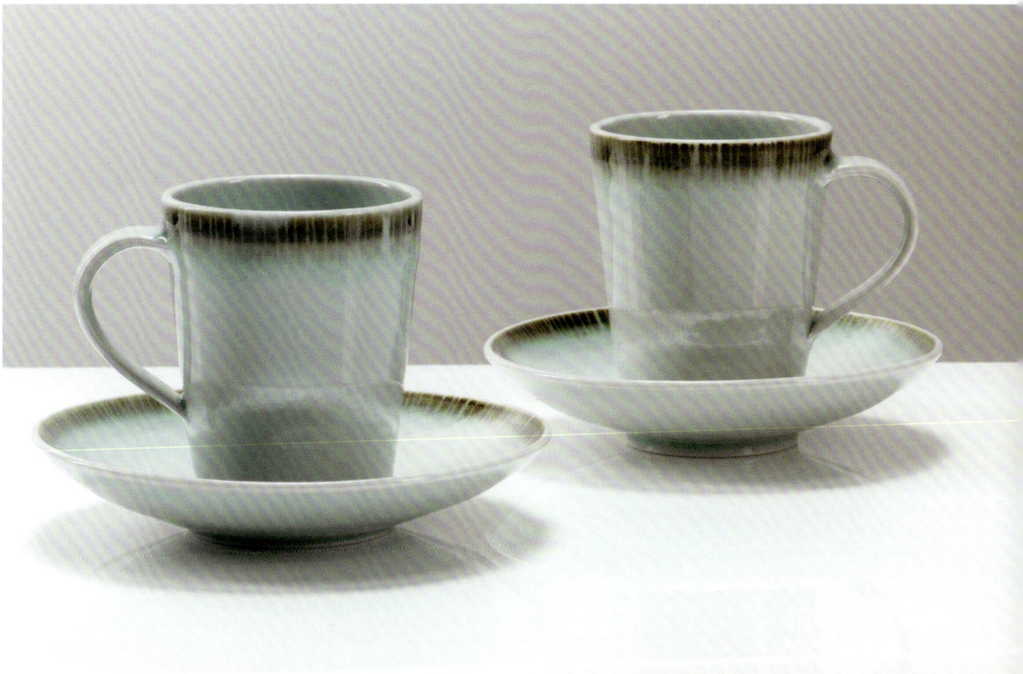

Chris Keenan, cups and saucers, 2010. Thrown porcelain with sgraffito rims, height: 11 cm (4¼ in.). *Photo: Michael Harvey.*

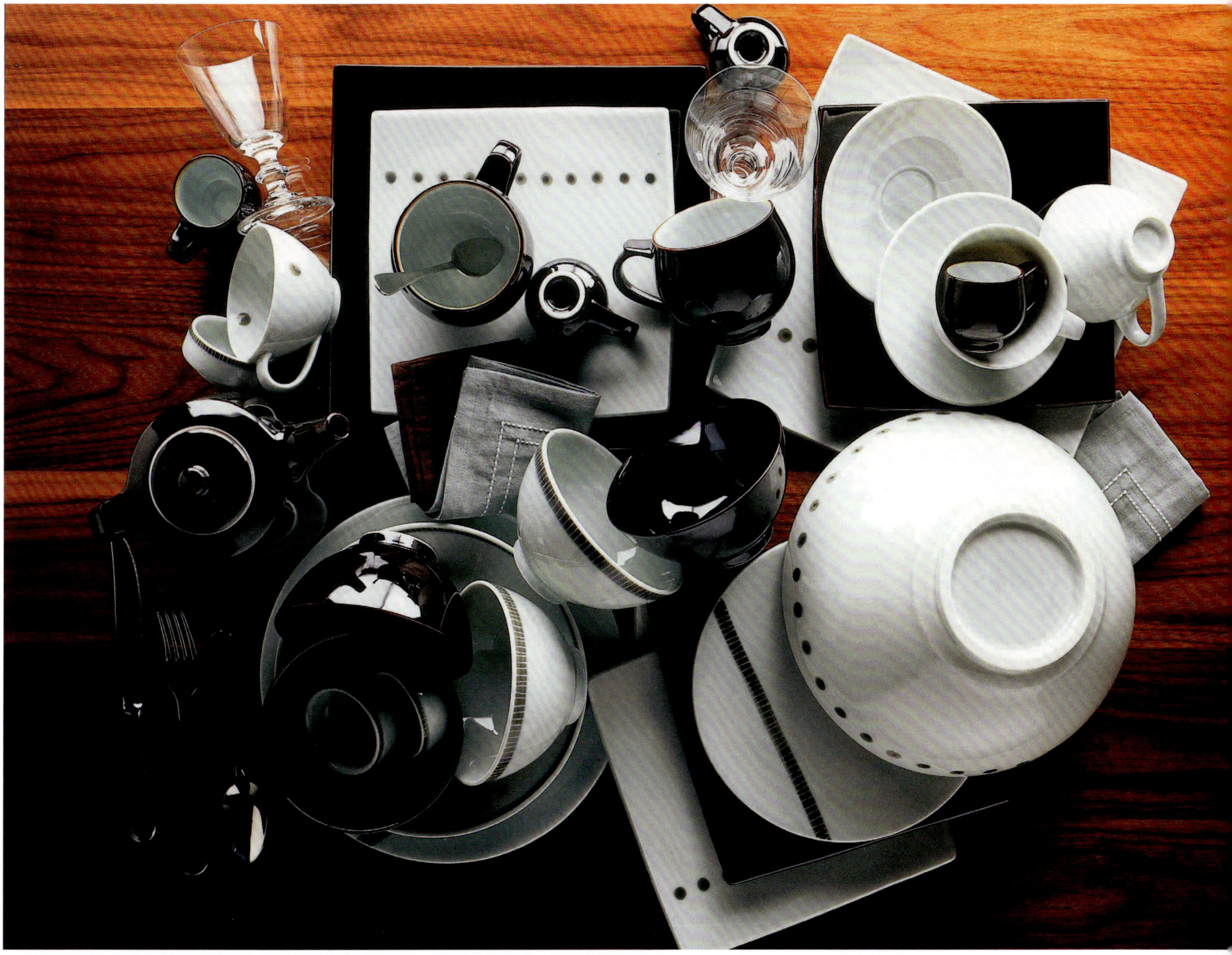

Chris Keenan for Habitat, SORA range, 2006. Porcelain, maximum diameter: 29.5 cm (11½ in.). *Photo: Henry Bourne.*

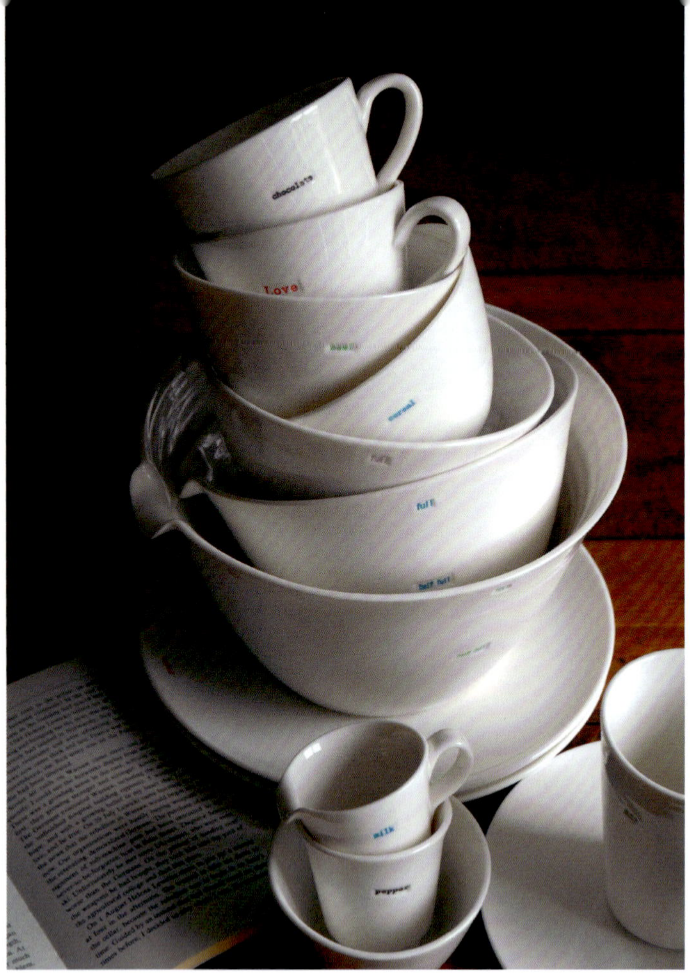

Keith Brymer Jones for Make International

Keith Brymer Jones works in his studio, the Old Bakery in Whitstable. He started his career throwing pots for Heal's, Habitat and many other large retailers in the UK, and also for stores overseas. Now as a director in his capacity as head of design for Make International, he has developed his own brand, 'Keith Brymer Jones', with his business partner and fellow director Dominic Speelman. His thrown pieces are used to make moulds for mass production in China. He works closely with the factories in China and has a studio there, where he throws prototypes. Brymer Jones is interested in using words as decoration, impressed into the clay using old typesets. His most popular tableware is the KBJ Word range in white porcelain with a coloured word impressed into each piece. His table and kitchenware uses bold, simple shapes with a modern feel. His favourite design is a bucket-shaped mug (the Bucket Mug) impressed with a word – for example, 'tea', 'coffee' or 'love'.

Make International, KBJ Word tableware, 2008. High-white porcelain, designed by Keith Brymer Jones, diameter: 26 cm (10¼ in.). *Photo: Petersen PR.*

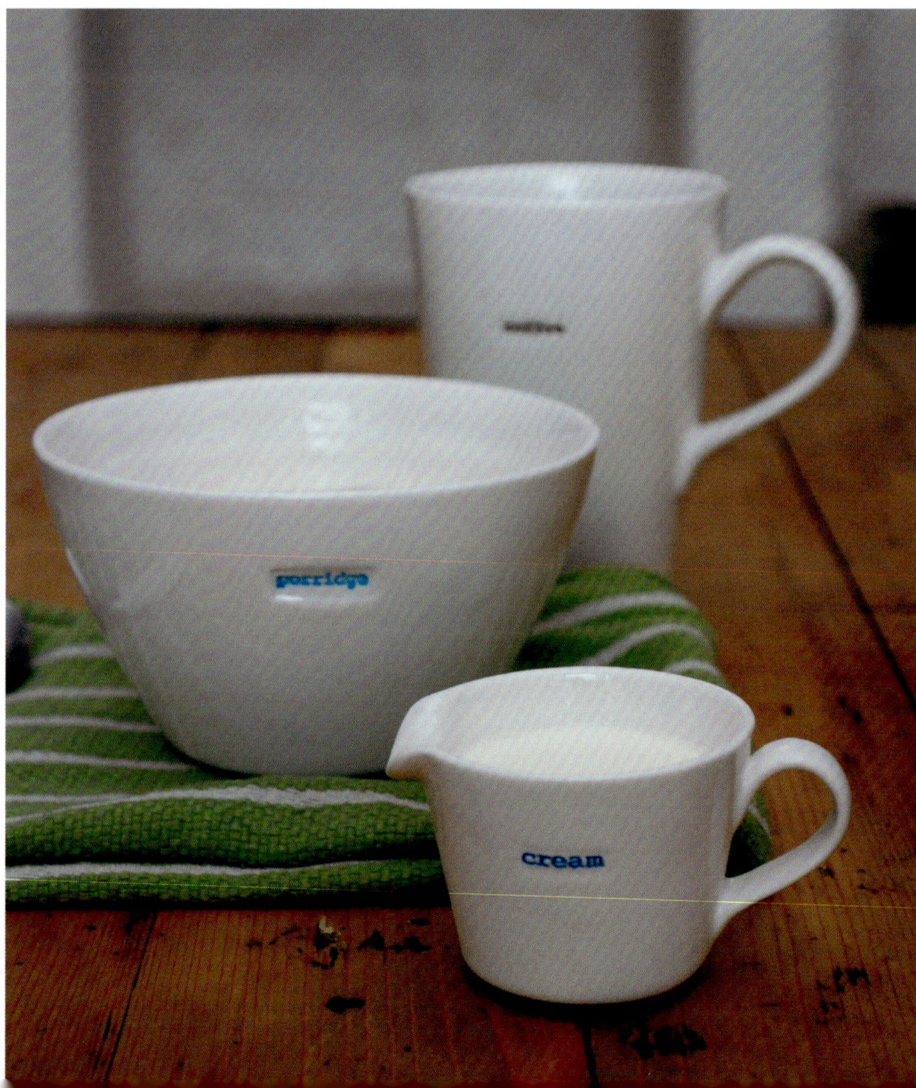

Make International, KBJ Word porridge bowl, coffee mug and cream jug, 2011. High-white porcelain, designed by Keith Brymer Jones, diameter: 13 cm (5 in.). *Photo: Polly Hancock.*

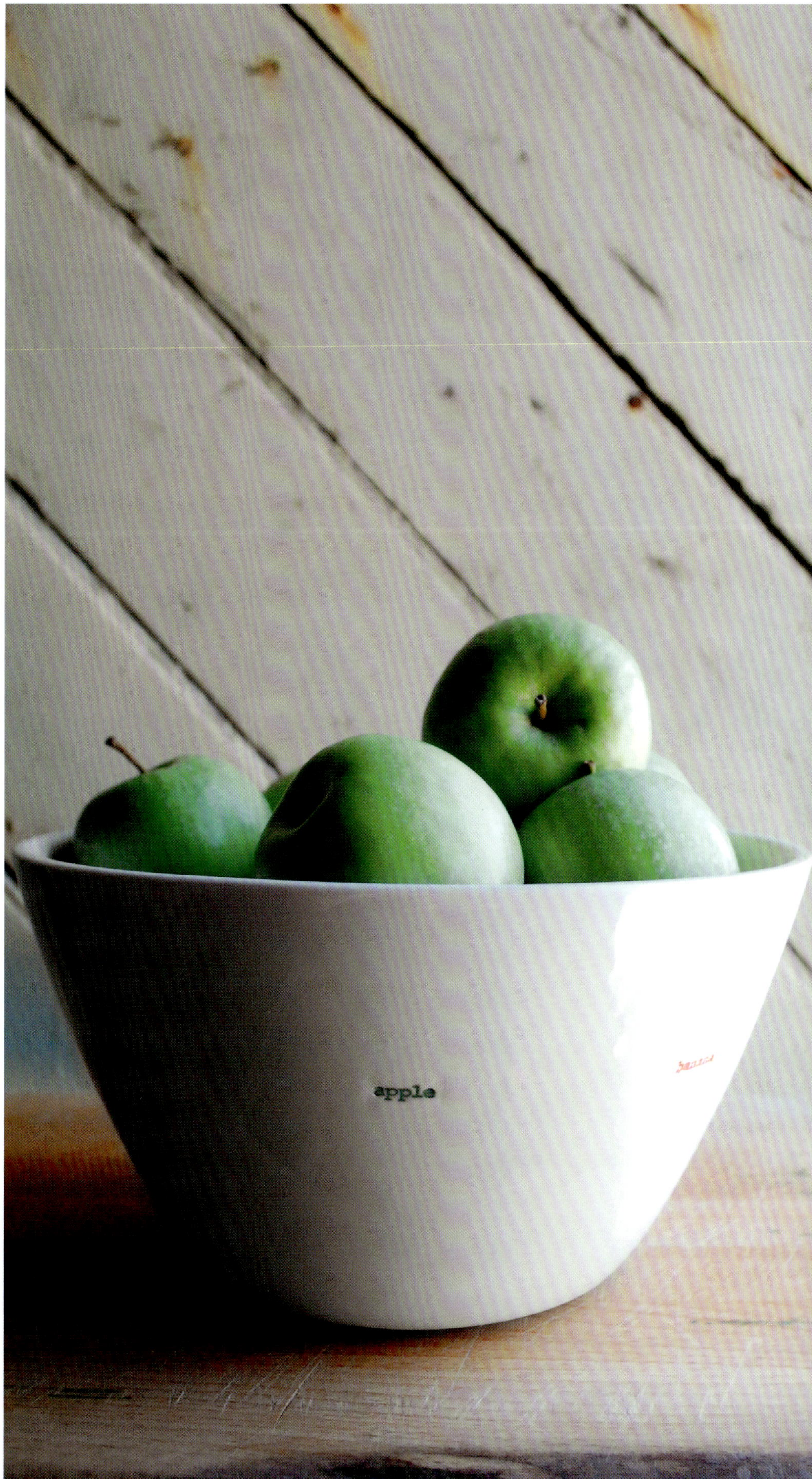

Make International, KBJ Word fruit bowl, 2011. High-white porcelain, designed by Keith Brymer Jones, diameter: 24 cm (9½ in.). *Photo: Polly Hancock.*

Bodo Sperlein for Nikko

Bodo Sperlein is a German-born, London-based designer who works primarily with bone china but has also designed in metal and wood. He had an early interest in clay as well as engineering and studied three-dimensional design at Camberwell College of Art. He has worked with porcelain companies Nymphenburg and Lladró, and more recently has collaborated with Japanese manufacturer Nikko to produce a fusion of European modernist design and Japanese tradition.

The Blossom range consists of fluid biomorphic bowl and plate shapes in gentle colours inspired by the sea, sky and cherry blossoms: pink, jade, aqua, blue and grey. The same colours are used in the Cloud range, where a spot of colour is placed in the centre of each plate, fading towards the edge like a drop of ink in a pool of water. In the Macaroon range, the colour spreads right across the plate, intensifying in the centre. Sperlein has also designed the Voyage tea set, which is influenced by both Eastern and Western shapes and rituals. These ranges can be mixed together and used in different combinations.

Bodo Sperlein for Nikko, Blossom dessert bowls, 2011. Bone china, diameter: 16.4 cm (6½ in.). *Photo: Graeme Duddridge.*

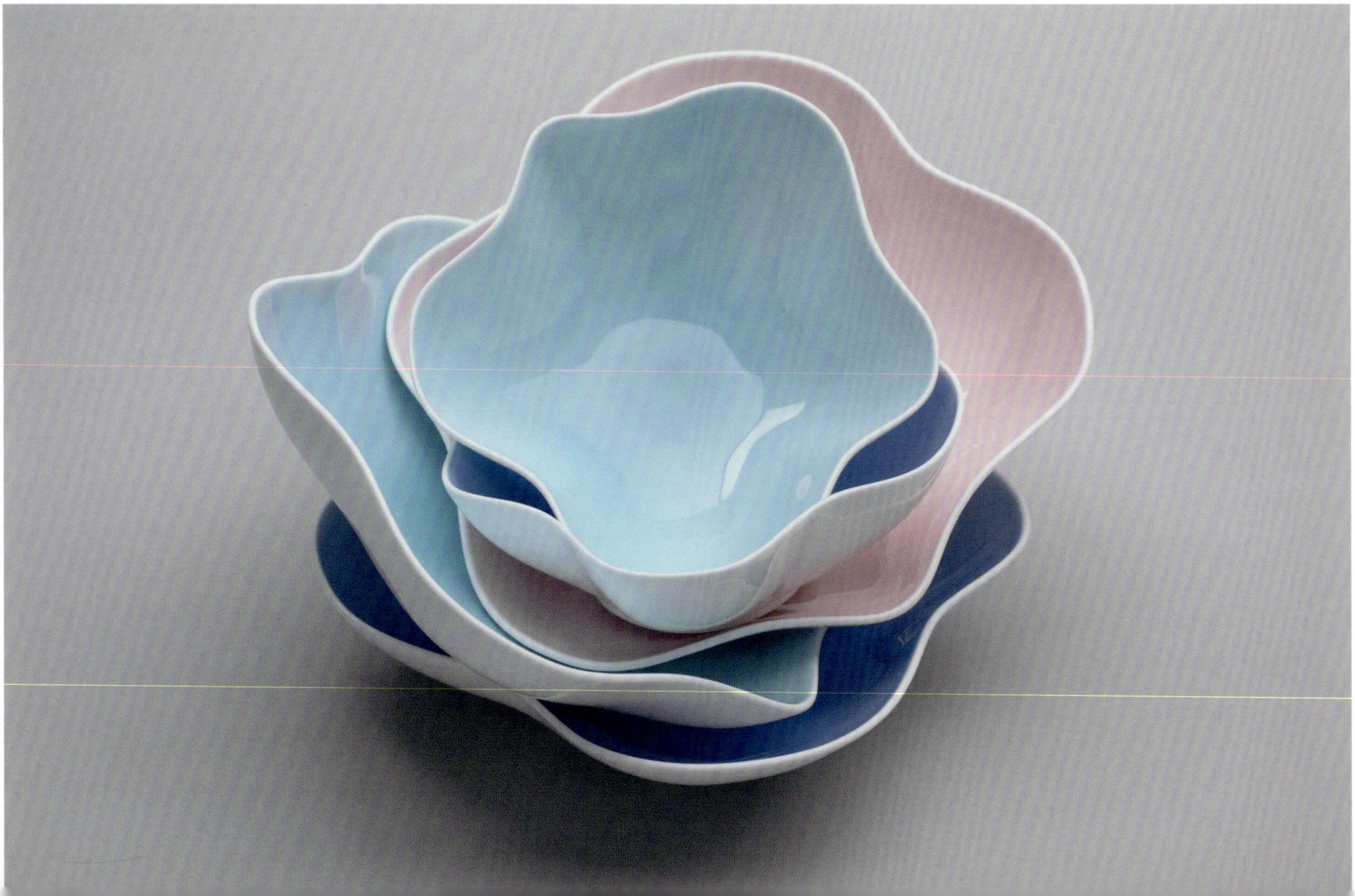

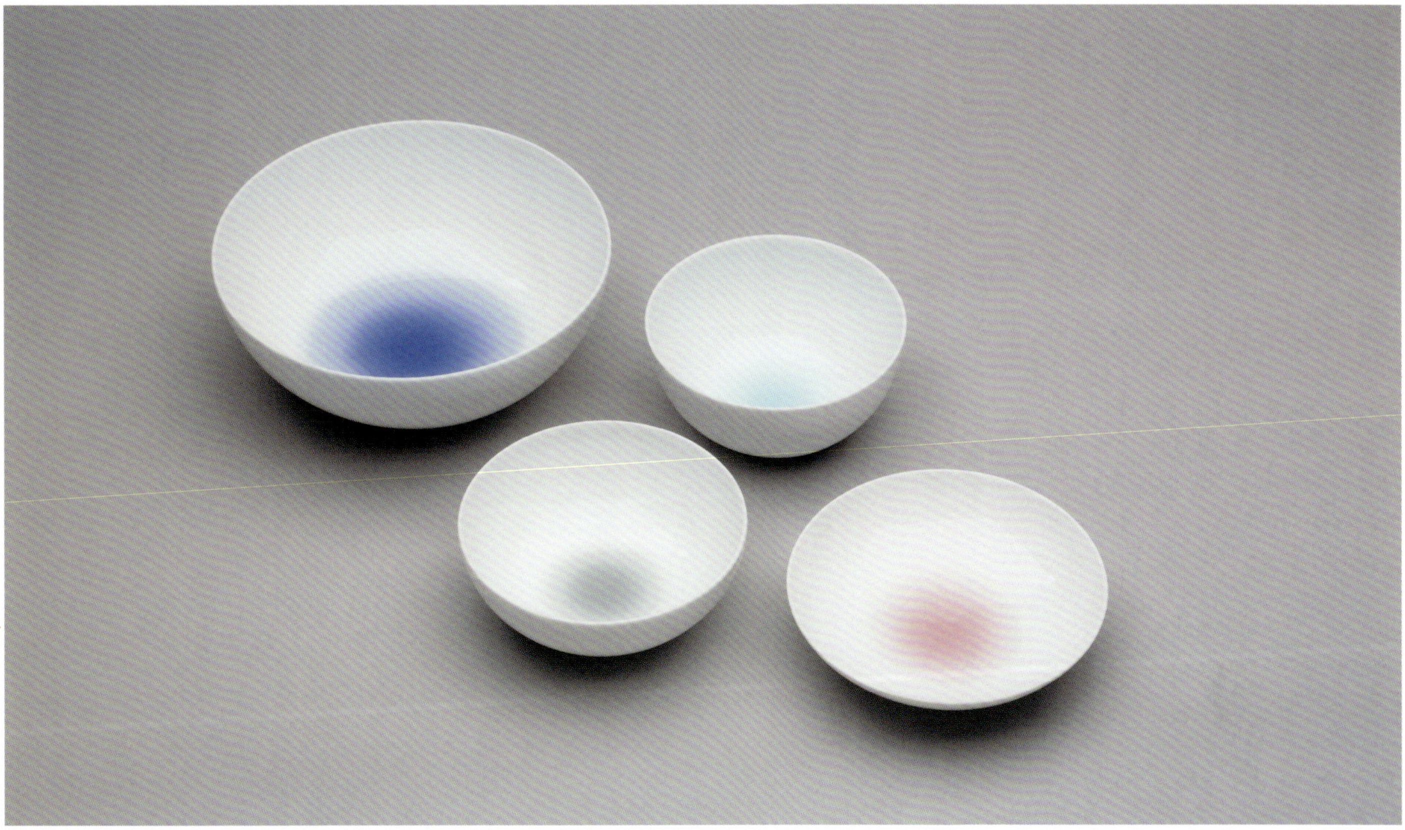

Bodo Sperlein for Nikko, Cloud bowls, 2011. Bone china, diameter: 14–22 cm (5½–8½ in.). *Photo: Graeme Duddridge.*

Bodo Sperlein for Nikko, Macaroon saucer, Voyage teacup, sugar bowl and creamer, 2011. Bone china, saucer diameter: 14.3 cm (5½ in.). *Photo: Graeme Duddridge.*

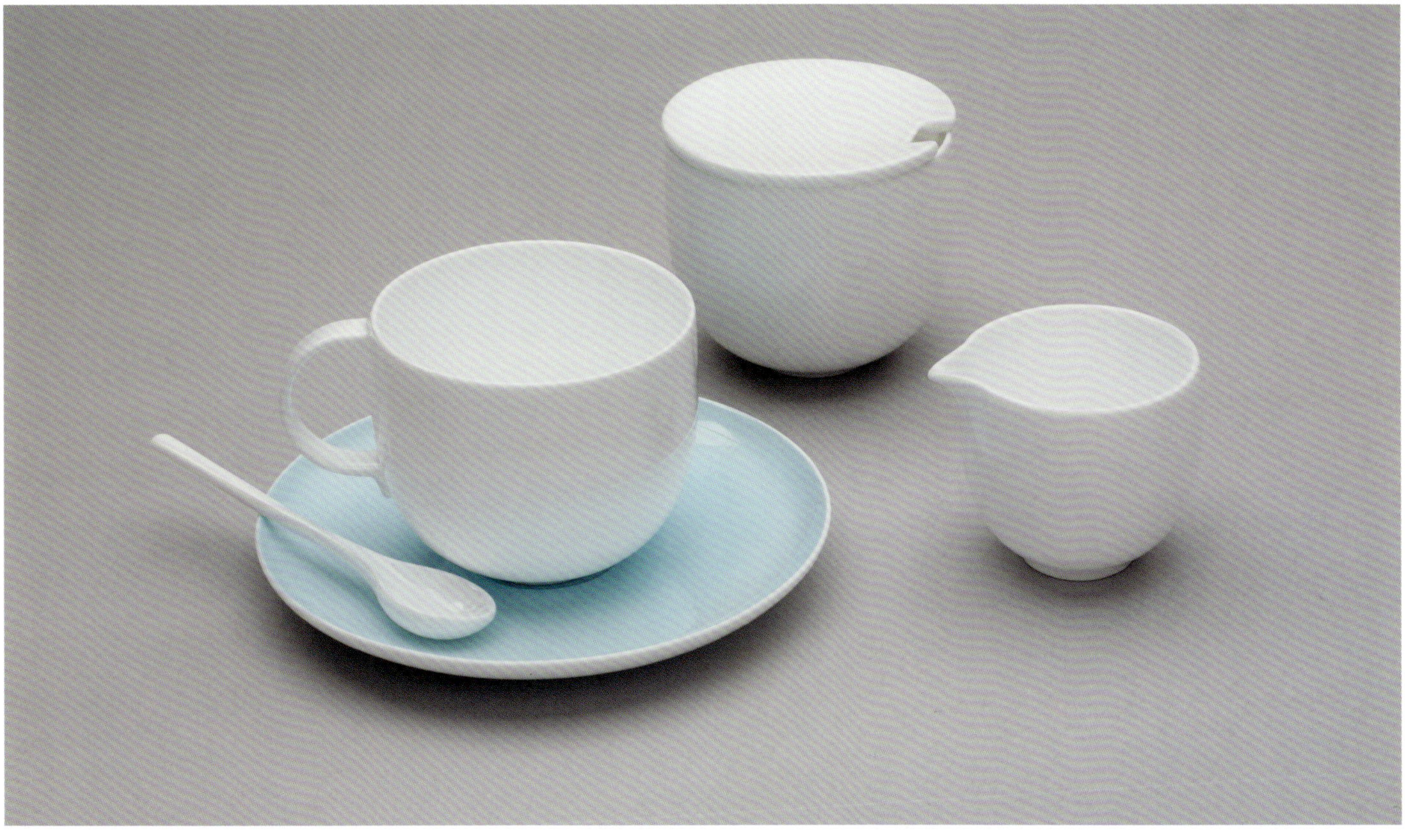

12 Teapots

It is very important that tableware should perform its function well and this is especially true of the teapot, the most complex functional form commonly made by the potter or ceramics manufacturer. Teapots should pour without dribbling. Glazes should fit well to withstand thermal shock, a particularly important requirement for teapots. Bases should be wide enough for good stability, and handles should be comfortable to hold.

Teapots are usually made from a number of parts joined together. The teapot body, spout, lid and handle must be assembled so that the teapot looks balanced and functions well. When designing a tea set, it is important to unite the teapot, sugar pot and milk jug in form and decoration.

Four-piece mould of Linda Bloomfield thrown teapot, by Nathan Smallman, Stoke-on-Trent. *Photo: Nathan Smallman.*

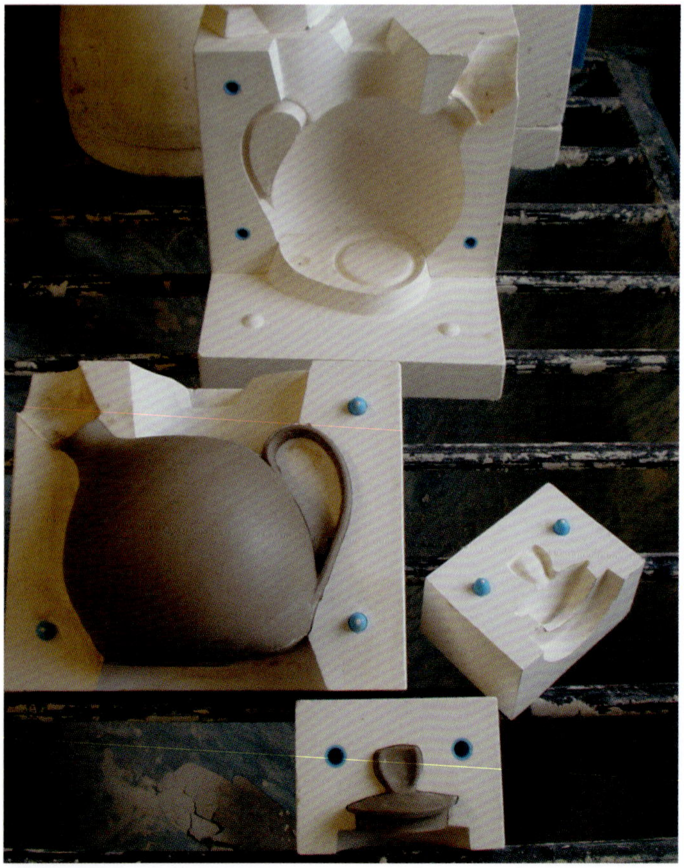

Teapot body

The traditional teapot shape, which originally came from China, had a spherical body. This is the best shape for infusing the tea and preventing turbulence when pouring. If the spout is joined high on the body, the strongest tea at the bottom of the pot will be poured last. Teapots from China and Japan were often small, containing only enough tea for one person. The Elers brothers, who made red earthenware teapots in Stoke-on-Trent in the late 17th century, often made cylindrical shapes turned on the lathe. They were influenced by both the imported Yixing teapots and by English silver teapots.

The use of Plaster of Paris to make moulds at the beginning of the Industrial Revolution in the mid-18th century enabled the production of tea, coffee and chocolate sets, with matching teapot, sugar basin and milk jug. Tea sets were expensive and kept for special occasions. A popular teapot form of the time was a rounded, globular shape with a crabstock handle (shaped like the branch of a crab apple tree). In France, particularly in the Sèvres porcelain factory which was supported by Louis XV, tea sets were made in the Rococo style, highly decorated and with elaborately scrolled handles.

It was not until the late 18th century, when the price of tea dropped, that it became an everyday drink. In Victorian times Brown Betty earthenware teapots were made with a Rockingham brown glaze containing manganese. These teapots could be large, holding several cups of tea, and were cheaply produced in large numbers.

In the Middle East and Europe, coffee pots were traditionally made of metal and had a tall, conical shape. Conical and cylindrical teapots became popular again more recently in the 20th century, but at the beginning of the 21st century their use is decreasing as many people make tea with a teabag in a mug.

Lid

Teapot lids should have a small hole to allow air into the teapot while pouring. The lid should sit on a gallery in the neck of the teapot body. A deep flange on the lid helps to prevent it falling off while pouring. Some lids have locking devices. Oriental teapots often have an integral tea strainer, which sits under the lid.

Spout

The tip of the spout should be positioned higher than the highest water level in the teapot and cut at an angle so that it is sharp enough to cut off the flow and prevent dripping. The tip should also be turned outwards at the end so that it is horizontal while pouring. Holes to strain the tea leaves may be cut in the teapot body where the spout is attached. For optimum flow, the total area of holes should be greater than the cross-sectional area of the tip of the spout.

Handle

Japanese teapots often have side handles or handles that reach over the top of the lid, sometimes made from bamboo or akebia vine. Western teapots more often have a handle on the side of the teapot opposite the spout, which gives a balanced look. The handle can have a thumb grip, a small knob of clay which prevents the thumb from slipping while pouring. Very large teapots may need a lug handle above the spout, as well as the main handle, to ensure ease of pouring.

Making methods

Chinese Yixing teapots are made by handbuilding or moulding slabs of red earthenware clay. These are burnished but not glazed and can absorb the flavour of the tea, so each teapot is only used for one type of tea. Earthenware has insulating properties and can withstand sudden temperature changes. Teapots can also be thrown on the wheel, with the teapot body, lid and spout being thrown separately and then assembled. The handle can be pulled from a short, thick roll of clay and attached to the pot, then pulled further from the teapot body.

In industry, teapots are made by slipcasting from a three-or four-piece plaster mould, with a separate mould for the lid. It is also possible to combine thrown and slipcast components.

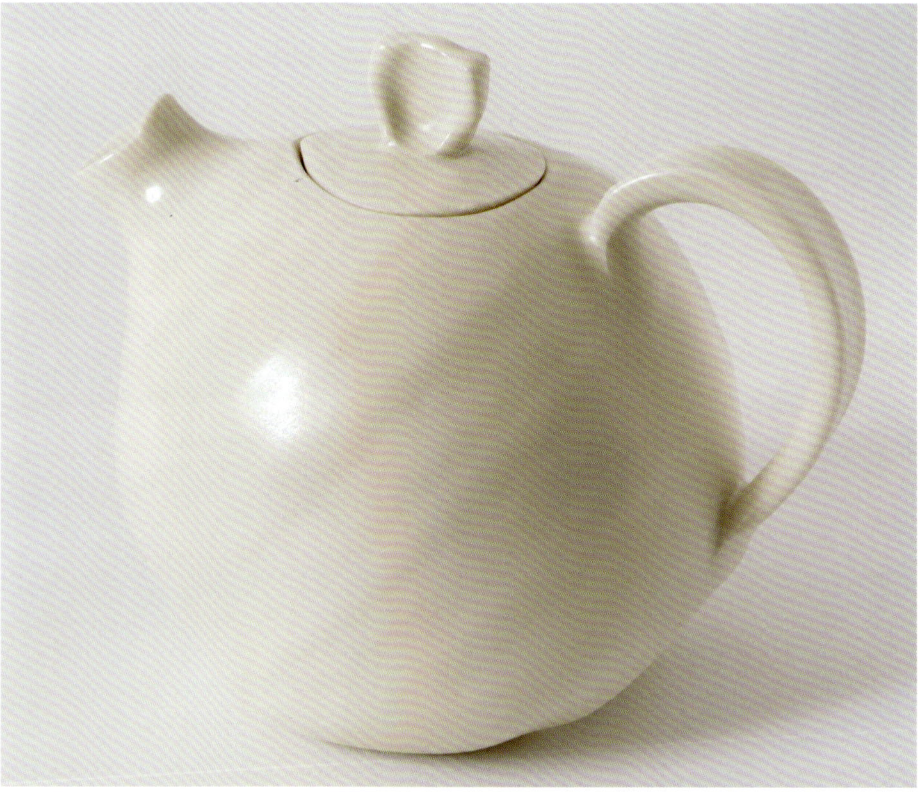

Linda Bloomfield, Organic teapot, 2008. Thrown porcelain, height: 15 cm (6 in.). *Photo: Jacqui Hurst.*

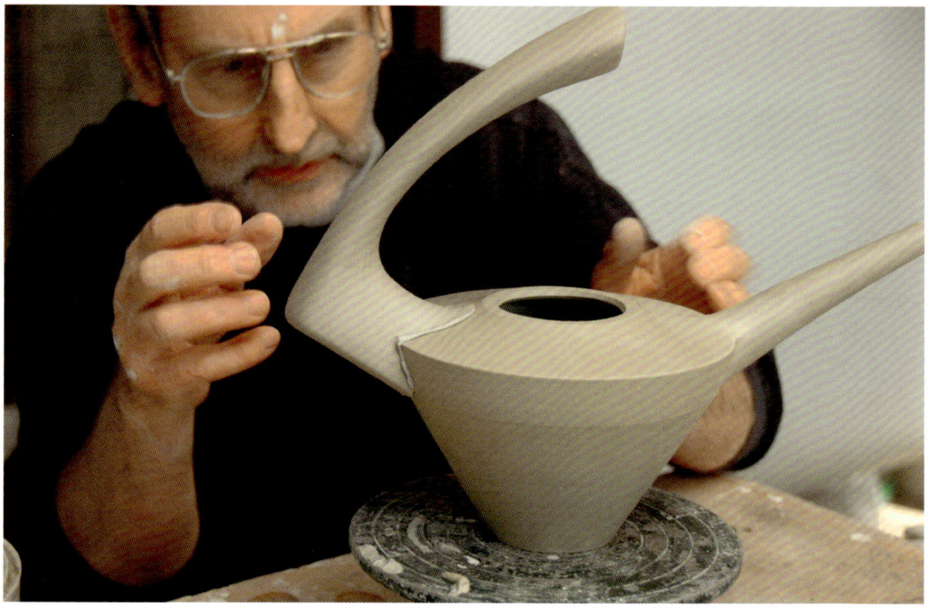

Jeremy Nichols attaching a slipcast teapot handle and spout to a thrown body. The underside of the handle is pierced with a pin to allow air to escape during firing. *Photo: Henry Bloomfield.*

Jeremy Nichols, teapot, 2008. Thrown body with slipcast spout and handle, salt-glazed stoneware, height: 23 cm (9 in.). *Photo: courtesy of the artist.*

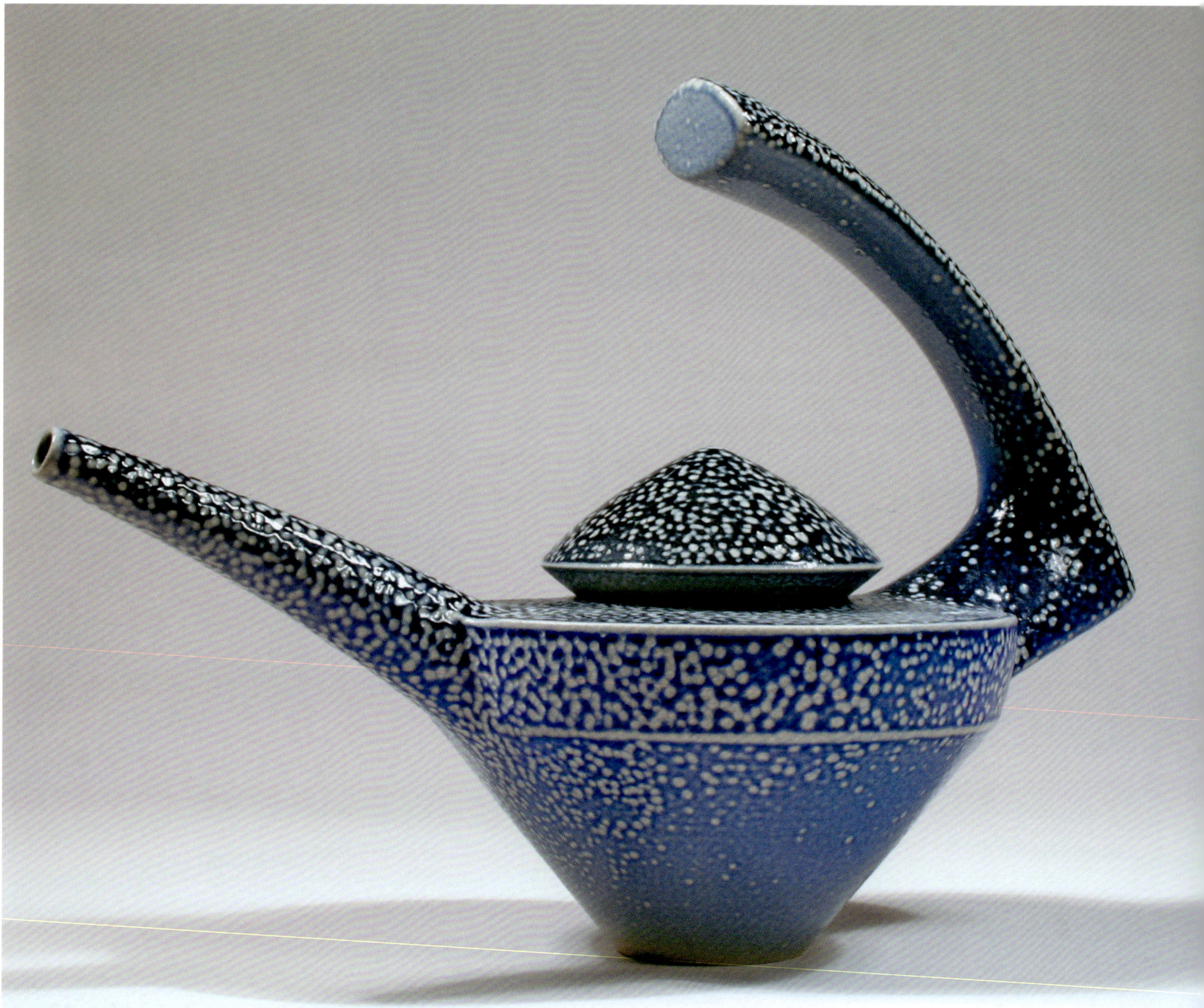

Glaze fit

The glaze should fit the teapot well and should be shiny and easy to clean, particularly on the inside. Crazing of the glaze (where the glaze is too small for the body and forms a network of cracks) is undesirable. But the opposite, shivering (where the glaze is too big for the body, causing glaze to flake off at the rim), is worse, as this can cause the teapot to crack when boiling water is poured in. The glaze and body expand and contract at different rates, causing thermal stress. This can be reduced by ensuring the glaze fits the body well, and that the teapot walls are an even thickness. The best way to test the glaze fit and check for cracking is to pour boiling water into the teapot. If crazing occurs, a small amount of silica (quartz or flint) can be added to the glaze. To correct the opposite problem, shivering or cracking, feldspar can be added.

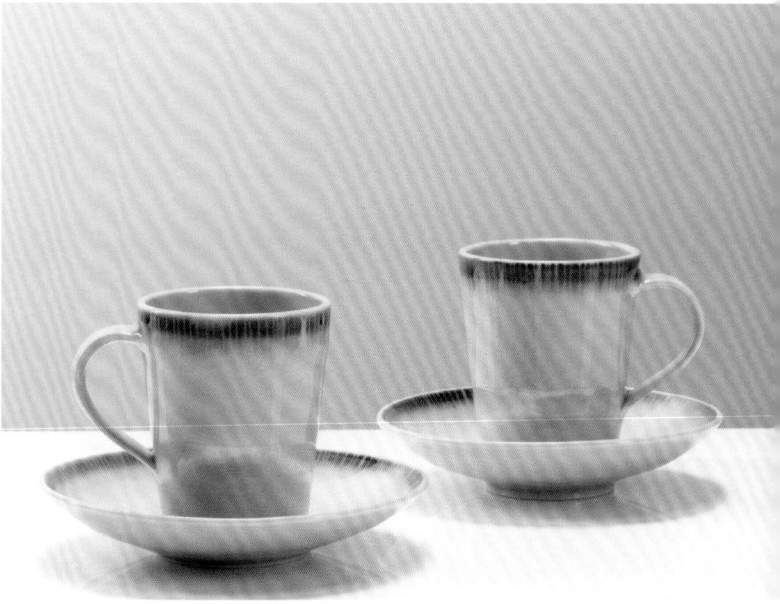

Chris Keenan, tea set, 2010. Thrown celadon with mulberry wood tray, height: 18.5 cm (7¼ in.). *Photo: Michael Harvey.*

Derek Wilson, thrown porcelain tea set on handbuilt stoneware tray with grey engobe, 2011. *Photo: Christopher Martin.*

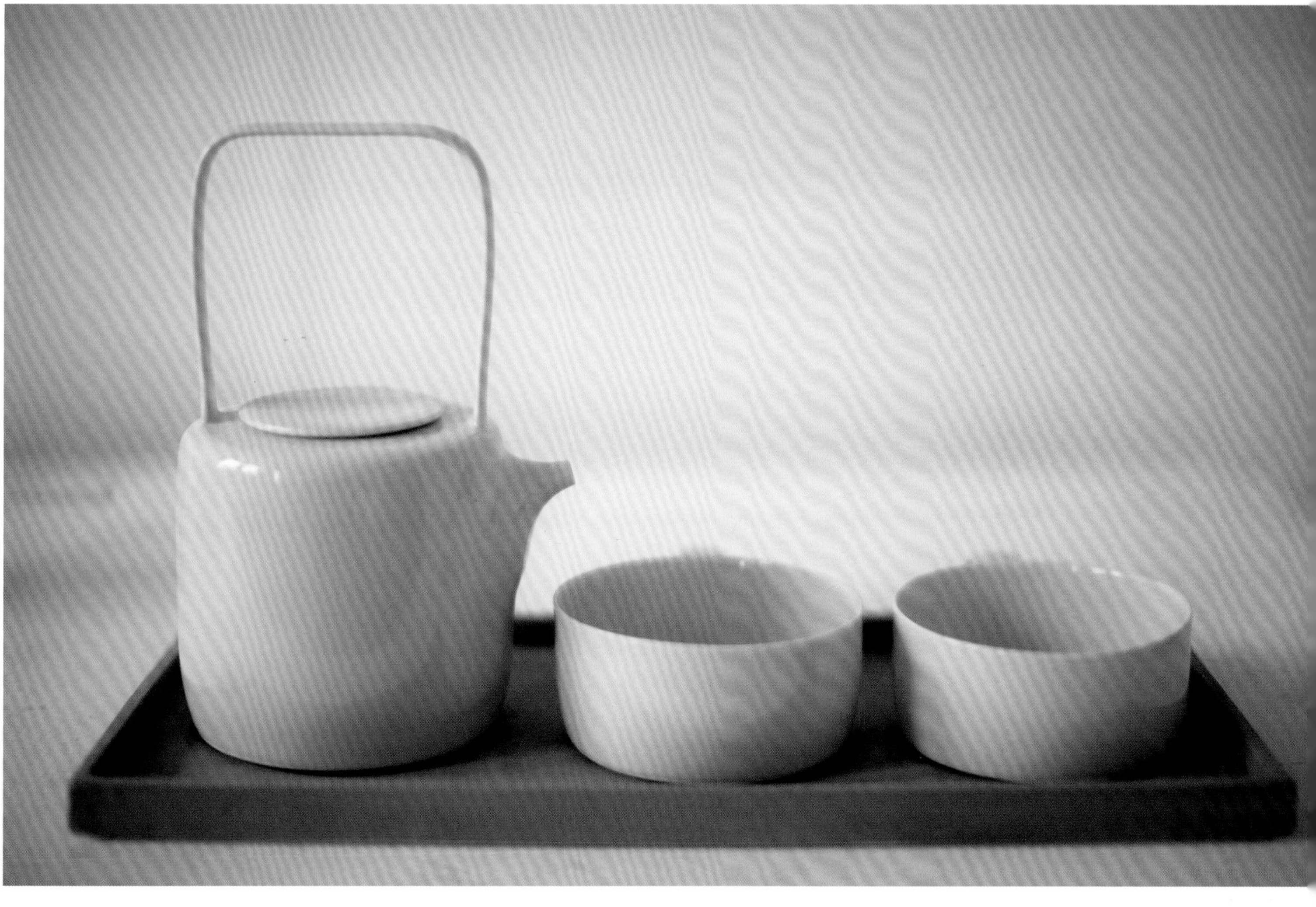

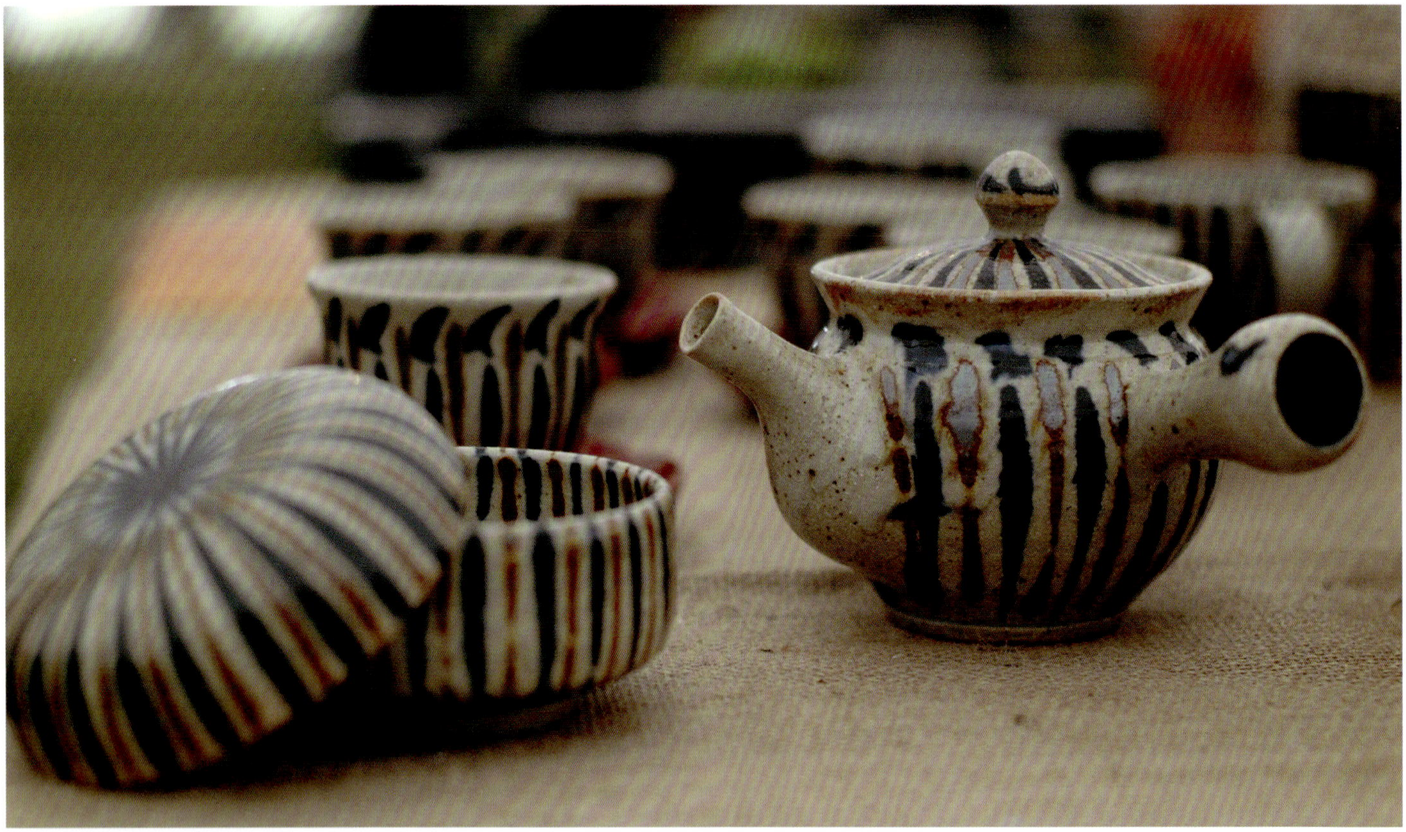

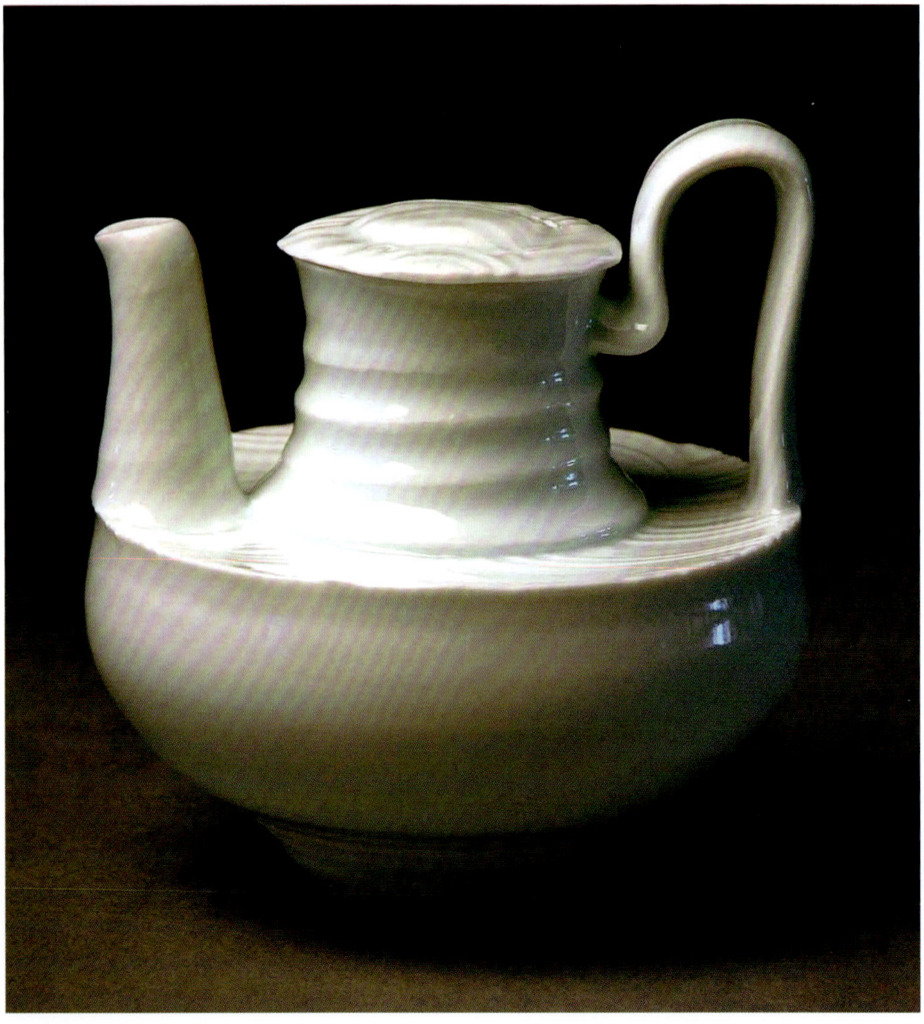

Reiko Nagata, tea set, 2011. Stoneware with iron and cobalt decoration, height: 10 cm (4 in.). *Photo: Henry Bloomfield.*

Takeshi Yasuda, thrown and assembled porcelain teapot, 2004. *Photo: courtesy of the artist.*

Akiko Hirai, Dobin, thrown stoneware teapot with vine handle, 2011. *Photo: Toshiko Hirai.*

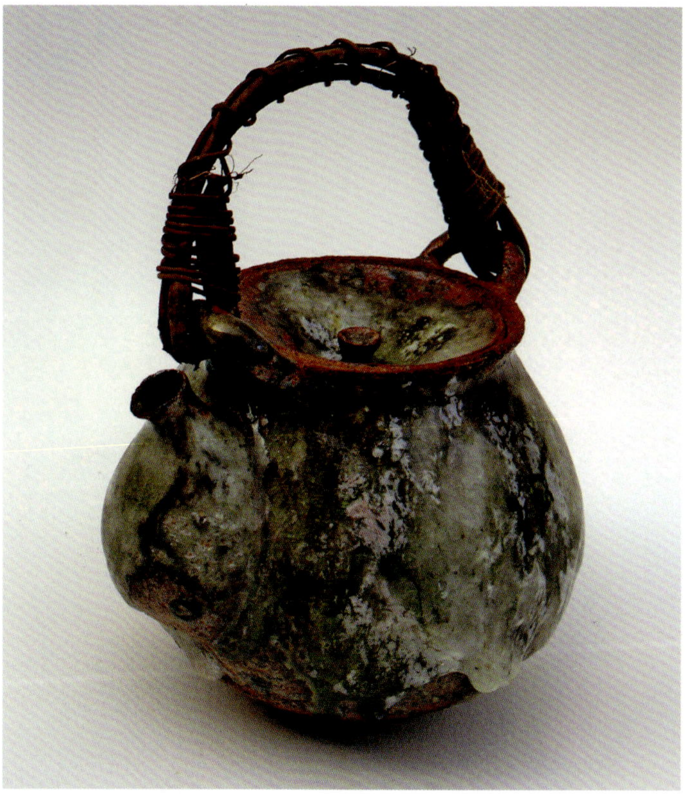

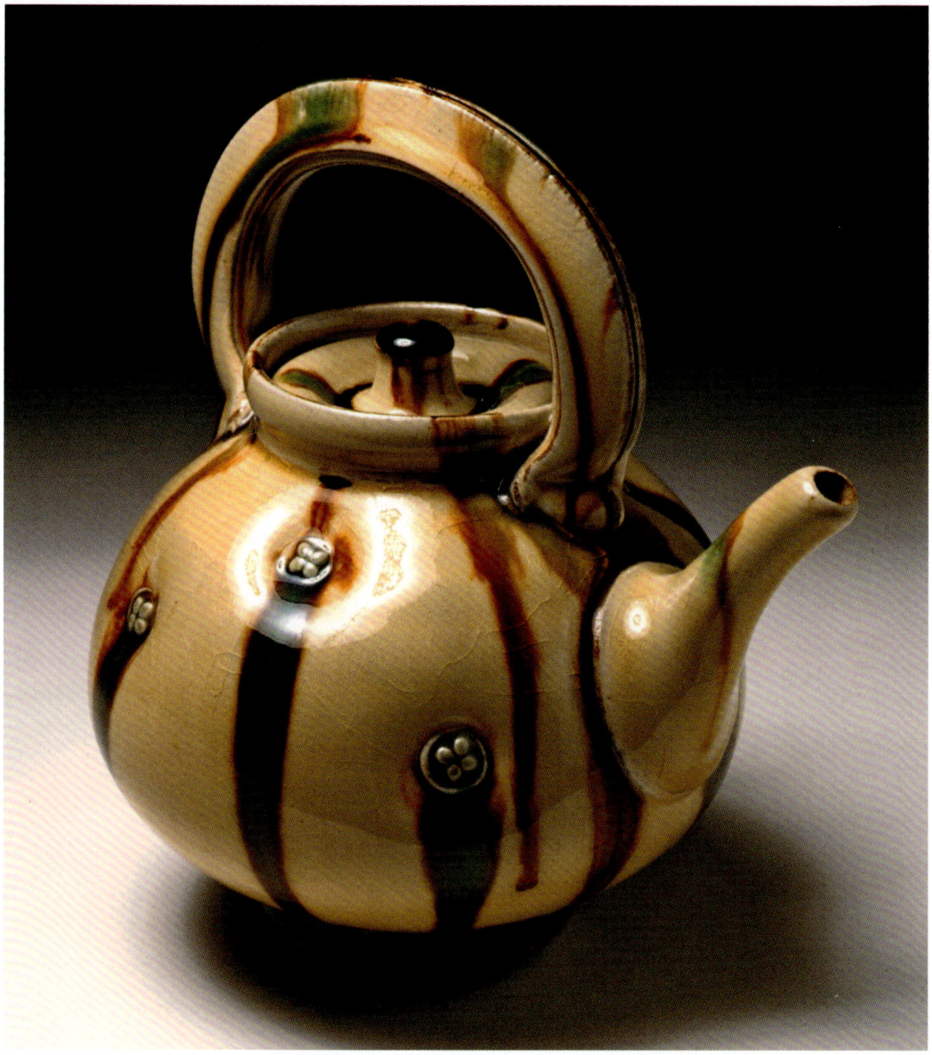

Takeshi Yasuda, sprigged stoneware teapot, 1990. Sancai (three-colour) decoration in copper and manganese, height: 24 cm (9½ in.). *Photo: courtesy of the artist.*

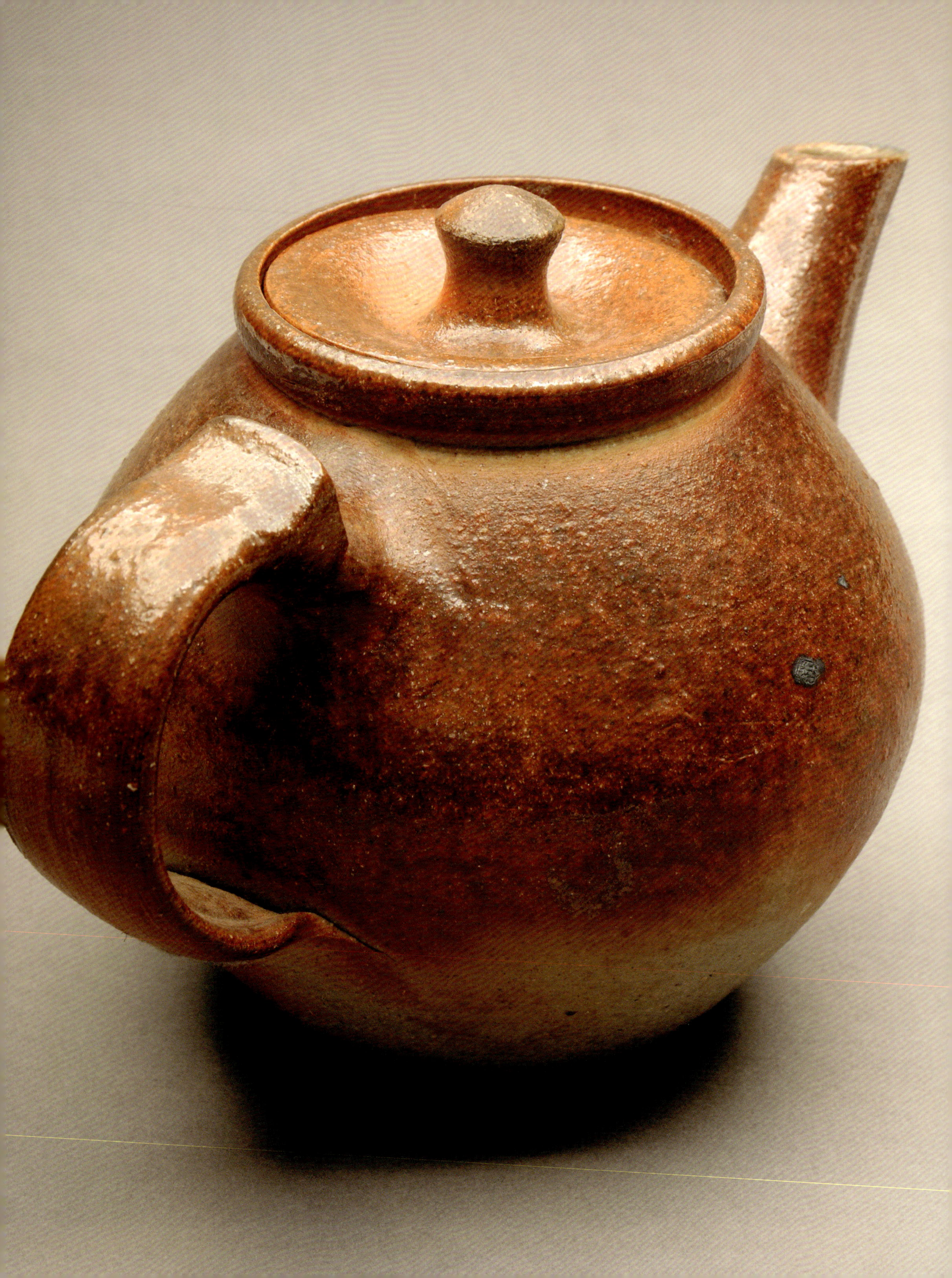

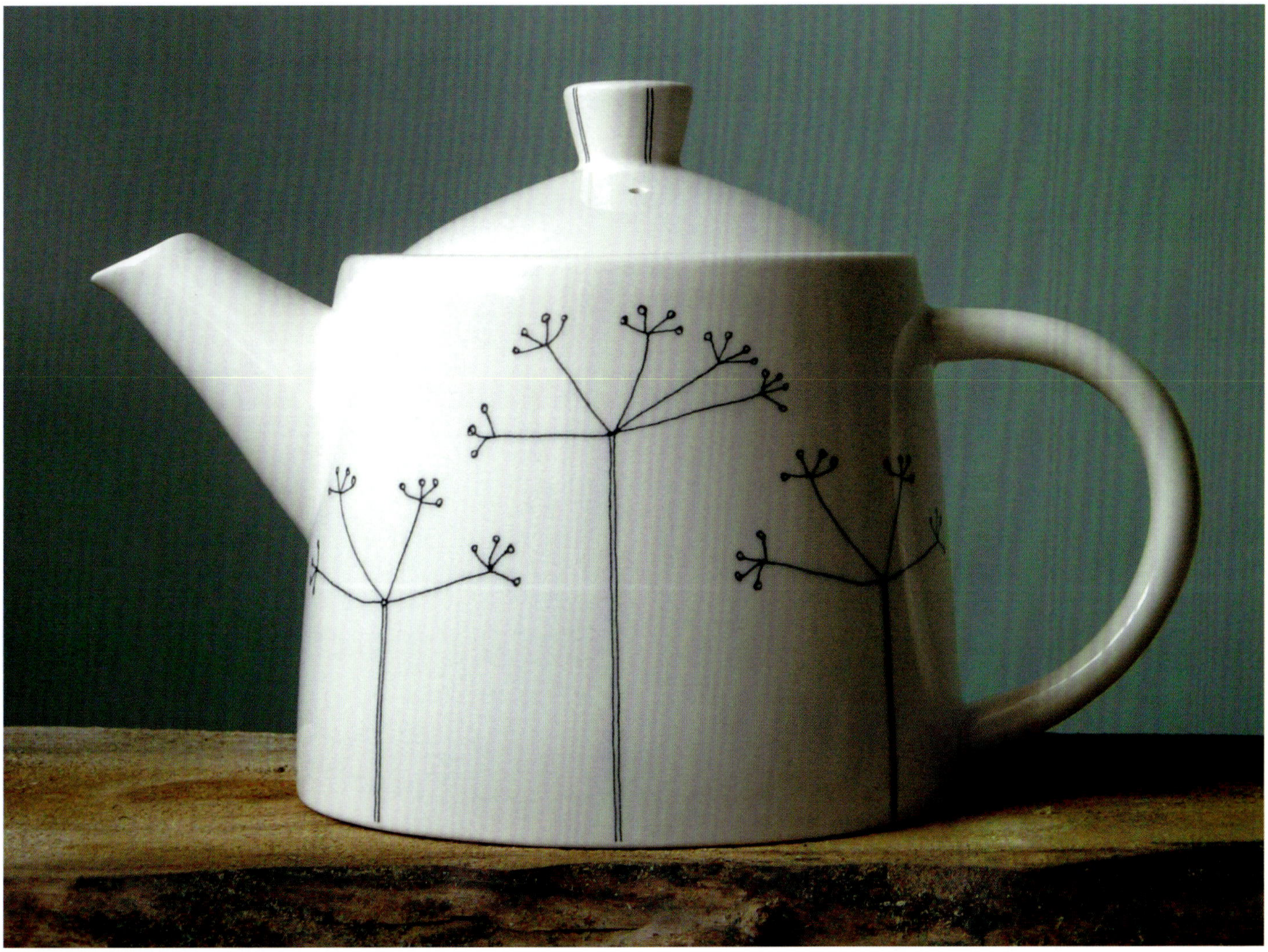

Rachel Barker, Coriander teapot, manufactured in Stoke-on-Trent, 2005. Slipcast earthenware, 23 x 14.5 cm (9 x 5¾ in.). *Photo: Rachel Barker.*

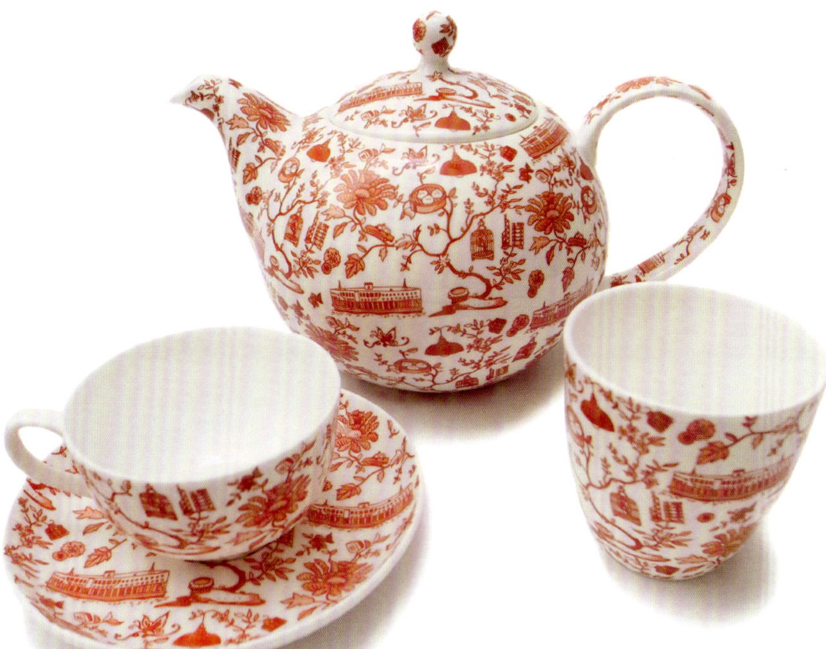

Mariko Jesse, Hong Kong Toile tea set, 2011. Teapot height: 14.5 cm (5¾ in.); cup and saucer width: 13.5 cm (5¼ in.); Chinese teacup height: 7.5 cm (3 in.). *Photo: Mariko Jesse.*

Svend Bayer, teapot, 1990s. Wood-fired stoneware, height: 12 cm (4¾ in.). *Photo: Jonathan Thompson.*

13 Bowls

Bowl shapes

Bowls have been used in the Far East for thousands of years, mainly for serving rice and noodles. The traditional Chinese shape is rounded, with a wide foot-ring and a fine, out-turned rim (see p. 11). Japanese rice bowls often have a narrow foot and a more conical shape. Bowls are also used for drinking tea and soup. In medieval England, large pancheons were used for settling milk or mixing bread dough. They were made of earthenware, glazed on the inside, and were conical in shape with a flat base.

Bowls vary in shape and size depending on intended use. Kitchen bowls need to be sturdy and stable for mixing. They include lipped bowls for pouring and colanders for draining. Serving bowls should be light enough to pick up and pass around. Dining bowls should be fine, with an easily cleaned glaze on the inside surface, and should stack easily so they take up as little storage space as possible. Tea bowls need a fine rim so that they are pleasant to drink from.
There are two basic bowl shapes: tall and deep or wide and shallow. The deeper ones are good for keeping soup hot, while the shallower bowls can be used for pasta or noodles. Bowls can be rounded or conical, with round ones having a greater volume for the same height. Wide bases will be more stable, while narrow, footed bases look more elegant.

Making methods

Bowls can be thrown on the wheel and the foot-ring turned when leatherhard (see p. 116). In industry they are usually made in rotating jolley moulds in a mechanised version of throwing but can also be slipcast or made from slabs pressed by hand into a mould.

Linda Bloomfield throwing a large bowl, 2009.
Photo: Henry Bloomfield.

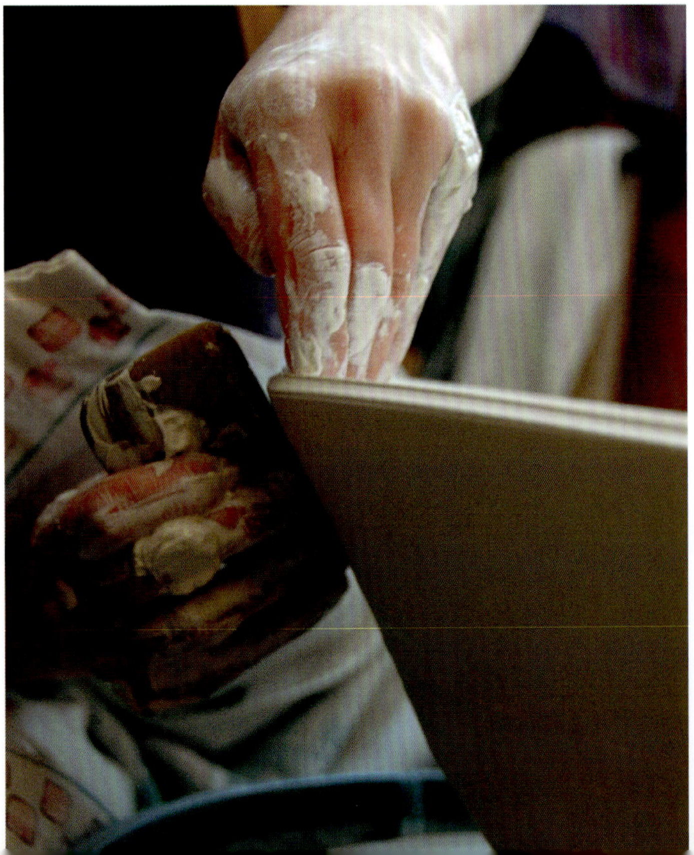

Rebecca Callis, stack of bowls, 2010. Thrown porcelain, cobalt, manganese, titanium and zinc glazes fired to 1240°C (2264°F), 5 x 12 cm (2 x 4¾ in.). *Photo: courtesy of the artist.*

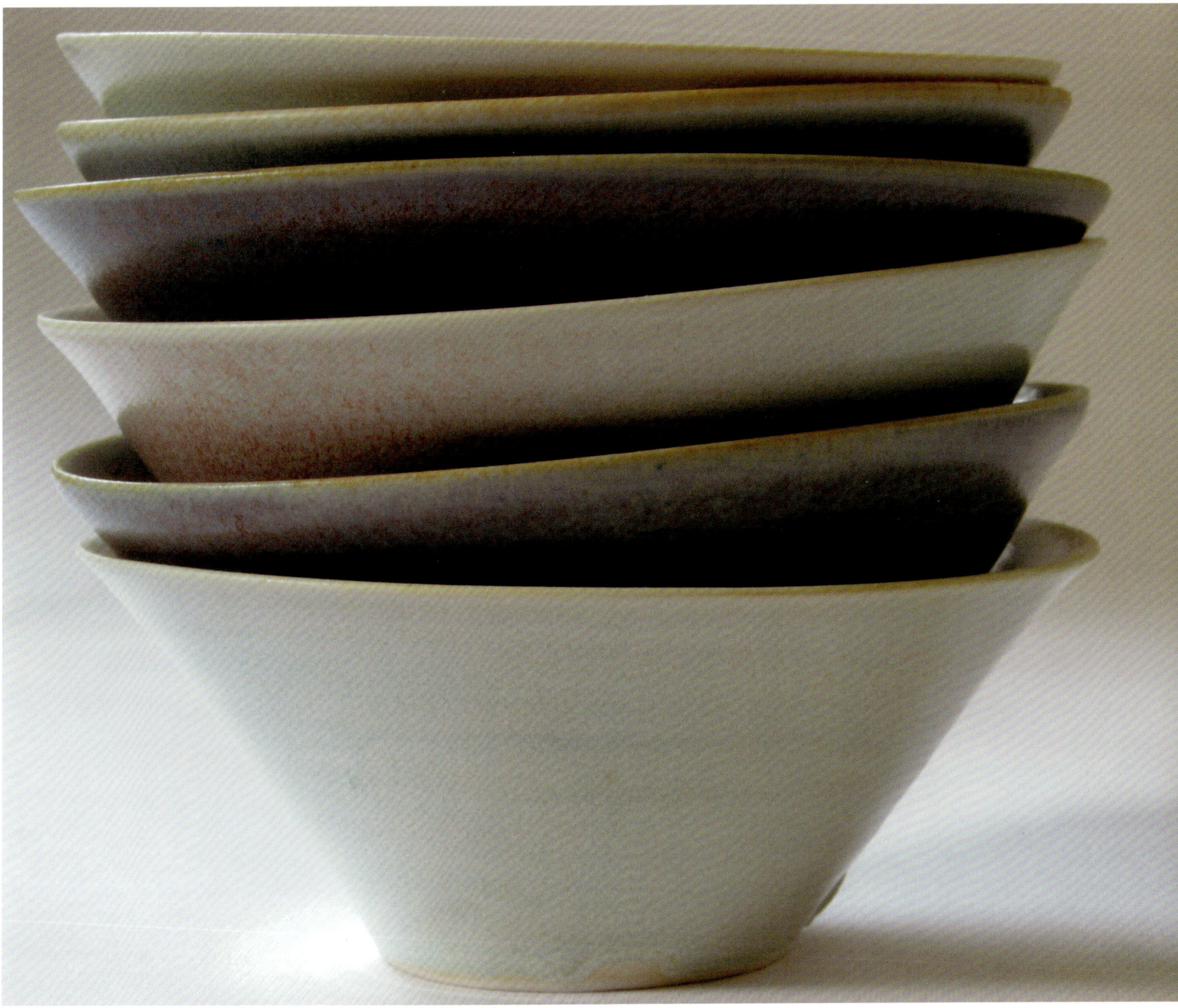

Kitchen bowls

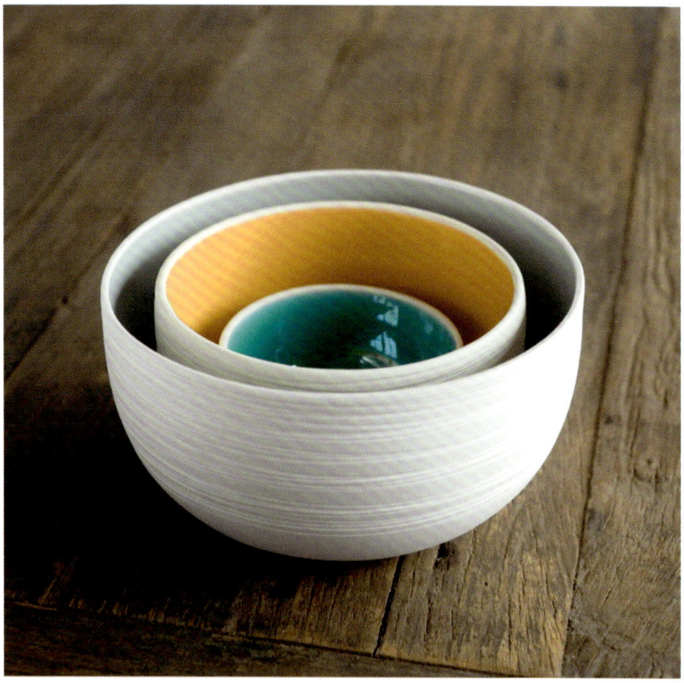

Pigeon Toe Ceramics, Portland, Oregon, Scribble Nesting Bowls designed by Lisa Jones, 2010. Thrown porcelain, glazed on the inside, width: 20 cm (8 in.). *Photo: Lisa Warninger.*

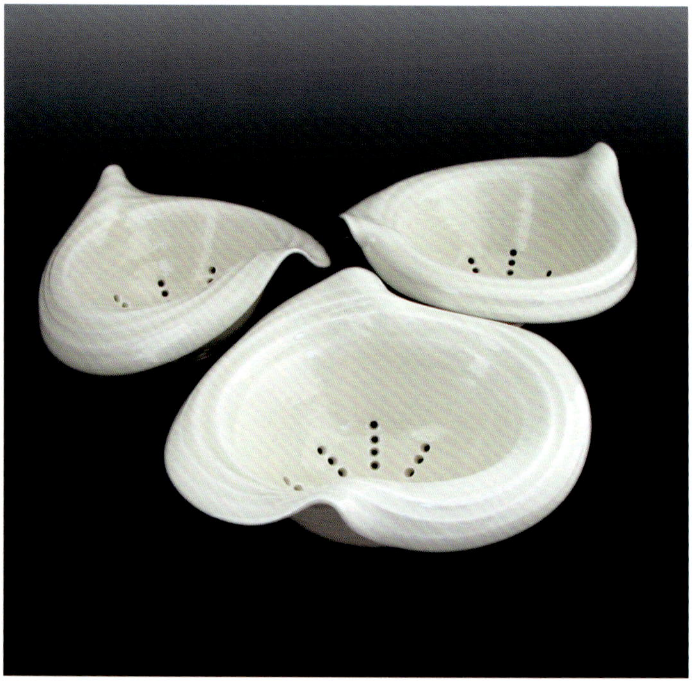

Karen Morgan, thrown and altered colanders, 2008. Porcelain, width: 26 cm (10¼ in.). *Photo: by the artist.*

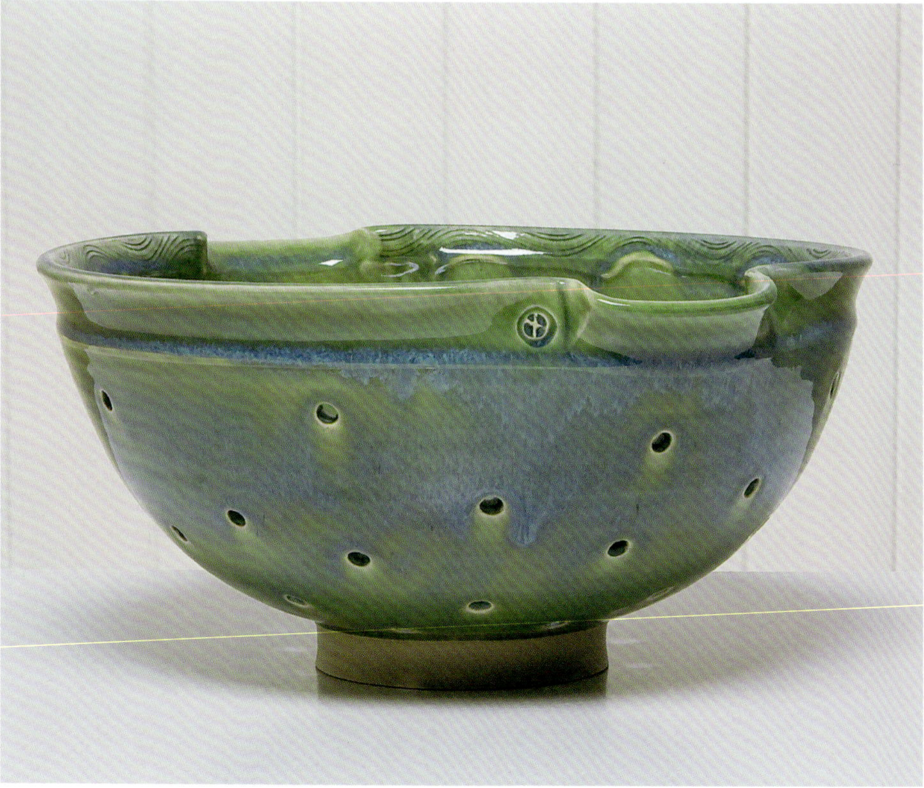

Arwyn Jones, colander, 2009. Thrown stoneware, diameter: 18 cm (7 in.). *Photo: Tony Burdett.*

Serving bowls

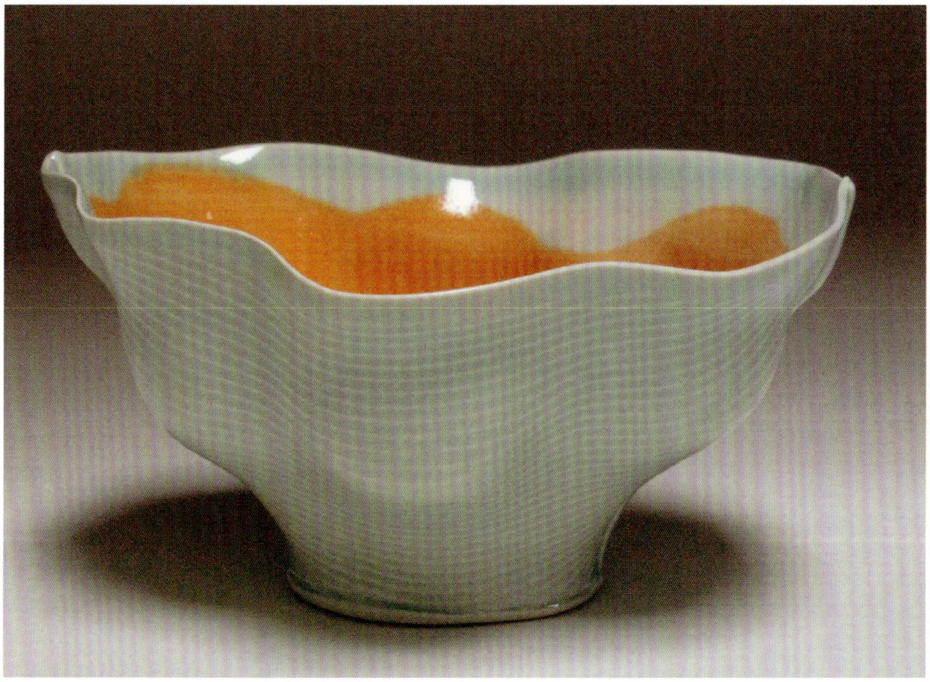

Scott Jennings, San Francisco, vortex bowl, 2010. Slab-built white stoneware, fired to cone 5 (1200°C/2192°F) in an electric kiln, width: 20 cm (8 in.). *Photo: courtesy of the artist.*

RAMP Ceramics (Rupert Johnstone and Alice Hartford), very large bowl, 2009. Thrown earthenware, slip-decorated. *Photo: courtesy of RAMP.*

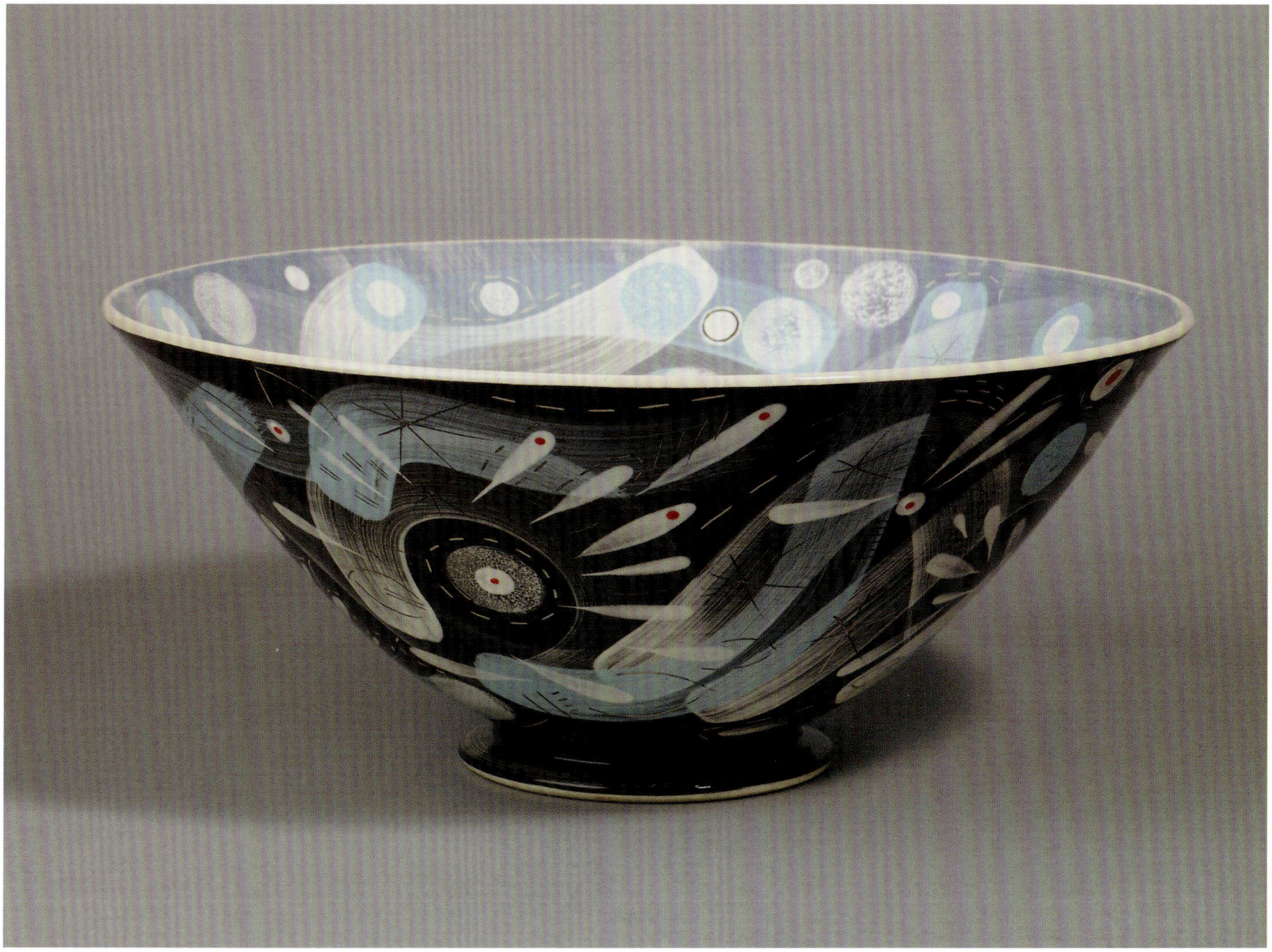

Dining bowls

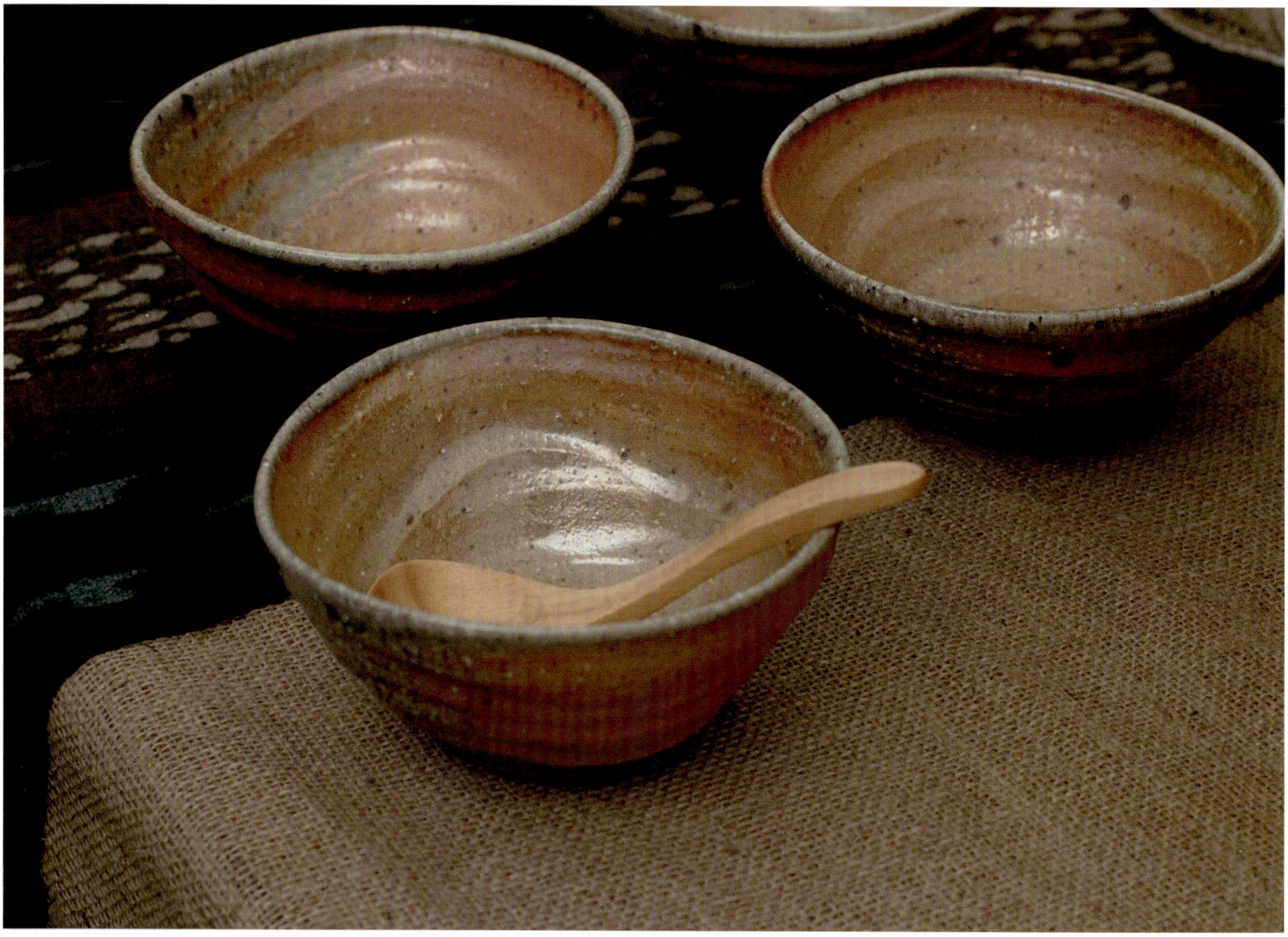

Peter Seabridge, bowls, 2011. Wood-fired stoneware. *Photo: Henry Bloomfield.*

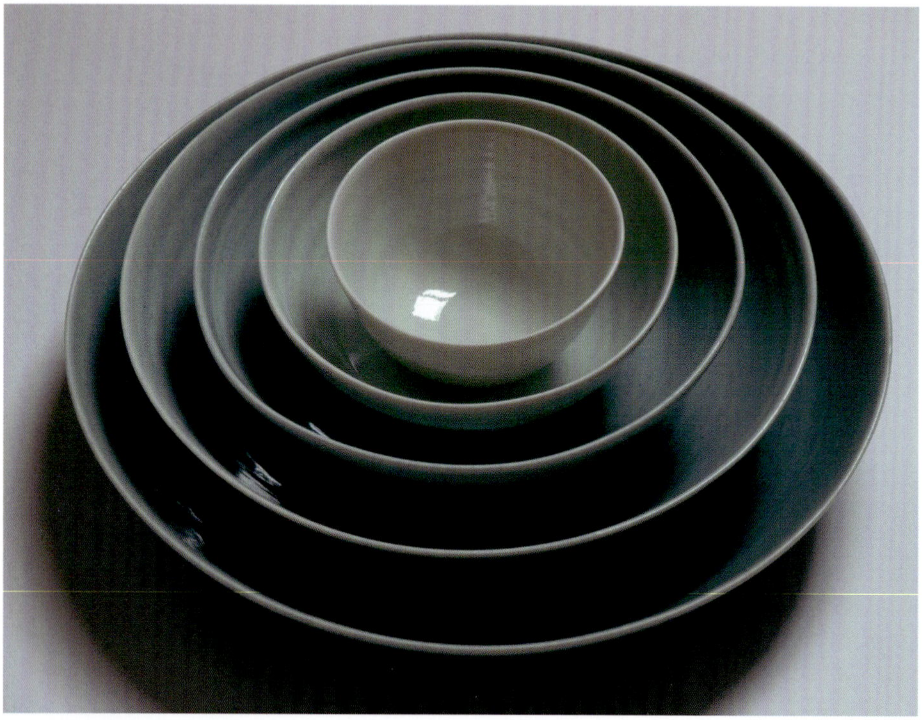

Daniel Smith, nest of five bowls, 2009. Finely thrown porcelain, diameter: 21 cm (8¼ in.). *Photo: Sonja Read.*

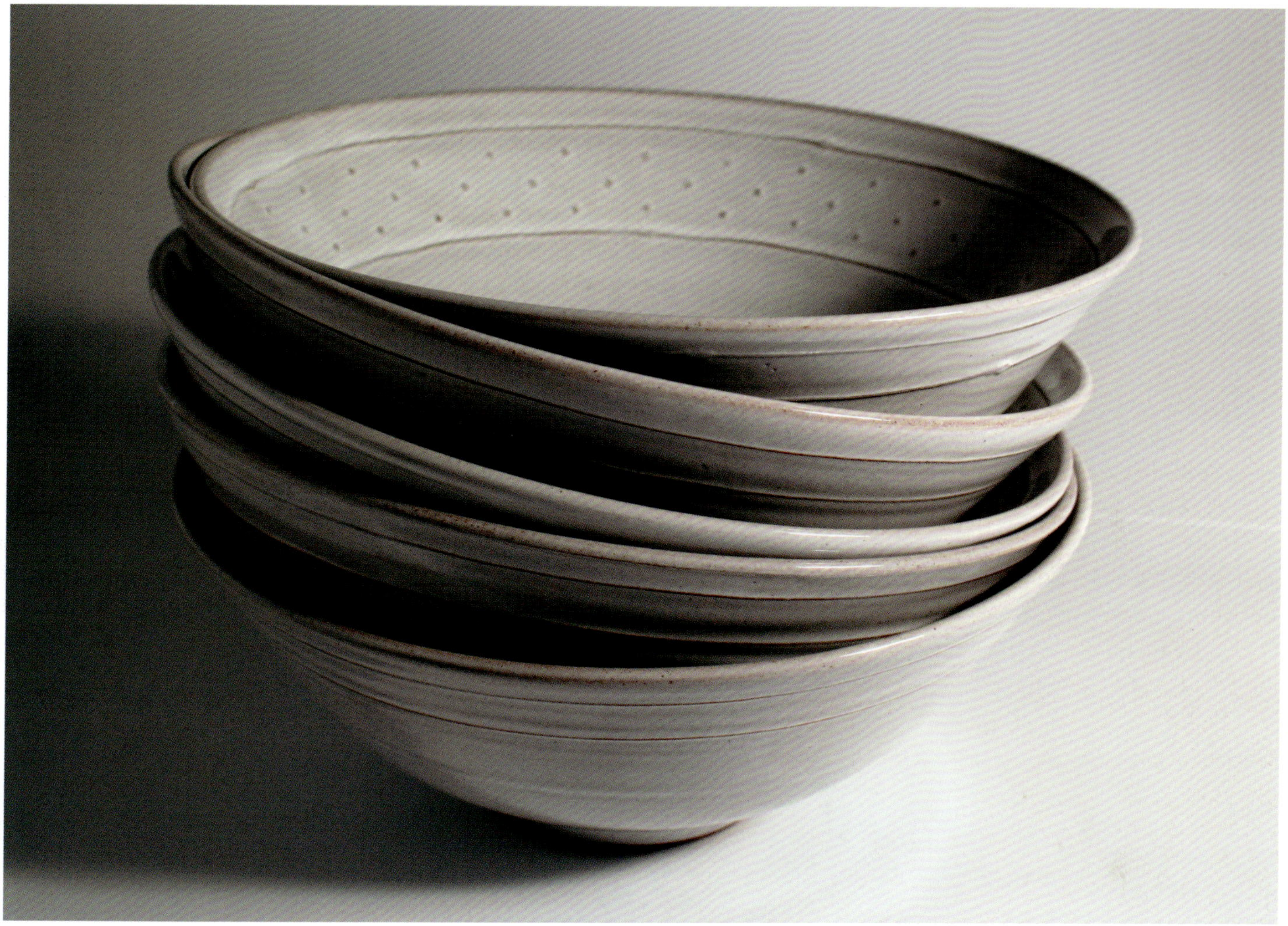

Kate Scott, bowls, 2011. Slip-trailed decoration, tin-glazed red earthenware, width: 17.5 cm (6¾ in.). *Photo: Kate Scott.*

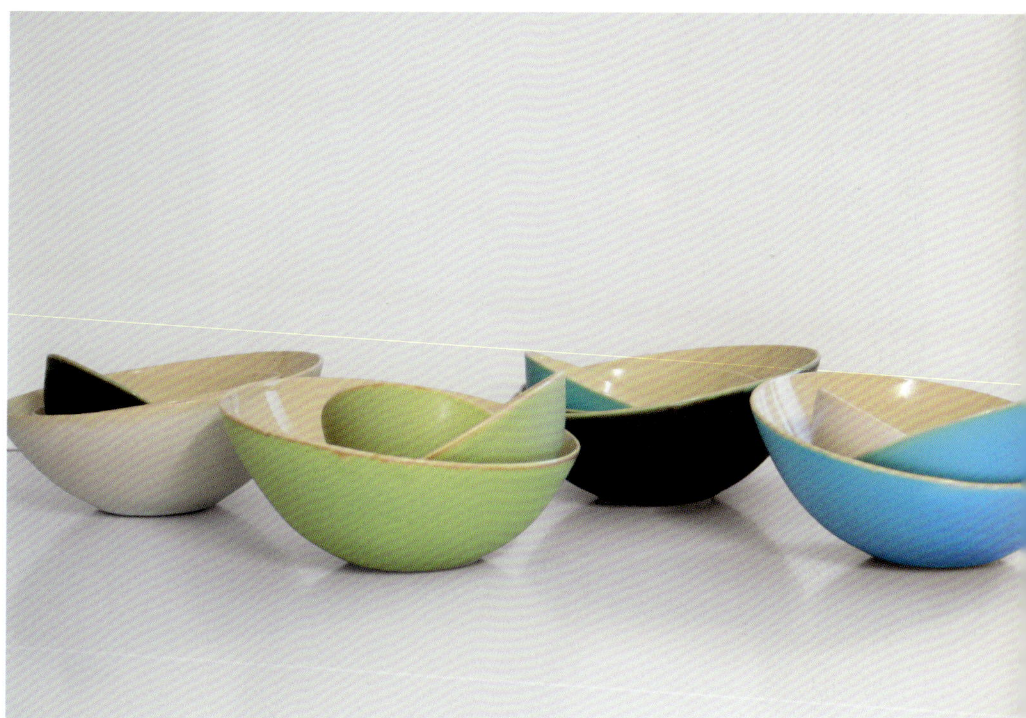

Sue Ure, Luna bowls, 2012. Thrown stoneware and porcelain mix, matt glazes. *Photo: by the artist.*

14 Cups, saucers and mugs

Functional shapes for cups and mugs

Mugs first appeared in England in the late medieval period, around the 14th century. They sometimes had grotesque modelled faces (hence the word 'mug', which is still used as slang for 'face' today). In China, small porcelain teacups without handles have been used since the Ming dynasty for drinking tea. Porcelain cups and saucers were first exported to Europe in the 17th century. Cup handles were added in the 1740s when European porcelain factories started making them, although the French still used footed bowls for drinking cafe au lait. When handles were added to cups, saucers needed to be shallower, so that there was space between the rim of the saucer and the handle to be able to pick up the cup. Saucers did not initially have a central well to prevent the cup from sliding around, but these appeared during the 18th century. At the beginning of the 20th century Jutta Sika of the Wiener Werkstätte designed a porcelain tea set including a cup with a pierced handle, and a saucer with a well to one side and space for a pastry on the other. The tea set was made by a porcelain factory in Vienna and decorated with abstract geometric patterns.

A cup on a saucer is usually filled with tea poured from a teapot, whereas a mug of tea is more often made using a teabag in the mug. Mugs therefore need to be able to withstand the thermal shock of having boiling water poured in, and the glaze should fit the clay body well to make it resilient to thermal stress.

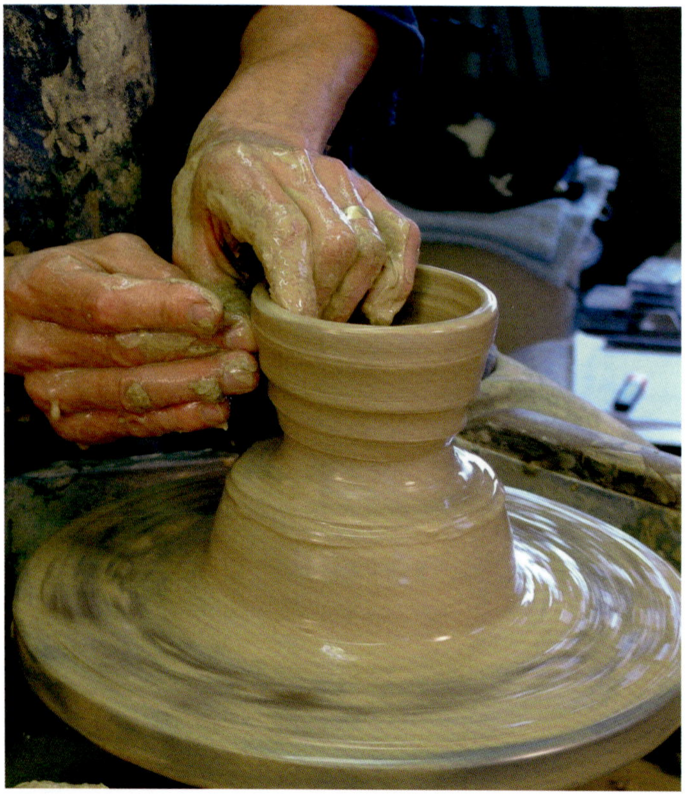

John Mathieson throwing a stoneware tea bowl off the hump. *Photo: John Mathieson.*

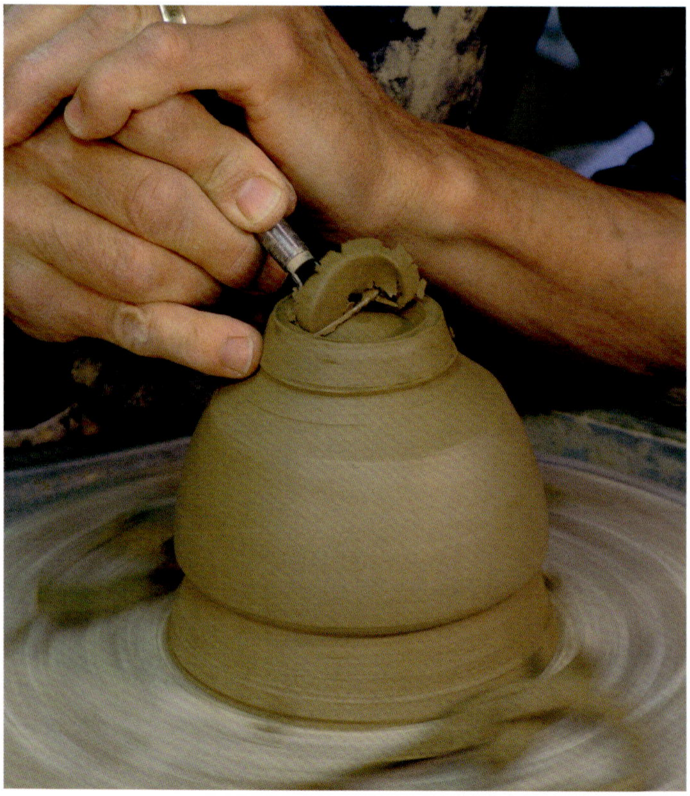

Turning the foot of a tea bowl placed upside down on a chuck. Foot-rings are sometimes notched so that water can drain out after they are washed. *Photo: John Mathieson.*

Oriental cups and beakers used in China and Japan usually have no handles. They are held at the rim with a supporting hand or saucer under the base. They are small and are filled frequently from a small teapot. Western mugs are often cylindrical or slightly flared, although rounded, full-bellied shapes of the same height have a greater capacity. Cups should have a fine, thin rim for drinking from and handles should be large enough to allow one or two fingers through without touching the hot cup. Handles are usually strap-like or oval in cross section and should be strong but comfortable to hold.

Egg cups can be made in the form of a cup on a stem or as a small, slightly flared beaker, which should fit a range of egg sizes. The important measurement is the inside diameter, which should be the same as that of a large egg, or about 4.5 cm (1¾ in.). Egg cups are used in Europe to eat soft-boiled eggs but are not common in the US.

Making methods

Mugs and cups can be made by throwing, slipcasting or jolleying methods. They can also be slab-built or made by extruding a hollow tube and adding a base. Handles can be pulled, extruded or slipcast, and attached when leatherhard. The cup and handle should be at the same state of dryness when they are joined, otherwise the different shrinkage rates will cause them to come apart. Saucers are made in a similar way to bowls or plates (see p. 130).

Lars P. Soendergaard Gregersen trained as a production thrower at Brangstrup Stoneware in Denmark. He moved to London and set up Soendergaard Design in 1995, settling at his current workshop in Suffolk in 2000. His work is functional, with clean lines and a Scandinavian feel. He makes thrown porcelain tableware with softly coloured matt glazes fired in a gas kiln to 1260°C (2300°F). His pots have flat bases with no foot-rings and minimal turning to enable fast production. He is able to make 8,000 pots a year by hand, with the help of one part-time assistant. He produces several different ranges for retailers including David Mellor, Nicole Farhi Home and Toast.

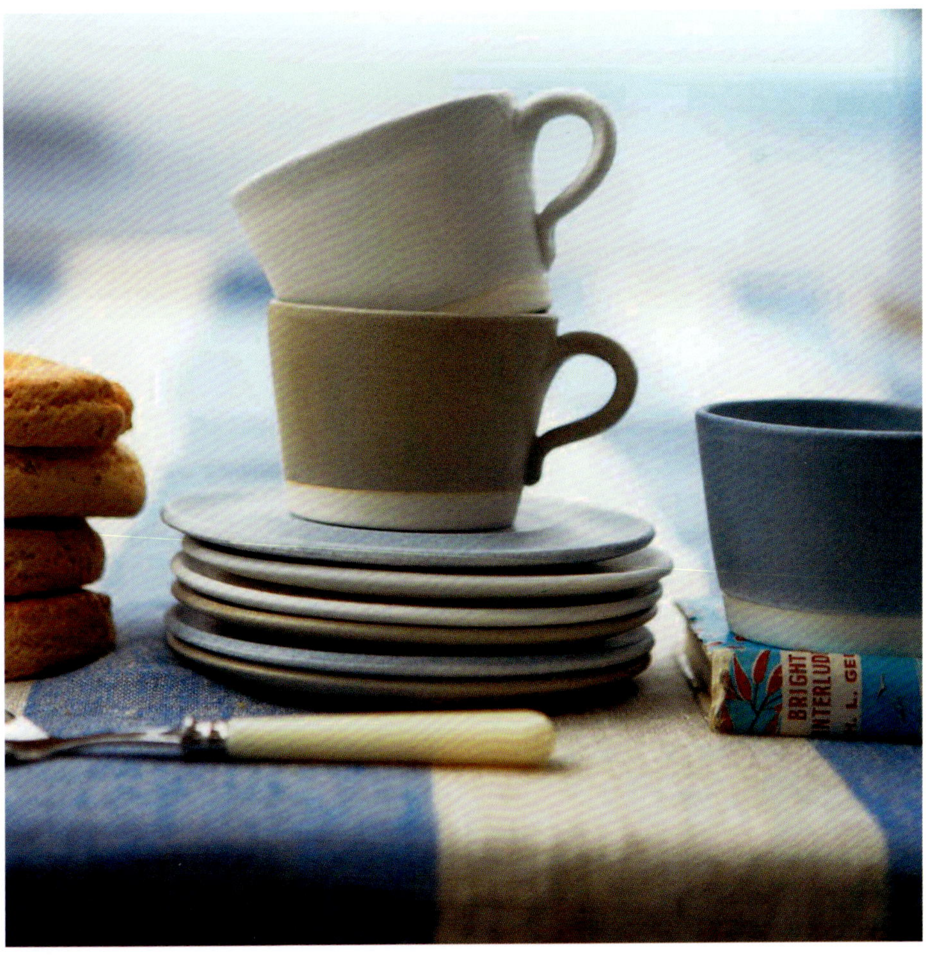

Soendergaard Design, Eve cups and saucers for Toast in stone white, sage grey and blue, 2011. Cup height: 5.7 cm (2¼ in), saucer diameter: 13 cm (5 in.). *Photo: Jonathan West for Toast.*

Cups and saucers

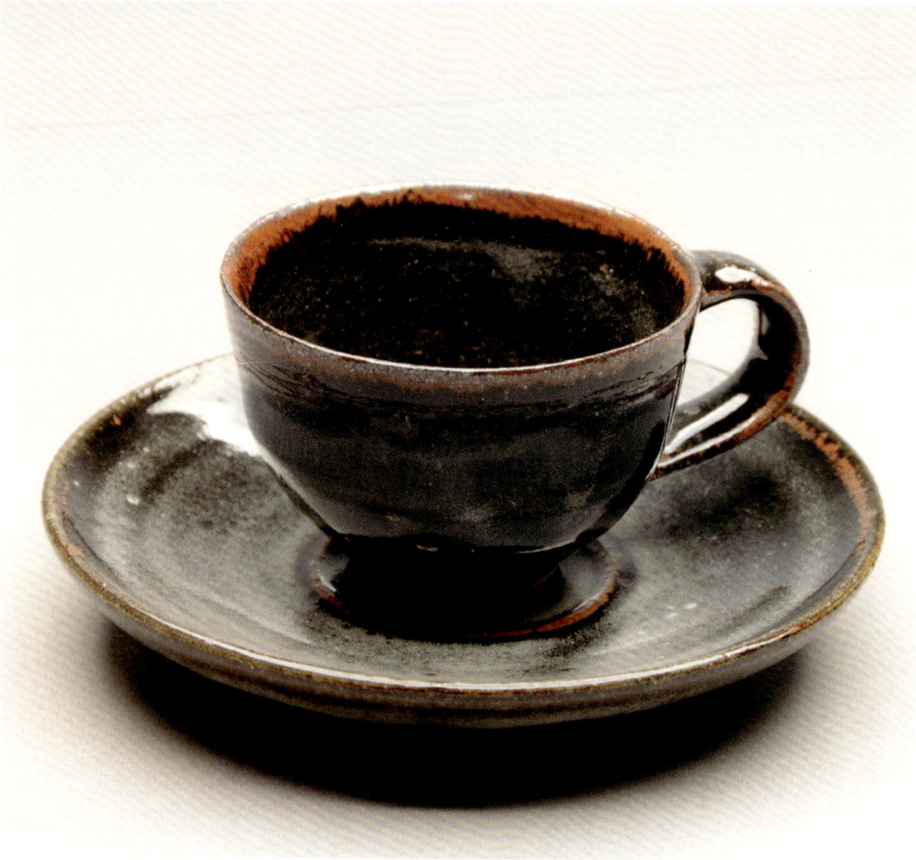

Peter Gboko, stoneware cup and saucer, 1960s. Made at the Abuja Pottery, Nigeria, run by Michael Cardew. *Photo: Jonathan Thompson.*

Arwyn Jones, coffee cups and saucers, thrown and stoneware, 2009. Diameter: 11 cm (4½ in.). *Photo: Tony Burdett.*

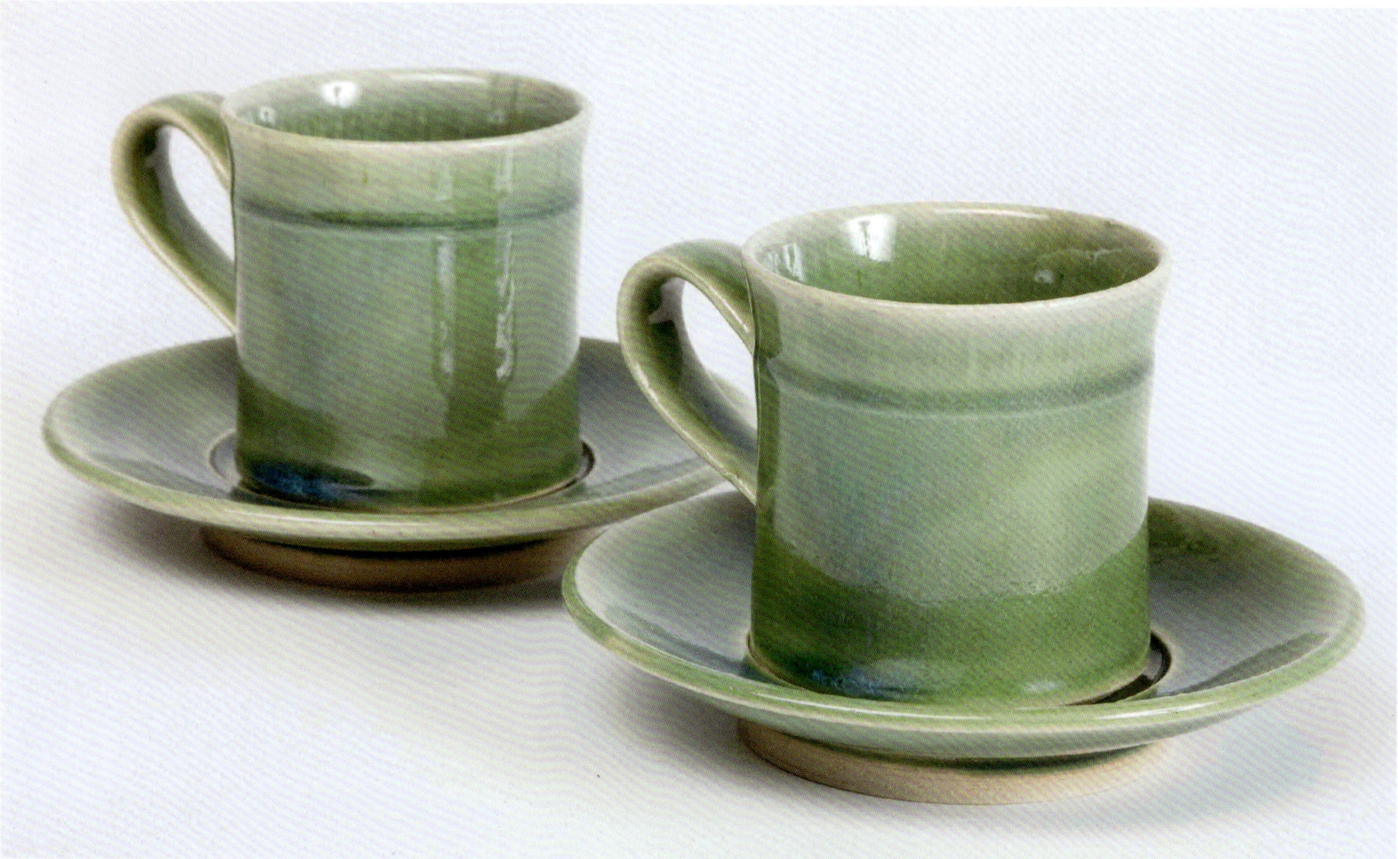

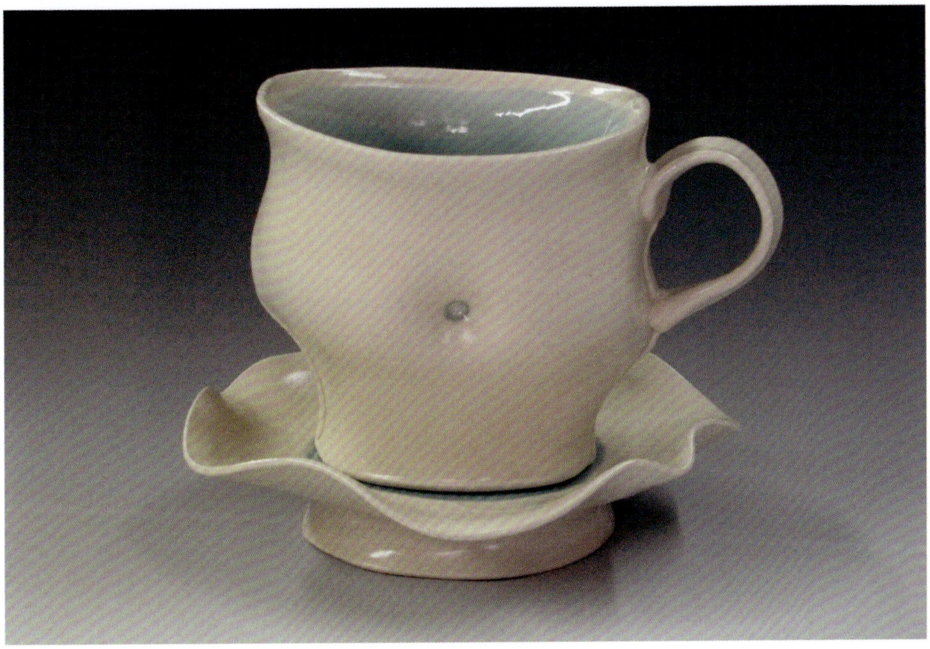

Scott Jennings, San Francisco, pillow cup and saucer, 2010. Slab-built white stoneware, fired to cone 5 (1200°C/2192°F) in an electric kiln, height: 13 cm (5 in.). *Photo: courtesy of the artist.*

Mini Moderns for Magpie, Festival porcelain espresso cups and saucers, 2011. Launched on the 60th anniversary of the Festival of Britain, designed by Keith Stevenson and Mark Hampshire, diameter: 11 cm (4¼ in.). *Photo: courtesy of Mini Moderns.*

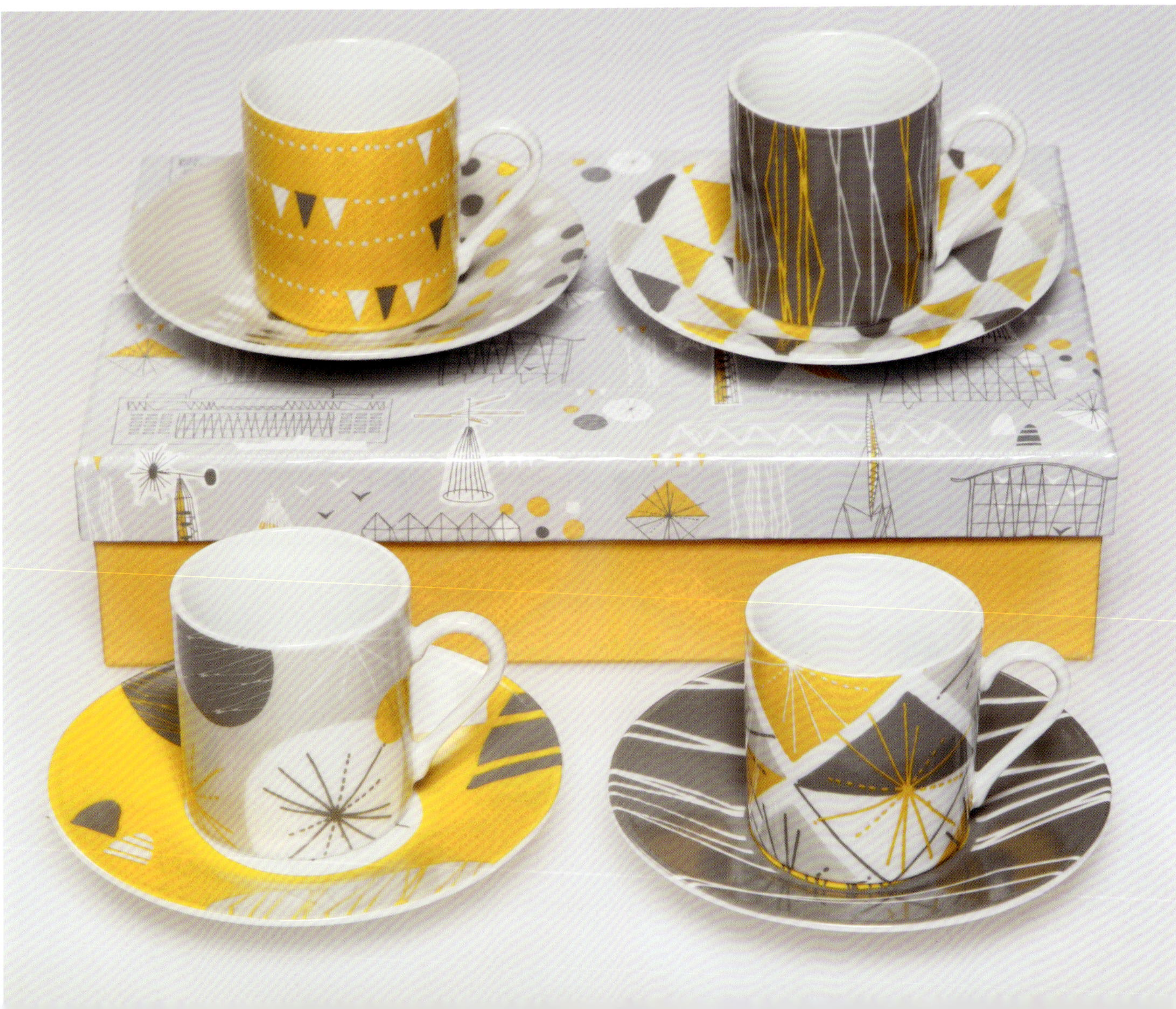

Mugs

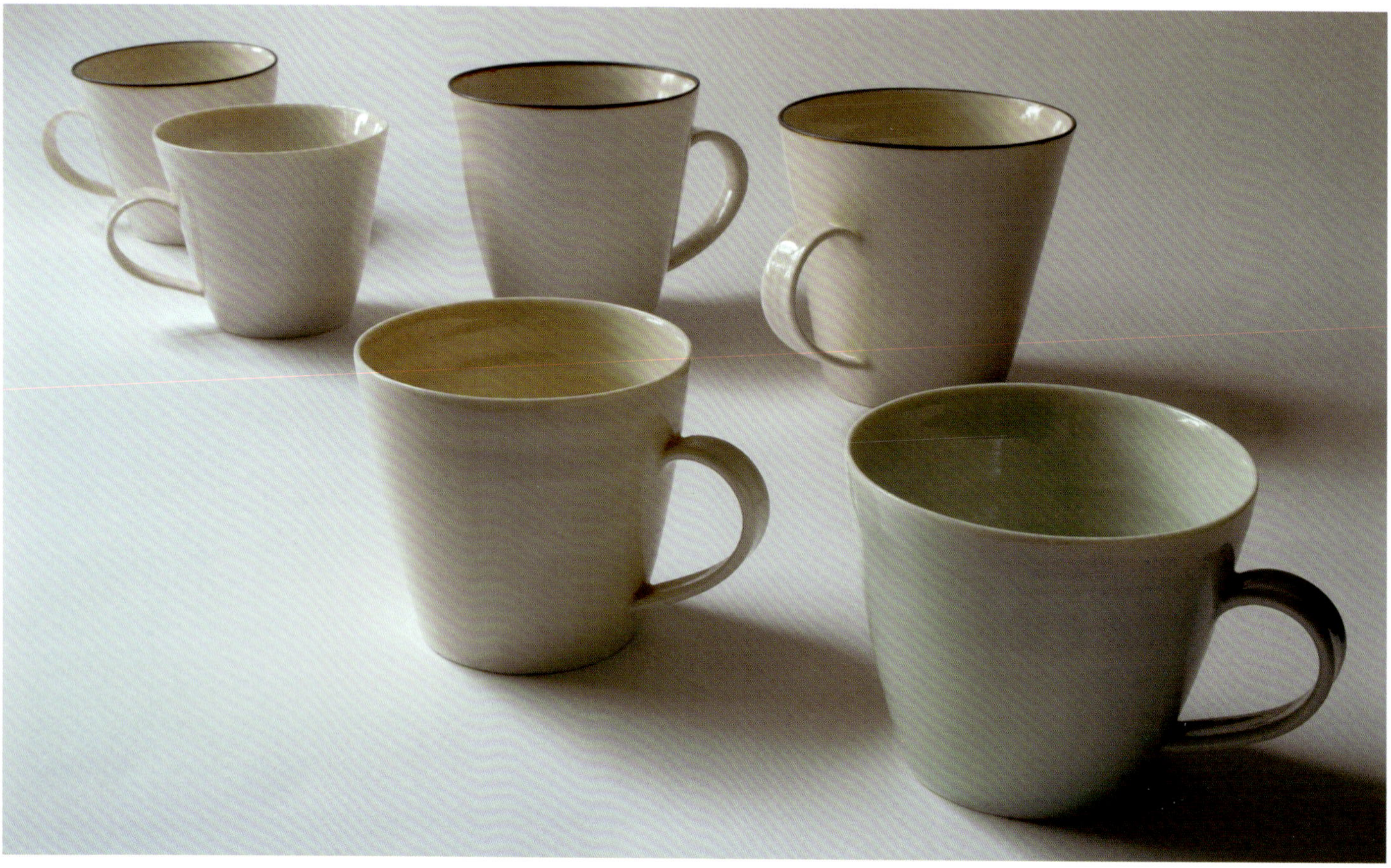

Daniel Smith, large mugs, 2009. Finely thrown porcelain, some mugs with iron oxide on the rim, height: 10 cm (4 in.). *Photo: Sonja Read.*

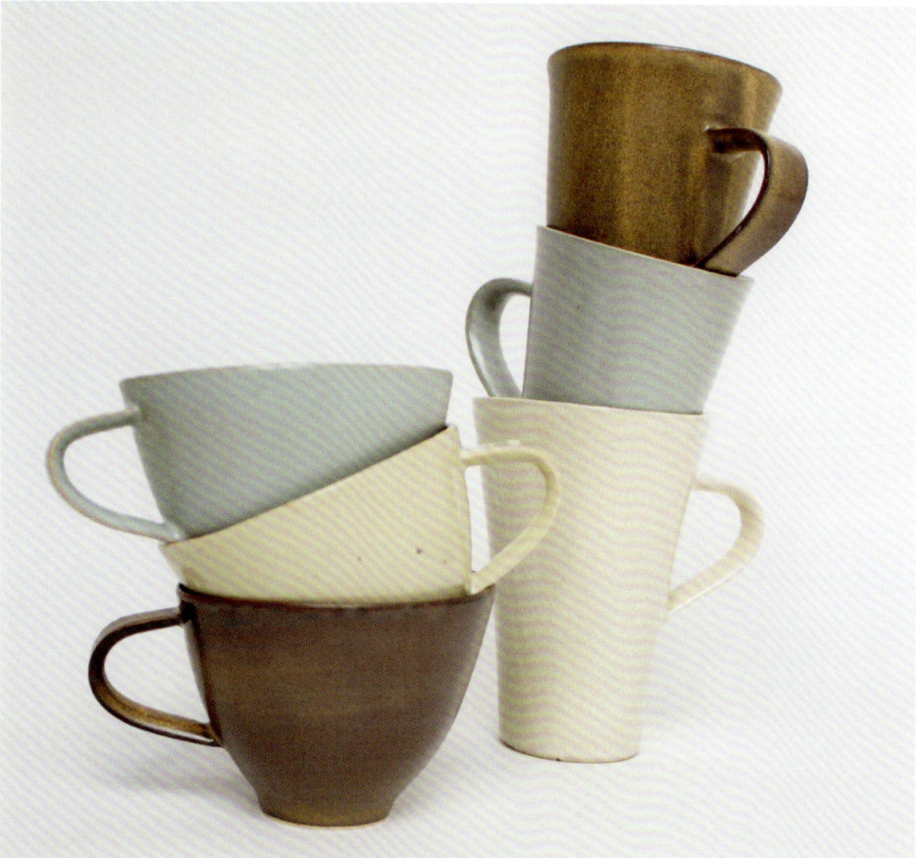

Stuart Carey, coffee cups and mugs, 2011. Thrown stoneware with matt glazes, height: 12 cm (4¾ in.). *Photo: Stuart Carey.*

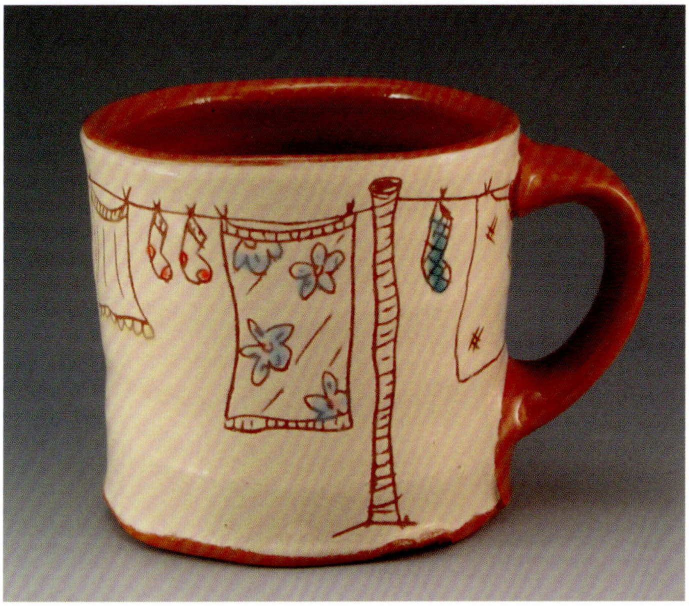

Ron Philbeck, North Carolina, Laundry Line mug, 2010. Slip-decorated earthenware, fired to cone 04 (1060°C/1940°F) in oxidation, height: 9 cm (3½ in.). *Photo: courtesy of the artist.*

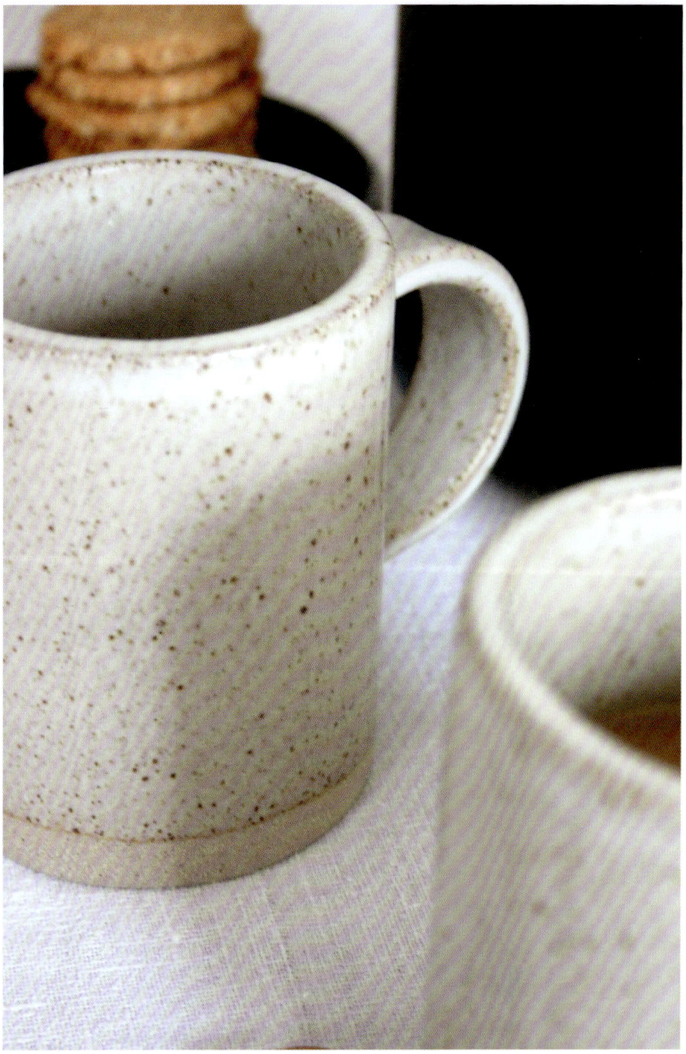

Tom Butcher, extruded mugs, 2011. Loch Long Stoneware range, height: 11 cm (4¼ in.). *Photo: Rosie Brown.*

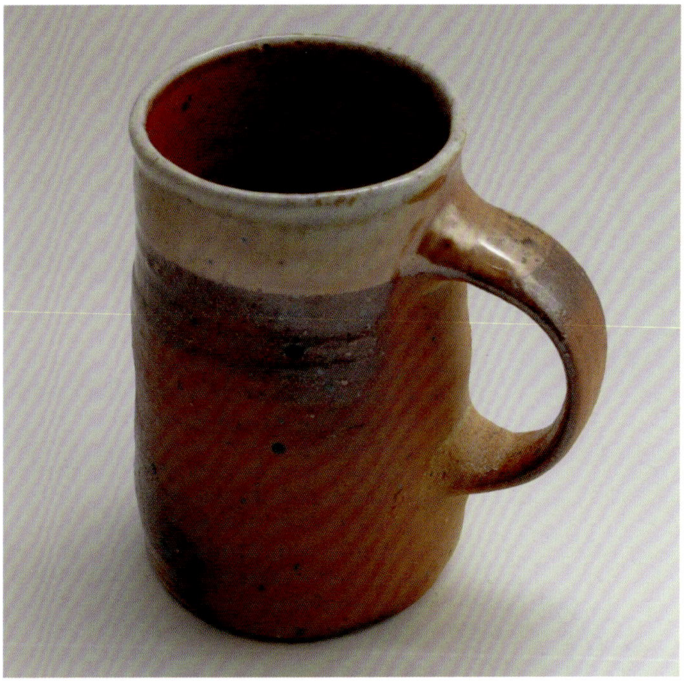

Nic Collins, wood-fired stoneware mug, 2009. Shino glaze, height: 11 cm (4¼ in.). *Photo: Henry Bloomfield.*

Beakers and egg cups

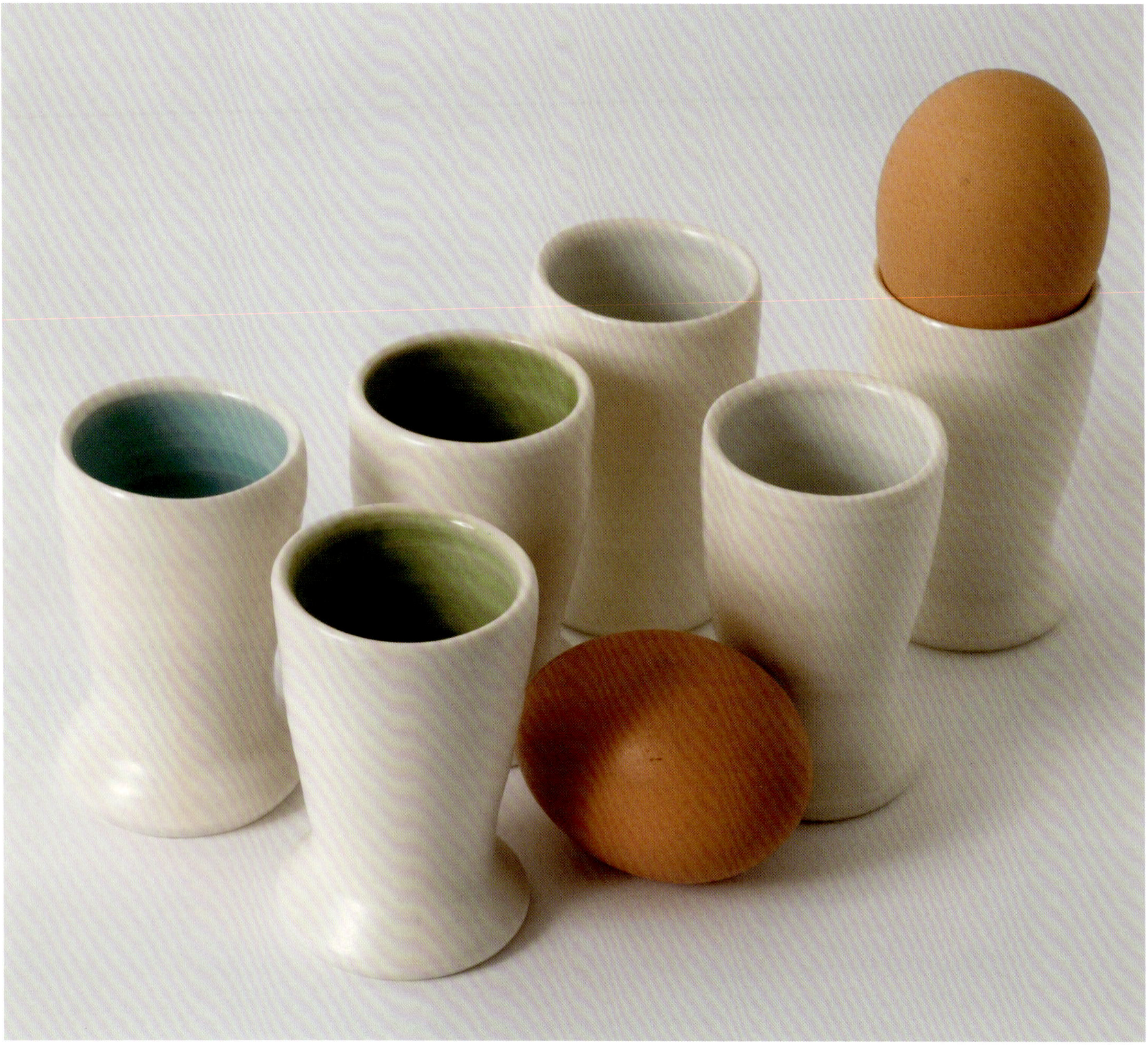

Linda Bloomfield, egg cups, 2007.
Thrown porcelain, coloured glazes, height:
7 cm (2¾ in.). *Photo: Jacqui Hurst.*

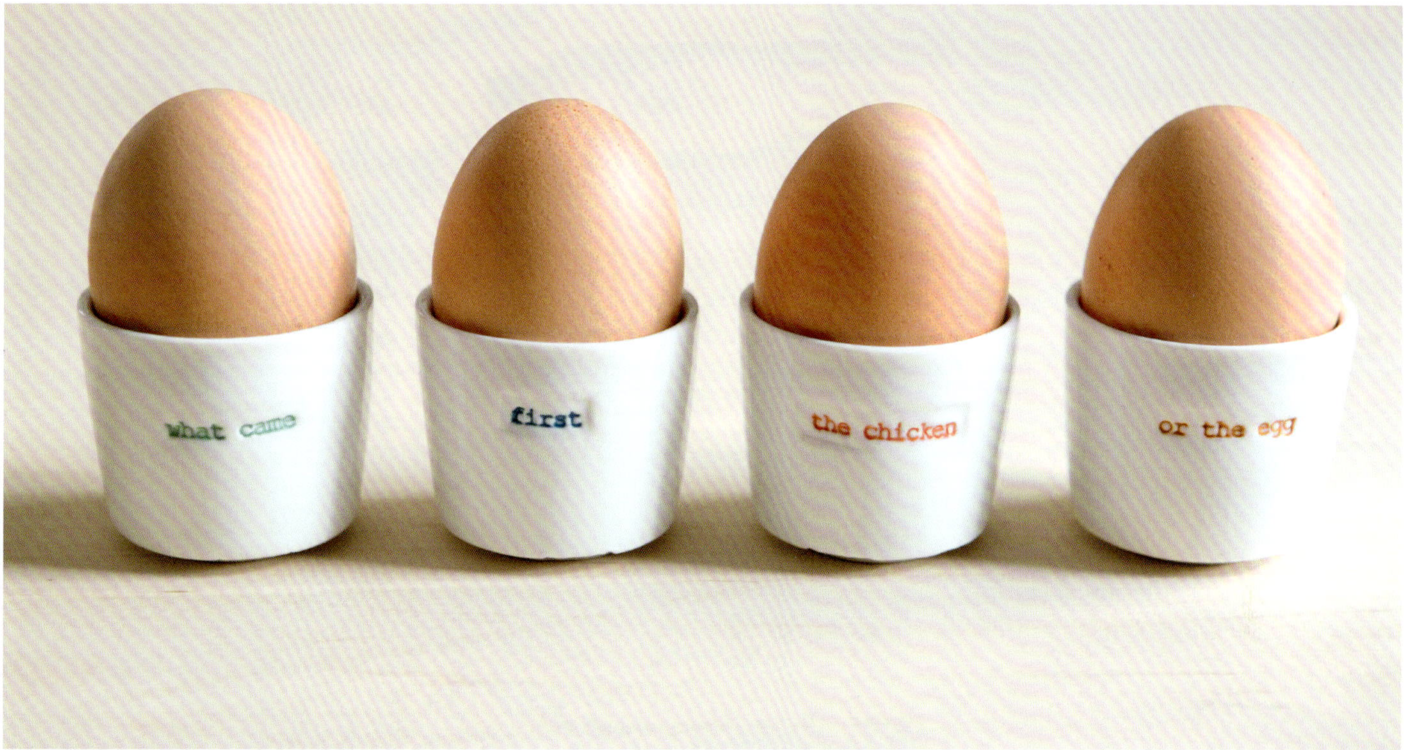

Make International, KBJ Word range egg cups, 2009. High-white porcelain, designed by Keith Brymer Jones, diameter 4.8 cm (2 in.). *Photo: Jake Fitzjones.*

Derek Wilson, thrown, squashed tall porcelain beakers with dark celadon glaze, 2011. *Photo: Christopher Martin.*

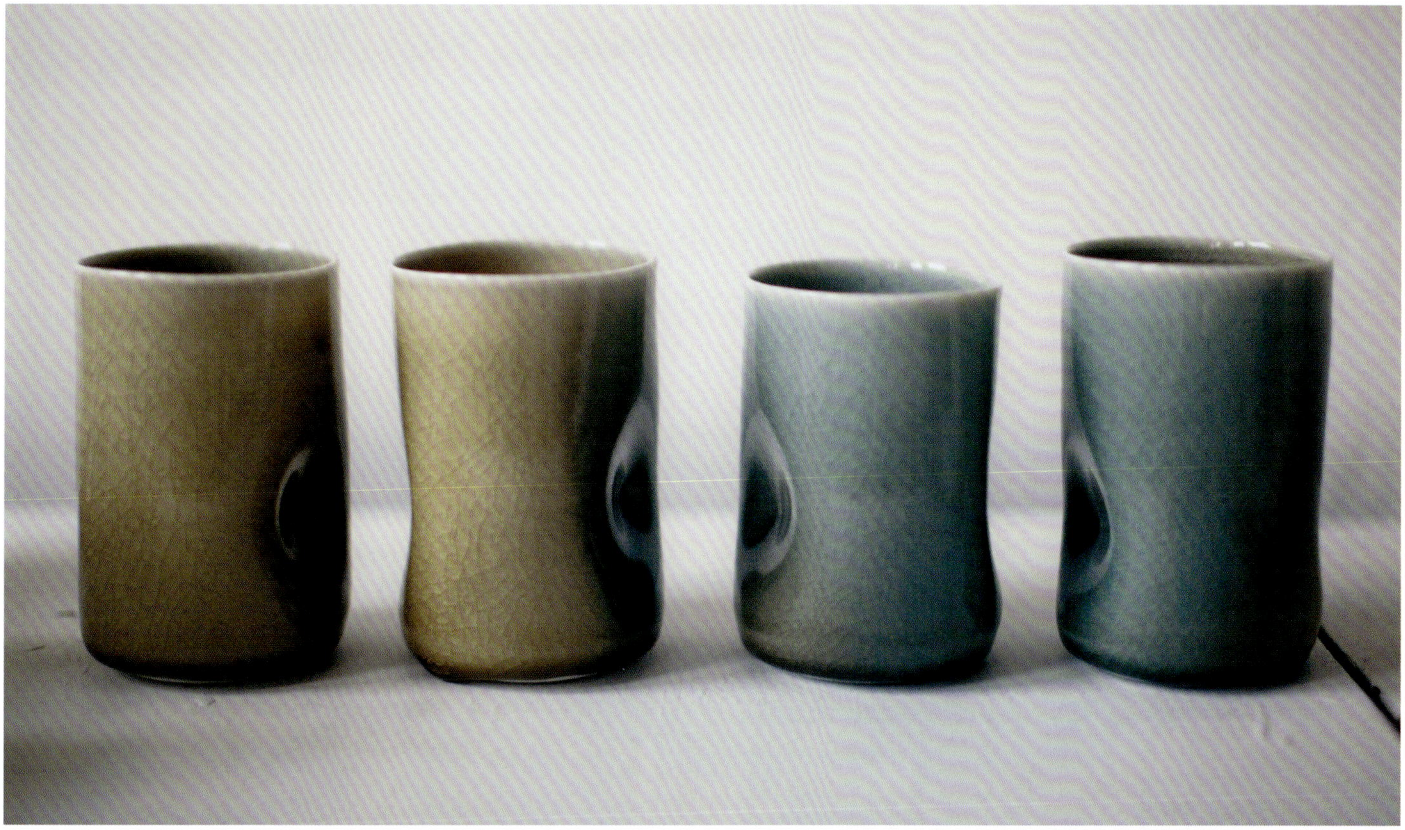

15 Jugs

Jug forms

One of the most appealing forms is the traditional jug or pitcher. Jugs can be cylindrical, conical or full-bellied. Medieval baluster jugs consist of a wide, stable foot, a swelling belly and a tall, narrow neck. The widest part of the belly of a jug was traditionally high up, to raise the centre of gravity for ease of tipping and pouring. Traditional English jugs have a round, robust form with the handle starting at the neck and ending at the widest part of the belly. When lifting a large jug, the hand fits easily through a handle stretching from neck to belly. Shorter, rounder jugs were also made in a range of sizes. However, the handles on smaller jugs must spring out further from the body in order to accommodate several fingers. Some jugs have a thumb stop, which prevents the hand slipping while pouring (see Ray Finch's jug with stopper on p. 127). A strap handle with a rectangular or oval cross section gives a better grip than a round one, although round side handles are easy to grip (see Reiko Nagata's teapot on p. 106).

Sauce boats became popular in the 18th century when French sauces such as mayonnaise were introduced. Sauce boats are often oval with a high-walled lip for better

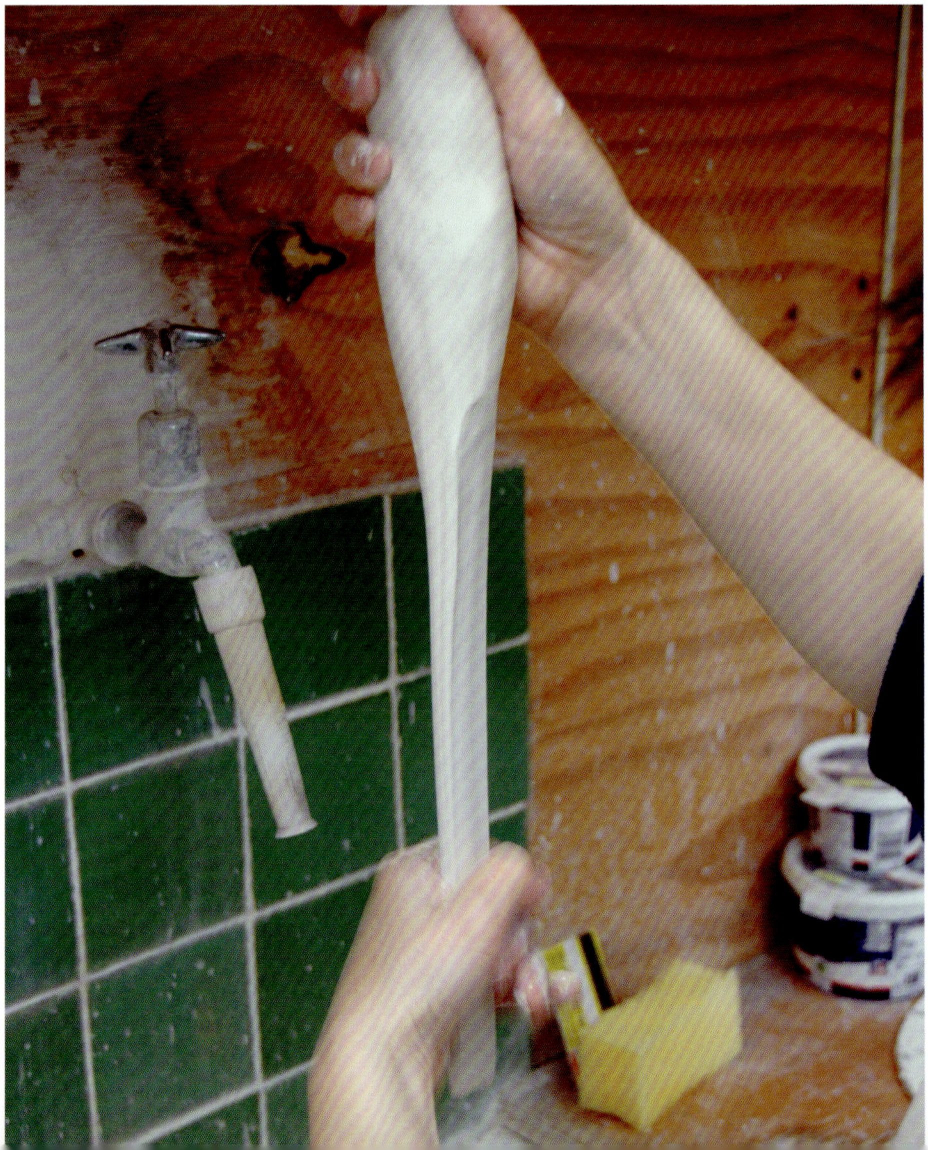

Pulling a handle. *Photo: Henry Bloomfield.*

pouring (see p. 29). Lipped bowls work best for thick sauces, which are poured slowly. Oil and vinaigrette can be stored in and poured from tall, bottle-shaped jugs.

In Victorian times jugs were sometimes cylindrically shaped with wide ribs like a milk churn. Jugs copied from the Dutch style had a rounded body with a short cylindrical neck. The rim of the jug was sometimes cut away to make the lip higher than the rest of the rim for better pouring (see Judi Tavill's creamer on p. 67). A narrow base makes a jug look elegant but is less stable than a wide base.

Making methods

Jugs can easily be made by throwing on the wheel, particularly with very plastic clays like red earthenware. Pouring lips can be pulled up and thinned while the pot is still on the wheel, then formed into a lip using a wet finger. The lip should be sharp enough to cut off the flow of the liquid without dribbling, but not so sharp that it chips easily. Some potters make the inside edge of the rim higher than the outside edge, so that the sharp rim on the inside will be protected from chipping. Jugs can also be extruded as a hollow tube or slipcast from a mould made from a thrown or modelled master.

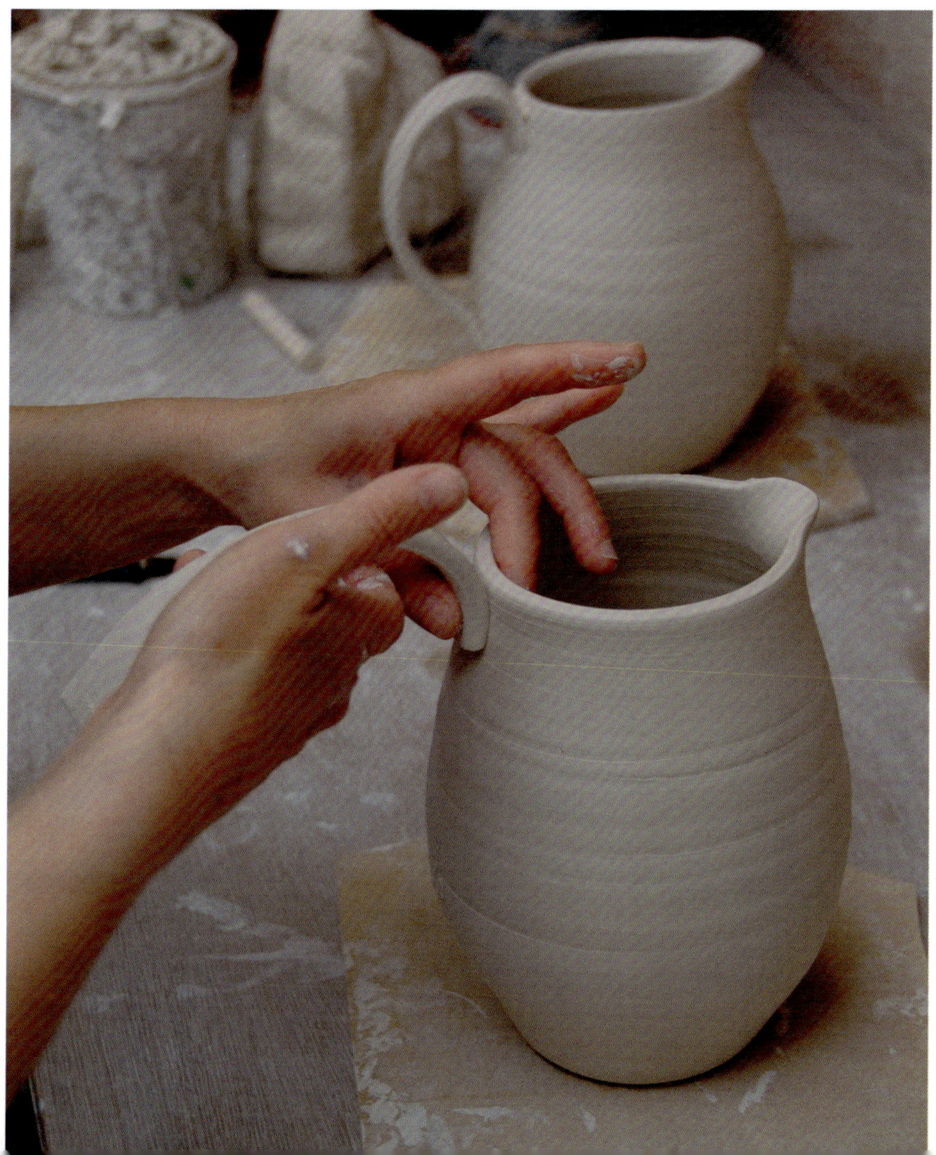

Attaching the handle to a jug after scoring with a knife and applying slip. *Photo: Henry Bloomfield.*

Tall jugs

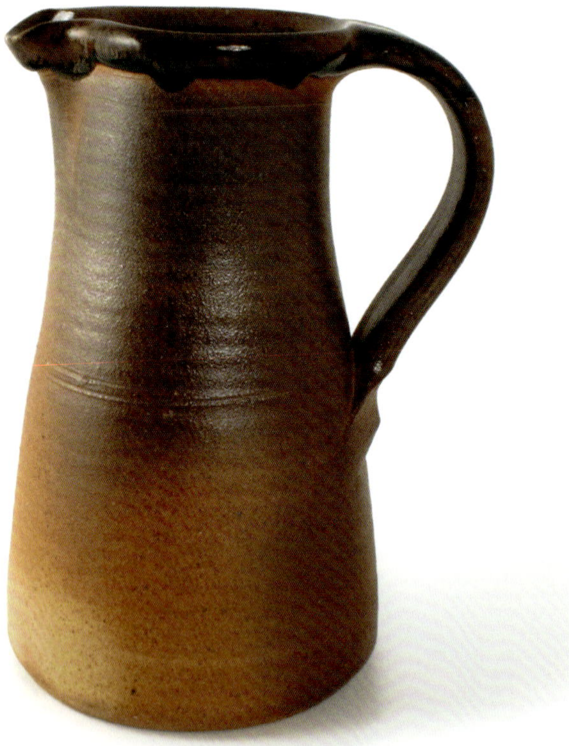

John Leach, large jug, 2010. Wood-fired stoneware with tenmoku glaze on the inside, height: 24.5 cm (9¾ in.). *Photo: Carole Melbourne.*

Tom Butcher, extruded vinaigrette jug, 2011. Loch Long stoneware, height: 11 cm (4¼ in.). *Photo: Rosie Brown.*

Kate Scott, thrown jugs, 2011. Slip-trailed decoration, tin-glazed red earthenware, height: 20.5 cm (8 in.). *Photo: Kate Scott.*

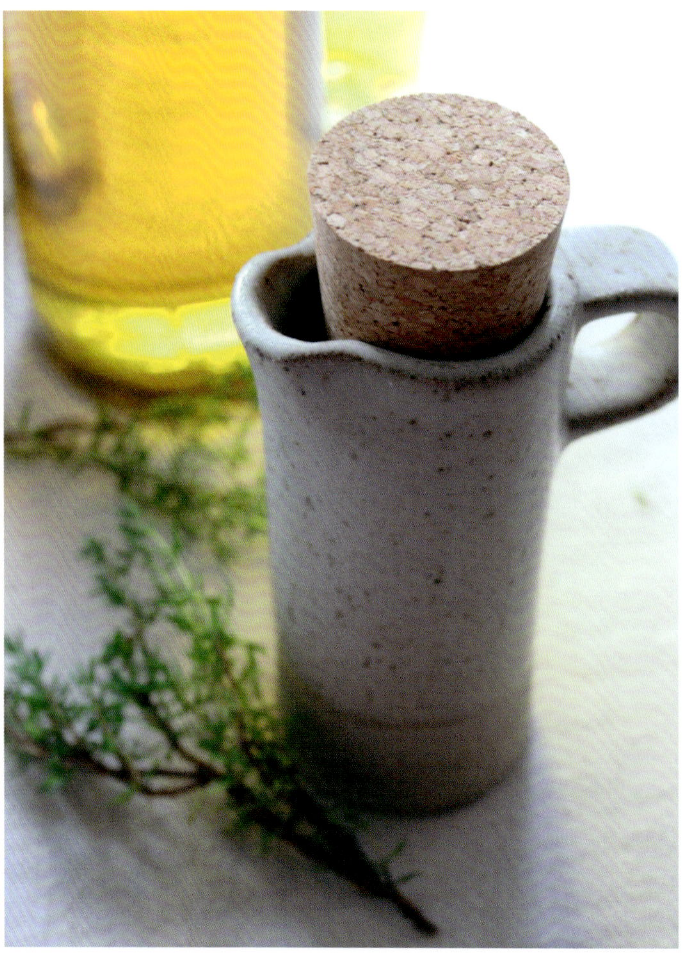

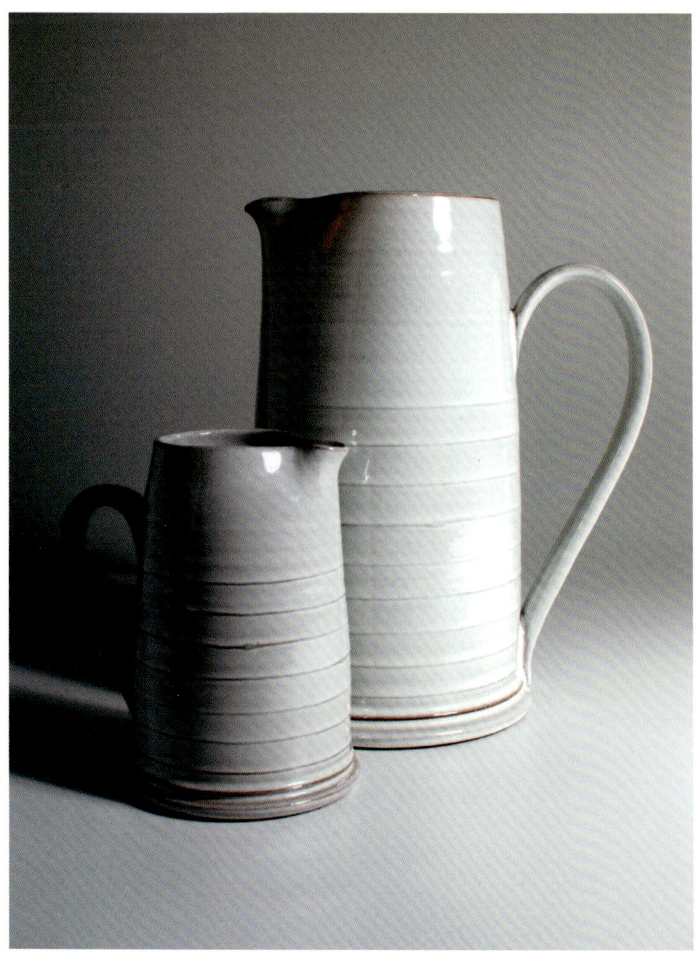

Rounded jugs

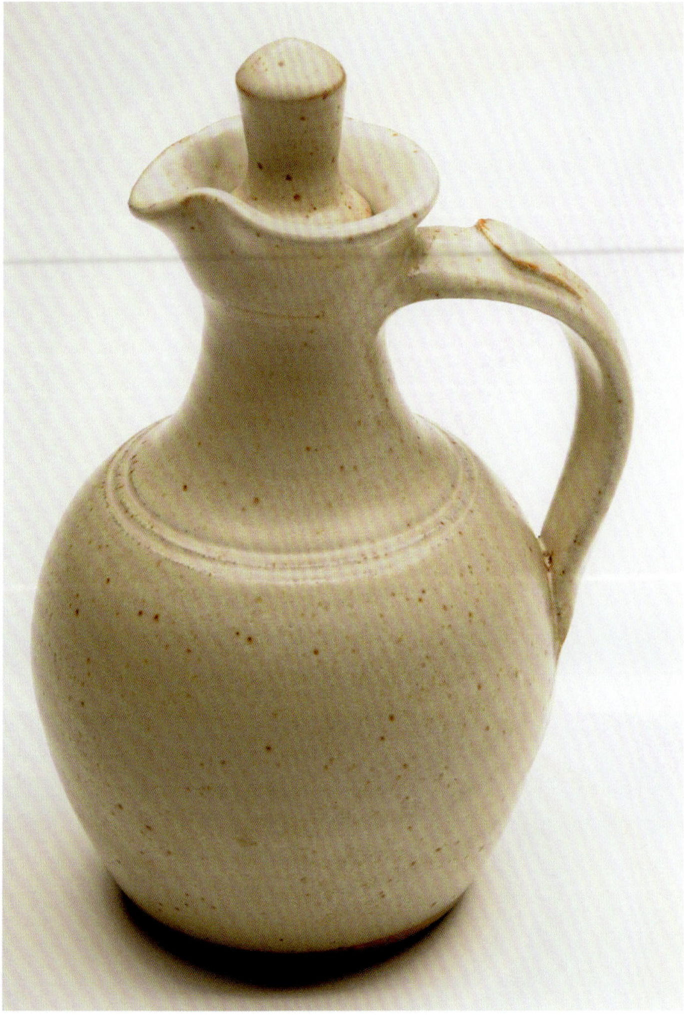

Ray Finch, Winchcombe Pottery, jug with stopper, 1990s. Thrown stoneware with oatmeal glaze, height: 12 cm (4¾ in.). *Photo: Jonathan Thompson.*

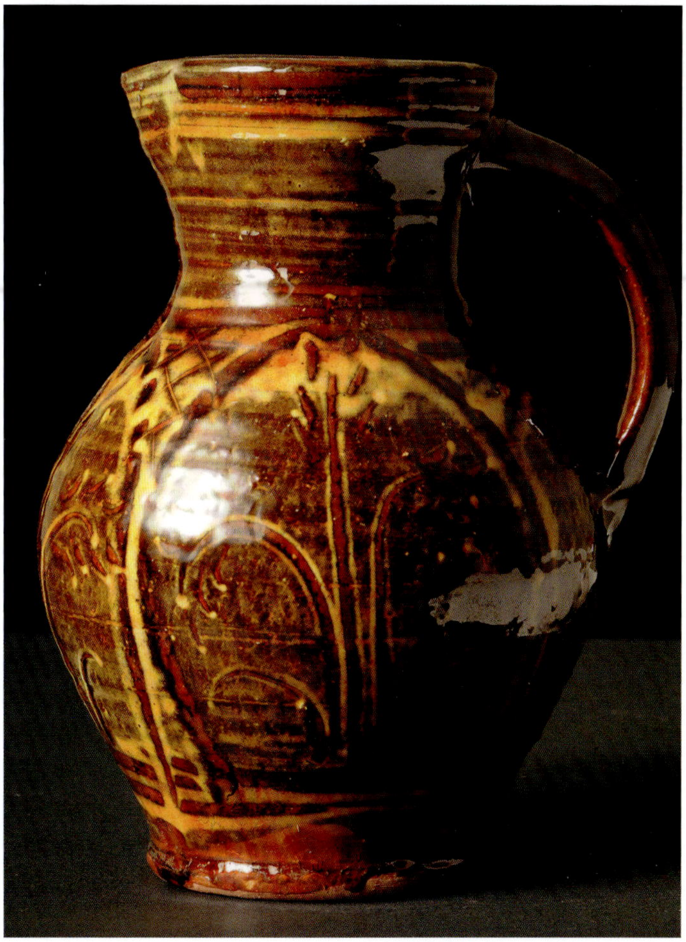

Doug Fitch, jug, 2011. Thrown red earthenware with slip decoration and galena glaze, wood-fired, height: 23 cm (9 in.). *Photo: Jonathan Thompson.*

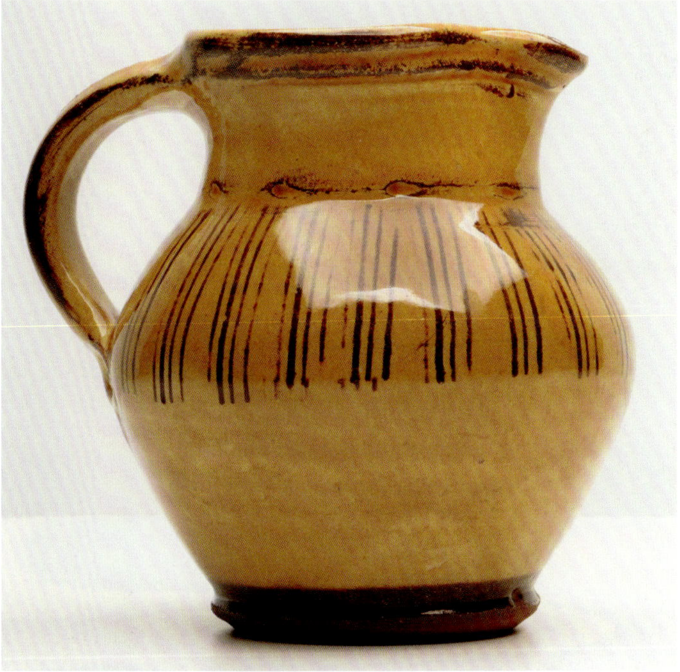

Deborah Mitchell, Cornwall, jug, 2009. Thrown red earthenware with sgraffito decoration through white slip, height: 13.5 cm (5¼ in.). *Photo: Jonathan Thompson.*

Susanne Lukàcs-Ringel, Germany, jugs, 2011. Salt-glazed porcelain, height: 20 cm (8 in.). *Photo: Christoph Ulrich.*

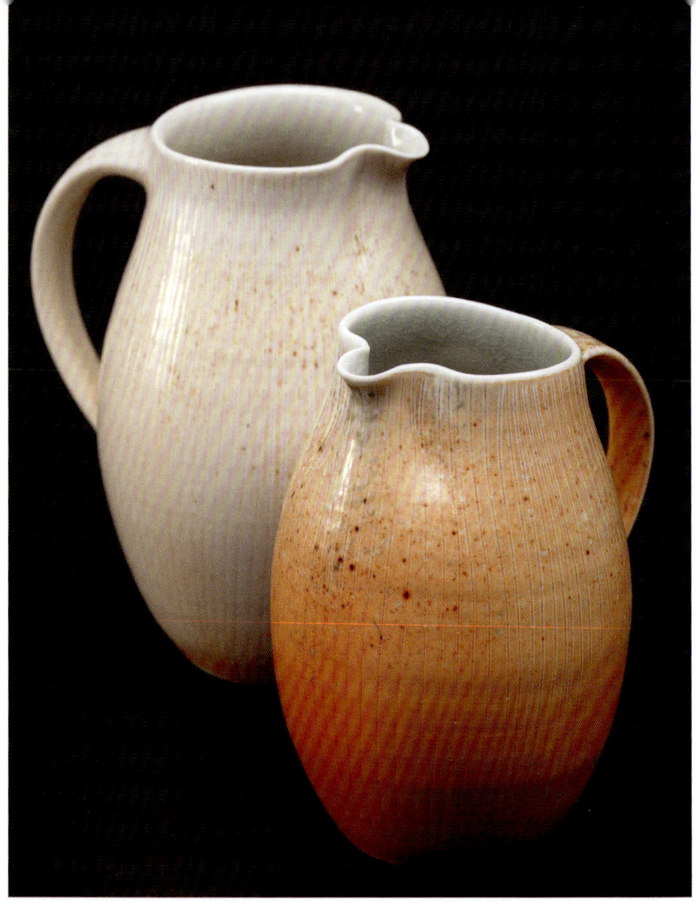

Courtney Murphy, ewers, 2011. Mailoica-decorated earthenware, fired to cone 02 (1120°C/2048°F), height: 21.5 cm (8½ in.). *Photo: by the artist.*

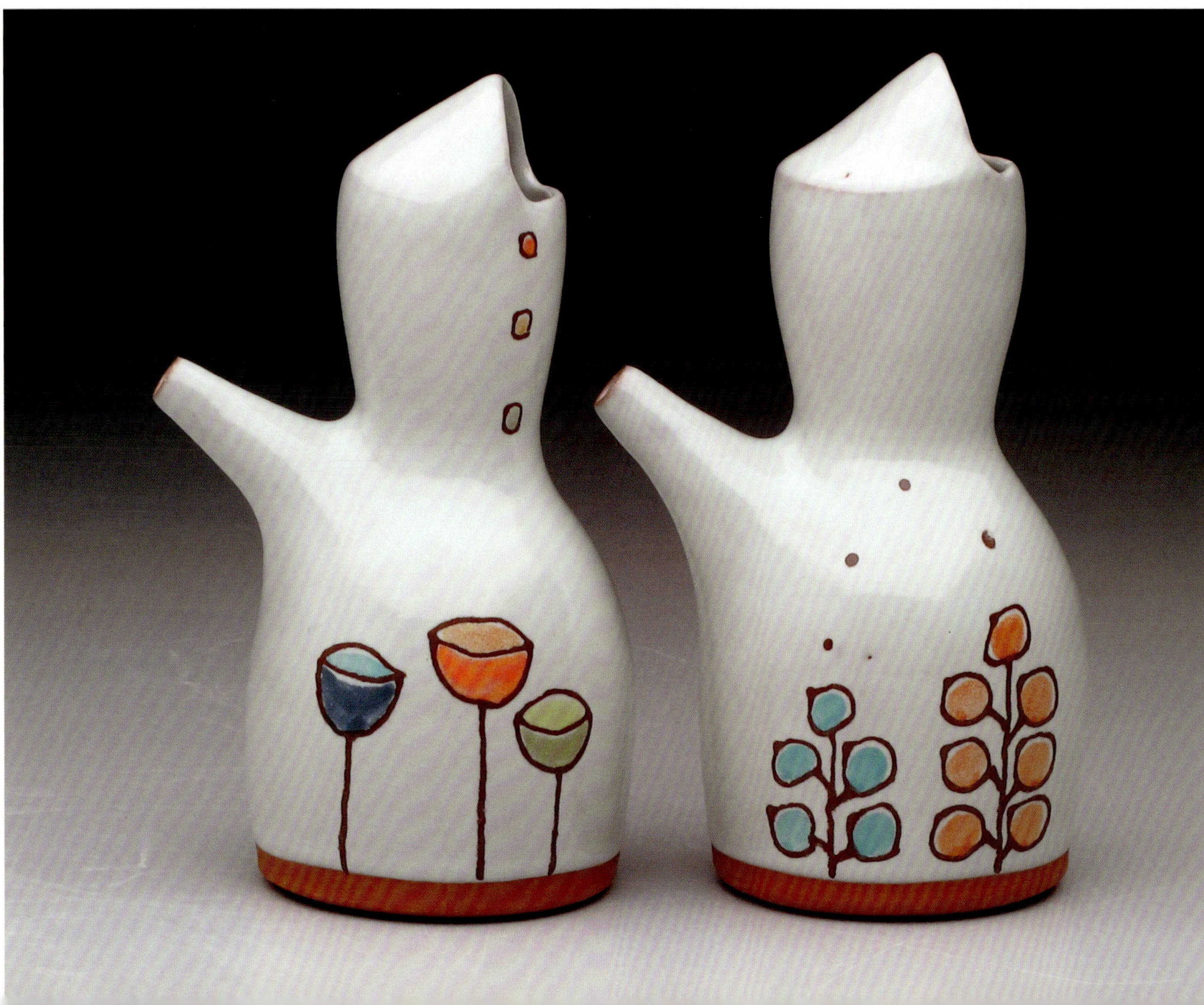

Small jugs

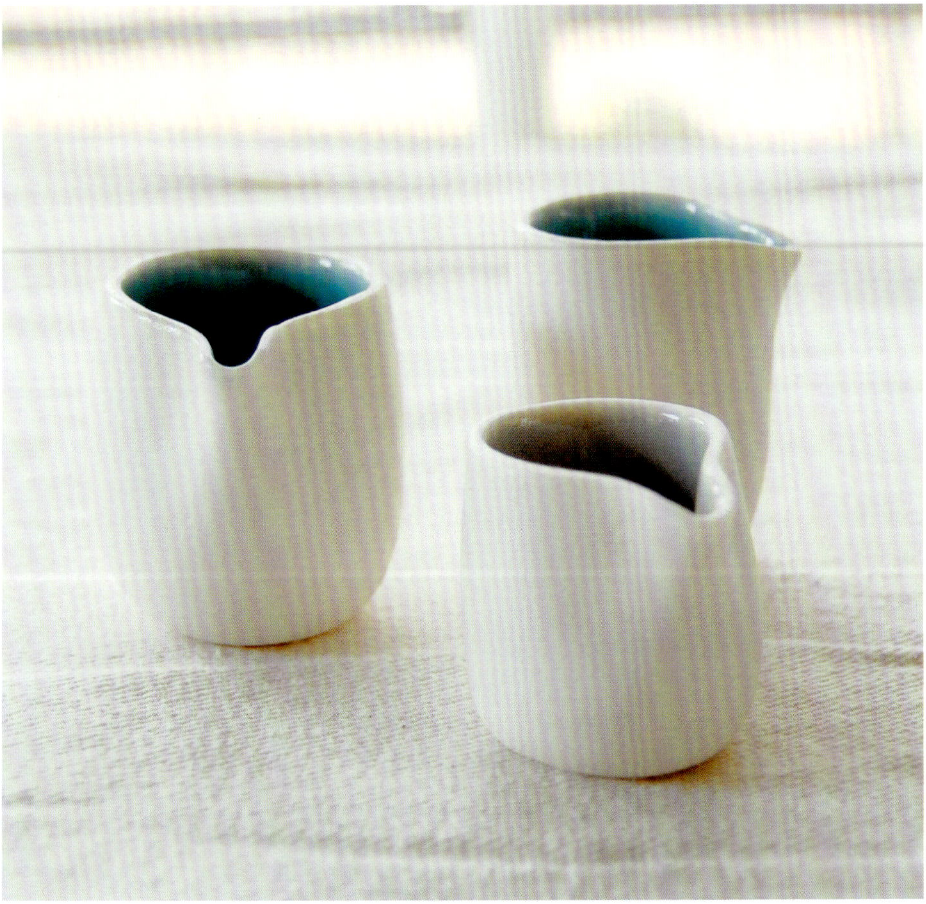

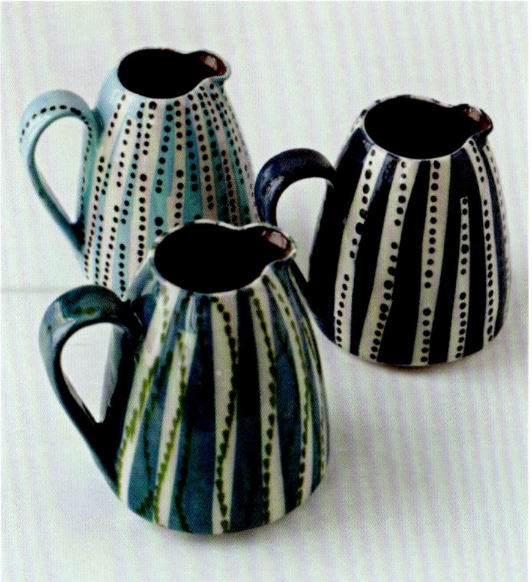

Katrin Moye, dotted stripe jugs, 2010. Thrown earthenware, slip decoration, height: 13 cm (5 in.). *Photo: Helen Shere.*

Pigeon Toe Ceramics, Portland, Oregon, mini creamers designed by Lisa Jones, 2010. Thrown porcelain, glazed on the inside, height: 6 cm (2¼ in.). *Photo: Lisa Jones.*

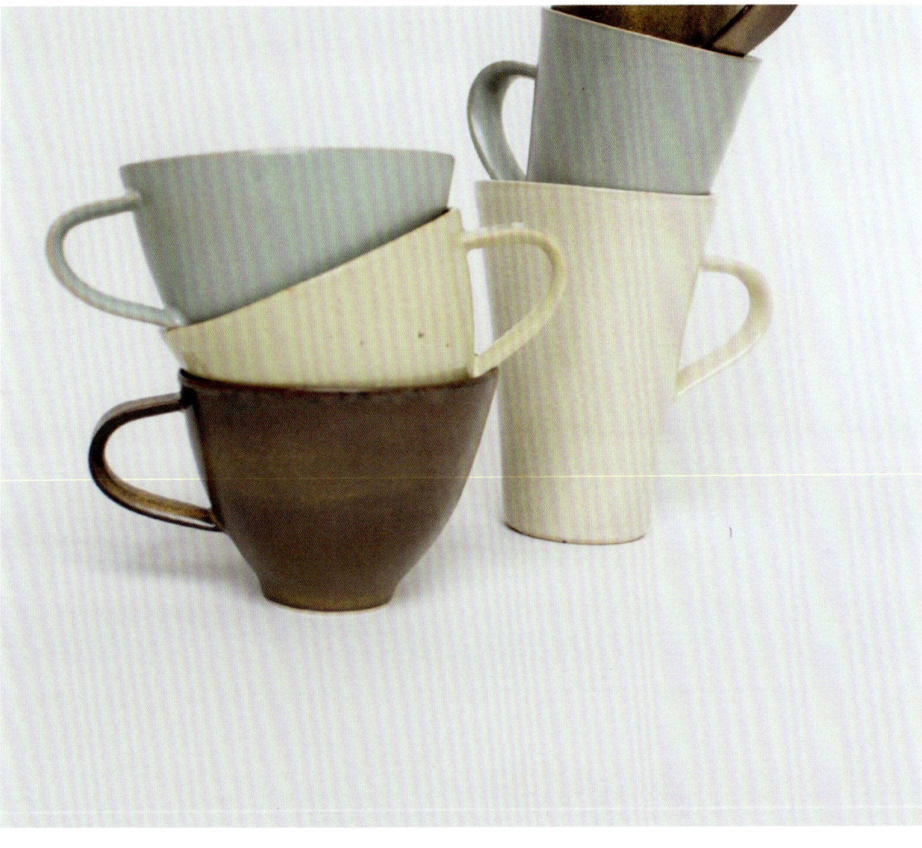

Stuart Carey, hot serving jugs, 2011. Thrown stoneware with matt glazes, width: 16 cm (6¼ in.). *Photo: Stuart Carey.*

16 Plates

Dinner plates have only been used in the West since the 17th century. Few potters are able to make fine, light plates by hand; they can be thrown on the wheel or made in a press mould, but when making in large quantities it is easier to form them on a jigger-jolley machine, with a profile pressing down onto a rotating mould. Plates often have a wide foot-ring, sometimes two concentric rings if they are large. They traditionally have a wide rim, but flat, rimless 'coupe' plates are easier to make by hand and have a wider usable area for the same overall diameter. Plates are often used by potters and designers as a blank canvas for decoration, although many modern chefs prefer them to be plain, with the main decoration provided by the food placed on them. Some of the best are the fine, white bone china plates made by Wedgwood since 1920. Several contemporary chefs have designed tableware ranges, most of which are white.

Dinner plates are usually around 27 cm (10½ in.) in diameter although they can be larger. If they are too wide, however, they will not fit in a standard kitchen cupboard or dishwasher.

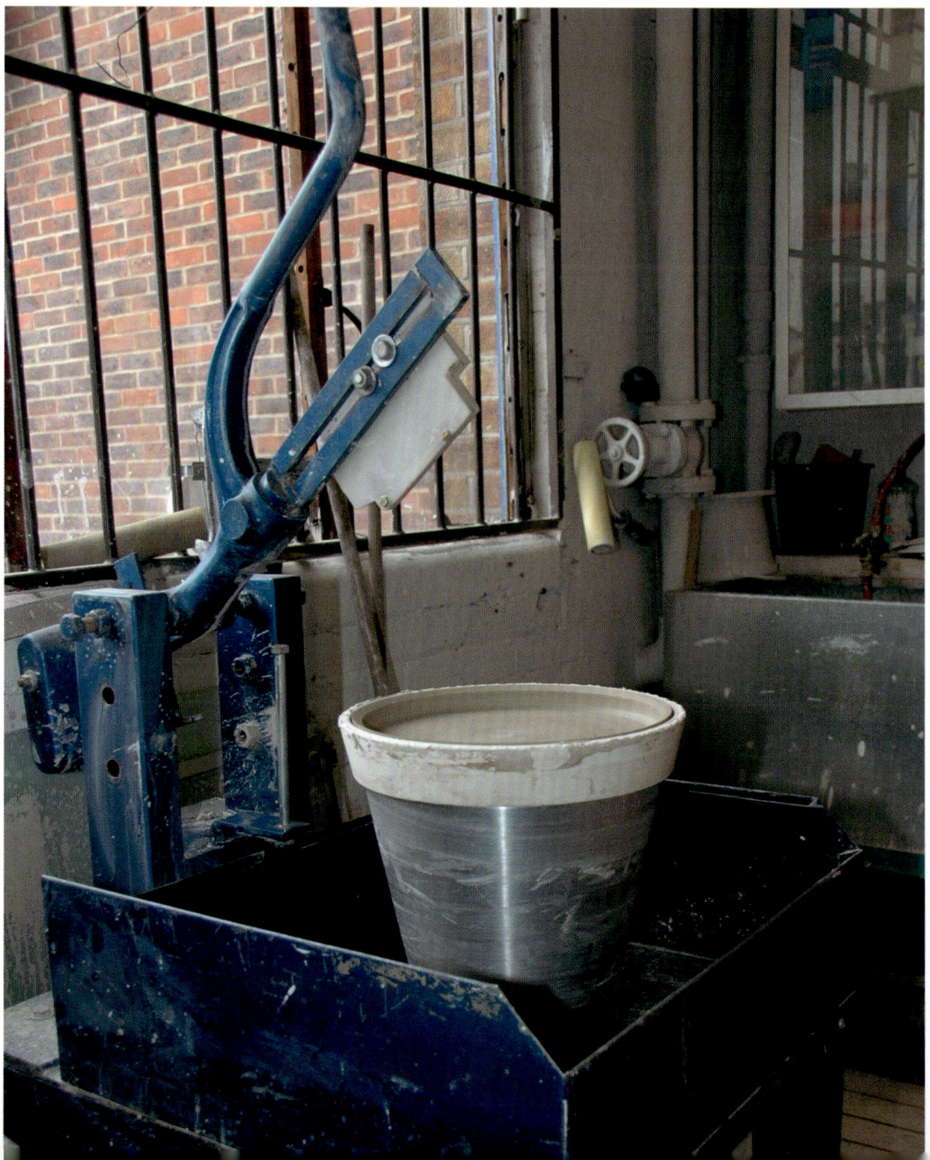

Owen Wall, Tower plate made in a jolley mould, with a profile for the internal shape, 2009. These plates are designed to be stacked in a tower. *Photo: Linda Bloomfield.*

Brickett Davda make press-moulded earthenware bowls and plates in their studio in Brighton. They use a range of coloured slips which are poured into the forms while these are still in the mould. Their colours are inspired by the grey skies and sea of the British coast and countryside.

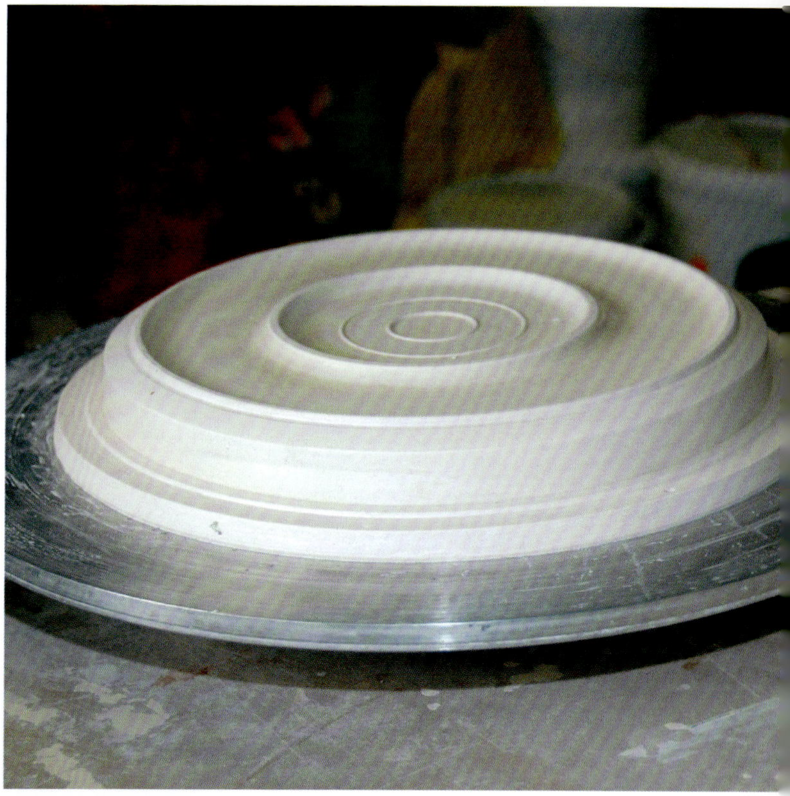

Owen Wall, master model for Tower plate, 2009. This shows the underside of the plate, which has two concentric foot-rings. *Photo: Linda Bloomfield.*

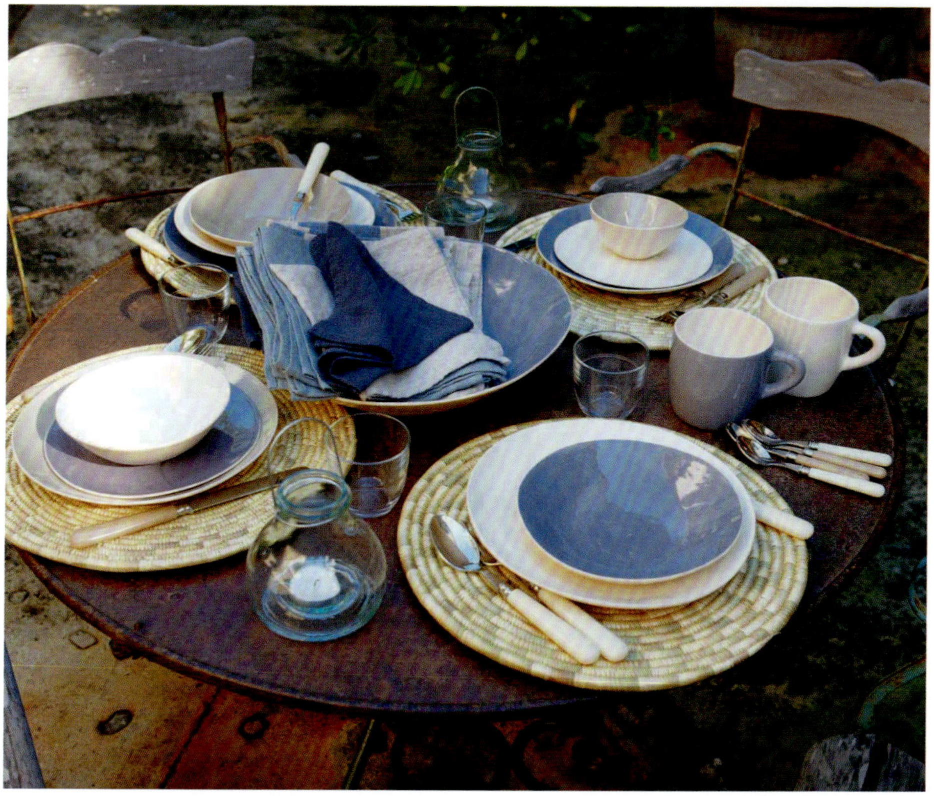

Brickett Davda for Toast, mugs, bowls and plates in blue, white and taupe, 2011. Earthenware, large plate diameter: 29 cm (11½ in.). *Photo: Jonathan West for Toast.*

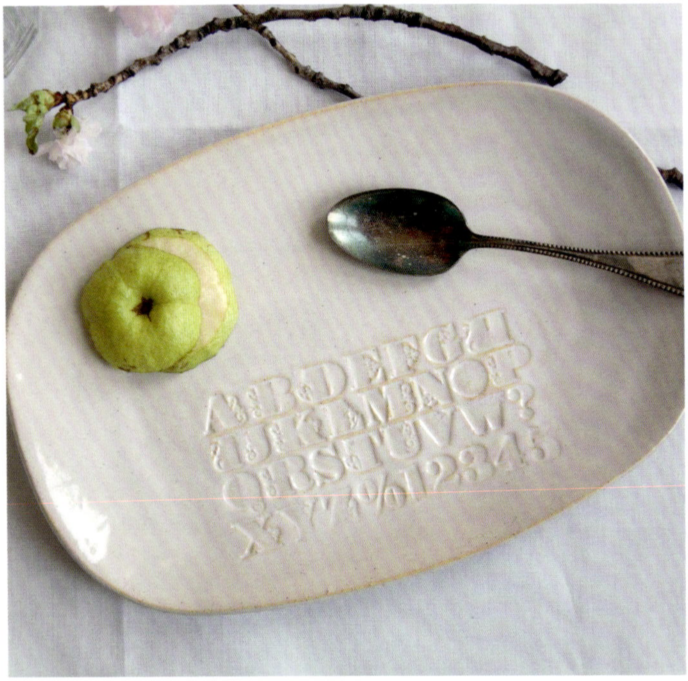

May Luk, Alphabet Platter, 2010. Embossed stoneware, 20 x 30 x 2 cm (8 x 12 x ¾ in.). *Photo: Jessica Marquez.*

Dartington Pottery was originally set up in the 1930s in Shinner's Bridge, south Devon by Bernard Leach. Potter Marianne de Trey produced successful ranges of tableware there from 1949, first in tin-glazed earthenware and later in stoneware. In 1975, Dartington Pottery became a training workshop run by a group of potters, then during the 1980s Janice Tchalenko designed some very successful tableware ranges with vibrant glazes and patterns. Some of these are still produced today, including one called Poppy, which is brushed and trailed with a floral design in bright primary colours. In 2005, production moved to Grayshott Pottery in Surrey.

Dartington Pottery, Blush tableware range, Donna Cockram and Janice Tchalenko, 2008. Reduction-fired stoneware, plate diameter: 26.5 cm (10½ in.). *Photo: Stephen Course.*

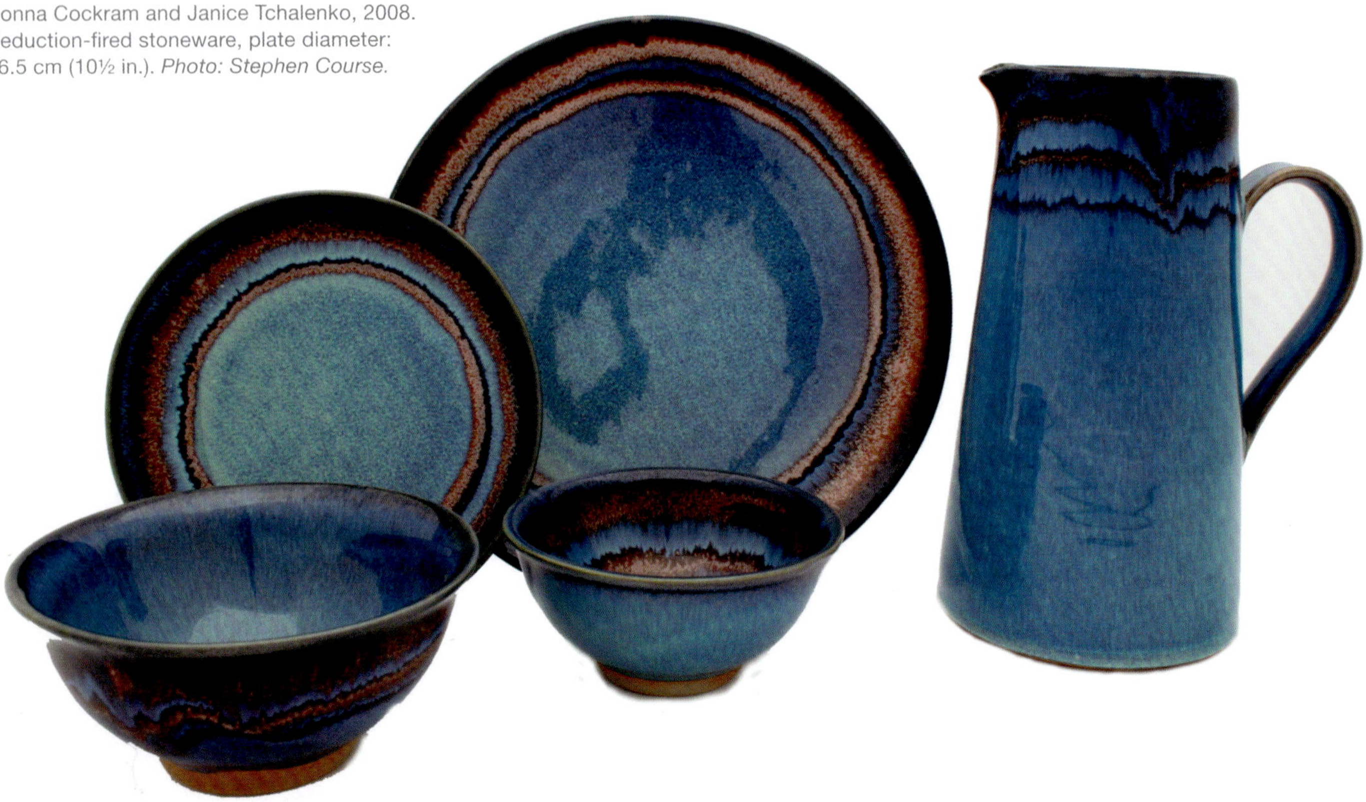

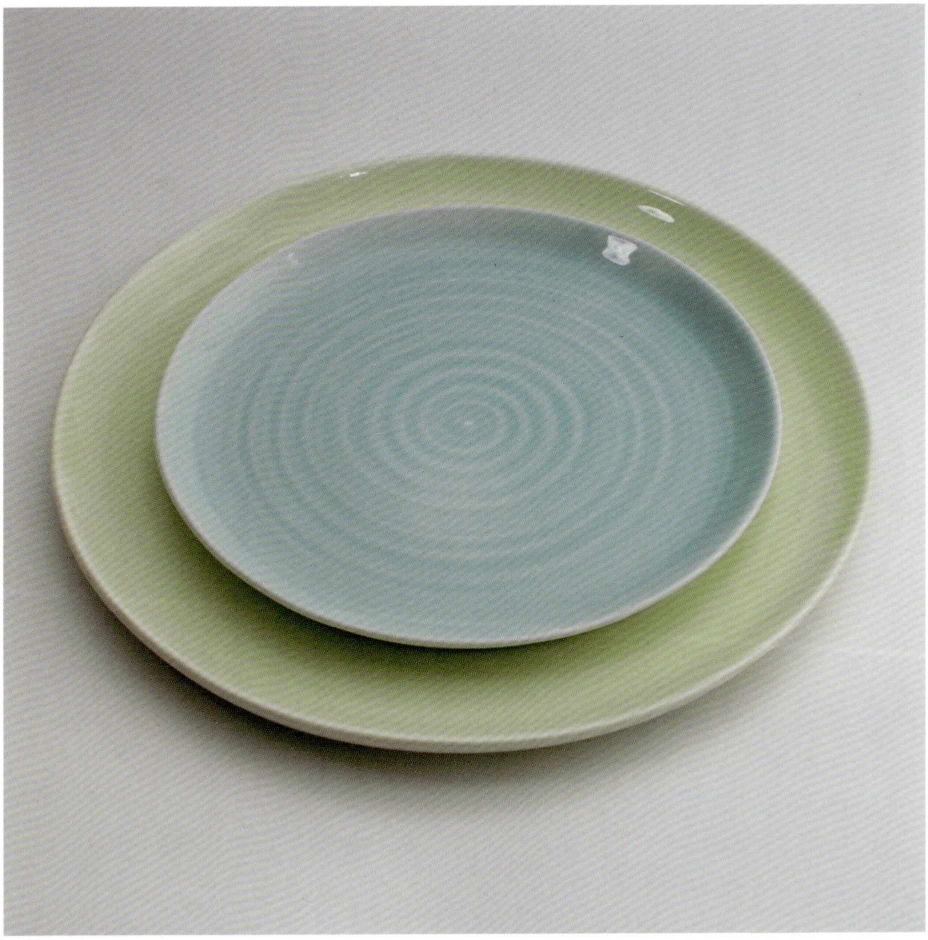

Linda Bloomfield Design, factory-made plates, 2011. Porcelain, diameter: 27 cm (10¾ in.). *Photo: Henry Bloomfield.*

Christiane Perrochon, Italy, hand-thrown and press-moulded bowls and plates, 2010. Stoneware. *Photo: Willer.*

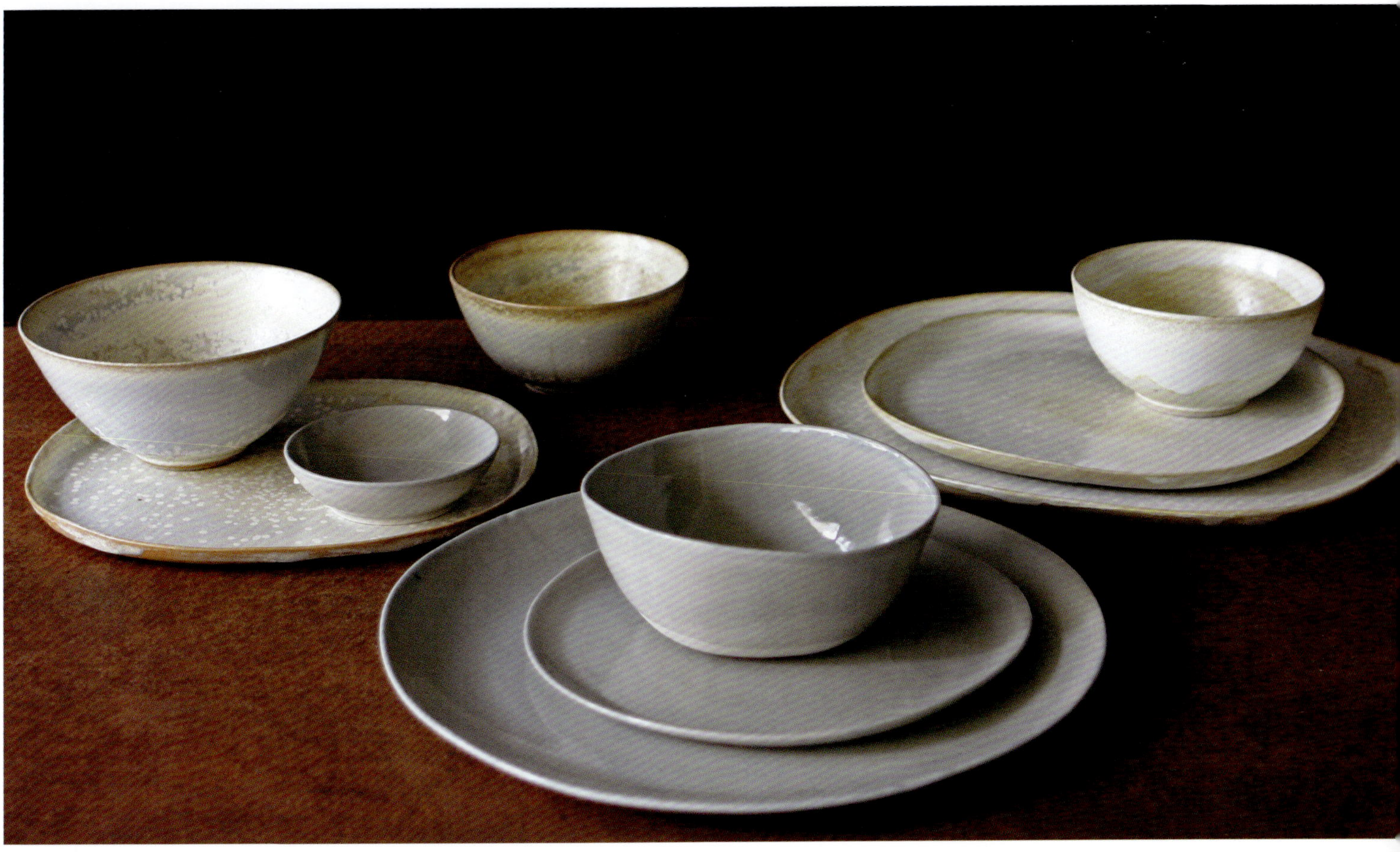

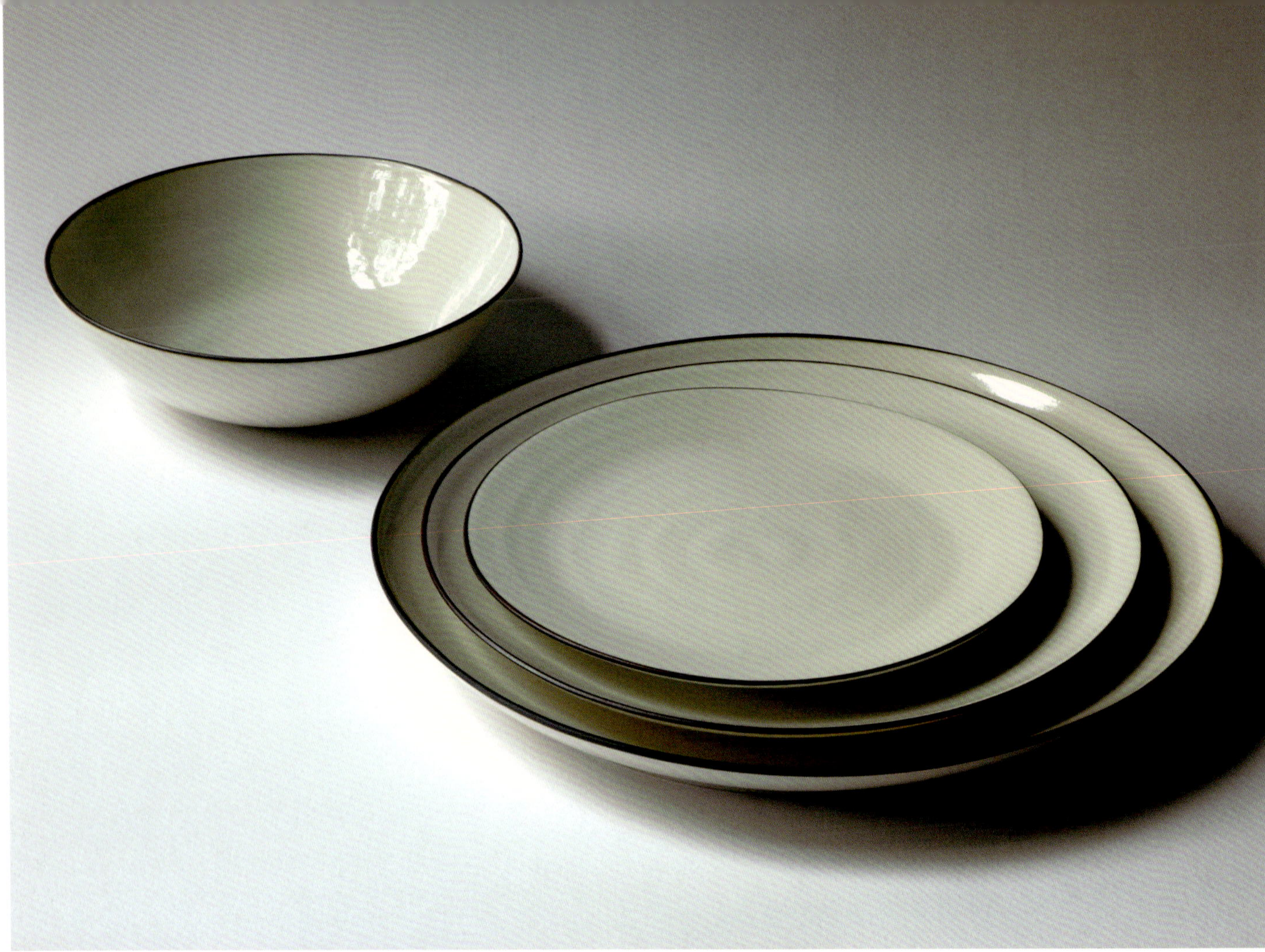

Daniel Smith, place setting, 2009. Finely thrown porcelain with iron oxide on the rim, diameter: 26.5 cm (10½ in.). *Photo: Sonja Read.*

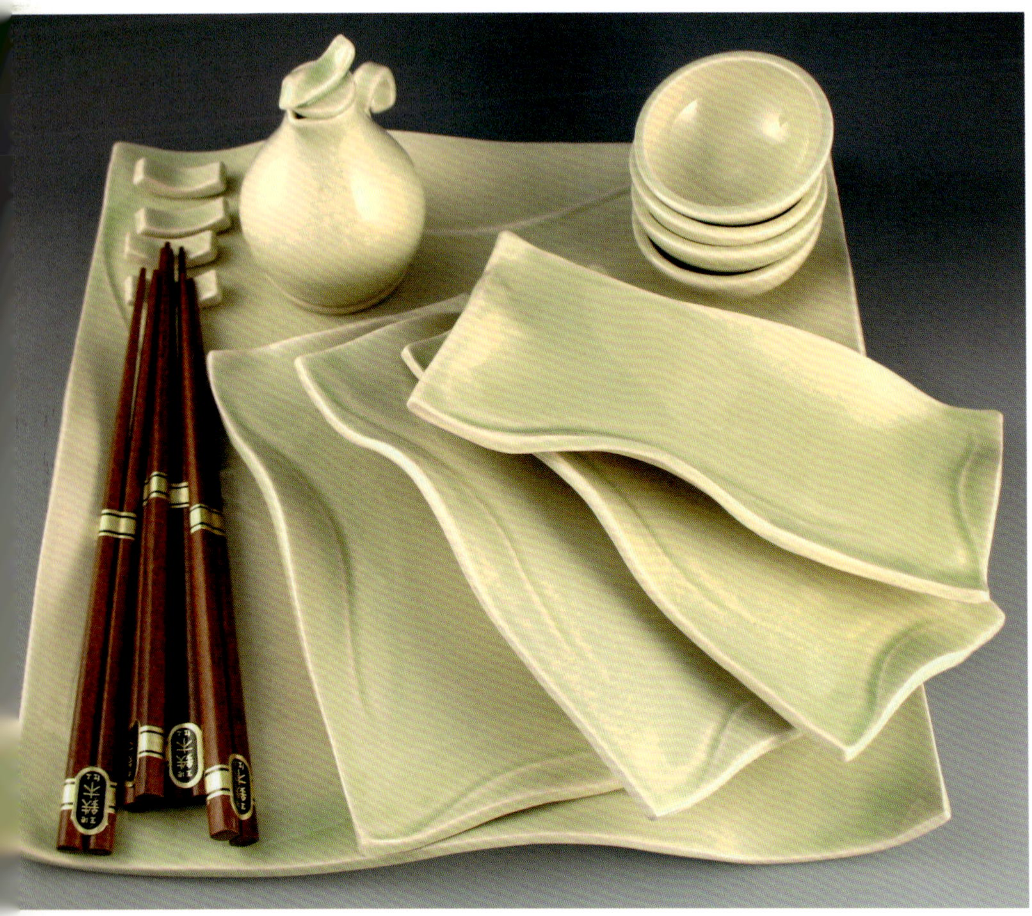

Judi Tavill, sushi set, 2010. Thrown and slabbed stoneware, width: 28 cm (11 in.). *Photo: Judi Tavill.*

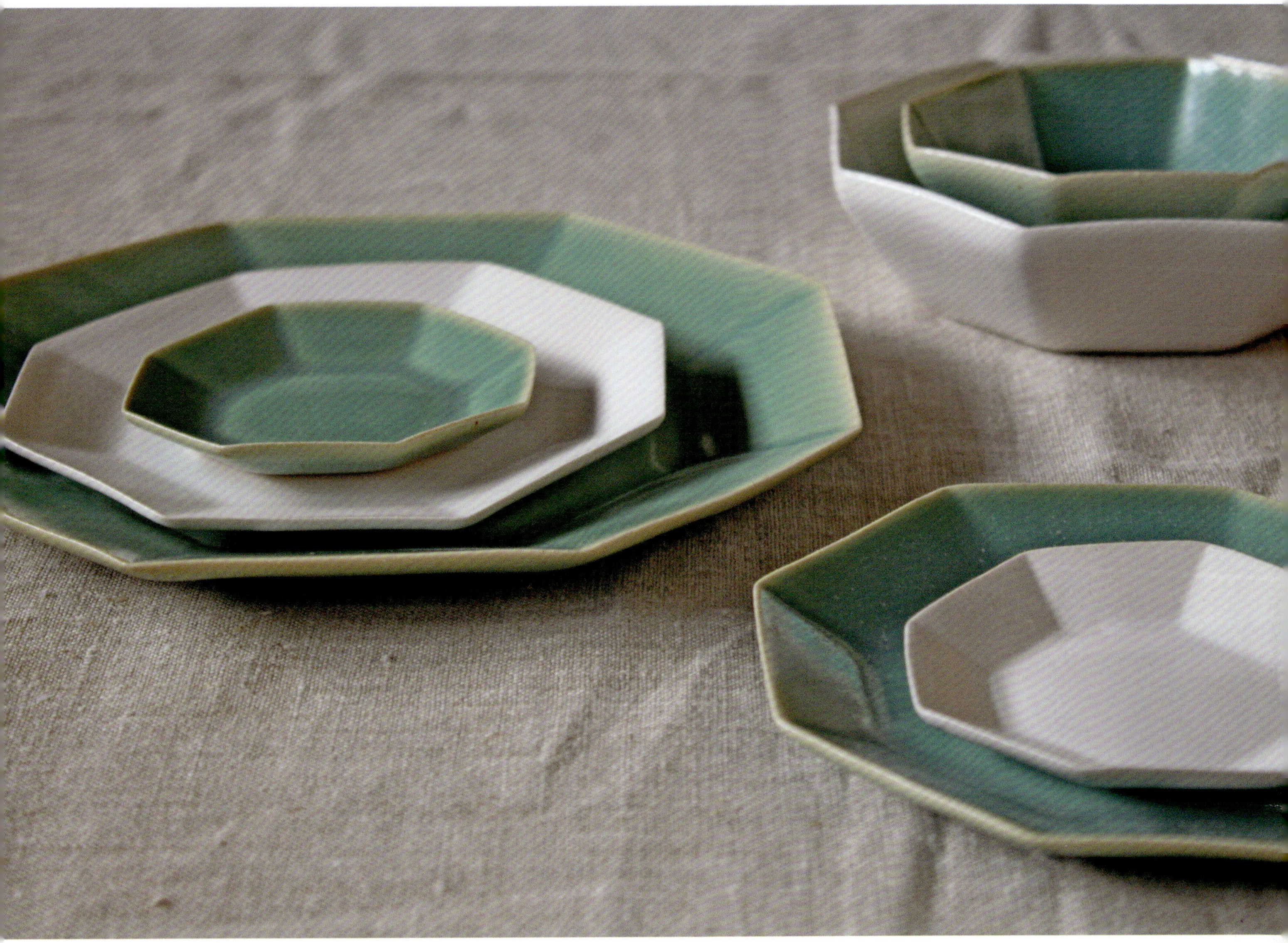

Mizuyo Yamashita, Camellia octagonal plates and bowls, 2011. Slabbed and hump-moulded stoneware, fired to 1260°C (2300°F). *Photo: by the artist.*

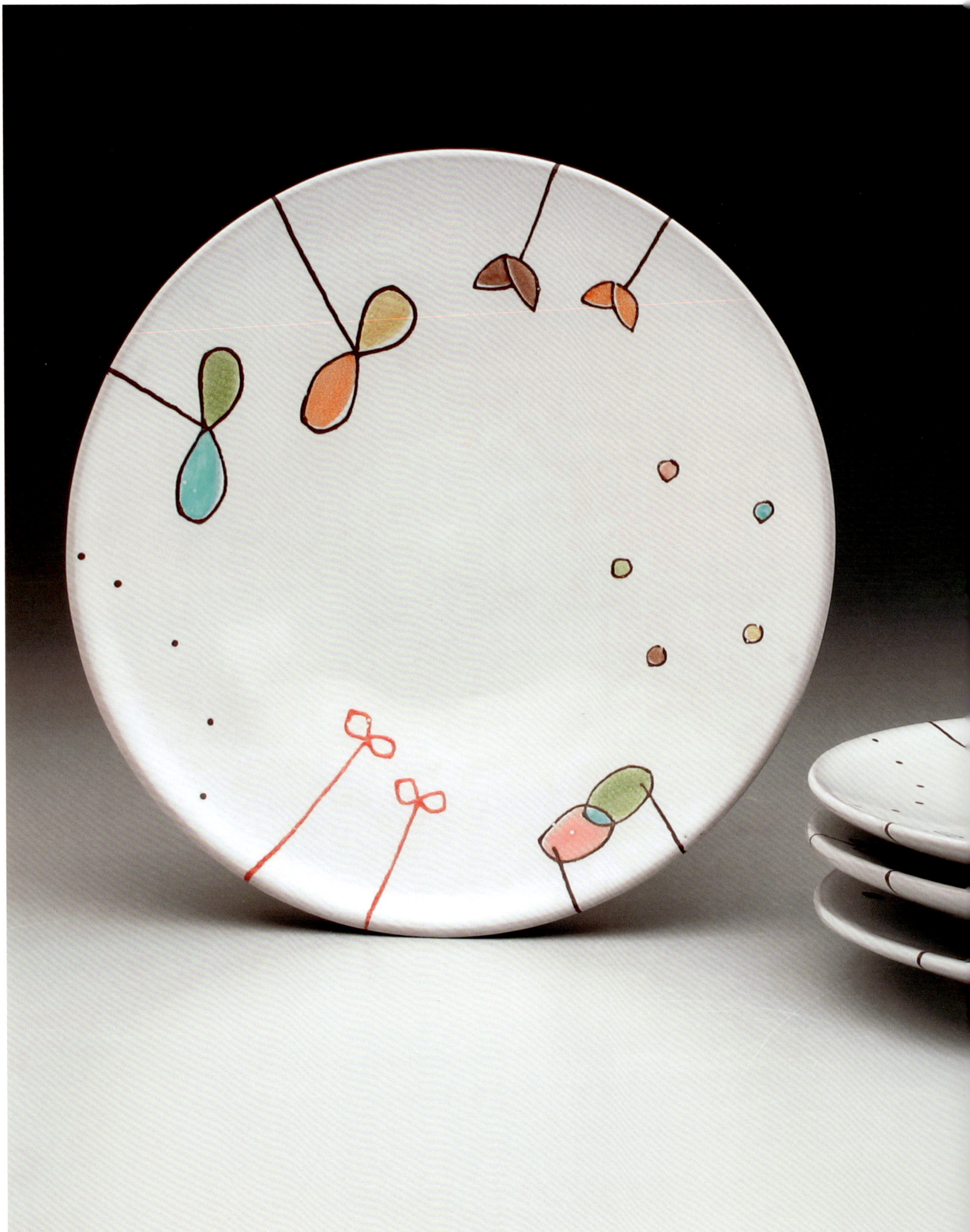

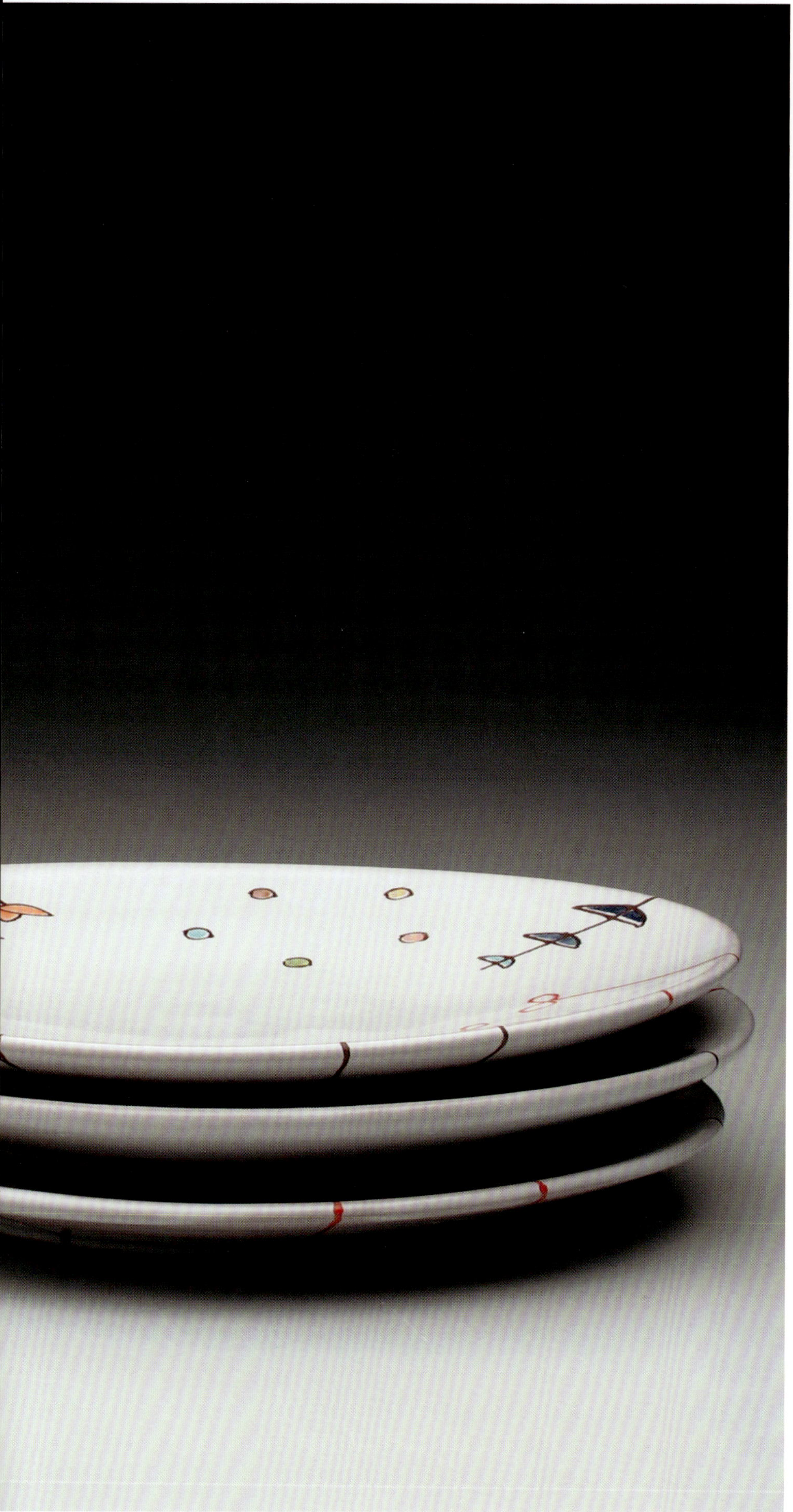

Courtney Murphy, plates, 2011. Mailoica-decorated earthenware, fired to cone 02 (1120°C/2048°F), diameter: 21.5 cm (8½ in.). *Photo: by the artist.*

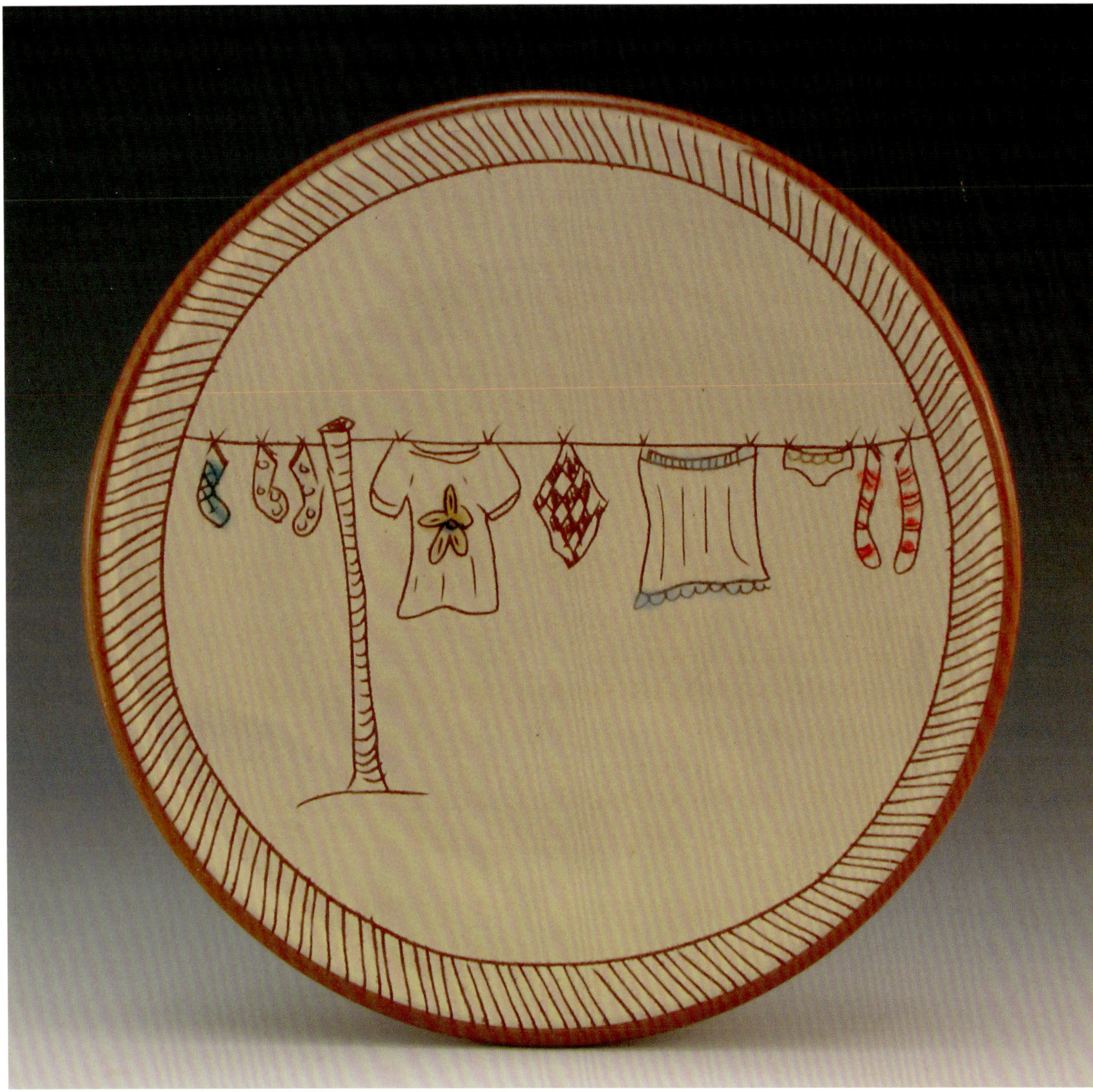

Ron Philbeck, North Carolina, Laundry Line plate, 2010. Slip-decorated earthenware, fired to cone 04 (1060°C/1940°F) in oxidation, diameter: 24 cm (9½ in.). *Photo: courtesy of the artist.*

Ron Philbeck, plate, 2008. Earthenware with slips and sgraffito fish decoration, diameter: 22 cm (8½ in.). Collection of Doug Fitch. *Photo: Jonathan Thompson.*

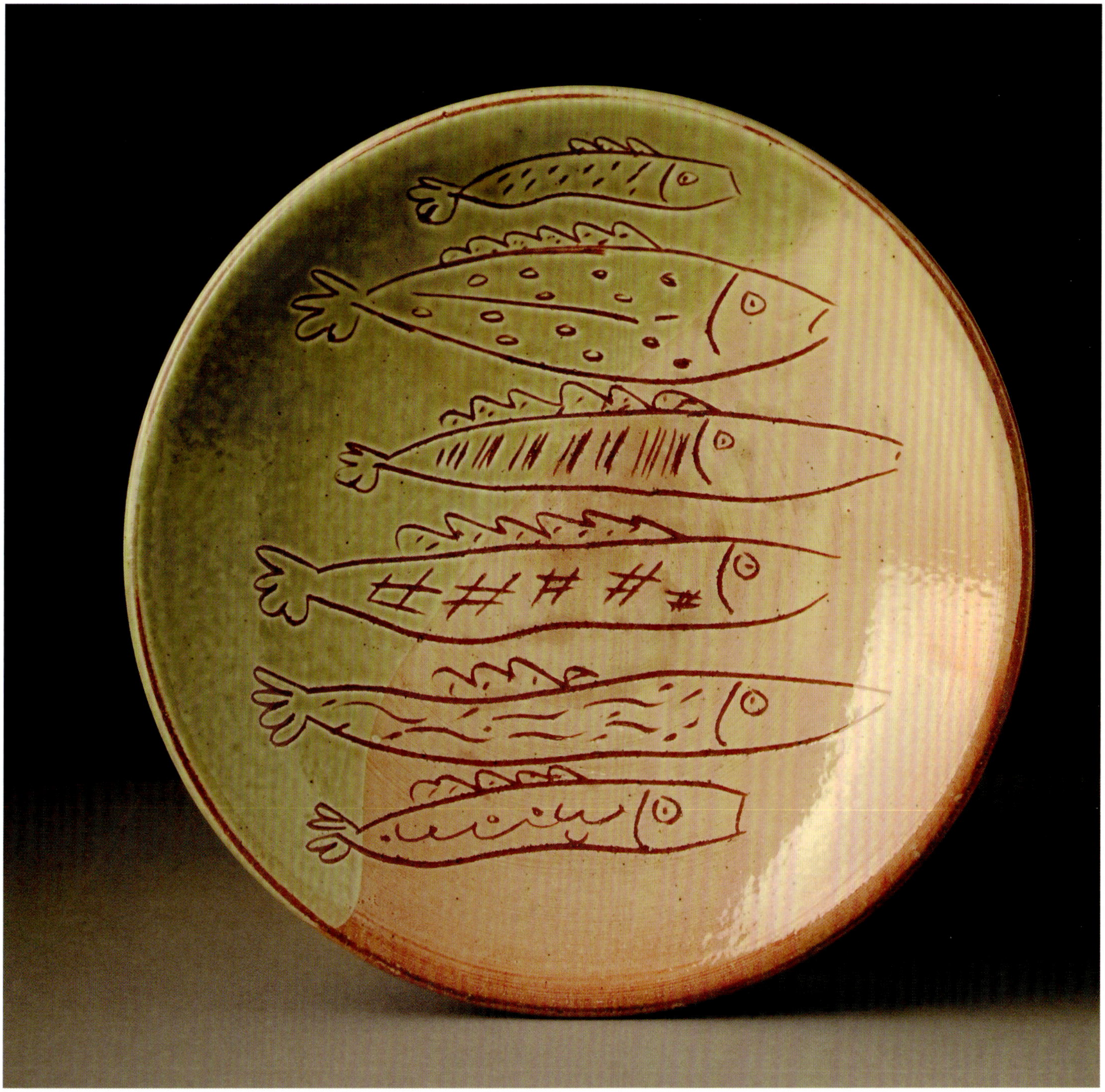

17 Serving dishes

During the Industrial Revolution, large quantities of highly decorated tableware were produced, much of it with blue and white patterns. The early 19th century brought the introduction of dinner service in the Russian style, with many courses brought to the table sequentially: soup, fish, meat, game, pudding, cheese and biscuits. Formal dinner services with many pieces, including plates, oval serving platters and tureens, were popular. In Victorian times there was a huge range of serving dishes, compote dishes and fruit stands, and pudding and pie plates, many shown in the illustrations in *Mrs Beeton's Book of Household Management*, published in 1861.

Modern dining more often involves serving dishes in which the food can be both cooked in the oven and served at the table. Oven-to-table ware must be sturdy, easy to hold with oven gloves and able to withstand sudden temperature changes. Pie dishes should be deep enough to hold a generous amount of filling and can be round, oval or square. Homemade pastry is usually rolled out in a circle, while shop-bought pastry is sold in rectangular block or sheet form, making a rectangular pie dish easier to use and less wasteful. Oven-to-table ware also includes ramekins, which are small, deep dishes for making individual soufflés or desserts.

Christine Hester Smith, extruded dish section from a pug mill with attached expansion box. *Photo: Christine Hester Smith.*

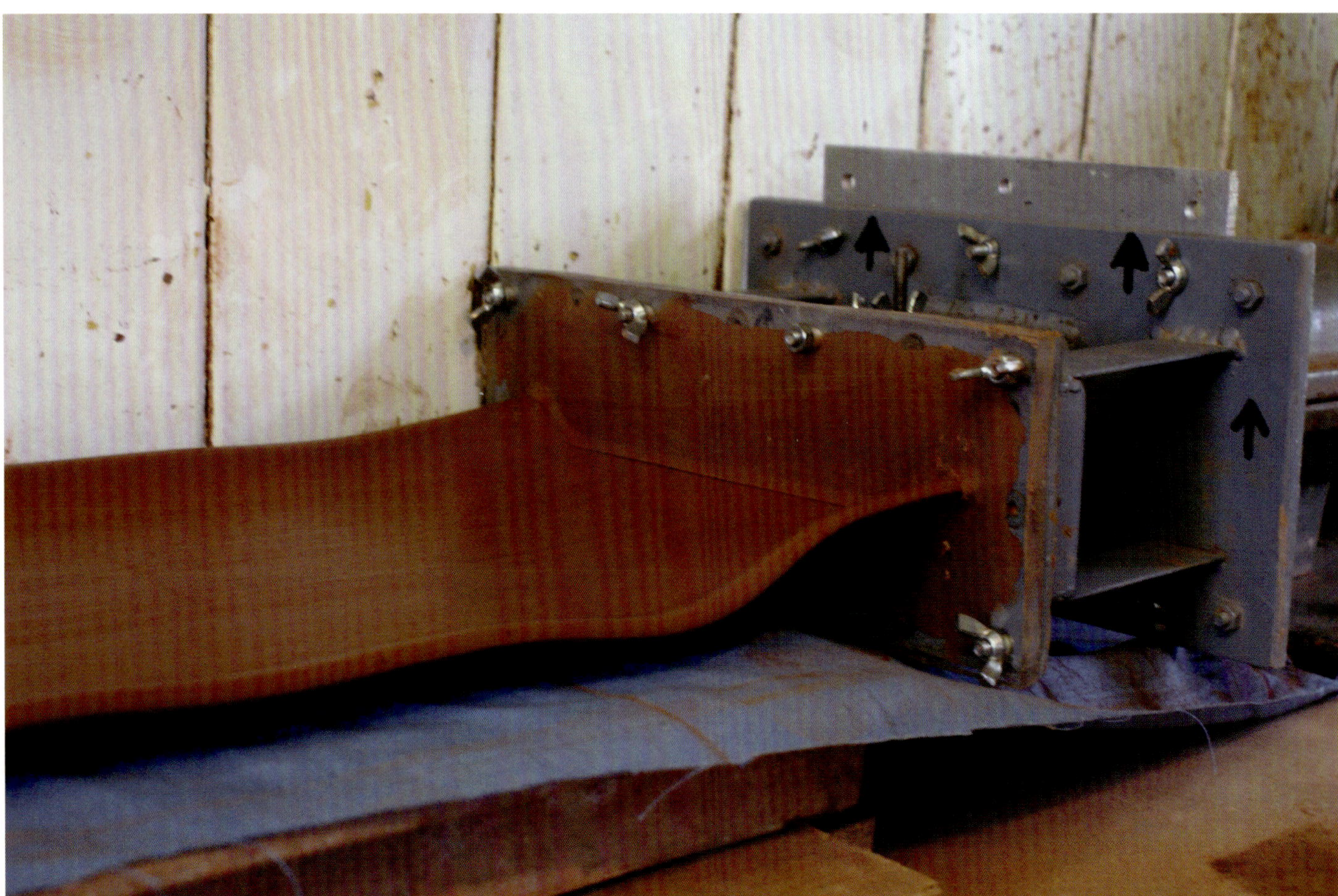

David Mellor porcelain, designed by Corin Mellor, 2010. Square deep plates, width: 8.5 cm (3¼ in.) and 14 cm (5½ in.). *Photo: David Mellor Design Ltd.*

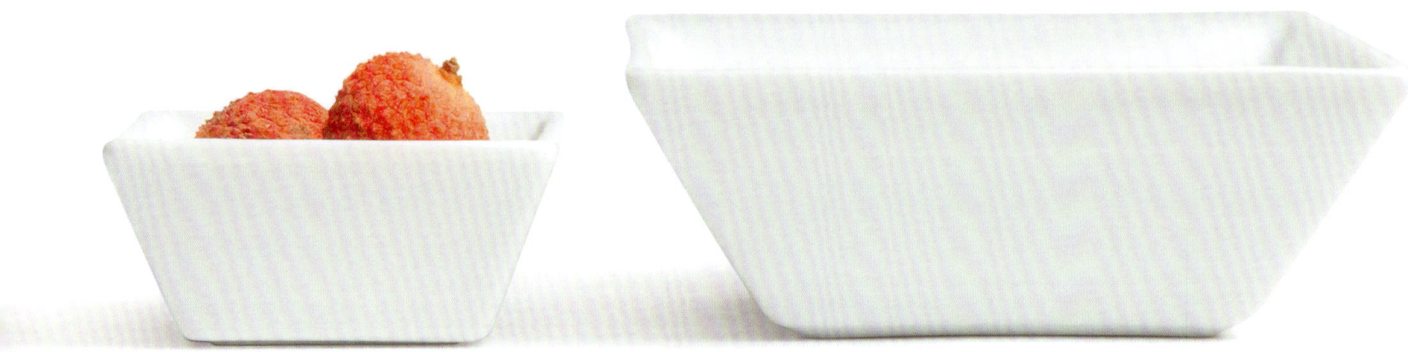

Adrienne Baba, square sushi plate and chopstick rest, 2010. Slabbed stoneware with matt glaze, fired to 1260°C (2300°F) in an electric kiln, width: 18.5 cm (7¼ in.). *Photo: Keiko Oikawa.*

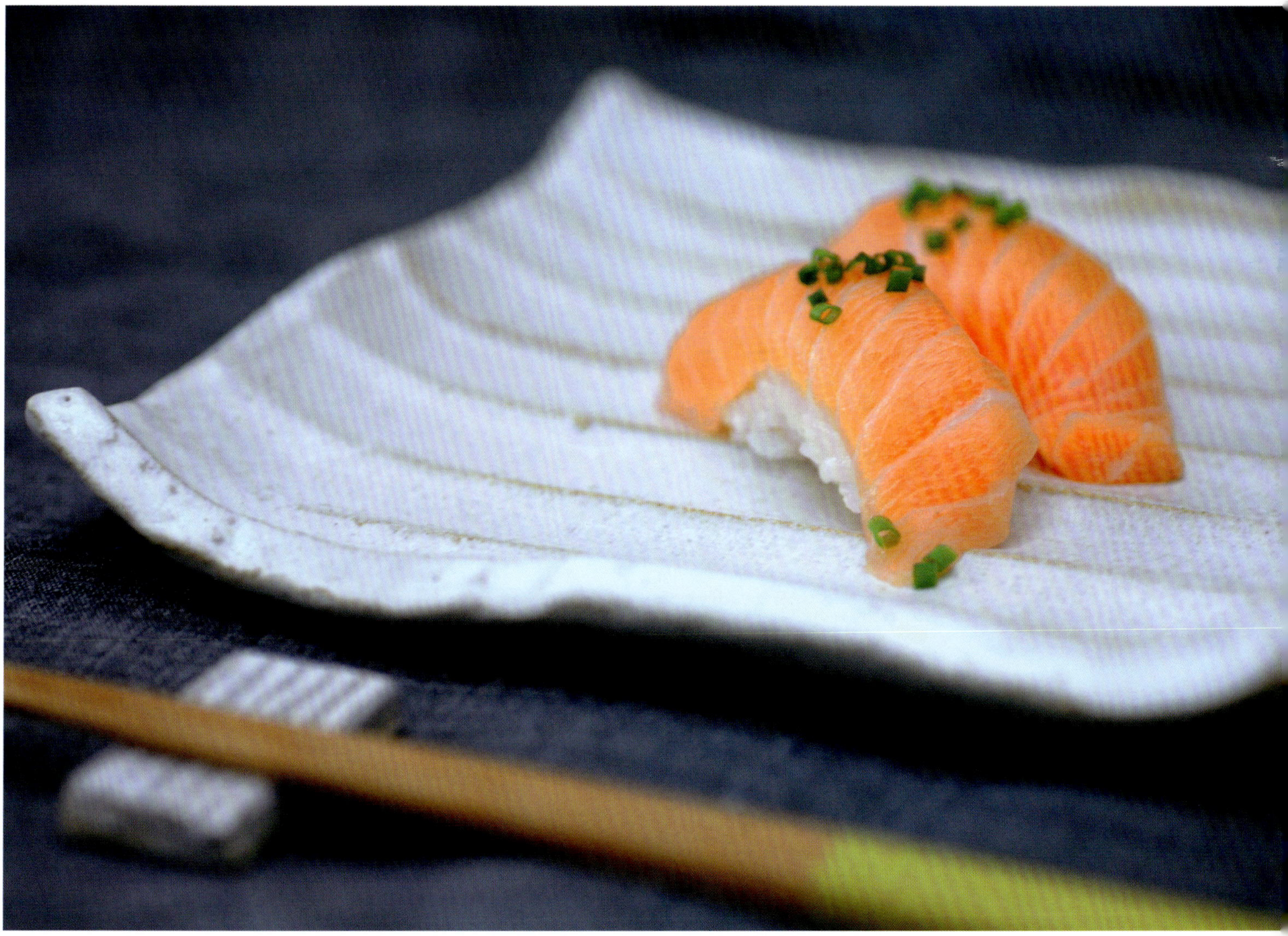

Platters need to have a wide flat base, unlike many plates, which have a wide rim and only a small flat area in the centre. Cake stands are made by joining a flat plate to a foot-ring, which is sometimes done after the pieces have been fired, to prevent warping. Compote dishes can be made by joining a bowl to a stem. Influences from Japan have resulted in the appearance of rectangular and square platters and serving dishes.

Making methods

Platters can be thrown or made in a mould. Rectangular platters are sometimes extruded but can also be made from a slab of clay supported at the sides while drying.

Rigmor Als, Copenhagen, oval bowls, 2008. Slipcast porcelain, 33 x 15 cm (13 x 6 in.). *Photo: Rigmor Als.*

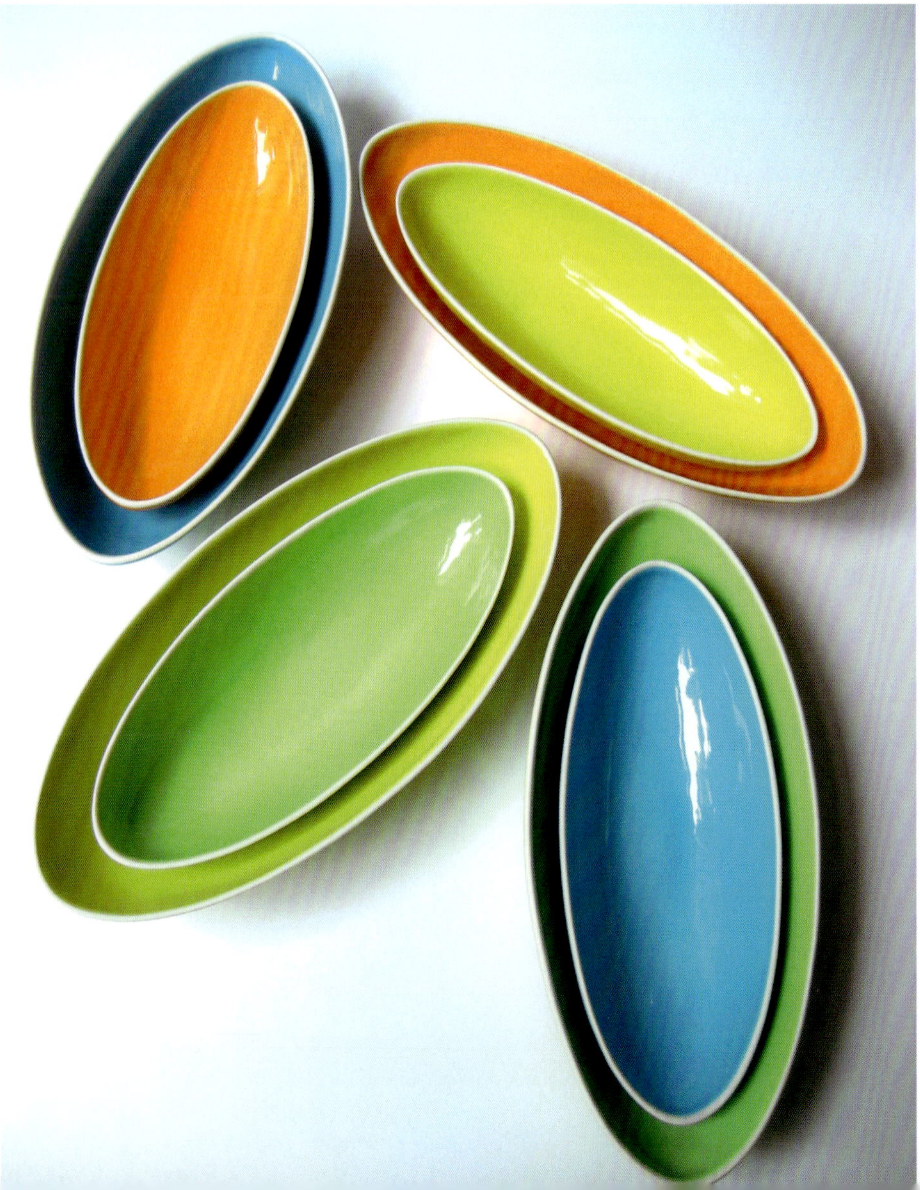

Hannah McAndrew, slip-trailed pie dishes, 2010. Red earthenware, diameter: 26 cm (10¼ in.). *Photo: Shannon Tofts.*

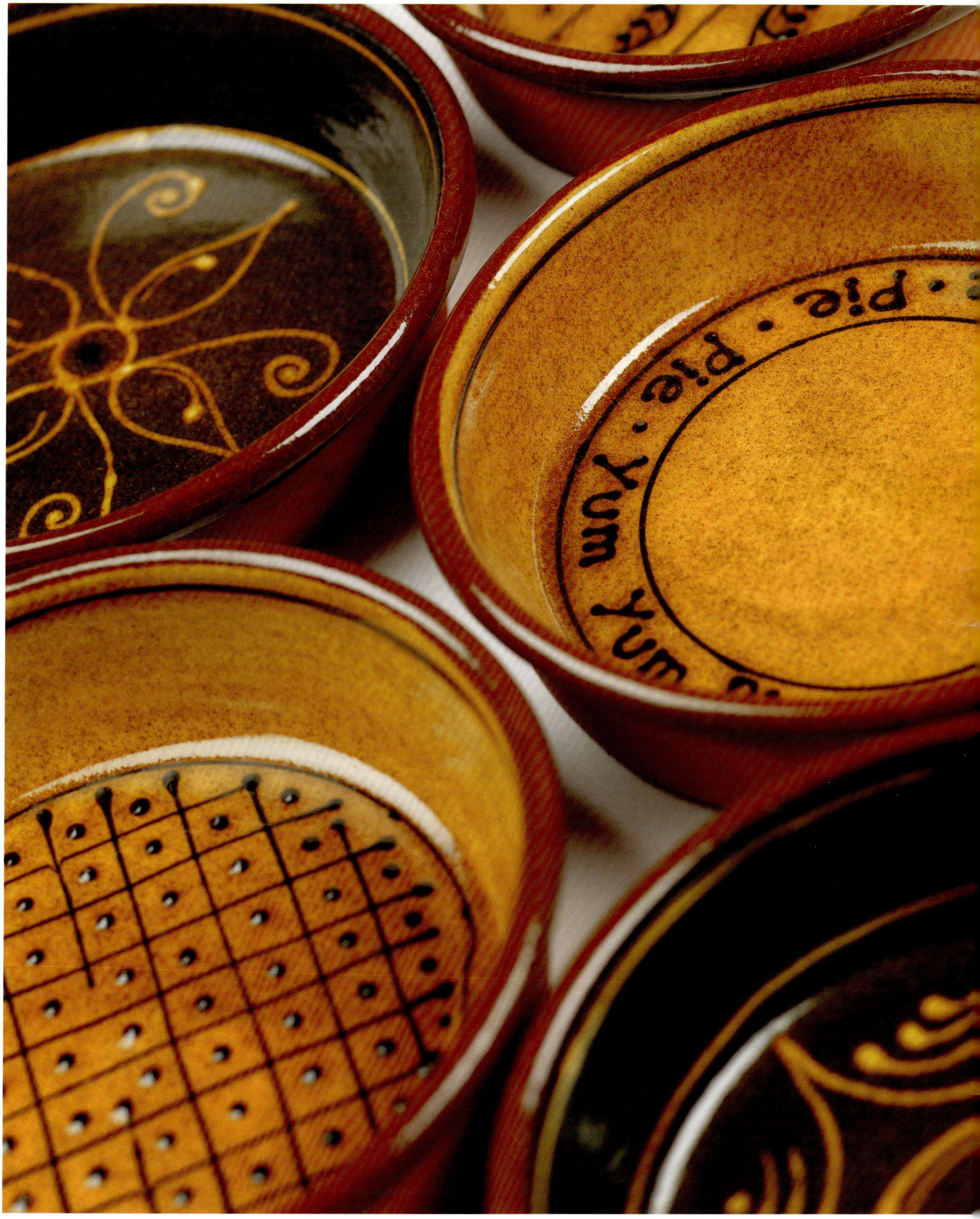
Yum Yum · Pie · Pie ·

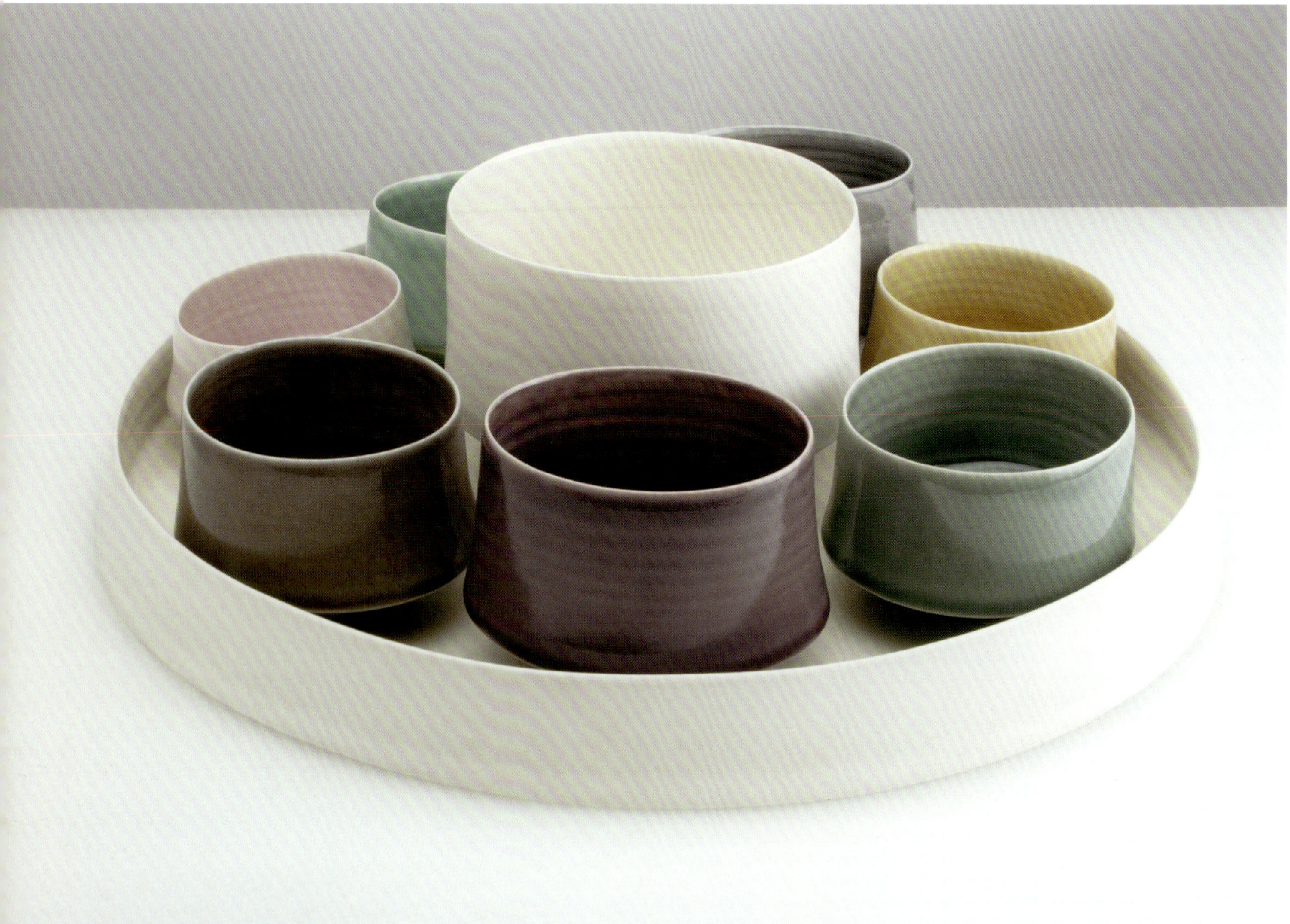

Louisa Taylor, Oriole supper set inspired by 18th century dining vessels, 2010. Thrown and assembled porcelain, diameter: 56 cm (22 in.). *Photo: Matthew Booth.*

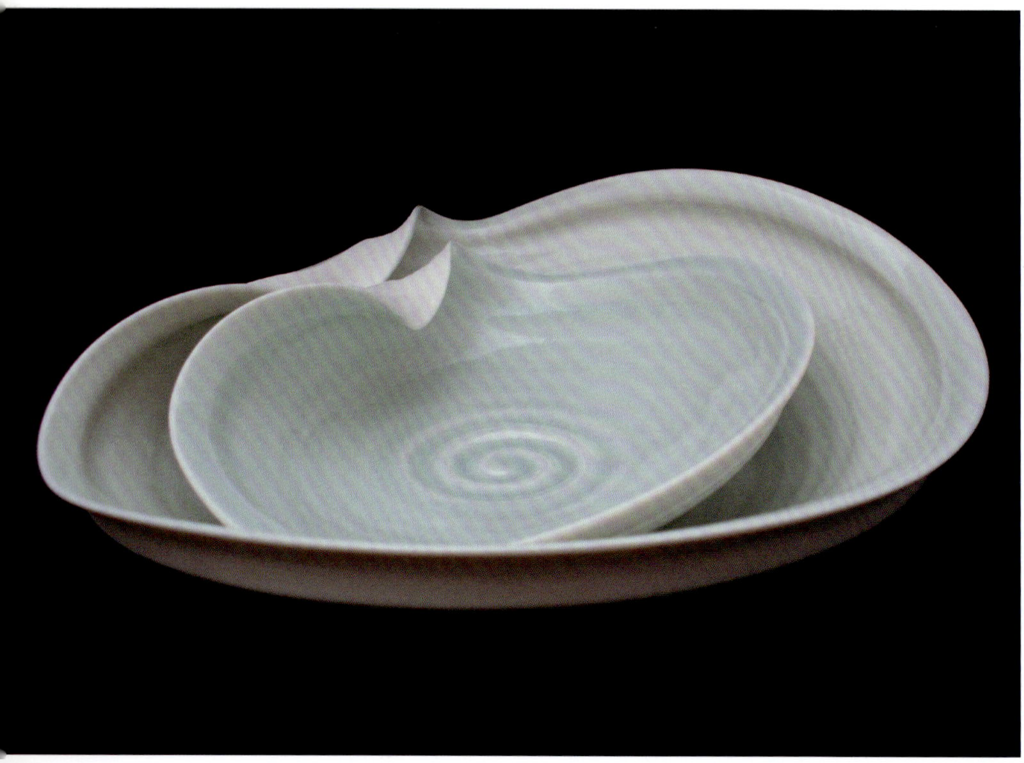

Karen Morgan, thrown and altered platters, 2008. Porcelain, width: 35 cm (13¾ in.). *Photo: by the artist.*

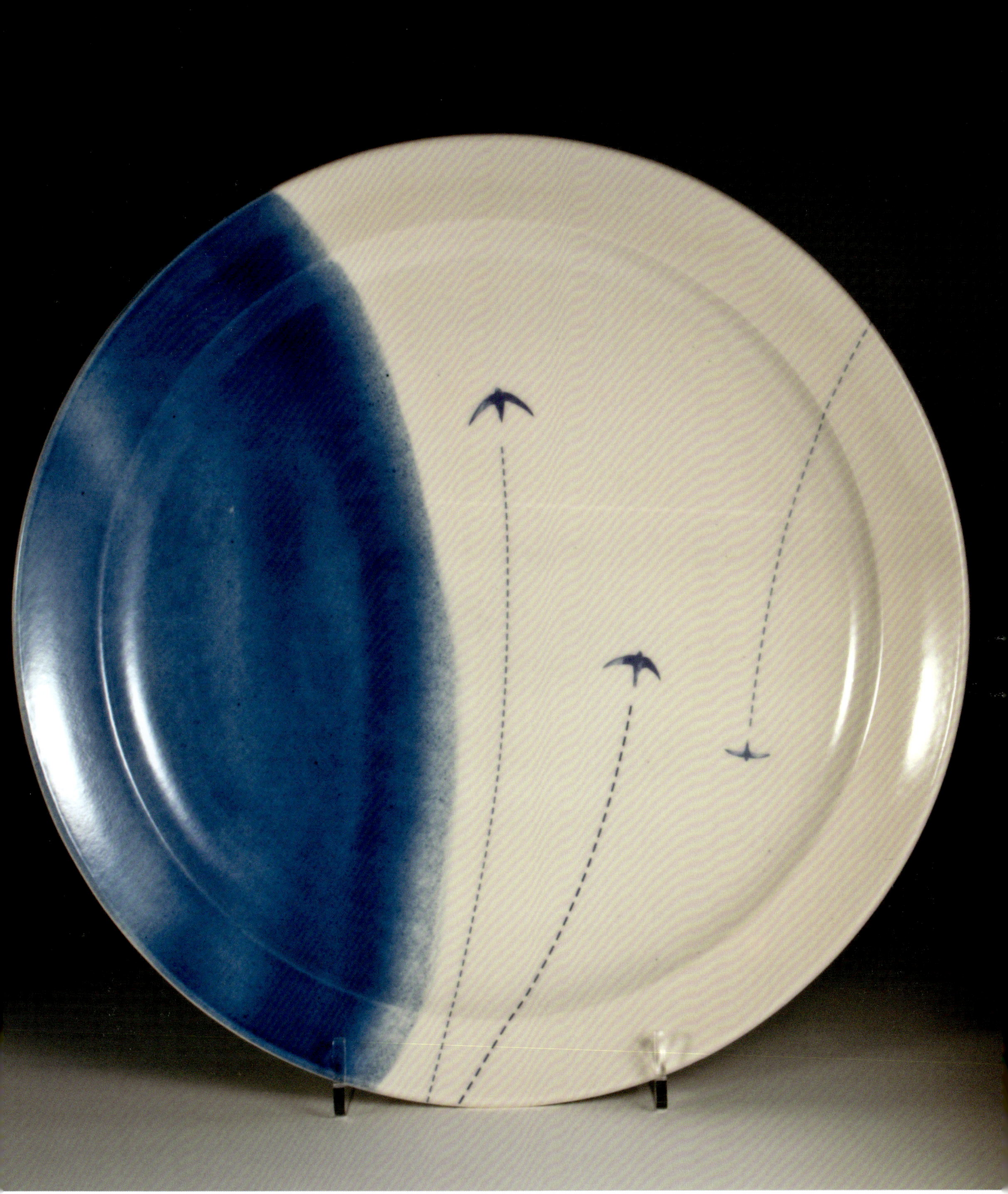

Matthew Tyas, Swift Skies platter, 2010.
Thrown stoneware, decorated with
ceramic decal, diameter: 42 cm (16½ in.).
Photo: Matthew Tyas.

Laura de Benedetti, thrown jug and platter, 2009. Porcelain, diameter: 35 cm (13¾ in.). *Photo: Sussie Ahlburg.*

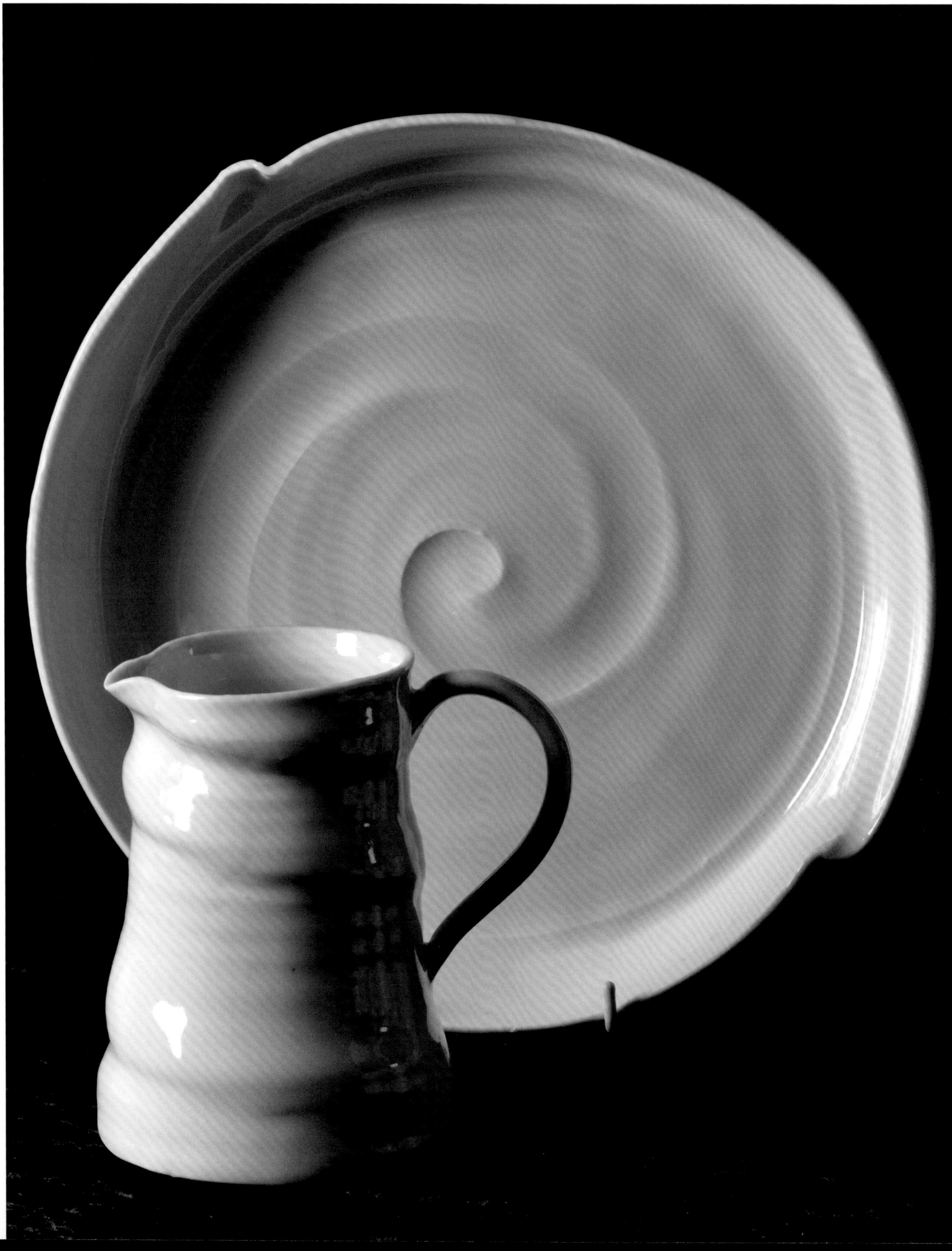

Katrin Moye, Fox and Hens cake stands, 2010. Thrown earthenware, slip-trailed decoration, diameter: 30 cm (11¾ in.). *Photo: Iwan Essery.*

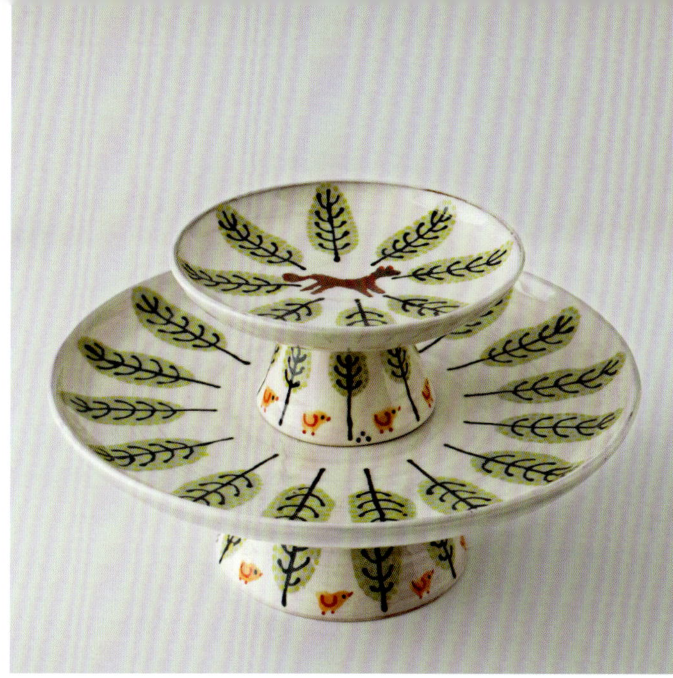

Make International, KBJ Word range cake plate, 2010. High-white porcelain, designed by Keith Brymer Jones, diameter: 27 cm (10½ in.). *Photo: Jake Fitzjones.*

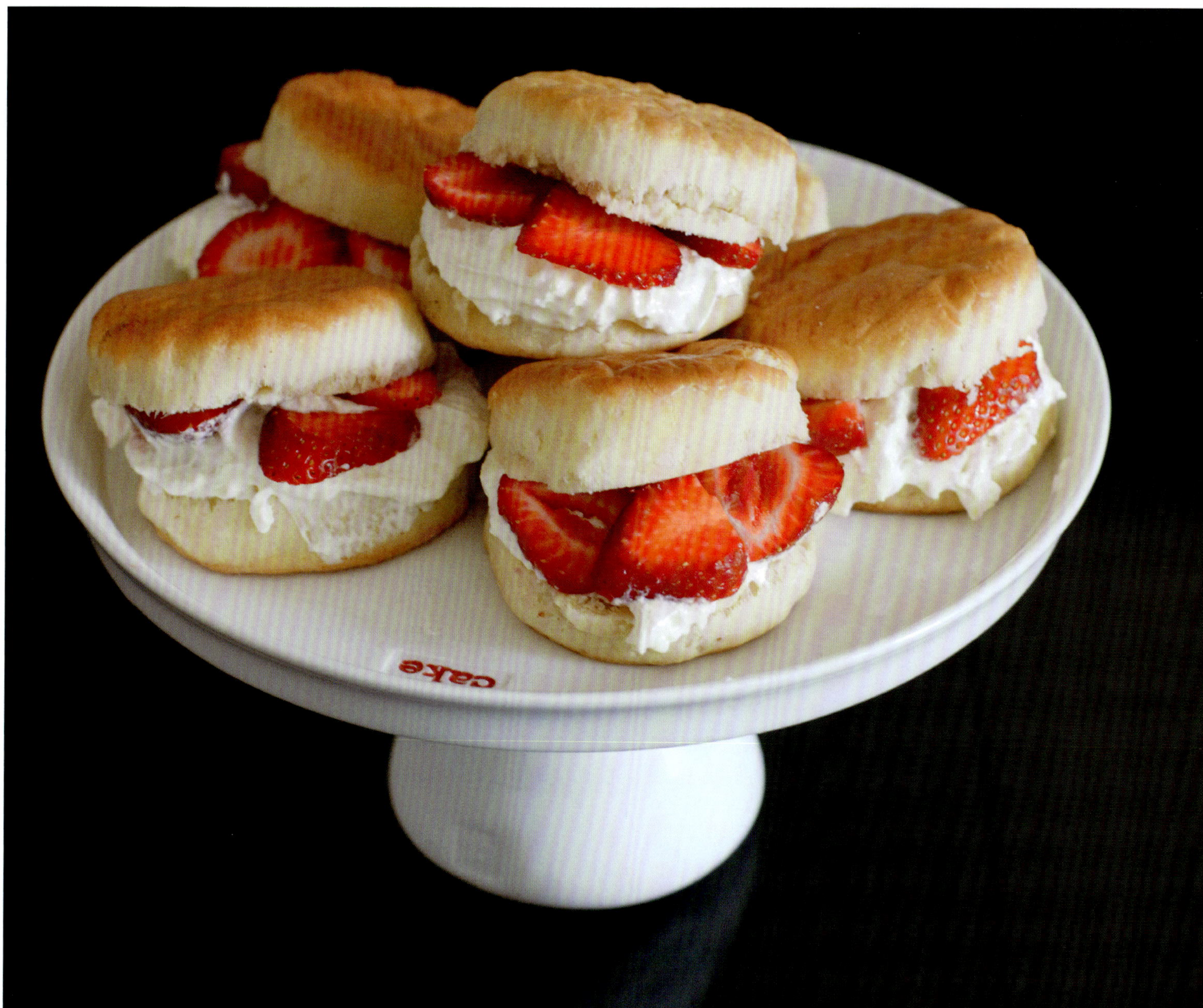

18 Lidded pots

Storage jars have traditionally been made of pottery and used to store food such as bread, flour, sugar and butter. They often have a domed lid with a knob or strap handle. Covered vegetable dishes and tureens are used for serving vegetables or soup at the table on formal occasions. Casseroles were originally made from earthenware and used to bake food in the oven. The pottery must be resistant to thermal shock and stoneware is now often used for this reason, particularly clay bodies containing petalite or talc. The pot should be easy to grip wearing oven gloves and should have either a collar, a generous rim or lug handles. Lug handles are made by pulling, extruding or slipcasting and attached to the pot when leatherhard.

A wide range of small, lidded pots is made for condiments such as mustard or sugar, sometimes with a notch in the lid for a spoon. Some potters make storage pots for garlic with holes to allow air to flow through.

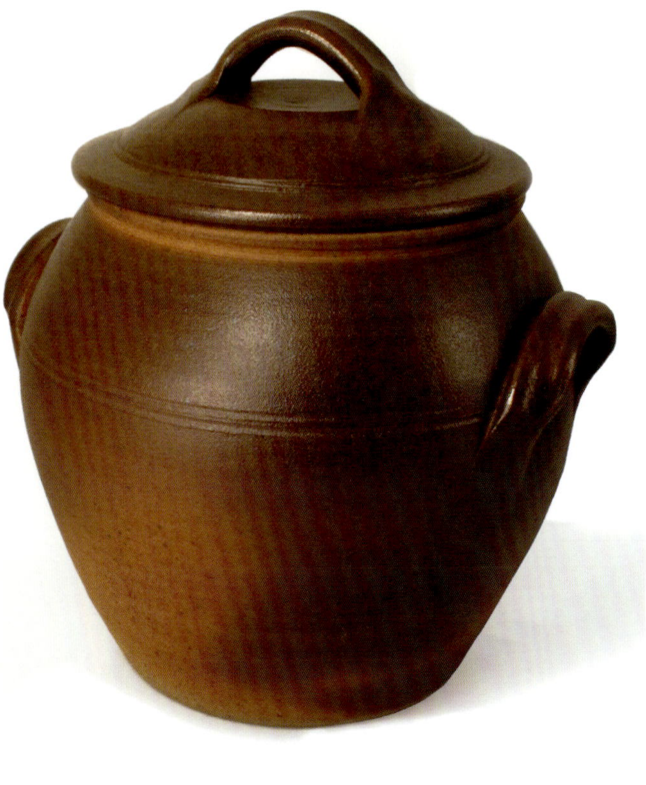

John Leach, bread crock with lug handles, 2010. Wood fired-stoneware, height: 29.5 cm (11½ in.). *Photo: Carole Melbourne.*

Arwyn Jones, small oval casserole, 2009. Thrown and altered stoneware, width: 19 cm (7½ in.). *Photo: Tony Burdett.*

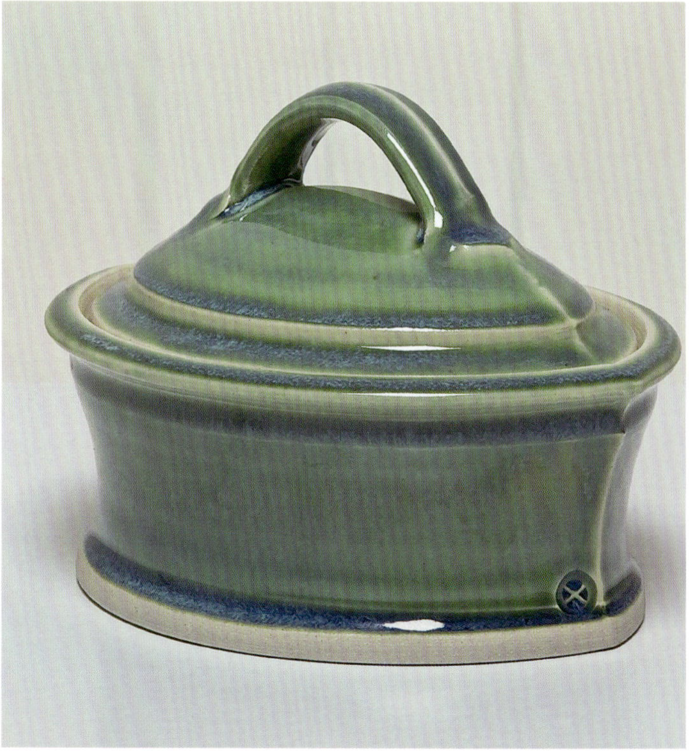

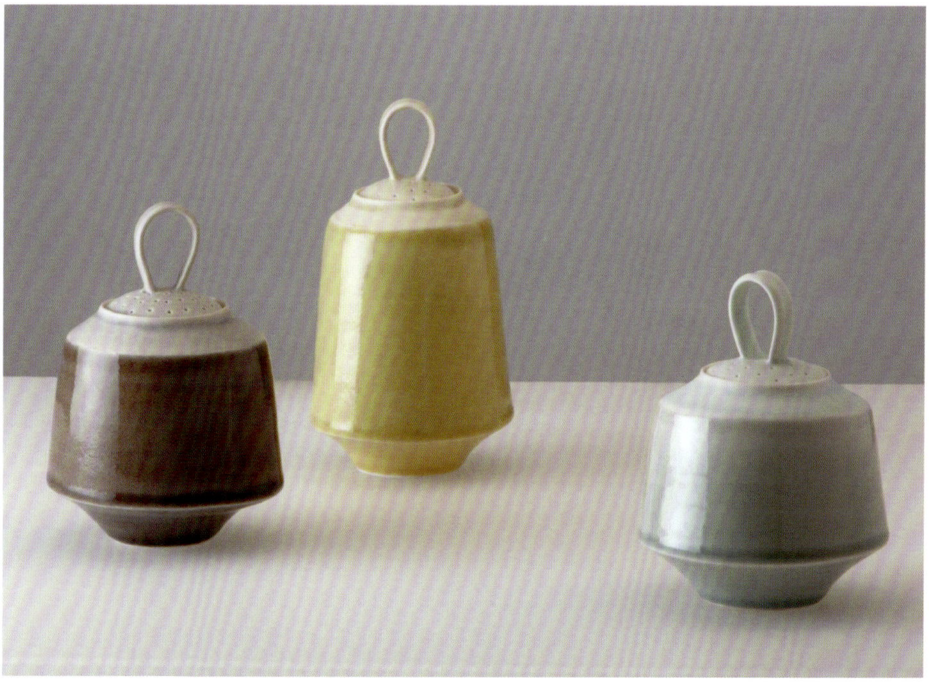

Louisa Taylor, castor pots, 2011. Vented storage jars influenced by an 18th-century castor shaker in the York museum collection, height: 25 cm (10 in.). *Photo: Matthew Booth.*

Winchcombe lidded pots by Charlie Tustin (top left), Sydney Tustin (centre) and Ray Finch (far right), from the collection of Doug Fitch. Three of these are early (1930s) slip-decorated earthenware and the other three were made after the pottery converted to stoneware in the 1960s, height: 6.5 cm (2½ in.). *Photo: Jonathan Thompson.*

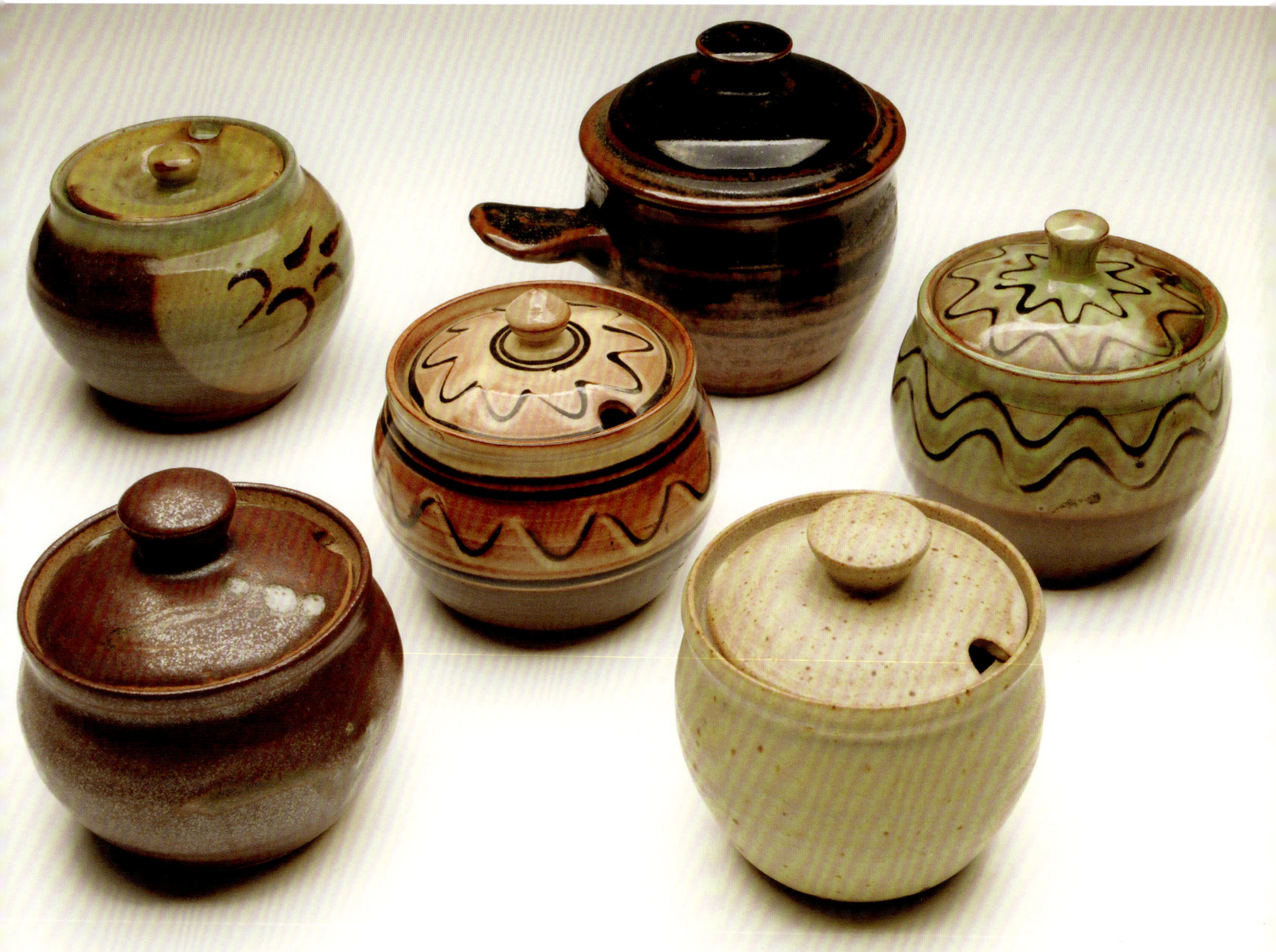

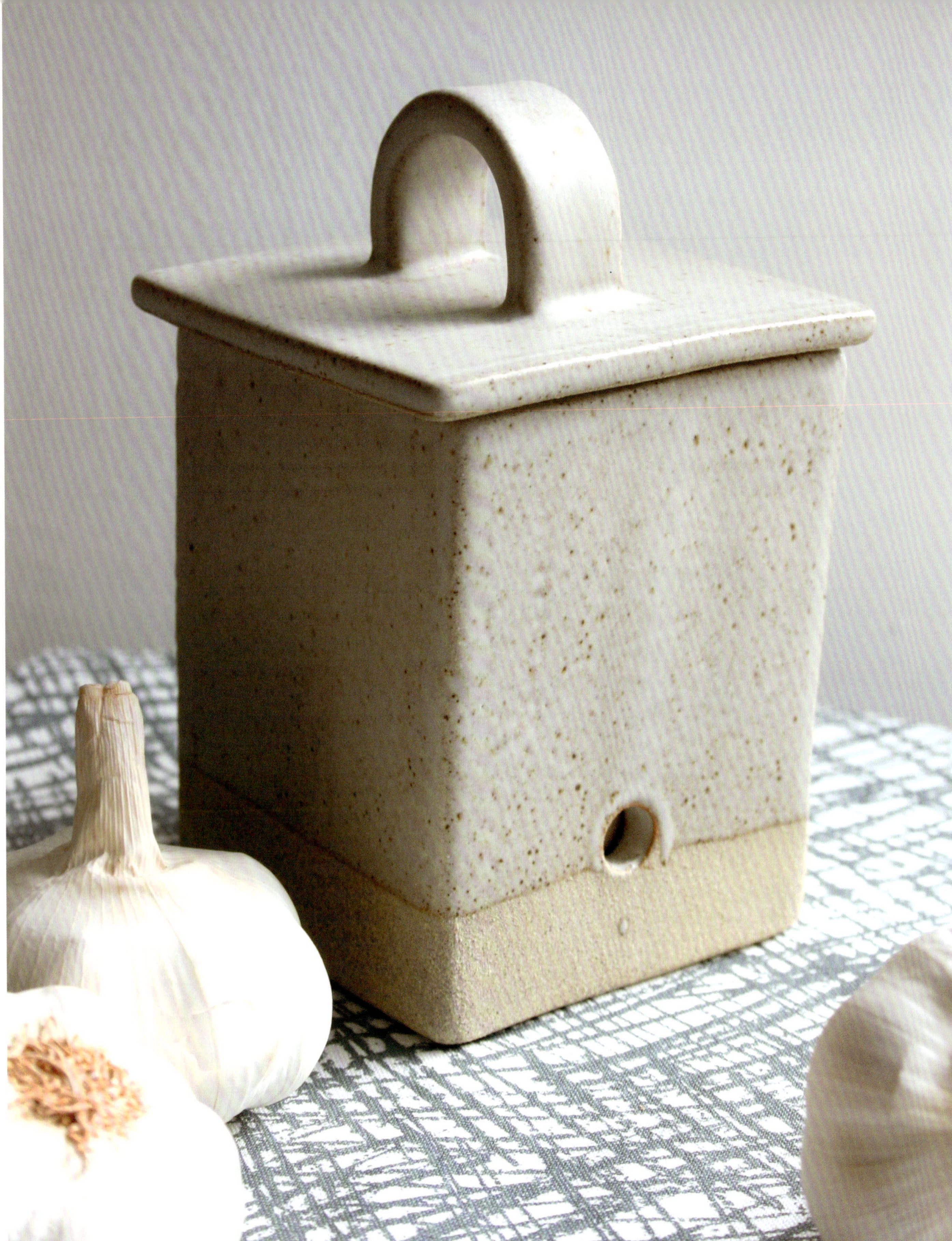

Tom Butcher, extruded garlic pot, 2011.
Loch Long stoneware, height: 11 cm (4¼ in.).
Photo: Rosie Brown.

Bento boxes are used in Japan to serve a selection of small portions of rice, fish and pickled vegetables. They are usually divided into compartments and can have more than one layer. They can be used as portable lunchboxes and are traditionally made of lacquerware and occasionally pottery. Tiffin boxes, used in India for carrying lunch, are based on a similar idea but are made of metal. Stacking and nesting dishes are useful and can be stored in a small space (see Adam Frew's stacking dishes, right).

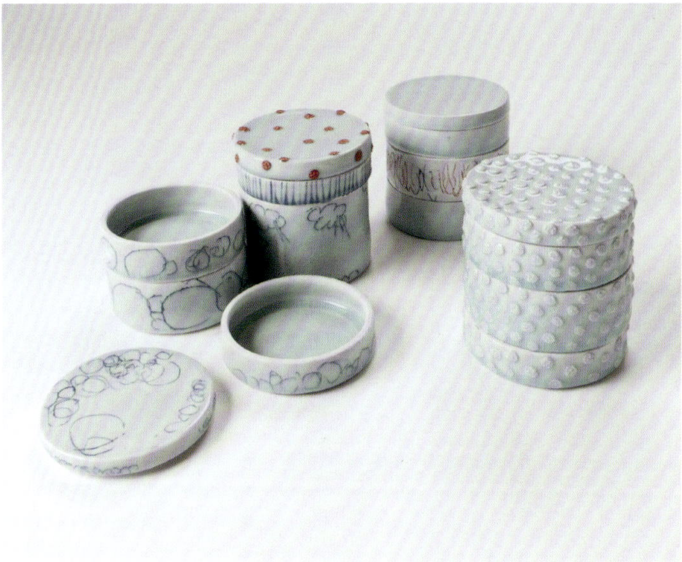

Adam Frew, Stacking dishes, 2011. Thrown porcelain, height: 20 cm (8 in.). *Photo: Glen Norwood.*

Reiko Nagata, Bento box, 2011. Stoneware with enamel overglaze decoration. *Photo: Henry Bloomfield.*

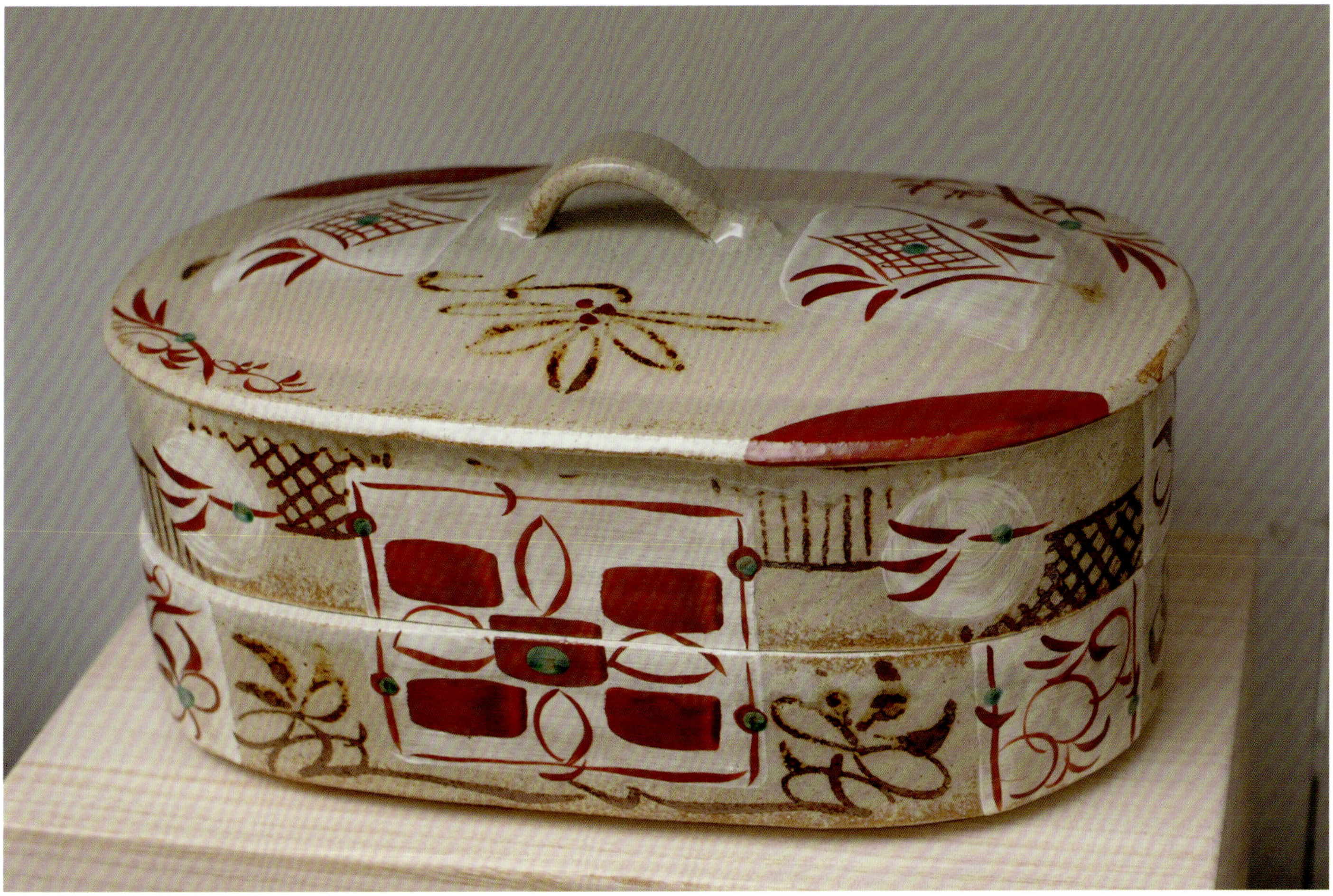

Making methods

Storage jars and casseroles can be thrown on the wheel, while rectangular butter dishes are more easily made by slipcasting from a mould. In Europe, butter is sold in rectangular 250 g (8 oz) blocks, while in the US it is sold in long, narrow, quarter-pound 'sticks'. Butter dishes can be made according to the size needed.

Lids can be made by throwing a shallow bowl, then inverting it, and turning and adding a knob or strap handle when leatherhard. Lids can also be thrown on the wheel in one piece, the right way up, by forming a knob in the centre of a small dish (see Winchcombe lidded pots on p. 149). A gallery to support the lid can be formed by splitting the rim of the pot and pushing down the inner half. Lids must be measured very carefully with calipers and, if necessary, turned when leatherhard to fit. Lids can also be made of other materials such as wood.

Measuring the diameter of a pot that has a gallery. *Photo: Henry Bloomfield.*

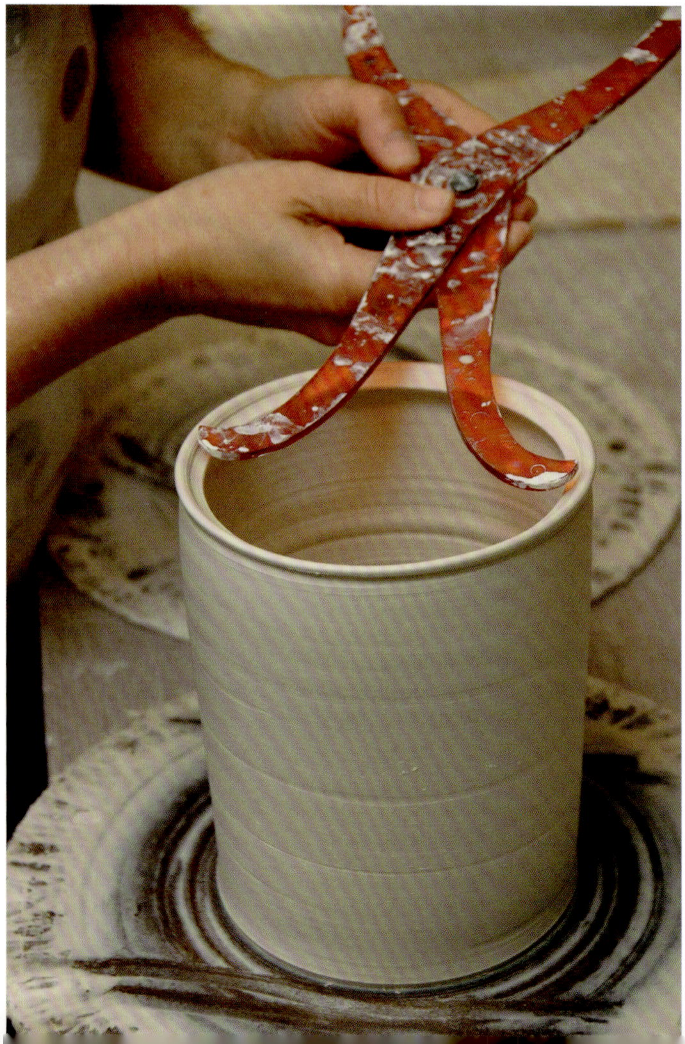

Measuring the lid. This will be turned and a strap handle added. *Photo: Henry Bloomfield.*

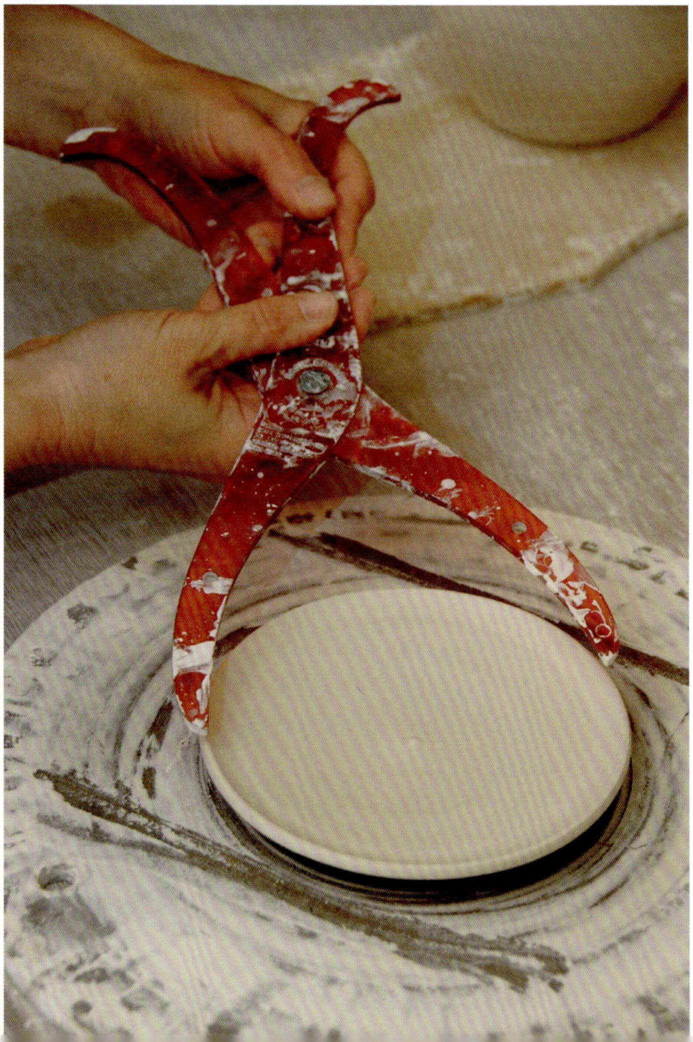

Rachel Barker, Crabapple Butter Box, manufactured in Stoke-on-Trent, 2005. Slipcast earthenware, width: 14 cm (5½ in.). *Photo: Rachel Barker.*

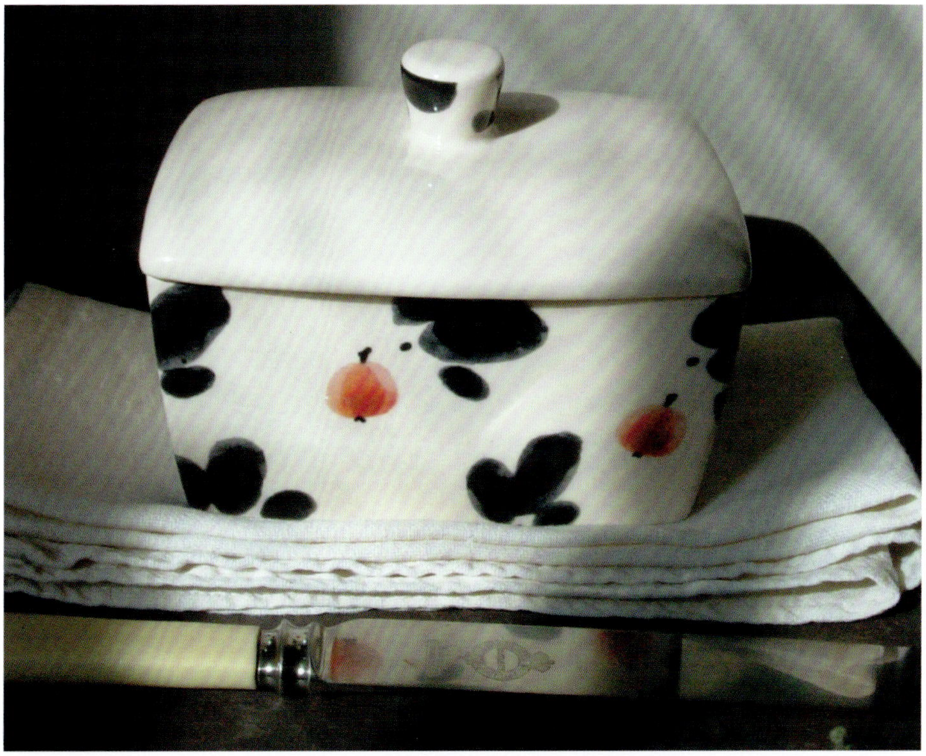

RAMP ceramics, thrown porcelain jars, 2009. Slip inlay, oak lids, height: 18 cm (7 in.). *Photo: courtesy of RAMP.*

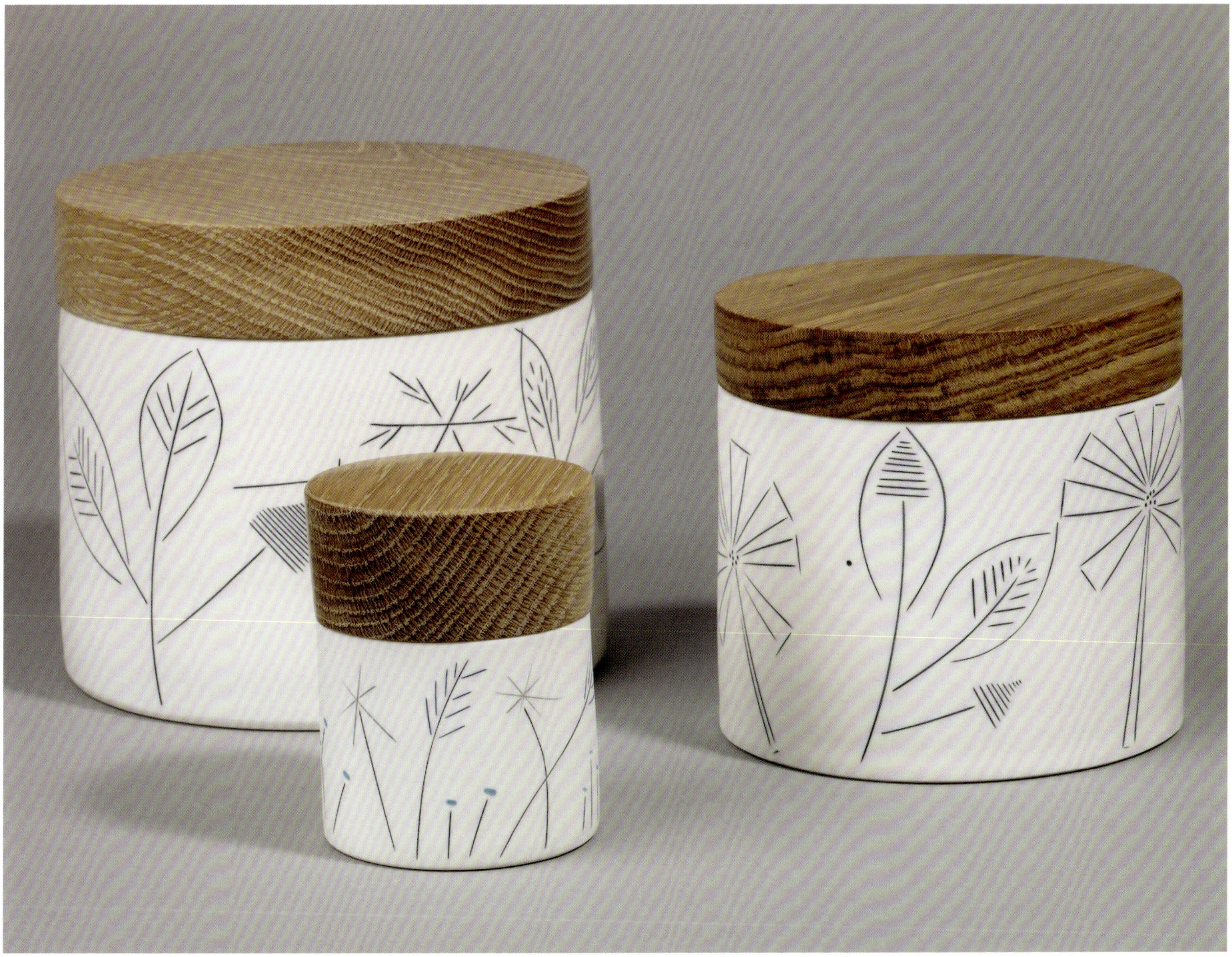

Glossary

Ball clay Fine-grained, plastic, secondary clay.

Baluster jug Jug in the shape of a baluster in a balustrade.

Biscuit A first firing to around 1000°C (1832°F) before glaze is applied. The term is also applied to fired ware.

Bone china A fine, translucent clay body containing up to 50% bone ash.

Calcining Heating in a kiln to drive off volatile compounds, for example, heating calcium carbonate to produce calcium oxide.

Celadon A type of pale grey-green or blue-green glaze containing iron, first developed in China.

China clay Pure, white clay (kaolin).

Cornish stone A type of feldspar found in Cornwall, used in clay bodies and glazes.

Crazing A network of fine cracks in a glaze, caused by poor glaze fit, with the glaze contracting more than the body. See *Shivering*.

Creamware Cream-coloured earthenware with a transparent lead glaze, first developed by Josiah Wedgwood.

Decal Transfer applied to glazed ware and fired to 800°C (1472°F).

Earthenware Clay which is fired to a low temperature, below 1150°C (2102°F), where the body remains porous and not vitrified.

Extrusion Forcing lengths of clay through a shaped die.

Feldspar Mineral derived from granite containing potassium, sodium, calcium and alumino-silicate.

Flux A material which helps to lower the melting temperature of a glaze or vitrify a clay body.

Foot-ring An unglazed ring of clay on the base of a pot.

Galena Lead sulphide. Poisonous lead ore once used in glazes. Frits are now preferred.

Gallery A ledge inside the rim of a pot to support the lid.

Jigger Mechanical method for making plates, using a wheel-mounted hump mould and a metal profile which shapes the foot of the plate.

Jolley Mechanical method for making bowls and cups, using a wheel-mounted press mould and a metal profile which shapes the inside of the pot.

Leatherhard Clay which is firm enough to handle without distorting.

Maiolica Decorated, tin-glazed earthenware thought to have originated in Malaga and spread throughout Spain and Italy.

Oatmeal glaze A cream matt stoneware glaze with iron speckles.

Oxidation Firing in the presence of sufficient oxygen, usually in an electric kiln.

Pancheon Large conical bowl used for settling milk to remove the cream.

Pinholes Small holes in glaze, caused by burst bubbles which have not healed over during firing.

Plaster of Paris Calcined, hydrated calcium sulphate (gypsum) used for making moulds.

Plasticity A property of clay that enables it to hold its shape when worked.

Porcelain A white clay fired to 1250–1400°C (2282–2552°F), becoming translucent and vitrified.

Pug mill Machine with rotating blades which mixes and compresses clay ready for use.

Reduction Limiting the air available during firing so that oxygen is drawn from the clay and glaze, usually in a fuel-burning kiln.

Salt firing Using salt thrown into the kiln at a high temperature, where it combines with the silica in the clay to produce a glaze on the surface.

Sgraffito Scratching a pattern through slip to show the clay body beneath.

Shivering Glaze flaking off the rims and the edges of handles. Caused by poor glaze fit, with the glaze contracting less than the body; the opposite effect to crazing.

Silica Silicon dioxide. Quartz, flint or sand.

Slip Liquid clay, made from clay mixed with water.

Slipcasting Pouring liquid clay into a mould.

Slip trailing Drawing lines or dots of thick slip with a nozzle.

Slipware Earthenware decorated with coloured slip.

Soda firing Using soda (sodium carbonate) sprayed into the kiln, where it combines with the silica in the clay to produce a glaze.

Sprigging Applied relief decoration, sometimes made in a mould.

Stoneware Clay which is vitrified or non-porous, fired to a high temperature (above 1200°C/2192°F).

Tenmoku A type of oriental high-iron glaze, which is usually black, breaking to brown.

Throwing Making pottery by hand on a potters' wheel.

Transfer printing Patterns printed onto paper and transferred onto biscuit ware.

Trencher A square slab of stale bread or wood used as a plate in medieval times.

Turning Trimming away clay using sharp tools on a potter's wheel or lathe.

Underglaze Colouring oxide or stain applied under a transparent glaze.

Vitrified A property of clay when fired to a non-porous, glassy state.

Bibliography

Arnold, A 2002, *Briglin Pottery*, Briglin Books, London.

Beeton, I 1861, *Mrs Beeton's Book of Household Management*, Samuel Orchart Beeton, London.

Bloomfield, L 2011, *Advanced Pottery*, Robert Hale, London.

Cardew, M 1976, 'Slipware and Stoneware', *A collection of essays*, Crafts Advisory Committee, London.

Cooper, E 2000, *10,000 Years of Pottery,* The British Museum Press, London.

de Waal, E 2003, *20th Century Ceramics,* Thames and Hudson, London.

de Waal, E and Clare, C 2011, *The Pot Book*, Phaidon Press, London.

French, N 1998, *The Potter's Directory of Shape and Form*, A & C Black, London.

Garson, S 2000, 'Home Cooking – A Case for Handmade Tableware', *Pottery in Australia*, vol. 39.

Heath, S 2004, *The inspiration of Marianne de Trey: necessity and decoration from cloth to clay*, Crafts Study Centre, Surrey.

Hopper, R 2011, *Functional Pottery: Form and Aesthetic in Pots of Purpose*, The American Ceramic Society, Westerville, OH, USA.

Kaplan, K 2011, *California Design, 1930–1965: Living in a Modern Way*, MIT Press, Cambridge, USA.

Klausner, A 2007, *Heath Ceramics,* Chronicle Books, San Francisco.

Leach, B 1940, *A Potter's Book*, Faber & Faber, London.

Wood, K A 1999, *Tableware in Clay*, Crowood Press, Marlborough, UK.

Yanagi, S 1972, *The Unknown Craftsman*, Kodansha International, Tokyo/New York.

Young, L 2003, *Eva Zeisel (Compact Design Portfolio)*, Chronicle Books, San Francisco.

Acknowledgements

Thank you to Doug Fitch and photographer Jonathan Thompson for photographing Doug's collection of pots and to Charles Randall for taking photographs of production in a factory in China.

Thanks to Linda Styles, Gillian Naylor of Repeat Repeat and Keith Brymer Jones of Make International for writing text for the book, and to Chris Keenan and Kevin Millward for answering questions. Many thanks to Angie Wickenden for information on archaeological pots and Jon Cullum for access to pictures of medieval pots.

I am indebted to the Victoria and Albert Museum, the British Museum, David Mellor Design and John Lewis for inspiration from their collections.

Thanks to the following for images:

Adam Frew, Adrienne Baba, Aiga Siceva-Sattler, Akiko Hirai, Alex Huxley, Ann Van Hoey, Arwyn Jones, Billy Lloyd, Bodo Sperlein, Branksome China, Chris Keenan, Courtney Murphy, Daniel Smith, Dartington Pottery, David Mellor Design, David Pier, Derek Wilson, Esther Coombs, Hannah McAndrew, Hatty Fawcett of Seek and Adore, Heath Ceramics, Hollis Engley, Jeremy Nichols, Jiří Pelcl, John Leach, John Mathieson, Jonathan West for Toast, Judi Tavill, Kaori Tatebayashi, Karen Morgan, Karin Eriksson, Kate Scott, Katrin Moye, Keith Brymer Jones of Make International, Kevin Millward, Laura de Benedetti, Leach Pottery, Linda Styles, Louisa Taylor, Mariko Jesse, Mark Hewitt, Marshall Colman, Matthew Tyas, May Luk, Mini Moderns, Miratis, Mizuyo Yamashita, Nathan Smallman, Nick Fleming, Paul Jessop, Peter Saenger, Peter Seabridge, Pigeon Toe Ceramics, Piret Kändler, Portmeirion Pottery, Rachel Barker, Rachel Dormor, RAMP Ceramics, Rebecca Callis, Repeat Repeat, Rigmor Als, Ron Philbeck, Rupert Spira, Sarah Spackman, Scott Jennings, Stuart Carey, Sue Ure, Susanne Lukàcs-Ringel, Takeshi Yasuda, Tom Butcher, the Victoria and Albert Museum, and Willer for Christiane Perrochon.

Potteries

UK

Branksome China
35 Shaftesbury Street
Fordingbridge
SP6 1JF
England
+44 (0)1425 652010
www.branksomechina.co.uk

Brickett Davda
Factory 17
17 Gordon Road
Portslade
Brighton
East Sussex
BN41 1GL
+44 (0)1273 414 765
www.brickettdavda.com

Emma Bridgewater,
Lichfield Street,
Stoke-on-Trent,
ST1 3EJ
0844 243 9266
+44 (0)1782 407733
www.emmabridgewater.
co.uk

Grayshott Pottery
School Road
Grayshott
Hindhead
Surrey
GU26 6LR
+44 (0)1428 604404
www.grayshottpottery.com

Leach Pottery
Higher Stennack
St Ives
Cornwall
TR26 2HE
+44 (0)1736 799703
www.leachpottery.com

Muchelney Pottery
Muchelney
nr Langport
TA10 0DW
+44 (0)1458 250324
www.johnleachpottery.
co.uk

Portmeirion Group UK Ltd
London Road
Stoke-on-Trent
ST4 7QQ
+44 (0)1782 744721
www.portmeirion.co.uk

Repeat Repeat Ltd
The Old Co-op
153 Smithpool Road
Fenton
Stoke-on-Trent
Staffordshire
ST4 4PW
+44 (0)1782 845870
www.repeatrepeat.co.uk

Soendergaard Design
Fressingfield House
Church Street
Fressingfield
Suffolk
IP21 5PA
+44 (0)1379 586200
www.soendergaarddesign.
co.uk

Winchcombe Pottery
Broadway Road
Winchcombe
Cheltenham
Gloucestershire
GL54 5NU
+44 (0)1242 602462
www.winchcombepottery.
co.uk

Denmark

Rigmor Als
Keramikbutikken
Blågårds Plads 12
DK 2200 København N
(+45) 26 37 29 81
www.rigmorals.dk

USA

Bauer Pottery Company
27430 Main Street
Highland, CA 92346
888-213-0800
+1 909-425-5700 from
outside the US
www.bauerpottery.com

Heath Ceramics
400 Gate Five Road
Sausalito, CA 94965
415-332-3732 x13
+1 415-332-3204
www.heathceramics.com

Pigeon Toe
727 SE Morrison Street
Portland, OR 97214
+1 503-709-5479
www.pigeontoeceramics.
com

Index